Ritual, Religion, and the Sacred

Ritual, Religion, and the Sacred

Selections from the

Annales

Economies, Sociétés, Civilisations

Volume 7

Edited by

Robert Forster
and
Orest Ranum

Translated by
Elborg Forster
and
Patricia M. Ranum

The Johns Hopkins University Press
Baltimore and London

The Johns Hopkins University Press, Baltimore, Maryland 21218
The Johns Hopkins Press Ltd., London

Library of Congress Cataloging in Publication Data
Main entry under title:

Ritual, religion, and the sacred.

   1. Christianity—Europe—Addresses, essays,
lectures.   2. Europe—Religion—Addresses, essays,
lectures.   3. Rites and ceremonies—Europe—Addresses, essays,
lectures.   4. Europe—Social life and customs—Addresses,
essays, lectures.   I. Forster, Robert, 1926-   .   II. Ranum,
Orest A.   III. Annales (Paris, France: 1946)
BR746.R57   209'.4   81-48184
ISBN 0-8018-2776-0   AACR2
ISBN 0-8018-2778-7 (pbk.)

Contents

Introduction

Marriage rituals. Parades of carefully polished, decorated, and honking cars filled with boisterous young people appear in many parts of the world today as parts of marriage rituals. Ritual? The term seems more appropriate to describe momentous ceremonies of state and religious services, not something so banal as a parade of honking cars. Nonetheless, the ethnographer's eye discerns patterns of meaning in signs and gestures in everyday life—not just in grand ceremonies. The rituals of everyday life occur in society so integrally, and so repetitively, that they are routine. Onlookers have no difficulty in interpreting the significance of the honking-car ritual; motorists encountering the parade may join in it by also honking their horns. The more sober onlookers may express annoyance at the noise and take offense at the double meaning of "Hot Springs Tonight!" printed in bold letters on the trunk of the wedding car, but ritual behavior it is, in all its banality and routine.

Births, baptisms, betrothals, marriages, deaths, and funerals are occasions of such moment in Western societies (and others, to be sure) that rituals accompany them. The relations between individuals and families, individuals and communities, and individuals and communities and the divine—and the diabolical—are made manifest and overt at such moments. Notions of true self, masculinity, femininity, family, and society are defined in and through rituals, and it is for this reason that ethnographers and historians study them. Rituals allow the search for patterns of behavior in society and structures of meaning in everyday activities. The very repetition of the same rituals—despite their infinite variations—permits the study of society; roles that otherwise might only exist in thought become actions and therefore more explicit and observable. It is usually not too difficult to determine who is the bride in a wedding procession in Western societies, or the newborn, the godparents, family mourners, pallbearers, and so forth, even today. The roles are familiar to everyone, even in an age when many believe that the amounts of ritualized behavior and the meanings of ritual have declined or lost their significance. There may be resistance to playing these familiar roles or attempts to create a counterritual on the part of some, but the ethnographer and historian search for the presence of rituals in society and use them for understanding relations between groups, classes, parties, religions, sects, and institutions.

The "loss" of a son or daughter from a family in the founding of a new household is a momentous occasion for a family and community. Nicole Belmont stresses how marriage rituals are encounters between families and communities, as brides are processed from their own families to those of their husbands. In popular culture this "procession" was more important than any other part of the ritual, and the evidence for this derives from the adaptation of the Roman Catholic Church to accommodate popular rituals. The noisemaking at weddings and the charivari are suggestively related by Belmont; an aspect of society that might not otherwise be perceived contributes to historical understanding in the best sense. Community approval of a betrothed couple constituted a significant step in social relations, regardless of class.

The second article on marriage rituals is by André Burguière, who explores roles played by the Church in Northern and Southern France from the sixteenth to the eighteenth centuries. There was no clear separation between popular and Church rituals of marriage, even in regard to such parts of the ritual as the blessing of the marriage ring and the exchange of vows. As in Belmont's article, however, we find again that church-society relations in the marriage ritual were altered by the decrees of the Council of Trent. While priests continued to celebrate what had been decided by families and approved by communities, the emphasis upon the chastity of the bride increased even as couples sought help in coping with fears of childlessness and evil.

The work of Christiane Klapisch-Zuber takes us to a still deeper level of meaning in marriage rituals, while exploring the same themes. Popular marriage rites in Florence flourished longer than in France; the religious blessing was less important than that of the community for a much longer time, with the result that the unconscious rivalries between the groom and the bride's father and between the groom and other males in the community manifested themselves not only in rituals but also in art. Popular attitudes were translated into biblical iconography in the depiction of Saint Joseph, the elderly victor over younger suitors. The conflict between age groups revealed in these paintings disappeared, however, from religious painting as a result of the implementation of the decrees of the Council of Trent. Popular marriage rituals also gradually became secondary to the religious rituals at the same time that marriage became more of a private family affair and less one of the community.

Françoise Zonabend's work elucidates kinship ties in a Burgundian village by studying the selection of godparents and the ritual of baptism in the modern period. Here again the theme is the synthesis of the familial and community rituals with those of the religious and cosmic. Note how she stresses that her approach is "both historical and ethnographic." There is the family ritual, "the asking" of relatives to serve as godparents, and the consequent choices of first names for the child that will be stated publicly before parents and godparents as the priest lifts water with his hand to the child's head in the religious ceremony of baptism. Who could offer to serve as godparents? Why were childless couples very often asked to serve as godparents? Zonabend's research provides a clarification not only of family ties beyond the nuclear family but also of the structure of roles played by all the participants in the rituals of an individual's life, especially on the occasion of an early death of the child or at first communion.

Perhaps because of the scarcity of other than what Evelyne Patlagean calls "narrative" sources, such as wills and laws, it is much more difficult to discern the relationships between social conventions and religious rituals in early and Medieval Byzantium. Since voluntary kinships, such as the adoption of brothers and the adoption of children were customary in Byzantine society before Christianization, Patlagean contends that "Christian ritual was superimposed" upon these older customs. Yet in other instances the sources suggest that the Church's doctrines are actually shaping society. Once again it seems evident that "social" and religious rituals cannot be studied separately, even though each seems to meet different needs of families and communities. Voluntary kinship in Byzantine society, just as in Burgundian society, turned on issues of property and status, while the religious rituals seemed to serve primarily to legitimize and sanctify decisions made among families.

For Christianity to have succeeded in implanting itself so deeply and thoroughly in Byzantine society, it had to be present in the key events of an individual's life. This presence could not be taken for granted, but rather consisted of an ongoing entrenchment or retrenchment of religious rituals in society. We have already observed how late the religious rite came to be important in Florentine marriages. All the articles in this volume stress the importance of studying individual and community contacts with the sacred—and the diabolical. Aline Rousselle's implicit definition of religious faith ought to be mentioned here because it suggests the complexity of religious-social bonds. It is the belief in the possibility of a cure for some physical condition. The social foundations of the great religious institutions that the churches became were not to be found in the deliberations of councils of bishops or university faculties, but rather in the vague, almost not thinking and routine gesture of seeking help from a holy person for an ailment or infirmity. Attitudes about good and evil, sickness and health, poverty and wealth, were directly linked to cosmic powers, and these powers became manifest in objects, special sites such as sacred springs, altars, and in holy men and women. Missionaries met specific needs in society, as the career of Saint Martin of Tours in Gaul testifies. Again, as in Patlagean's research, we find shifts from pre-Christian to Christian rites and social values. There seem to have been no boundaries between medical science, magic, and pagan beliefs prior to Christianization in

Gaul, and we should therefore not be surprised to find that the powerful synthesis of healing with conversion in the career of Saint Martin of Tours played such an important role in the Christianization of the region.

The early miraculous works and teachings of the saints would continue to inspire veneration for centuries to come, but occasionally, quite nonmiraculous experiences, such as the theft of something sacred, might be fabricated into a miraculous event only centuries later. Anne Lombard-Jourdain's work on the miracle of Le Lendit is a piece of careful detective work about how, in the sixteenth century, donors, clergy, and artists created a visual image of a miracle from what had clearly been only a theft in the thirteenth century. The shifts from written text to stained glass and tapestry, back to credulously written historical text, and finally to critical historical analysis reveal something about the mechanisms through which beliefs were consolidated in rituals and works of art.

Whereas Rousselle gives us a glimpse into the process by which meanings and social continuities were transferred in Gaul, M. H. Froeschlé-Chopard offers a more structural analysis of the same phenomena in her study of iconographic programs in chapels of the local churches in Southern France during the eighteenth century. The precise ways in which the sacred was related to the communities are suggested, and moreover, the community itself is defined by the saints it venerates. The patron saint as represented in the central painting of the high altar of the parish church and the special devotions on that saint's festive day provided a special identity for the community that veneration of members of the Holy Family and the "universal" saints did not. Note the way Froeschlé-Chopard defines the manner in which the paintings of saints perform for the community—they "manifest the sacred." The early Christian heroic activity of the type performed by Saint Martin, particularly the curing of the sick and the tortures endured by martyrs for the faith, continued to be represented down through the centuries in hundreds of altar paintings and sculpture. There was a great diversity of saints, but the distinction between local and universal saints was always upheld. The influence of the sixteenth-century reform movements—often described in a shorthand fashion in these articles by alluding to the Council of Trent—continued down into the eighteenth century. This is evident from the reformist centralization of the Church that continued to press for the placing of "universally" or generally well-known saints over the high altars. This, of course, meant displacing the pictures of the local saints. The issue of whether the old thematic program of the high altars would survive reveals the influence and counterinfluences of local and centralized religious institutions. Cleavages between elitist and popular expressions of spirituality may also be dimly perceived in this struggle in the form of old-fashioned versus more modern artistic styles.

In the sixteenth century, the destruction of altars and statues of saints by those who claimed to be reformers had divided Europeans into Protestants and Catholics as much as had theological differences. In some instances, brutal persecutions of minorities were carried out by local communities, whereas states as large and variegated as France used the law courts and troops to attempt to enforce religious uniformity. Denis Richet explores what was an intensification of religious life in the sixteenth century, with the splintering of doctrine and rituals into Protestant and Catholic. We have seen in numerous instances how religious reformism touched the rituals of society in fundamental ways; this same reformism eventually would shatter families, communities, and states. The results would be felt for centuries to come. Intensification of the religious life *in* society occurred along with the splintering of faiths that strained relations between local and national life after 1560 in France. The study of individual and community contacts with the sacred in baptisms, marriages, and funerals helps to clarify not only the relationships between religious and other institutions in society but also why hitherto peaceful individuals and communities became torn by conflict.

At various points in these articles there is also an implicit recognition that popular beliefs included belief in the devil. Attitudes toward evil were linked as directly to cosmic forces as were those toward good. Baptisms ought not to take place on certain days of the week because these were associated with disaster, bad luck, or some other expression of evil. Medicine did its work better at certain hours and on certain days, and couples performed special rituals to reduce the possibility of sterility. Fears of evil may have been very powerful and real, as were attempts to focus on what, or who, the sources of evil might be in the community. Robert Muchembled explores the meanings of evil and of the diabolical in popular culture, and once again the relations between individuals, their communities, and the church are the focus of study. Witchcraft represented a strategy for overcoming the fears of the world, as did the respect for the traditional belief that some catastrophe might take place if a baptism occurred on a certain day. Links between rituals and evils that occur, like the attitudes that favor the performance of rituals to occur only on certain days, are part of the same structure of beliefs about the "magical milieu" that included Christianity as well as witchcraft.

Together these essays constitute a rich and exciting introduction to a vast ethnographic and historical literature about ritual, religion, and society. They break new ground by cautiously and tentatively raising very general questions about how the study of ritual and religion in society may reveal previously hidden relationships and suggest a comprehensive wholeness in the human experience. The research techniques of the ethnographer and historian are also combined, in each instance, in highly individualized quests for understanding the present and the past without placing strict boundaries on the use of those disciplines.

Robert Forster
Orest Ranum

Ritual, Religion, and the Sacred

1

The Symbolic Function of the Wedding Procession in the Popular Rituals of Marriage

Nicole Belmont

The popular rituals connected with marriage are probably the most important and the most elaborate of all the European rituals. The reason for this is no doubt that Europe does not have (or has long ago abandoned) any rites of initiation designed to bring the adolescent age group into the adult group. In Europe this function is fulfilled by the large set of rituals connected with betrothal and marriage.

I therefore cannot hope to retrace these rituals in all of their profusion, their richness, and their telling detail, even though as far as France and the periods for which we have rather complete descriptions are concerned, these rituals are much less elaborate than in other regions, especially in eastern and southeastern Europe. I shall therefore limit myself to describing what I consider to be the essential principle of this ritual. This principle is stated very clearly by abbé J.-B. Thiers in connection with the "superstitions concerning the time to celebrate marriages," for in this passage Thiers describes what I see as the very mainstay of the popular ritual of marriage.[1] He examines—in order to reject them—the various superstitions that prevented people from marrying in May, or on Wednesdays or Fridays. However, he adds, when the Church forbids the celebration of marriage during certain times of the year, it is not a matter of superstition, since the Church is guided by the Holy Ghost. He then lists the days and the times of the year during which the Church forbids weddings, adding: "If anyone contracts a marriage during these times with its [the Church's] permission, it must be done without the trappings deployed in leading the bride from her house to the church and

Annales, E.S.C. 33 (May-June 1978): 650–55. Translated by Elborg Forster.

from the church to her husband's house, a ceremony which in Latin is called the *traductio*. Moreover, it must be done without the feasting, dancing, and rejoicing that ordinarily takes place at weddings, for such things are not befitting for days of prayer and penitence."

The main feature of the popular ritual of marriage is thus the *traductio*, together with rejoicing, dancing, and feasting. This *traductio*, and the trappings connected with it, is more simply and more commonly referred to as the wedding procession (*cortège*), an expression that includes three stages: (1) the ceremony called in certain regions the *départie*, that is, the bride's departure from her house, marked by a great number of rituals, most of them rituals of separation as this term is used by A. Van Gennep in his analysis of the rites of passage; (2) the stop at the church for the religious ceremony itself; and (3) the arrival at the house of the groom or his father, marked by rites of reception. Between these three points, two ritual treks are executed, one from the bride's house to the church and the other from the church to the groom's house. This, then, is a spatiotemporal complex that, in my opinion, constitutes the schema and the essential principle of the popular ritual of marriage. Moreover, it is likely that this fundamental schema underlies the ritual of marriage throughout the Indo-European domain. This hypothesis is confirmed on etymological and philological grounds by E. Beneviste.[2]

The Indo-European languages do not have an original term for the action of getting married. In Latin, for example, the expressions used are secondary coinages essentially reflecting the male point of view. For the father it is *dare filiam suam* or *tradere filiam suam*, "to give his daughter in marriage"; and for the husband it is *uxorem ducere*, "to lead a woman" (to his house). These expressions reproduce the basic ritual scenario exactly: the father hands over his daughter to the husband, who takes her to his house. The religious ceremony, enacted midway in this process, serves to ratify it. "The woman does not marry," Beneviste adds, "she is married. She does not accomplish an act, she undergoes a change of condition."[3] She is like an object that is handed from one owner to another. It is probable that the many gifts and countergifts that used to circulate throughout the entire ritual of betrothal and marriage had the function, beyond their economic role, of representing and symbolizing the young woman, even if they were sometimes intended for her. In any case, given the essential purpose of marriage, which was to convey a woman from one house to another, the circulation of objects throughout the ritual was designed to facilitate symbolically the circulation of the woman herself. Such a passage did indeed call for a great number and a great variety of rites. It could not possibly be accomplished by the simple act of going from one point to another, for in this case it would amount to no more than a concubinage.

According to the abbé Thiers, it appears that the Church had great difficulties in eliminating from these popular rituals of marriage the noisy manifestations that accompanied the wedding procession. There is probably not one author who fails to report and describe this behavior.

The procession is preceded by a violin and a clarinet, the usual and traditional music of the village, in addition to the young men who do their part by shouting on top of their lungs their *thiou hihi va longué*, the customary expression of the noisy and at times somewhat savage joy of the mountaineers of the Vosges when there is something to celebrate, . . . not to forget the old custom of their forebears which consists of frequently firing their pistols near the bride, sometimes even aiming between her legs. We are told that far from being frightened by these sudden bursts of gunfire, she appears to be greatly entertained by it, for she is quite sure that her wedding would not be properly celebrated with a paltry and insignificant consumption of gunpowder; especially since this would also mean that once she had become a mother she would not be *good for milk*, that is to say, a *good wetnurse*.[4]

The inhabitants of the Médoc . . . celebrate their weddings with more *éclat*. Shouting and screaming accompany the celebration, rather than the calm and pure joy that makes this bond so beautiful. . . . The procession takes place . . . amidst the most piercing cries, which are more reminiscent of the *evohé* and the *io bacche* than of the modest strains of peaceful hymen.[5]

The father of the groom, and in his absence his closest kinsman, brings the bride to the house. Here again, muskets and pistols are fired into the air and the followers shout with all their might in order to bring the townspeople to their doors and windows. The fiddler plays his instrument.[6]

In reporting facts of this kind Thiers is in a quandary, for he cannot condemn them outright as superstitions or useless observances. He therefore chooses to call them insolences, as in the following passage, which deals with the betrothal.

We must call insolences, rather than superstitions, what is practiced in certain places, where the custom is to throw holy water on persons who have just become betrothed when they leave the church; to beat them up if they are from another parish; to lock them up in the church; to demand from them money for drinking; to seize them bodily and to carry them into the *cabarets*; to insult them and to make a great hue and cry, or a charivari, when they refuse to give money to those who ask for it.[7]

E. Westermarck also reports that the firing of muskets is a widespread European practice on the occasion of a wedding. In Durham county, England, the wedding procession was escorted as far as the church by men armed with muskets, which they fired very close to the ears of the bride and the bridesmaids. In Germany a great deal of shooting was done during the night before the wedding.[8] According to Westermarck, this custom had the purpose of chasing away the spirits and evil influences to which the bride and groom were particularly vulnerable at this time. Here the shooting had a purifying and protective function. Laisnel de la Salle recalls this practice for Berry and gives us a classic description of it. He adds that this was also done in Languedoc "for the purpose of chasing off evil spirits," but unfortunately he does not

provide any references.[9] Richard's indications for the arrondissement of
Remiremont would seem to indicate that this was a fertility rite, since he
states that unless muskets were fired at the wedding, the bride would not be
good for milk, that is, *a good wetnurse*.[10]

Sociologically speaking, there is no question that the noise connected with
the wedding procession fulfilled the function of attracting public attention.
In fact, one of the functions of the wedding ceremony as a whole was to make
public the union of two people by ensuring the presence of numerous witnesses. These witnesses were, first of all, the wedding guests, who were recruited among people belonging to the concentric social circles grouped
about the two spouses, circles that became wider and wider as they spread
from the immediate family to friends by way of the more or less close kin. But
even such public notice was not yet sufficient: the entire local community had
to be notified of the new union. This is why the wedding procession pursued
its noisy course through the territory in order to let the other members know
about the event. Monnier clearly states this intention for the Jura: "Shotguns
and pistols are fired again [this is the return of the procession], and loud
shouting brings people to their doors and windows." The same author, speaking of the case when the bride is taken after the ceremony to a village that is
not her own, says that "the horse-drawn carriage, all covered with ribbons,
must speed through the villages, *bourgs*, and towns along its way at full tilt;
above all it must arrive at its destination to the sound of repeated acclama-
tions and detonating firearms."[11]

Public notice was also demanded by the Church. There is no need here to
recall the obligation to have the banns published on the three Sundays before
the conclusion of the marriage, an exigency designed to make the intentions
of the couple public so that, in particular, persons who knew of an obstacle
could come forward. Thiers objected to nocturnal weddings as a practice the
Church had always forbidden and abhorred. "Marriages must be celebrated
in broad daylight and in the presence of three or at least two witnesses," and
he cites the ritual-books of several dioceses to lend weight to his assertion. He
incidentally also tells us why people wanted to celebrate their marriage at
night; it was in order to forestall evil spells against the groom, or in plain
words, from fear of the *nouement des aiguillettes* [impairment of the groom's
sexual potency] which a sorcerer or some other malevolent person could bring
about if the day of the wedding were known.

This reason may also account for another practice condemned by Thiers,
that of getting married in everyday clothes in a very simple ceremony, and
then reappearing in the church a few days later in festive apparel with all the
trappings of a wedding. It was, in other words, a matter of holding the celebration in secret and without public notice and of pretending to hold it a few
days later in order to outwit any potential malevolence.

These popular practices designed to attract public attention certainly did not originate in the Church's demand for public notice. I think that in this instance the religious and the popular ritual converged to fulfill one and the same need, though by different means. Curiously enough, the Church was not as demanding on this point as the popular ritual, insisting only that the banns be published, that the ceremony take place in broad daylight, and that two witnesses be present. The popular ritual, by contrast, called for an enormous amount of noise to make sure that the entire local community was notified of the formation of a new couple, as well as for a large number of witnesses, that is to say, wedding guests. In this connection one only has to think of the traditional Breton weddings, at which four hundred to five hundred guests might be present. And it is also curious that in the celebration of marriage the civil law makes the same demands as the Church, since it calls only for the publication of the banns and the presence of two witnesses, in addition to the mutual consent of the spouses, which is also demanded by the Church.

Why this emphasis on public attention? First and foremost, of course, there is the need to notify the social community that a new couple has been formed. But if the community must be notified, it is because it gives legitimacy to the new couple, and probably also because it can prevent its formation if it perceives an obstacle, the obstacle being essentially a prohibited degree of kinship. As a compensation for this kind of control, however, the community gives the new couple permission to enter without guilt into this new kind of existence, in which the two partners symbolically take the place of their father and mother. The fact that all the concentric circles of society have given their approval—which may be tacit or explicit—transforms the couple's sexual relations and their shared life into a social act, a marriage. The public character of the marriage ceremony brings with it the approval of the members of the community. In the traditional society this approval was given tacitly by the villagers who were notified of the marriage by the noisy procession; it was given, if not explicitly then at least implicitly, by the wedding guests who bestowed it on the couple by the very fact of their presence and sometimes even expressed it verbally. This is no doubt why invitations to a wedding were extended in an extremely ritualized manner. In many cases, in fact, such invitations were couched in stereotyped gestures and formulas.[12]

If one considers the period of three or four hundred years running roughly from the sixteenth to the nineteenth century, it appears that the Church was partially successful in eliminating the noisy manifestations occurring during the religious ceremony itself, which means that in this respect (and probably in other respects as well) a breach appeared between the religious and the popular ritual. Some authors of the early nineteenth century specify that the noise abated as the procession approached the church; the participants ceased their shouting, singing, and laughter, and the procession entered the church

only after silence had been established. This may seem to be a minor and
above all a very hard-won victory for the Church. Yet it was of capital importance in the long run, precisely to the extent that it brought about a clear-cut
distinction between the religious ritual and the popular ritual, a distinction
that eventually contributed to the demise of the latter.

At this point I should like to make another observation about the matter of
noisemaking at weddings. In reading the descriptions of various authors,
from very early ones such as Thiers to those of the late nineteenth century,
one comes to feel that between the noisemaking of a wedding and that of a
charivari there was no real difference in kind, only of degree. Even the nuance
of derision, which was very strong in the charivari directed against a second
marriage, was present at ordinary weddings, even those that were approved
by the social community. Recall, for example, the "roasting" of the wedding
night, which involved noisemaking, derision of the newlyweds, and even violence. Considering the matter in this light, we might be well advised to take
another look at the conventional ideas about the charivari and, in particular,
to try to understand the symbolic meaning of these rituals of derision.

What I have called the mainstay of the popular ritual of marriage, that
spatiotemporal complex that served to accomplish a young woman's passage
from her father's to her husband's house, might help us determine the nature
and function of ritual in general. There is nothing startling, of course, about
the statement that the ritual expresses itself not in words, but in bodily gestures and in the manipulation of objects. But, in the case that occupies us
here, one has the feeling that the gesture of fetching a woman at her father's
house in order to take her to her husband's house adheres to the reality of the
situation—in other words, that there is no room here for metaphor as there is
in language. Reduced to its fundamental schema, the gesture is the very one
that must be accomplished if a young couple is to begin living together. The
gesture has all the characteristics of an everyday action, yet it is a ritual gesture. And it is a ritual gesture because it makes use of both time and space.
Van Gennep has drawn attention to the importance of time in a certain
number of specific rites (the hiding of the bride, the flight of the bride),
pointing out that they "had the purpose of making the nuptial ceremony progress by degrees, stages, and steps," since "neither the separation from an
earlier milieu nor the reception into a new milieu can be accomplished in an
immediate mutation."[13] In much more theoretical terms Claude Lévi-Strauss
says something similar in *L'Homme nu.*[14] He remarks that the ritual always
proceeds by subdivision and repetition, thereby making use of two procedures that although seemingly fulfilling opposite functions (for one of them
differentiates among operations that would seem to be identical, whereas the
other endlessly repeats one and the same statement), in fact achieve the same
objective, which is to restore continuity to a human experience. What is actually subdivided in rituals is time, and it is this procedure that transforms

an everyday gesture into a ritual one. And one of the most effective modes of subdividing time is to inscribe a series of gestures in space: hence the outstanding importance of the wedding procession punctuated by three distinct stages. In conjunction with all the rites that have been grafted onto it, this ceremonial complex becomes a means of establishing the social and economic status of the new family cell that is being formed, a means, in other words, of anchoring a seeming change or mutation in the norms of everyday life. This theory advanced by Lévi-Strauss does not contradict Van Gennep's schema of the rites of passage, although it does, to be sure, go much further. Yet both authors stress that ritual is a matter of facilitating the community's acceptance of a change that upsets its economy by displacing persons, property, and values. This is why it is necessary to create time, a feat that, according to Van Gennep, is accomplished by a succession of stages, and according to Lévi-Strauss, by subdivision and repetition. Fragmented in this manner, time will be able to symbolize the much longer time that is normally needed to shape an organism as it undergoes gestation, evolution, growth, mutation, degeneration, or metamorphosis.

NOTES

1. J.-B. Thiers, *Traité des superstitions qui regardent les sacremens* (Paris, 1741), bk. 4, p. 565.

2. E. Beneviste, *Vocabulaire des institutions indo-européennes* (Paris, 1969), 1: 239–44.

3. Ibid., p. 241.

4. N.L.A. Richard, *Traditions populaires, croyances superstitieuses, usages et coutumes de la Lorraine* (Remiremont, 1848), pp. 198–99.

5. De Caila, "Recherches sur les moeurs des habitants des Landes de Bordeaux," *Mémoires de l'Académie Celtique* 4 (1809): 78–79.

6. M. Monnier, "Vestiges d'Antiquité observés dans le Jurassien," *Mémoires de la Société des antiquaires de France* 4 (1823): 359.

7. Thiers, *Traité des superstitions,* p. 477.

8. E. Westermarck, *Histoire du mariage,* trans. A. Van Gennep (Paris, 1934).

9. Laisnel de la Salle, *Souvenirs du vieux temps: Le Berry* (Paris, 1900–1902), p. 65.

10. Richard, *Traditions populaires,* p. 199.

11. Monnier, "Vestiges d'Antiquité," pp. 359, 361.

12. Descriptions of this kind can be found in the folkloric literature; see, for instance, Laisnel de la Salle, *Souvenirs,* pp. 51–52.

13. A. Van Gennep, *Manuel de folklore français contemporain* (Paris, 1943), 1: 325.

14. C. Lévi-Strauss, *L'Homme nu* (Paris, 1971), pp. 597–611.

2

The Marriage Ritual in France: Ecclesiastical Practices and Popular Practices (Sixteenth to Eighteenth Centuries)

André Burguière

The present research project was undertaken with a view to analyzing, by means of the symbolic modes of expression adopted by the marriage ritual, the collective representations that informed the relationship of the family group with the surrounding society and with the ecclesiastical power in France between the sixteenth and the eighteenth centuries. For this purpose, folklore furnishes abundant material. Ethnographers have often underscored the richness and abundance of ceremonial practices connected with marriage as a peculiarly European trait, noting that other rites of passage are more or less neglected in this cultural area.

There is hardly a local monograph in the plentiful collection of popular traditions assembled by travelers, administrators, and above all folklorists—from the survey of the Celtic Academy in the early nineteenth century to Van Gennep's *Manuel de folklore*—that fails to include a painstaking description of marriage customs (gifts, dress, propitiary or divinatory rites, and so on). But how can we reconstitute the history of these practices? Are they part—as the folklorists assert, and as the theologians claimed before them—of a pre-Christian cultural substratum, partially covered by sediments of Christian civilization? Or are they the expression of a recent surfacing, dating by and large from the eighteenth century, of peasant culture?

For the period before the nineteenth century we have many testimonies about marriage rituals. Aside from a few essays of the ethnographical type,

Annales, E.S.C. 33 (May-June 1978): 637-49. Translated by Elborg Forster.

however, which are of a fairly general character and tell us little about their sources of information (here De Gaya's book, *Les Ceremonies nuptiales de toutes les nations*, published in 1680, comes to mind), all of these works were written by churchmen. They were manuals of ritual published in each diocese for the use of the clergy, describing with great precision the sequence of events, gestures, and words to be used in the religious ceremony; synodal statutes and episcopal instructions which recommended or condemned certain practices; and finally, ecclesiastical compendia that listed and denounced popular superstitions.

These two types of source material are hardly comparable. In passing from one to the other, we come not only to a different period but to a different perspective as well. The illusion of the folklorist, who presents a set of popular practices and beliefs as an autonomous and immutable cultural system, impervious to social change and to the influence of the State, is supplanted by the normative illusion of the cleric, for whom any practice that strays from the ceremonies fixed by the Church amounts to deviance or the resurgence of old pagan customs. Yet for two reasons the ecclesiastical texts are more useful than the descriptions of the folklorists: they have a date, and they extend over a long time span. Not only do they provide a glimpse of the evolution of the ecclesiastical ritual by depicting its successive adjustments; their normative, indeed repressive, character also reveals the existence of practices that broke out of the official ritual and sometimes formed its counterpoint.

Yet the discontinuity of our source material must not mislead us; for there was no radical distinction between the religious ritual and the popular ritual, either with respect to their history or their function. Officially, the religious marriage ceremony had a juridical and sacramental purpose: the priest had to verify whether the two partners satisfied all the conditions that made their marriage valid (for example, that they had not contracted another engagement or that they were not related to a prohibited degree). He had to make sure that they freely consented to this marriage. Finally, by blessing the newlyweds and certain objects symbolizing their union (like the ring and the *treizain*), the priest did not administer the sacrament (the theologians had accepted the notion that the spouses administered the sacrament to themselves when they consummated the marriage), but added the sacred power of the Church to the consent of the spouses.

By way of compensation, scholars often attribute to the popular ritual an essential magic and social function: that of marking an individual's passing from the youth group into the adult group, or the passing of a woman from one family group to another, as well as the functions of warding off evil spells that might compromise the success of the new marriage and of predicting its fate. In reality, the religious ritual, which came into being by a series of adaptations and regenerations, absorbed many of the popular rituals. It preserved and even restored, after the Council of Trent, certain practices to which the population ascribed a magical function, such as the rite of exorcism (against the *nouement de l'aiguillette* [an evil spell over the groom's sexual potency]) or the blessing of the marriage bed (*benedictio thalami*) which was to parry the threat of sterility.

The popular ritual in turn often had a juridical purpose: it legitimized a relationship by celebrating it through forms of behavior that reinforced its public character (noise or derision, processions, the presence of large numbers of people) or through symbolic gestures and formulas that attested to its irrevocable character (such as the kiss or the joining of hands). In an article published long ago, E. Chenon[1] has shown how certain marriage rites that one would be inclined to interpret as so many symbolic expressions of the affective content of marriage have, in fact, essentially juridical origins and functions. This is the case for the kiss of betrothal, a legacy of the Roman custom that strengthened the fiancée's "betrothal right," entitling her, among other things, to gifts received "*ante nuptias*" in case of the groom's death. It is also the case for the joining of hands, a mandatory gesture for making a contract binding (the Roman law speaks of the *fides manualis*), as well as for the blessing of bread and wine, which illustrates the formula "sharing bread and pot" for the conjugal community.

As for the affirmation of the freely given consent of the spouses that inspired the major gestures and formulas of the religious ritual, it was not imposed by the thinking of the twelfth- and thirteenth-century canonists who made the validity of the sacrament contingent upon the couple's consent, but by the Roman law of the late Empire, which transformed the institution of marriage from a simple transfer of the woman into a consensual community. In reality, the Christian ritual was a patchwork of customs, some of them Jewish (the betrothal was expressed by an "earnest," that is, connected with a bride price), others Roman (it was a consensual contract) or barbarian (the agreement between the woman's father and the future husband was sealed by an exchange of tokens; on the wedding day the woman was handed over by her father to an intermediary, who might be a priest as well as a representative of the law).

When, after the tenth century, the Church began to shape the marriage ritual, it was only to the extent that it inserted into an already complex set of judicial operations the set of rules and regulations that followed from its theory of impediments. By and large, the reformers recommended that the popular customs be followed. By the end of the Middle Ages, the religious marriage ritual called for a certain number of obligatory gestures (the blessing of the rings, of coins, of the "earnest," of the newlyweds; the joining of their hands, and the transfer of objects symbolizing the union) and formulas (questioning the spouses, verifying their consent, the declaration of mutual giving). However, the manner in which these various sequences were fitted together, and hence the global sense of the ceremony, varied from region to region. Accord-

ing to J.-B. Molin and P. Mutembé,[2] these variants can be grouped around
two models, each of which corresponds to a dominant tendency of the religious liturgy. These authors cite the northern model, in which the juridical
aspect is predominant, and which is also called the Norman model, since it is
most coherent in Normandy, although it is also found throughout northwestern and western France. The other model is the southern one, in which the
sacramental aspect is predominant. It covers southern France and northeast-
ern France, from Champagne to Alsace.

One of the differences between these models lies in the place of the ceremony: in the Norman model the ceremony, to be followed in principle, but
not mandatorily, by a nuptial mass, takes place in front of the church (*ante
fores ecclesiae*), while in the southern model it takes place inside the church.
There is also a difference in the order of the proceedings: in the Norman model
the verification of the spouses' consent—essentially a juridical precaution—
precedes the joining of their hands during which the spouses pronounce a formula of mutual giving; whereas in southern and eastern France the gesture
that unites the spouses and the formulas of mutual giving come before the
verification of the validity of the commitment, that is, the verification of the
partners' freely given consent.

In the first case, priority is given to formal considerations and to the validity of the agreement. Here the priest acts primarily as a representative of the
law. He replaces or assumes the functions of the notary as the arbiter between
the two spouses—and especially between the two families—and as guarantor
of the legality of the union. In the second case, the reality of the relationship
takes precedence and indeed spawns the sacrament. The priest celebrates the
union more than he verifies its validity; he incarnates the authority of the
father rather than the control of the law. To a large extent, he uses his ecclesiastical power to deal with the sacred on behalf of the new spouses.

Many specific traits confirm this contrast. The simple fact that in the Norman ritual the ceremony took place outside the sanctuary indicates that the
Church intended to participate only in a formalized and limited manner. In
the southern model, by contrast, the celebration of the marriage inside the
church, with a pomp and a solemnity in which Molin and Mutembé see a
Visigothic legacy, underscores the desire of the ecclesiastical power to sacra-
lize this rite of passage and to absorb it completely into the religious life of
the community.

"Do the future spouses wish to have each other?" asks the priest in several
ritual books of the Norman type. One manual of Evreux adds: "When both
have given their consent, the dowry is to be presented." The tradition of the
giving of the ring and of the coins symbolizing the dowry constitutes a totally
separate operation. Inserted between the two parts of the ritual, the blessing
of the ring marks a pause designed to emphasize the distinction between the
giving to each other of two persons as expressed by the joining of hands and

the spouses' words of commitment, and the giving of material goods. This scenario, then, is informed by a strictly judicial logic: (1) The agreement is valid because it is freely consented to; (2) it involves a union between two persons; and (3) it involves a transfer of property.

In the southern rituals the priest sometimes asks: "Do the future spouses love each other?" The affirmation of the union by the giving of the spouses to each other precedes the verification of the validity of this union. Above all, one notes that instead of occurring one at a time, the ritual operations are tightly packed together so as to heighten the impact of the celebration. Thus, the giving of the ring (which is often blessed before the ceremony itself) takes place at the same time as the joining of the hands and the expression of the spouses' consent. In the accompanying formula spoken by the priest the ring becomes as much the symbol of the marital bond as of the goods pledged in the contract.

Does this mean that the marriage rite of northern France emphasized the transfer of property, whereas that of southern France emphasized love, and that southern France was most responsive to that which united two individuals, whereas northern France was more responsive to that which united two families? One cannot help but see a relationship between these opposing tendencies in the organization of the marriage ritual and the juridical practices that obtained in these respective regions, especially in the matter of succession. In Normandy and Brittany the law postulated complete equality among all the heirs. Since the father had no possibility of intervening in the transmission of the patrimony, the marriage contract became a precarious and perfunctory act. Under these circumstances it was almost natural that the priest should assume the juridical role of the notary, considering that the latter rarely had anything to do with the conclusion of the marriage. The rigidity and the formalism of this system of inheritance reinforced the contractual character of marriage. By casting the religious ritual in essentially juridical terms, the Church followed the bent of the local law. It went along with the lineage-orientation of the area.[3]

In regions where the right of the eldest [droit préciputaire] obtained, on the other hand, marriage was designed to exalt the authority of the father and the cohesion of the house. The priest had no reason to take the place of the notary, who was called upon by everyone, even the poorest families, to draw up the marriage contract. In this case, the priest acted on behalf of the father: his sacramental power metaphorically expressed the power of paternal authority. The Church acted on behalf of the house (or family), for the integration of the rite of marriage, underscored by a solemn liturgy celebrated at the altar, into the religious life of the community clearly shows what was really at stake in marriage: It was a matter of integrating the new wife carnally into her husband's "house," whose continued existence she was called upon to ensure. The importance accorded to formulas of mutual giving in the ritual confirms this preoccupation.

The sequence expressing the mutual giving of the spouses is no doubt the element of the ritual that had evolved most dramatically between the thirteenth and the sixteenth centuries; it also shows most clearly the plasticity of the ecclesiastical practices. Originally, only the husband spoke to accept the wife who was handed over to him and to promise that he would take care of her. Beginning in the thirteenth century, and under the influence of scholastic thought, which propounded the consensual nature of the conjugal bond, acceptance became mutual. It subsequently evolved, especially in southern and eastern France, into an increasingly active form of mutual giving. The Troyes ritual book of 1540, for example,[4] stipulates that the two spouses must declare, one after the other: "I take you to my wife (my husband) and to my wedded spouse, and I promise you that I will be faithful to you and that I will loyally share with you my body and my property, and that I will keep you in health and in sickness and in whatever state it will please God to place you. For better or for worse, I will not forsake you until death." Whereupon the husband, having received the ring from the priest, was to slip it onto the wife's finger saying: "With this ring I wed you, with my body I honor you, with my property I endow you."

This tripartite formula, corresponding to the threefold symbol of the ring, the joining of hands, and the pieces of money, became general in the sixteenth century. Yet certain ritual books of northern France were unwilling to adopt formulas of active mutual giving. Thus, the 1552 mass book of Amiens[5] has the priest say: "Jehan, I give you Marie; Marie, I give you Jehan." Whereupon he joins together their hands (*et debet sacerdos manus viri et mulier[is] insimul jungere dicendo*) and adds: "Jehan, you promise and swear that you will . . . loyally share with her your property . . . and that you will uphold faith and loyalty to her in your body and your property."

Does the formula of active mutual giving which progressively conquered northwestern France, a region traditionally bound by law and by consideration for the lineage, correspond to an improved condition of the conjugal couple? Here again, one cannot help but see a relationship between this ritual innovation and certain new successoral practices, such as the "universal community" or the "community limited to *acquêts* [property acquired during the marriage]," which appeared at that time in the Paris basin, but also in certain regions of the Southwest, such as the Bordelais.[6] As the ritual lost its clerical character, it began to favor the individual couple.

In fact, the Church's practices underwent a contradictory evolution in the course of the sixteenth century. On the one hand, the Church seemed more and more willing to adapt to the civil procedures. A ritual of betrothal (*verba de futuro*) was developed in response to strong social pressure to have the marriage concluded in several stages: the agreement and engagement between the two families, the signing of the contract, and the religious celebration. Among the 105 sixteenth-century books of ritual studied by P. Mutembé,[7] only 35 fail to call for some kind of ceremony of betrothal. Among those that do call for it, only 12 prescribe that it must take place in the church, and 16 mention other locations. Although some of these manuals recommend that the free choice of the betrothed couple be respected, the vast majority insist only that the agreement of the parents be obtained before marriage.

On the other hand, however, the Church strongly reaffirmed the sacramental character of marriage, especially in response to criticism voiced by the Protestants. Nor were the Protestants alone in criticizing the ecclesiastical rules. Humanists, jurists, and the royal administration—the latter concerned about the problem of clandestine marriages—all stressed the contradictions inherent in the institution.

Certain judicial sources can provide us with information as to how the religious ritual was perceived and used among the lower classes. A particularly helpful source in this regard is the rich *fonds* of the ecclesiastical tribunal [*officialité*] of Troyes, which is known to us thanks to the good work of an archivist who transcribed long extracts from it in the inventory of the archives of the department of Aube.[8] Between 1480 and 1540, many cases involving clandestine marriages, and especially betrothals, came before this tribunal. As always when dealing with judicial sources, one must receive the declarations of the defendants and witnesses with considerable prudence. But here the veracity of the testimonies is less important than the coherence and the homogeneity of the practices evoked in them. It turns out that the practices were remarkably similar, regardless of what may have been at stake in the statement made before the court.

Sometimes the case concerned a couple coming before the tribunal in order to have its union legalized. Sometimes it concerned a woman or a man seeking to be "adjudicated"—to use the tribunal's expression—a recalcitrant partner. Yet the scenario described is always the same. Take the case of Henriette, widow Legouge, versus Jean Binet (1483). Henriette declared that

since Christmas the defendant had several times asked her to become his wife. The latter had replied that she consented. Then, on the eve of Purification, the defendant came before Henriette's father and said that he would like to have the said Henriette for his wife if she were willing. Henriette said that she would be willing if her father were willing. The father said that he would be willing since his daughter was willing . . . .

Thereupon the father told his daughter to sit down at the table beside Jean Binet; then he poured wine into a glass and told Jean Binet to make his daughter drink from it in the name of marriage. Jean Binet obeyed without saying anything. Henriette drank without saying anything either. When this was done, Henriette's uncle said to her: "Make Jean drink in the name of marriage, as he made you drink." Henriette presented the glass to the defendant. He drank from her hand and then said to her: "I want you to receive a kiss from me in the name of marriage," and he kissed her.

Then those who were present said to them: "You are betrothed [*crantez*] to one another; I call the wine to witness."

The defendant replied: "This is right."

The popular ritual described here uses the same procedure as the religious ritual. The conditions that give it validity are fulfilled with an exactitude that is suspiciously reminiscent of a lawyer's brief: Henriette agrees to pledge herself because her father consents to the marriage; the father gives his consent because his daughter wants to get married. The ceremony is public, since Henriette's uncle and other persons are present. The wine drunk together by the couple attests to the agreement in the most classical manner. The kiss given "in the name of marriage" also gives expression to the agreement; as the symmetrical counterpart to the wine offered by the young woman, it confirms the reciprocity of the pledge. Those who witness the scene, finally, underscore the effectiveness of the symbols used ("I call the wine to witness") and the irreversible character of the agreement.

None of the other cases invoked in this source presents as scrupulous and as accomplished a ritual as this. Some of them attempt to give proof of a minimum of validity by citing the more or less public exchange of an object performed "in the name of marriage." Marguerite, daughter of Jean Gueux, declares that two years earlier, on the occasion of the quiltmakers' festival at Troyes, Guillaume Foucher offered her a pear, which she ate "in the name of marriage." The women who were present said to her: "He is your husband." But most of the plaintiffs had to fall back on the solemn exchange of an object "in the name of marriage" as presumptive proof of an engagement. Certain objects were specifically designed for this ritual exchange. This is the case with the *chanjon*, described by Jean Paisseley, a witness in the case of Jean Simon versus Jeanne Lepage (1530) as "a belt which the *cranté* (that is, the fiancé) gives to his fiancée, and she to him, and which is called *chanjon* because of this exchange." But it could also be a pin (same case), a flute (Marguin Pyot vs. Marguerite Royer, 1530), a tin goblet (Jean Bertrand, a fuller of Troyes, vs. Jacquette Gaudouart, 1506), a string of wool (Catherine Mongin vs. Pierre Gaytat, 1517), or a branch of "prune blossoms" (Jeanne Guiot vs. Colas Regnault, 1516).

Sometimes the exchange was altogether incongruous. Marguerite, widow Jacomat, claimed in 1532 that Pierre Pellart, who had carnally known her, had promised to marry her. She told the court that the defendant, holding her in his arms in bed, had said to her: "Marguerite, so that you will not be afraid that I will abuse you, I put my tongue into your mouth in the name of marriage." The invention is not without humor, but it was perfectly faithful to the spirit of the ritual. The bond was not created by the object that was exchanged, but by the exchange itself; moreover, what really counted in the exchange was not its reciprocity—and indeed we rarely hear of an exchange in the strict sense of the word—but the transfer. In 1483 Bernarde put her hand into Jean Geoffroy's gamebag, pulled out a handful of coins, and asked him: "Do you give me this to do with as I please?" "I do," replied Jean Geoffroy. Whereupon she gave back his coins to him, saying: "Well then, I give them back to you in faith of marriage." Perrette, interrogated in 1504 about the manner in which she had become betrothed to Thomas Belle, said that he had taken from her a ring that she was wearing and given it back to her in the name of marriage.

Men and women, then, drank from a goblet that was offered to them; they touched their lips to a flute that was handed to them; they ate a pear that was given to them; and whenever these objects were presented "in the name of marriage," they became invested with magical power, and the slightest physical contact with them could create an irreversible bond between the person who touched the object and the person who presented it. It would be absurd, of course, to reduce the popular ritual of marriage and its connection with the religious ritual to this belief in the magical efficacy of the objects exchanged. The same judicial source contains several descriptions of a civil ritual that faithfully reproduced the gestures and formulas of the religious one. On the occasion (1502), for example, when Jean Bourgeois was caught in amorous dalliance with Henriette Parigot, who lived in the household of Pierre d'Egremont, seigneur of Eclance, the latter improvised in the middle of the night, in the presence of witnesses who were awakened for the purpose, a somewhat forced ceremony of betrothal. A witness asserted that Pierre d'Egremont threatened to cut off Jean Bourgeois's ears unless he "*créantait*" [promised marriage to] Henriette. For the ceremony, Pierre d'Egremont took the hands of Henriette and Jean Bourgeois and said to Henriette: "You promise to take in proper marriage dictum reum [the said defendant]?; quod et fecit dicta adjuncta [and the said plaintiff did promise]; et vice versa dictus d'Egremont eidem reo dicendo [whereupon the said d'Egremont turned to the said defendant saying]: You promise to take in proper marriage dictam adjunctam [the said plaintiff], quod et fecit ipse reus [which the defendant did]."

The presence of a nobleman, no doubt a man of at least some learning, may account for a better knowledge of the ecclesiastical ritual: the joining of hands and the declarations of mutual giving are here performed in the proper canonical form (even though, by that time, the ritual of Troyes called for a less active participation on the part of the officiating agent).

The practice of anchoring the popular ritual to the exchange of symbolic objects may have been a recent phenomenon in the early sixteenth century. Far from viewing the development of a religious ceremony of betrothal as an adaptation of the ecclesiastical practice to a custom with which they were familiar, people were often confused by it. The betrothal divided the religious ceremony into two parts: at the time of the betrothal one declared (in the *verba de futuro*) that one was "beginning a marriage"; at the time of the wedding one declared (in the *verba de praesenti*) that one was "concluding a marriage begun earlier."

The betrothal also made for a period of uncertainty at the very time when families expected the Church to sanction the bond and to demonstrate clearly its irreversible character. It is possible that, in the face of this uncertainty, the popular imagination tended to invest in the objects themselves the sacramental efficacy and the power of legitimation which the Church no longer seemed to impart as clearly.

Is it possible, however, that we are being misled by our source? Could it be that our witnesses concentrated their testimony on the objects exchanged purely as a matter of juridical tactics? Was this the way to prove that a situation had arisen that called for reparation? The many demands for execution of promise of betrothal brought before the ecclesiastical tribunal at the end of the seventeenth and in the eighteenth centuries—and I was able to verify this for Troyes as well as for Paris and for Beauvais—all mention an object given or an exchange made as a pledge to keep a promise or pay a financial compensation. Here the object, which was usually given as the pledge of a promise, always had a considerable material value, while in the *crantailles* [betrothals] of the early sixteenth century it was transferred and manipulated symbolically and almost never had any real value.

To stay in Troyes, let us take the case of Marie Garnesson, who in 1686 was made to return the "earnest" she had received in exchange for a promise of marriage which she did not wish to keep. She made the following deposition to the clerk of the court: "A fur muff in its case. Two ells of cloth, two ells of fine lace, one candle of gilded silver, one candle of silver, a pewter-ring, ten sols for a pair of gloves, and six livres in silver." In this case, the pledge was essentially of a pecuniary character.

In 1667 Joachim Simon, a writing master of Troyes, in a suit against Savine Dieu, daughter of a master braidmaker of that town, who no longer wanted to marry him, referred to the "promises made to him by the said defendant . . . surely of her own free will and accord, since she had even come to the plaintiff's father's house in order to reciprocate the visits the latter had paid to her; and since she had come in person to the goldsmith to choose the rings she wanted, as well as to a house where the plaintiff had invited and treated an honorable company to a collation." The reciprocity of the visit was to prove that the agreement had been freely consented to, and the expenses incurred called at least for compensation.

At the end of the seventeenth century, popular practice continued to invest the manipulation of objects and of the formulas of the marriage ritual with a magical power to bind. But it is clear that the Church no longer accepted this practice. The Catholic reformation that swept France in the wake of the Council of Trent profoundly transformed the ecclesiastical marriage ritual. To begin with, the ritual was progressively unified, so that by the end of the seventeenth century, Pope Paul V's Roman ritual had everywhere replaced the multiple regional variants. In addition, the ritual was brought back under the control of the clergy; all the ceremonies, whether it be the betrothal or the wedding, had to take place in the church. Henceforth, the presence of the priest was indispensable, not only for verifying the validity of the union but also for making the ceremony effective. The priest's "Ego conjuguo vos" had come to replace the different formulas of mutual giving and the joining of hands that had earlier been left to the couple.

The Church was determined to impose a new form of piety, one that would be quiet, chaste, and scrupulously subservient to the guidance of the Church. No longer was devotion conceived as the individual or collective expression of awareness of the sacred that included exuberant joy as well as sadness, earnestness as well as high spirits; it had become an exercise in asceticism and discipline. Popular practices that the Church had long accepted as normal concomitants of the marriage ritual—perhaps even as particularly fruitful ground in which to plant its own roots—had now become unacceptable because of (1) the forms these practices assumed, which were henceforth considered to be "disreputable" and scandalous; (2) the power to censure or to legitimize that was asserted in them; and (3) the religious concepts they conveyed, which were henceforth rejected as "superstition" and "paganism."

Characteristic in this connection is the Church's change of policy with respect to the betrothal, an old institution of the customary law and a vital part of the marriage procedure for most people to the extent that it sealed the agreement between the families of the future spouses. Having made a strenuous effort throughout the sixteenth century to integrate this civil practice into the religious ritual by greatly developing the religious ceremony of betrothal, the bishops now attempted to play down its importance and to turn it into a means of moral improvement. In regions where the population did not seem to be very attached to it, roughly speaking, in southern France, the bishops preferred to prohibit it altogether.[9] Elsewhere it became one of the steps in the verification of the validity of the projected marriage and a device for moral education.

Until the middle of the seventeenth century the promise of marriage inaugurated a period of tolerance during which the betrothed couple began to live together. These premarital relations, which in certain regions were consistent with solid traditions of sexual permissiveness and fairly well controlled by the family or the age group, were accepted by the couple's families all the more readily as the latter were not always very sure at what point in the religious procedure the union was consecrated and therefore became both legitimate and irreversible. Henceforth the Church made a forceful effort to combat such tolerance: "Since a shared domicile and the overly intimate frequentation between betrothed persons, and even between those whose banns have begun to be published, often lead them into sin, we very expressly forbid them to live in the same house before they are married, and we forbid their fathers and their mothers, guardians and relatives, masters and mistresses, and all those who have power over them, to favor and permit their living in this manner. Moreover, we enjoin the parish priests to do their utmost to prevent this," stated an ordinance of the bishop of Auxerre, Monsignor Colbert, in 1695.

In certain dioceses this prohibition was repeated by synod after synod, a sure sign that the Church had trouble enforcing it. In order to reduce this ambiguous period of transition as much as possible, the date of the betrothal, which initially had to take place before the publishing of the banns, was later placed closer and closer to the date of the wedding. Having become a simple formality, the austere betrothal of the seventeenth century eventually became totally antiquated and turned into a folkloristic ritual.

The blessing of the marriage bed underwent a similar evolution. Like many other aspects of the popular ritual, this old fertility rite had been discreetly taken over by the Church. It took place long after the blessing of the marriage, usually after the wedding banquet, at the home of the newlyweds. In the sixteenth-century manuals, the exordium spoken during the blessing placed the main emphasis on the harmony, fidelity, and fecundity of the couple: "Ut in tua voluntate permaneant et in tuo amore vivant et senescant et multiplicantur in longitudinem dierum" [that they may remain faithful to your will, and that in your love they may live and grow old and multiply in the fullness of time], states the manual of Autun (1514); this expression is repeated in those of Laon (1524), Amiens (1552), and Chartres (1604). The priest's exordium was usually accompanied by ribald songs and jests, which provided a popular counterpoint to the propitiatory evocation of good understanding and sexual prosperity for the couple.

The post-Tridentine reform maintained the "benedictio thalami," but turned it into a celebration of conjugal chastity. In the 1646 ritual book of Paris, most of the exordium is devoted to a commentary on the story of Tobias, the symbol of chastity and even abstinence within marriage. In that of Chartres (1689) the priest is enjoined to bless the marriage bed only in the presence of the parents of the newlyweds and two or three persons of venerable age. The text adds: "Monebitque conjuges et assistantes ut risis aut ludicia inhonesta non admisceant ne per nujusmodi actus illicitos et profanos sanctitatem sacri connubii . . . polluere aliqua ratione videantur" [He will admonish the spouses and all those present that they must not engage in laughter or unseemly banter, nor by any illicit and profane behavior . . . appear to pollute the sanctity of holy matrimony in any manner whatsoever].

The ritual books and the texts promulgated by the synods of the seventeenth century objected not only to the lewd banter that accompanied the blessing of the marriage bed but indeed to all the exuberant forms of popular piety, such as the "disguises and indecent acts which offend the honor of the temples and the sanctity of this sacrament" (statutes of the synod of Soissons, 1673), "disreputable singing and dissolute dancing" (Châlons-sur-Marne, 1657), and every kind of musical accompaniment: "The priests are not to tolerate oboes, violins, and other similar instruments in the church on the occasion of a wedding" (Beauvais, 1699).

This determination to break with the traditional forms of behavior led reform-minded prelates to take a repressive stand against all rejoicing and noise, as we can see from the following directives for the celebration of marriage issued by Monsignor de Clermont (Laon, 1696): "Desiring that our diocese be cleansed of that pomp and that profane display which the peasants are in the habit of deploying there, we herewith forbid the future spouses to be led to the church to the sound of violins, whether it be for the ceremony of betrothal or for the wedding; we also forbid the ringing of the bells for the betrothal, as well as the trappings that go under the name of welcomes, bouquets, and similar displays, all of which are imbued with the spirit of paganism."

It is difficult to decide whether the noisy forms of behavior were condemned because they ran counter to the quiet and reserved piety that the Church henceforth wanted to impose or because they asserted a form of publicity, a power to legitimize that competed with the ecclesiastical authority. I have elsewhere analyzed the evolution of the Church's attitude toward the charivari,[10] a demonstration that involved both noise and chastisement and was henceforth condemned by the Church on those two grounds. Also condemned were the extortion of money and of "wedding wine" (seven of the ritual books I have analyzed cite this "wedding wine"), two traditions that expressed the young bachelors' defense of their right to the local girls. In September 1657 Nicolas Porcher, the ecclesiastical judge [*official*] of the diocese of Paris, sent out an admonitory letter condemning "several superstitions, insults and acts of violence committed by the young bachelors of the village of Montrouge when a marriage is celebrated in the church," stating "that they continue these insults at the time of the blessing of the marriage bed and that, on the day after the celebration of the marriage, they capture the newlyweds and to that effect lead them . . . to a shallow pond at the edge of the village, force her [the bride] to genuflect and even make her drink the water of the said pond, to dip into it and then to kiss the doors and entryways of nearby houses and [to engage in] other actions marked by paganism."[11]

These "disorderly acts," whose perpetrators were threatened with excommunication by the ecclesiastical judge, represented a rather well-known and widespread practice. De Gaya's book *Les Cérémonies nuptiales de toutes les nations*, written twenty years later, mentions it for France: "In some places the poor new bride is not free to go to bed when she is ready. She is first made to suffer a thousand pains, and very often she is led through thorn bushes, through marshes and brooks, before she is returned to her husband on the next day."

It was a matter of introducing the new wife to the community—and it is likely that this was done when she came from outside the village—by a series of initiatory ordeals designed to acquaint her with the space she was about to appropriate. What the Church condemned here was, to be sure, the element of mockery that colored this practice, but also the claim to control over the village's marriages asserted by the local youths on these occasions.

Commenting on the 1536 ritual book of Périgeux, J.-B. Thiers wrote [in 1701]: "When the betrothal was concluded and when the priest had said: 'Now kiss each other in the name of the marriage that will be if it please God,'* this same priest makes them drink in the name of marriage. . . . This ceremony, which I dare not call superstitious because of the book in which it is written down, is among those that have since been deleted from the ritual books."[12] This text reveals the extreme suspicion with which the Church, well aware that its efforts to standardize the existing practices represented a break with its own tradition, viewed any form of active participation. The ecclesiastical ceremonial became imprisoned in a tight circle of suspicion, as if in some strange way the suppressed practices were poised to return, and as if all the old practices, unless expressly ordered by the priest, could only be inspired by paganism. The manuals no longer limited themselves to prescribing the gestures and words of the ceremony; they also warned against uncontrolled upsurges of symbolic content.

The priest was to be very careful to bless only one wedding ring: "Annulus . . . benedicendus sit unicus, argenteus, simplex . . . caveatque maxime Parochus ne plures simul uni sponsae tradendus benedicat" [Only one simple ring of silver is to be blessed . . . the priest must be very careful not to bless several to be given to one spouse], states the 1646 ritual book of Paris. This warning is expressed in the same terms in the ritual books of Boulogne (1647) and Châlons-sur-Marne (1649); and that of Chartres (1689) adds: "Deinde oblatum a sponso annulum unicum (insignum rejectae a christo polygamiae) ante non benedictum benedicit" [Having been handed by the bridegroom a single, not previously blessed ring (an emblem of Christ's rejection of polygamy), he blesses it]. This justification of the single ring as a symbol of the rejection of polygamy simply adds another argument to the warning against popular practices. Similarly, the priest must be careful not to drop the ring when he slips it onto the couple's fingers: "Caveat sacerdos ne ex digito extrahatur aut data opera, cadat annulus" [The priest must be careful that the ring is not taken from the finger or that it falls to the ground during the ceremony] (Ritual book of Boulogne, 1647). J.-B. Thiers mentions among the "superstitions concerning the marriage celebration and the nuptial benediction" that "brides let the ring fall to the ground in order to fore-

---

*In *patois* in the text.—Trans.

stall evil spells." He also mentions the custom of having several rings blessed. Pointing out that in the past the diocese of Bordeaux used to give a ring to each of the spouses (ritual book of 1596), our superstition hunter adds: "But I do not believe that this could be done today without superstition."[13]

Thiers seems to indicate that, in his day, the Church rejected as superstition what it had earlier accepted as one among many formulas of the religious practice. Several historians have recently insisted on the separation wrought by religious reform (Protestant as well as Catholic), which created a gap between the rationalistic, moralizing, and often ascetic devotion of the Church and the superstitious popular devotion that remained confined within its magical universe.[14] Considerations of space do not permit me to enter here into a study of the mental categories that found expression in these superstitions; but these mental categories were still intact in the folkloric customs described for the nineteenth century. Suffice it to say that the principles underlying superstitious practices, according to E. Delcambre,[15] (for example laws of contrast, similarity, and contact), are equally applicable to the conditions that made for effective popular rites of betrothal and marriage, such as those described in the statements made before the ecclesiastical tribunal and in the warnings sounded by the seventeenth-century books of ritual.

By its repressive attitude, and by the new principles of conformity which the Catholic reformation sought to impose on devotional practices, the Church forced the popular ritual practices relating to marriage into a new and specialized category. Yet the two practices were neither totally competing nor totally separate. Certain customs by which the youth group imposed a brief period of abstinence on the newlyweds after the religious ceremony seem to transfer into the popular ritual the emphasis on asceticism that had come to permeate the ecclesiastical ceremonial. Conversely, the Church's continued attachment to rites and prayers of exorcism (against evil spells and sexual impairment, the so-called *nouement des aiguillettes*) clearly shows that it did not intend to break completely with the magical universe that sustained the imagination and the anxieties of the people.

One has the impression, however, that the popular practices henceforth became concerned primarily with social integration (hence, perhaps, a development of those rites that asserted the territorial rights of the local community, such as the "wedding-wine" exacted at the "gates"), whereas the responsibility for moral guidance and the juridical and administrative supervision of marriage was left to the Church.

NOTES

1. E. Chénon, "Sur quelques rites nuptiaux," *Nouvelle Revue historique du droit français et étranger* (1912).

2. J.-B. Molin and P. Mutembé, *Le Rituel du mariage en France du XIIe au XVIe siècle* (Paris, 1974). The authors also distinguish a third model, which they call the "common" one, but it seems less clearly delineated in time and space.

3. Cf. E. Le Roy Ladurie, "Système de la coûtume," *Annales, E.S.C.* 27 (July-October, 1972): 825–46. Translated in R. Forster and O. Ranum, eds., *Family and Society: Selections from the Annales, E.S.C.* (Baltimore, 1976).

4. *Rituale seu manuale ecclesiae trecensus* (Troyes, 1540).

5. *Missale ad insignis eccl. ambianensis* (Amiens, 1552); text dating from 1498.

6. J. Lafon, *Régimes matrimoniaux et mutations sociales: les époux bordelais (1450–1550)* (Paris, 1972).

7. P. Mutembé, "Le Rituel de mariage au XVIe siècle," unpublished typescript (Paris, 1973).

8. This very rich *fonds*, which is preserved in series G of the departmental archives of Aube, has been partially transcribed in the inventory. My analysis is based on this transcription. For a more systematic study, see Beatrice Gottlieb, "Getting Married in Pre-Reformation Europe: The Doctrine of Clandestine Marriage and Court Cases in Fifteenth-Century Champagne" (Ph.D. diss., Columbia University, New York, 1973).

9. C. Piveteau, *La Pratique matrimoniale en France d'après les statuts synodaux.*

10. "Repression religieuse et pratique du charivari en France (XVe-XVIIIe siècle)" in *Colloque sur le charivari* (forthcoming).

11. Archives nationales, Paris, Z^{10}, 129.

12. J.-B. Thiers, *Traité des superstitions qui regardent les sacremens* (Paris, 1704).

13. Ibid.

14. See, for example, Keith Thomas, *Religion and the Decline of Magic* (New York, 1971); and Jean Delumeau, *Le Catholicisme de Luther à Voltaire*, Collection "Nouvelle Clio" (Paris, 1972).

15. E. Delcambre, *Le Concept de sorcellerie dans le duché de Lorraine* (Nancy, 1948).

3

Zacharias; or The Ousting of the Father: The Rites of Marriage in Tuscany from Giotto to the Council of Trent

Christiane Klapisch-Zuber

Between 1300 and 1500, one iconographical theme, the Marriage of the Virgin, or *Sposalizio*, became surprisingly popular in the art of central and northern Italy. It was not, of course, the only theme to deal with marriage. Millard Meiss has drawn attention to the appearance in fourteenth-century Tuscan painting of several novel themes in the treatment of the family, the couple, and the child.[1] Does this mean that the *Sposalizio* is simply one among other testimonies to the new concern with family and domestic life among the middle classes of Italy?[2] Its pervasive flowering on the walls of the sanctuaries of Tuscany, and eventually of Umbria and other regions of Italy, also suggests that the Church found it a useful tool for the edification of the faithful. But to what ends was it used? I will attempt to shed light on the originality of the iconographical premises of the *Sposalizio* by relating them to the contemporary ritual practices followed in the conclusion of alliances and marriage. In doing so, I shall use the *Sposalizio* as the indicator of the evolution of the rites of marriage and their takeover by the Church,[3] a phenome-

Annales, E.S.C. 34 (November-December 1979): 1216–43. Translated by Elborg Forster.

This study is the latest in a series of articles in the *Annales* (1978) devoted to the rituals of kinship. Its elements were assembled for a seminar on this subject held between 1975 and 1977. They were submitted to the criticism of American colleagues during a lecture tour in January of 1979. I would like to thank the following colleagues for their criticisms and suggestions: M. Becker, G. Brucker, S. Chojnacki, S. Cohn, R. Goldthwaite, D. Herlihy, R.˙Lopez, E. Muir, R. Starn, R. C. Trexler.

non that has already been most perceptively analyzed elsewhere. I will therefore adopt a frankly historical perspective. My purpose is to prepare the ground for a full-scale reflection on the place of ritual in Tuscan society.

Before the Council of Trent, the Church, in its efforts to gain control over the ceremonies connected with marriage, had to deal with a wide variety of situations in the Western world. The rituals of alliance had evolved in a largely autonomous manner since the late Empire, even if borrowings and adaptations seemed at times to create similarities between rites observed in provinces far removed from each other. But by the fourth century, and in the Western Empire, the *matrimonium justum* was already founded above all on the wish to be married. Customs and rites of marriage had to demonstrate this wish, although the validity of the marriage was not attached to any particular forms. In keeping with this general tendency, the Church very soon adopted the policy of letting its flock observe the "local customs," provided that the spouses were permitted to give free expression to their consent. The consent expressed by the partners was thus to become the basis of Christian marriage, and this pattern tended to assign secondary importance to the other means of access to "just marriage," i.e., the validation of the union by nothing more than recognition of conjugal cohabitation or the conclusion of an alliance legally contracted by written documents, dowries, and donations.[4]

In its earliest stages this evolution thus favored one of three avenues leading to marriage without, however, imposing any mandatory forms upon the gestures, words, and acts surrounding the conclusion of the alliance. "Freedom of form" was the motto that, in western Christendom, allowed the historical evolution of marriage rituals to take an independent course until the Council of Trent. In 866 Pope Nicolas I sent a reply that was to become famous to the Bulgarians, who had already become instructed in the Greco-Byzantine rite; his statement stressed the concept of the nuptial rites that had become prevalent in the West, where they were subordinated to the "consent of those who contract the conjugal bond and of those who have authority over them." Unlike the Eastern Churches, the Roman Church did not feel that the absence—caused by poverty, for example—of *iura nuptiarum* tainted a freely consented marriage with illegitimacy.[5]

The emphatic affirmation of the principle of consent given by the spouses "and those who have authority over them" as the most important obligation that validates and institutes marriage allowed ancient popular rituals of marriage and a wedding liturgy to subsist and develop in the western provinces of Christendom. It appears that this autonomy of the ritual forms of alliance in relation to the Church's doctrinal content permitted France and Italy and their various provinces to individualize the agents, gestures, words, and objects of the ceremony in their own ways by inserting them into differing contexts and arranging them in ritual scenarios that varied greatly from region to region.

Yet in France, beginning in the eleventh century and especially the twelfth century, the religious authorities made a concerted effort to standardize these procedures as part of their increased desire for control. In this endeavor they pursued a threefold goal: to make the partners aware of the sacramental nature of the bond that was about to unite them, to verify the licitness of the projected union, and to make sure that the consent was freely given.[6] In certain regions this threefold endeavor spawned a number of transformations that invested the ritual with entirely new significances. These transformations included changes in the place where the ceremony was performed, the transfer of functions from one actor to another, and modifications in the symbolic value explicitly attributed to the gestures, words, and objects involved in the liturgical ritual.[7] In Italy, the Church achieved its goals with greater difficulty and later than in France. Could the reason be that the ecclesiastical model of marriage, such as Georges Duby has defined it for twelfth-century France, remained less distinct in Italy, and that the Italian clergy was not as determined to impose it?[8] My study of the nuptial scenario, the shifts and internal substitutions it underwent, and finally the ideal model proposed by the *Sposalizio* will attempt to elucidate the original features of the evolution of the Italian rituals in relation to those of France or northern Europe.

The Stages of the Wedding in Fourteenth- and Fifteenth-Century Florence

What sources exist for this investigation? Such historians of marriage as E. Chénon for France[9] and F. Brandileone for Italy[10] have largely used documentation of a normative or repressive character, as well as notarized documents. In addition, Brandileone was also wise enough to analyze a long description of aristocratic weddings in Rome, written shortly after 1500 by the humanist M. A. Altieri. This important and extraordinarily interesting text[11] may be the first attempt at systematic reflection by a European about the rituals of alliance, marriage, and the wedding celebration in use among his contemporaries or their immediate forebears. It soon becomes clear that this layman's perception of the Roman rituals of marriage is informed by a double cultural identity, Christian and ancient at once, which suggests to him more than one "transcultural" interpretation. His description of the marriage customs of the fifteenth century is therefore as valuable for the mass of information it conveys as for the symbolic reevaluation to which it subjects the ritual elements analyzed. There is, to be sure, a normative and pedagogical bias in his discourse, for Altieri makes no secret of his intention to inform the fictional interlocutors of his dialogue about the nature of the aristocratic wedding in the good old days, a model that since 1500 has become corrupted by a pervasive acquisitive attitude. But it is important to note that he condemns a number of civil practices of his time from a layman's point of view. His criticisms therefore go beyond the areas of concern that circumscribed the clergy's denunciations of certain popular superstitions, and by the same token his description of the popular ritual of marriage includes far more than the strictly liturgical matters treated in the diocesan manuals of ritual.

The charge of bias does not apply to texts emanating from the civil authorities. For the most part, these relate to the sumptuary regulations enacted by the Italian communes to deal with the customs and abuses arising from festive occasions.[12] Moreover, my investigation can gain considerably wider scope by using sources of a juridical nature relating, if not to actual forms of behavior, which are still not well known for Italy, then at least to the many more or less succinct accounts of the nuptial drama that have been left by the protagonists themselves, the givers in marriage and those who were married. Numerous instances of such texts can be found in the household books kept by the Florentines, which exist in great profusion for the period 1300–1550.[13] I shall examine here this body of texts from Florence only,[14] but it is certain that the investigation could make use of similar texts elaborated in other Italian cities.

In describing the marriages of their close kin and the expenses incurred for the festivities, these "merchant-writers" provide a clear picture of the high points and the various stages of the ceremonies involved, the actors and the attitudes and gestures expected of them, the gifts and objects that circulated among them, and some of the words they had to pronounce in order to give substance to the projected marriage. These domestic chroniclers certainly experienced the ritual of marriage as a coherent whole and felt that its various phases naturally complemented each other.[15] Indeed, the system constituted by the phases of this ritual guided their writing to such an extent that they treated it as a single entity, which they endeavored to describe on one page, even if its elements were spread out over a certain lapse of time. In this manner, accounts of alliances and marriages were usually inserted *en bloc* into the entries about domestic events that were kept up, day after day, by these Florentines. To be sure, their accounts are very often condensed and stereotyped;[16] moreover, they describe only the customs observed by a limited social milieu, that is, the middling bourgeoisie and the families belonging to the merchant oligarchy or the urban aristocracy. Despite these reserves, what we learn from them can be considered extremely revealing of the unique character of the Italian customs of marriage in a Tuscany profoundly marked by Lombard influences. It can also serve to set these customs apart from the French marriage ceremonies, which had been imposed long ago by the Church.

Two distinctive traits manifest what one might call the archaic nature of the popular Italian rituals, which were still strongly marked by Roman and Lombard influences and largely impervious to the pressure brought to bear by the Church. To begin with, the set of ceremonies that constituted the marriage ritual was organized around several poles, and it is difficult to decide, at first sight, which of these was the predominant one.

The architecture of the nuptial scenario can be compared to a triptych. Its predella would be the first negotiations and the preliminary agreement between the parties, without which the matter clearly would not go any further. These preliminary negotiations, which have been described in detail by Altieri[17] as well as by many Florentine *ricordanze*, were mediated by a professional *sensale* or by a more or less interested friendly soul who took it upon him or herself to propose a profitable match. These negotiations then proceeded with the help of one or several *mezzani*, friends of the two families who acted as buffers between their conflicting interests. They culminated in a first meeting between the two parties, that is to say, between the parents of the future spouses, accompanied by three or four close relatives. The purpose of this meeting was to "set up the alliance" (*fermare il parentado*). In the fifteenth century the terms of the agreement were set down in writing and this *scritta*, a private act, was kept by the accredited intermediaries.[18] In fact, this agreement very often remained confidential at this point, and many domestic chronicles stress the fact that the parties have pledged themselves not to reveal it before a certain amount of time has elapsed, either because the spouses are still too young or because they have to wait for a dispensation, for the preparation of the final arrangements concerning the dowry, or other matters of this kind. Symbolic gestures sanctioned this agreement. In Rome, where the ceremony went by the name of *abbocamento*,[19] its most important feature was the kiss on the mouth exchanged by the partners in the negotiation, who also did not fail to shake hands all around. The Florentines, in their ceremony of *impalmamento* or *toccamano*, favored the immemorial gesture of the handshake, the customary sanction of all contracts.[20] At this point the father could say that he had *impalmato* his daughter. As soon as this agreement was concluded, the future husband rushed to the house of his intended, usually bringing her a present—rings or jewelry—and was treated to dinner by her family.

The first panel of the triptych consisted of a solemn and public meeting between the two parties, both accompanied by the largest possible number of friends and relations. On this occasion, however, only the male members of the families who planned the alliance and their in-laws were present. Not even the "betrothed bride" was invited to this masculine affair, and it was the person who "had authority" over her who promised the future husband that he would give her to him as his wife and that he would prevail upon her to give her consent. The future husband in turn promised to take her as his wife within the period of time and under the conditions agreed upon, and in Rome another *baso di bocca* ritually expressed the validity of the publicly proclaimed agreement.[21] Meanwhile, the notary had drawn up the *instrumento delli futuri sponzalitii*, as Altieri calls it, a document that stipulated the dowry and other financial terms of the marriage.[22] Guarantors and arbiters were appointed; they would be called upon to implement the terms of the contract and to supervise its execution—the paying off of the dowry in particular, but also the dates of the ensuing festivities. This sequence of events, which had different names (in Florence it was usually *giure* or *giuramento grande*, and *sponsalia* or *sponsalitium* in notarized documents; in Rome it was *fidanze*), was found throughout central and northern Italy. It constituted the act of alliance *par excellence*, since it stated and guaranteed the terms of the exchange, which involved a woman and property.

This engagement was extremely binding; it could not be broken without the most serious consequences. It is recognizable as an avatar of the ancient Germanic *bewedding*.[23] The Florentines preserved the crudely contractual character of these *sponsalia*; the woman, a mere object of this trade, had no part in it. The *giure* of the good Florentine families therefore bore only a very faint resemblance to the more intimate ceremony of betrothal with which the Church was trying to replace it in certain regions of France.[24] In Florence, where the promised bride was not present (and in some of the oldest texts she was not even specifically mentioned among all of a family's daughters),[25] no actual banns were published. It is true that the archbishop of Florence, Saint Antonino, stressed the role of the public *sponsalia* of great families, saying that they took the place of duly published banns "in certain places where they are publicly celebrated long before the marriage."[26] The public character of the agreement of alliance, in other words, made it possible—in theory— for potential opponents to voice their doubts as to the licitness of the union before the wedding took place.[27] But at this stage of the procedures an intervention that threatened to jeopardize an alliance without producing "good reasons" was likely to trigger nothing less than civil war in the fourteenth century and a long-lasting grudge between the offended families in the fifteenth. As for the normal space of time between the *impalmamento*, the first direct but not yet public agreement, and the solemn *giure*, it was usually much too short to allow for any serious verification from the outside. Under these circumstances the application of the rules governing impediments to marriage as established by Lateran IV was bound to remain rather vague. By and large, only their own genealogical knowledge could prevent the Florentines from committing an error that would threaten public tranquillity and bring dishonor to the families contracting the alliance.

The setting of the second panel in the triptych was the bride's house. Present were her relatives by blood and alliance, men as well as women. They had been invited by her father, brother, or guardian, who had also summoned a notary. The future husband arrived with his relatives and friends. At this point the notary asked the questions prescribed by the Church in order to receive the couple's express agreement to the union negotiated by their families. Thereupon he took the woman's right hand and led her to the husband, who slipped the wedding ring onto her finger. The notary recorded this sequence in the *instrumentum matrimonii*.[28] Next, according to Altieri,[29] came the presentation of the gifts brought by the husband and his entourage to his in-laws, followed by a collation or a banquet provided by the wife's family. In Florence this ceremony was usually called the "ring day," after the solemn bestowal of the symbolic object that was most apt to strike the imagination. The notaries and canonists called it *matrimonium*, but the words *sponsalia, sposalizio,* and *desponsatio*, which in the fourteenth century were used most frequently to designate the *giure*,[30] were still widely applied to the ceremony involving the exchange of consent and the *anellamento* in the fifteenth century.[31] These nuptials were called *arraglia* in Rome, a term in which Altieri, with some hesitation, detects the old meaning of "earnest of marriage" (*arrhes de mariage*) and which he willy-nilly applies to the dowry itself, as the "pledge of the future marriage."[32] In Florence the Latin expression *subarratio per annulum* refers to the same root, and in the Florentine countryside, far into the fifteenth century, brides were still said to be *subarrate, anellate, waidiate* after this ceremony, that is to say, "pledged."[33] By the end of this day the spouses were considered to be husband and wife.[34] But before it was considered "complete," the marriage had to be consummated, though not before public notice of its celebration had been given to the entire community.

The third panel of the triptych is devoted to the ceremony of "publicity" during which the new bride was conveyed to the house of her husband, whose relatives and friends received her with a feast and rejoicings that were sometimes spread out over several days. Traditionally the union was physically consummated at the end of this wedding day. Among the Florentines and among the Romans, this sequence presented all the classic features of a rite of passage as described by Van Gennep.[35] The bride bade a tearful good-by to her kin and solemnly betook herself to her husband's house, led by the friends of the latter. Crowned and decked out in all her finery, she rides through the town at night by torchlight, mounted on a white palfrey, escorted by her husband's "friends."[36] In Rome, by contrast, according to Altieri, the spouses met on Sunday morning at a church, where they attended a mass at the end of which the priest blessed them.[37] In fourteenth- and fifteenth-century Rome the liturgy was thus an integral part of this marginal phase of the long ritual of marriage. As I shall discuss, this was not the case in Florence, for here the bride's way to her new domicile did not include a stop at a sanctuary. In this manner, the wedding festivities explicitly notified the entire community of the consent that had united the new couple, provided the bride's new kin with the opportunity of honoring her, and conveyed the new couple to the marriage bed, thereby putting the crowning touch to the union that had slowly come into being.

In recapitulating the major episodes of the Florentine ritual of marriage, I must insist on the distinction between the contractual phase that regulated the juridical transfer of the woman from one group within society to another, the very ritualized, festive phase that marked her physical transfer to her husband in full view of the entire community, and her actual reception into the group of married and adult women. Yet in Tuscany as elsewhere, the *desponsatio* had become split into two parts; some of its contractual aspects spilled over into the public *giure*, a ceremony that can hardly be seen as a "betrothal" in which the future spouses exchanged the *verba de futuro* as recommended by the Church. On the other hand, the consensual nature of the marriage found expression in the "ring day," which also included the juridical formalities that settled the delivery of the bride to the husband and the payment of the dowry. In the fifteenth century the ultimate phase, that of the wedding proper, was often reduced to minor importance, owing to the imbalance introduced into the scenario as a whole by the increasing emphasis on the earlier ceremonies. An investigation of the days that were chosen to celebrate the various ceremonies will enable us to judge this pattern more accurately.

Indeed, it is rather instructive to be able to locate these ceremonies in time and to attach them to specific days of the week with a view to understanding the economy of the nuptial scenario and judging the means of control which this scenario afforded the Church. Altieri provides a few chronological benchmarks. In the Rome of his grandparents (late fifteenth century), whose rites he sets out to describe, Sunday, a day of solemnity which could be expected to bring together the greatest number of people, and thus witnesses, was always chosen for the public transfer that brought the new union to everyone's attention. Altieri indicates that this Sunday of the wedding was also the day when the new bride received a special benediction on the way to her new abode. But while he speaks about the delays between the first three acts (one to two weeks between the *abboccamento* and the *fidanze*, a week between the *fidanze* and the *verba de praesenti*, and as much as a year between the last and the wedding), and while he painstakingly describes the chronological sequence of the immediate preparations for the wedding, he says almost nothing about the days chosen for the first three ceremonies.[38] Fortunately it is possible to fill in the gaps in this time chart with indications from the Florentine narrators, whose household books outline every detail of these phases. Their habit of keeping a daily record of the ordinary run of family matters dates their accounts of the proceedings so precisely that it is possible to break down the process by which a woman came into a new family into a number of distinct phases. Whenever these writers do not indicate the day of the week, it is easy to calculate it with the help of other chronological indications.

For the three principal ceremonies that marked the high points of the ritual, the Florentines frequently chose Sunday; however, Thursday and Wednesday turn out to be, individually or together, almost as attractive as Sunday. Of the 126 "ring days" mentioned in these Florentine texts between 1300 and 1530, one-fourth took place on a Thursday and a good one-third on Sunday. In this manner, the Florentines divided their preference between the day of *Juno pronuba* and the Lord's day when it came to bestowing the greatest solemnity on the exchange of consent, the very foundation of marriage. A more minute periodization shows that the tendency to hold the "ring day" on a Thursday may be a late development. Before 1430, the giving of the ring took place on a Thursday one time out of six or seven; thereafter it was almost one time out of three. The preference for holding the wedding ceremony on Sunday is undeniable, indeed almost exclusive; between 1300 and 1530, 45 percent of a cohort of 122 new brides were "led" to their husbands on a Sunday. Here again, the marked preference for Sunday seems to have become accentuated later; before 1430 the number of solemn transfers undertaken on Wednesday and Thursday combined was equal to the number of transfers undertaken on Sunday (40 percent for Wednesday and Thursday together; 40 percent for Sunday alone), while in the second period, around the time when Altieri recorded his parents' customs, Sunday was chosen in almost half of all cases for celebrating weddings in Florence.

What conclusions can we draw from these facts and from these rudimentary statistics? To begin with, the predominant position of Sunday as the day when certain of the most important nuptial ceremonies were enacted undoubtedly reflects the wish to give the the widest possible publicity rather than the desire to integrate them into the religious ceremonies that took place on Sunday. I shall return to this point in connection with the clergy's participation in these rites. Second, one wonders whether shifts in the location and in the importance attributed to the various phases of the nuptial pageant are a reflection of profound mutations in the ritual as a whole. In order to shed light on the value attached to these different poles of the ceremony, finally, I shall examine the moment chosen by the new couple for the consummation of the marriage.

Altieri attributes to his Roman forebears a wise restraint, which prompted them to wait until the night of the wedding before bringing the wife into the conjugal bed, regardless of the length of time—a year and sometimes more— that had elapsed between the *matrimonium* and the wife's departure for her husband's house.[39] It appears that the same custom was also widely practiced in fourteenth- and early fifteenth-century Florence. Unfortunately, the texts under consideration here are not often explicit on this point, and among the Florentine *ricordanze* dating from this early period I have found only a handful (five, to be precise) of instances providing the date on which the spouses consummated the marriage. In each of these cases, the completion of the marriage took place on the night after the wedding day, after the woman, having been "sworn" (*jurée*), then "wedded" (*epousée*) or "ringed" (*annelée*), had been "led" to her husband. In the fourteenth century and still in the early fifteenth century, the expression *menare donna* unequivocally meant "to lead one's wife under one's roof"; it implied that the consummation followed the transfer. In a town in Lombardy, witnesses who had seen the passing of a wedding procession could infer that the union would be consummated shortly thereafter.[40] This *ductio uxoris in viri domum* was thus the ultimate precondition for access to the physical union. In the household *ricordanze* of the late fifteenth and early sixteenth centuries, explicit notations concerning the time when marriages were consummated become more frequent. Among some fifty precise notations, sixteen indicate that the marriage was consummated on the "ring day," following the exchange of consent, while nineteen cite one of the days between the ceremony and the wife's transfer to her husband's house. In both of these cases it is evident that the union was consummated at the home of the young woman's parents. Only ten of these notations indicate that the consummation took place on the evening of the day when the wife was brought to the conjugal home. In five cases, finally, the "ring day" and the wedding day seem to be one and the same, and the marriage was consummated on that day. Do these data warrant the conclusion that the exchange of consent gradually relegated the wedding procession and the public festivities to a secondary rank? Can it be said that a fundamental distinction came to be made between the necessary and sufficient condition fulfilled by the *verba de praesenti* and the popular rite imposed by "local custom," a respectable but not indispensable part of the ritual of marriage? If such an evolution could be proven, would it not provide evidence for the growing influence of the Church by the fact that it placed the main emphasis on the fundamental act of the sacrament of marriage, the free exchange of consent?

In the end, however, it could well be that the statistics will take away with one hand what they seemed to give with the other. The shifting meaning of the expression *menare* makes it extremely ambiguous and compels me to qualify the figures that suggested this interpretation to me. As a matter of fact, it is not rare for a domestic chronicler to write calmly that he "led and consummated" (or "slept with her") "in the house of [his father-in-law]" only to describe, three lines further down, how a few days later he "led her to his house." In the second statement, *menare* still has the meaning of leading the bride physically to her new home, but in the first it has obviously been contaminated by the notion of consummation with which it has long been associated and has come to mean the act of consummation itself! Consequently, it becomes extremely difficult to determine in the texts of the second period just what is meant by the expression *menare* when the context is not given. It is quite possible that whenever the date of the consummation is not specified, the many references to the "leading" of women may reflect the practice of the Trecento, when the consummation followed the transfer. This would mean that the evolution seemingly suggested by the distribution of the dates of consummation may take into account the exceptional cases, precisely because the writer felt obliged to be more accurate in his description.

Nonetheless, the testimony of contemporaries, whether they were preachers or simple observers, seems to corroborate this first impression of an increasingly close relation between the "ring day" and consummation.[41] Antonino[42] complained that in his day brides had a hard time preventing that "in their parents' home their fiancés (*sponsi*) did shameful things when they visited."[43] Bernardino of Siena severely criticized the custom of newlyweds, "encouraged by thoughtless parents," to "rush into the carnal union" as soon as the ceremony of *desponsatio* was over, and sometimes even before.[44] To his mind, these "brutal animals and dogs" were moved by base credulity, inspired by the devil and by "fear of spells and charms" that threatened the couple with impotence. Altieri also indicates that the Romans of his time were afraid of being "tied up by evil spells," especially on the day of the wedding procession, when the public nature of the event exposed the couple to every possible form of malevolence.[45] Consummating the union ahead of time—a course of action that was, after all, made licit by the preliminary exchange of consent—was therefore a means of forestalling the occult interference of some troublesome mischief maker.

Another reason, of an institutional and financial nature, further accounts for the haste with which well-to-do Florentines went about consummating the union just as soon as it was concluded. In the fourteenth century it was customary to celebrate the marriage, at least the wedding festivities and the wife's arrival at the husband's house, only after the dowry had been paid.[46] This norm was fraught with innumerable twists and exceptions. Yet it did subordinate the "completion" of the marriage and its culmination in the physical union to the at least partial execution of the agreement concerning the dowry. After 1434 a new financial institution, the *Monte delle Doti* enabled those Florentines who could afford it to invest at interest a capital sum earmarked to become, ten to fifteen years later, the dowry of their daughter.[47] When this "bond" came due, the husband received the sum, in full or in part, provided that the marriage was consummated and the tax on the dowry paid. This led to a veritable inversion of the traditional scenario. Whereas the payment of the dowry had traditionally been the precondition for the consummation of the union, the consummation now became the precondition for the payment of the dowry. What prompted the Florentines, with their strong allegiance to the old principle that the dowry must be paid before the final phase of the wedding, to make this change? The parents of a marriageable daughter no doubt found the new arrangement to their advantage, since it protected them against reconsideration of an already agreed-upon alliance and against a husband's refusal to receive his wife under his roof on the grounds that the dowry was not paid.[48] The shift in the moment when the marriage was consummated became acceptable and ceased to pose a threat to the honor of the families contracting the alliance as soon as the payment of the dowry by the State, a transaction that was firmly linked to the consummation of the union, made the obligation irrevocable for the son-in-law and his family.

This modification of the matrimonial scenario thus operated to the advantage of the "ring day," when the exchange of the *verba de praesenti* made the carnal union licit. Bright and early on the next morning the happy husband would rush to pay the tax he owed and then go to collect the sum owed him by the State or at least register his claim. The wedding proper might well be put off until later, or even omitted altogether; the essential part had taken place and the marriage was "complete." Here is one example among many others: when Messire Niccolò Altoviti married Antonia, the daughter of Bernardo Rinieri, he "attached her by oath and gave her the ring" on Thursday, 24 November 1485, and on that evening "led" her in the house [of B. Rinieri] without any other wedding celebration. On Monday, 28 November he collected the dowry, and it was not until 1 February 1486 that he sent his wife the traditional presents and had her brought to his house.[49] This case shows a veritable condensation of several phases of the scenario around the supremely important moment of the giving of the ring. However varied the motives for this concentration may have been, they all benefited the central ceremony and detracted from the other episodes, which were annexed or eclipsed by the "ring day." Around 1500, then, a long, drawn-out ritual of marriage, whose phases were dispersed among a number of poles, gave way to a new and much more focused pattern of ceremonies, all of them closely gathered about the *verba de praesenti* and amounting to an early foreshadowing of modern marriage as it would emerge from the Tridentine reform.

The fact that the financial institutions of the Republic guaranteed the payment of dowries testifies to a new attitude of the well-to-do classes toward State intervention in the affairs of their families. This dependence is even more striking among the families who were among the Prince's clients after 1470. The skill with which the Medici played the role of givers in marriage is well known and its political importance is evident, for it was a matter of using the marriage alliances of their clients for gaining control over their ties of fidelity and solidarity.[50] A few precise examples will serve to illustrate the nature and the timing of their interventions. A number of books of *ricordanze* show that, by manipulating the traditional position of the *mezzani*— the friendly intermediaries between families who contemplated an alliance— and of the arbiters, the Medici forcefully asserted themselves as the guarantors *par excellence* of the marriages concluded among the families of their clients and eventually among the entire urban aristocracy. In the third quarter of the fifteenth century the Medici often took it upon themselves to instigate the preliminary negotiations between such families; there were more and more cases in which their mere presence was sufficient to give binding force to an agreement concluded earlier between the two families. No need, in that case, for the solemnity and the public notice afforded by a church, nor even for the presence of all of the family's "friends and relations" to formalize the *giuramento*. Most of the *ricordanze* indicating that the *impalmamento* took place under the aegis of Lorenzo, in his chamber of the Palazzo della Signoria, at his bank, or at his private palace, either do not mention any other ceremony of *giure* or expressly note that no further ceremony was held.[51] The series of operations by which a marriage came into being was thus stripped of the essential sequence by which, a hundred years earlier, two lineages made their alliance public. Here again, the ritual was gathered more closely about the "ring day."

Do the modifications in the internal balance of the popular rituals of marriage testify to an increased power of the Church to shape the manner in which marriage rituals were enacted in Florence? In the light of what has just been said, the answer must be negative. Indeed, I am inclined to see this fact as the second archaic trait of the Italian rituals in comparison with those of France. Unlike the French rituals, which by the eleventh and twelfth centuries had already transferred to the vicinity or even the interior of the sanctuary rites that had earlier taken place in a domestic setting or in a public square and which had consolidated in the person of the priest a number of functions that had formerly been carried out by a layman,[52] the Florentine rituals persisted in attributing no more than marginal importance to the presence of the Church and to the religious consecration of the union. I shall briefly analyze the various aspects of this disregard for the Church's recommendations which the Florentines were to manifest until the Council of Trent.

Paradoxically, the Florentines considered Sunday as a particularly propitious day, and the sanctuary as a particularly propitious place for a nuptial ceremony only as long as the Church was not involved in the ceremony itself. As I have pointed out earlier, the choice of Sunday for the *giure*, for the "ring day," or for the wedding was not related to a desire to integrate these ceremonies into a religious rite. The formal character of the "peace" between the lineages who concluded an alliance or the ritual circuit of the bride was a function of the festive day on which it took place. Similarly, the custom of choosing the sanctuary or its purlieus for celebrating the *giure* seems to have been primarily a matter of creating a climate of neutrality and of giving a certain publicity to the peace sealed by the *osculum* and to the pledge made by the two families. In 1356, and again in 1384, when the city of Florence promulgated a decree ordering that the *sponsalia* take place in a church, this step was taken above all with a view to reinforcing this commitment to public tranquillity.[53]

Neither through its representatives nor in its legislation did the Church directly intervene in the ceremony of the *giure*. Its absence is equally noticeable on the "ring day." In medieval France the inroads made by the apparatus of the Church, its sanctuary and its clergy, in the rites of the *verba de praesenti* enabled the clergy to control and eventually to "liturgize" this supremely important moment. Yet for the Tuscan families under study here the ceremony in which the consent of the spouses was expressed remained largely a domestic event until the eve of the Council of Trent. The "ring day" was almost always celebrated at the house of the bride's father, guardian, or patron. I can cite only one case in which a priest officiated, and this exception precisely confirms the rule! On 19 September 1477 Filippo Strozzi married his second wife, Viagga Gianfiglazzi, at an estate in the country. The notary, who had been summoned to ask the requisite questions and to accept the spouses' consent, failed to appear. At that point Filippo fell back on a priest who happened to be there.[54] The matter could not be put more succinctly: the priest was used as a mere stopgap. Far into the sixteenth century, statutory texts and synodal legislation continued to assign these important functions to the notary.[55]

The most surprising aspect of the Florentine rituals of marriage and of their archaic autonomy, however, is their casual attitude toward the religious benediction. This was despite the fact that the archbishop of Florence, Antonino, in his *Summa*[56] and in his *constitutiones* of 1455,[57] had unequivocally insisted on the obligation to hear a mass at a first marriage, addressing himself especially to the *contado*, where the faithful were no doubt even more thoroughly ignorant than the city dwellers. Much better informed and guided though they were by the Church and its predication, the urban dwellers seemed scarcely more interested than the peasants in attending the wedding mass, which was not included among the festivities of the wedding day in Florence as it was in Rome. The household books very rarely indicate that a *messa del congiunto* was celebrated at any point in the nuptial scenario. Only twelve of these accounts (two before 1430 and ten after that date) report that the couple, or only the woman, heard mass and received the blessing of the Church. To judge from these few testimonies, the Florentine spouses who did sanctify their union preferably did so on the "ring day" itself, before the exchange of consent, and sometimes on one of the preceding days. None of these twelve masses was celebrated on a Sunday.[58] Should we assume that the religious ceremony was so automatic that a writer did not even feel called upon to record it, and that the expenses involved were so minimal that they were, with one exception, never noted among the other minor expenses incurred by the head of the household? It seems more likely to me that the Florentines had as casual an attitude toward the Church's blessing as the country people or as Macchiavelli's Nichomachus, and that they were quite simply content to handle the matter of marriage "like brute beasts" and to skip over this tiresome formality for the bride.[59] In the last analysis the need for it was determined by each individual's piety. The core of the ritual was elsewhere.

Among the popular classes the sequence of juridical acts surrounding the marriage was more concentrated and truncated by several episodes, but it did give the clergy a chance to play a more important role than it did in the families described in the *ricordanze*.[60] Notarized acts show us a great many "documentary films" of these marriages of artisans, even *contadini*.[61] We know little about the gestures and symbols of betrothal among the lower classes of Tuscany. Saint Antonino agreed that the engagement could be made in different ways, by means of a simple promise, by the gift of a "token of betrothal, such as money, jewelry, etc.," by the gift of a ring, by an oath or a promise similar to an oath, or by words spoken "with honorable and serious intent."[62] Several of these forms could thus easily accommodate all kinds of popular rituals that had been shunted into the background in the solemn *giure* of the patriciate. In his study of the notarized acts of alliance, Samuel Cohn found that only about ten percent of all the unions that gave rise to a notarized contract were preceded by an *instrumentum sponsalitii* drawn up at the time of the *giure*, and that virtually all of these concerned wealthy families.[63] The artisans and workers of Florence, by contrast, regularly went to a notary to record the dowry, however small, they gave to their daughter; the scrivener would, usually shortly thereafter, record the exchange of consent and the giving of the wedding ring. The ring of the poor, moreover, seems to have been bestowed more often under the dome of a church, before a priest or a few monks who served as witnesses.[64] Among the "people" the priest could almost naturally play the role of mediator and privileged witness to which he aspired, for the economic stakes of the marriage were not very high. Among the lower classes, finally, the new bride followed her husband immediately after the ring ceremony, provided that the dowry had been paid.[65]

Everything I have said thus far, whether it concerns the rich or the poor, shows that the religious blessing of the marriage, while by no means mandatory, was associated with the ring ceremony. To be sure, the spouses' exchange of consent, the very foundation of marriage, still took place in a domestic setting and eschewed the presence of a representative of the Church; yet the fact that the religious ceremony was drawn to the symbolic object given on this occasion, together with the feeling that this ceremony should be a preliminary to the sacrament of marriage, gave this object a role in a religious rite that had not yet come into its own.

The Role of the Wedding Ring in Tuscany and the *Sposalizio* of the Virgin

The ring as a symbolic object has a long history in the rites of marriage of the Western world; that story cannot be told here.[66] The meaning of the Roman engagement ring, the *anulus sponsalitius*, which was the token of a promise, was later enriched by the Eastern notion of an "earnest" of the dowry promised. In the late Middle Ages the ring became integrated into the Germanic ceremony of the *desponsatio*, which constituted a very binding commitment. Once the Church had found a way to impose its conception of marriage as a consensual union, so that a distinction was made between the preliminary ceremony in which the commitment of the families was expressed and the ceremony of the *verba de praesenti*, the *anulus sponsalitius* became associated with the second rather than with the first ceremony.[67] Here it preserved its character as the token of a promise that made the marriage definitive and conveyed the right to consummate the union. Yet the Roman idea that the ring was the token or pledge of a promise or an earnest of the promised dowry, though gradually overshadowed by a more intimate conception, was never completely discarded. In Florence by the fifteenth century the ring was no longer a "pledge" of material promises in the strict sense, and the bride who had received the ring [the *anellata*] was hardly ever referred to as *pledged* [*gagée*] as well. Yet whenever an educated Florentine said that the wedding ring he had slipped *maritali affectu* onto his wife's ring finger was a token of the promised faith, he meant, above all, the wife's fidelity. Moreover, while the exchange of consent was mutual, the giving of the ring was not. The husband, and he alone, gave a ring bearing, in the case of the aristocratic Romans described by Altieri,[68] the coat of arms of his lineage rather than one of the mottos of mutual fidelity favored by the ancients.[69] The ring thus did not affirm the affection and the personal bond of the union without implicit restrictions.

Owing no doubt to this long-standing connection with a wide variety of juridical and symbolic acts and to its deep roots in the popular ritual of alliance itself, the ring became a central symbolic object that lent itself to any number of new interpretations and to various readjustments that did little to change its mandatory character. This polysemia and this symbolic richness were not lost on the Church, which, at a very early date, found ways to make use of it in the liturgy of marriage as the only object that would universally remain a licit part of the religious ceremony.[70] Having undergone many changes of meaning throughout its long history, the ring also enabled the Church to change the course of an evolution which, as I have shown by means of the more flexible popular rituals of Florence, was still discernible well into the fifteenth century. It could easily be integrated into the new pastoral guidance that stressed the understanding of the consensual nature of marriage. And indeed it was the ring that was given a central place in the pictorial representation of the marriage of the Virgin in the fourteenth and fifteenth centuries.

The story of the marriage of the Virgin and the miracle by which Saint Joseph was designated as Christ's terrestrial father has undergone many transformations. The oldest Eastern version known is found in the proto-evangelium of James, an apocryphal gospel of the third century.[71] Mary, a tender young maiden (twelve years old) approached the age when her presence became a threat to the purity of the Temple where she had been brought up. The High Priest was bidden by an oracle to entrust her to one of the widowers of Judah; a sign, he was given to understand, would designate the chosen one. Then it came to pass that the divine dove emerged from a staff carried by Joseph, a kindly old man burdened with grown sons. Panic stricken, Joseph tried to declare himself incompetent for the task by alleging his sons and his old age. But it was no use; the priest entrusted him with the keeping of little Mary, although nothing was said about marrying the old man to the future mother of the Redeemer.

Four or five centuries later, in the apocryphal text of pseudo-Matthew, which is the more immediate source of the Western representation of the *Sposalizio*, the theme of Joseph's election appeared in a new guise.[72] Although the Church had long ago refuted the notion that Joseph was a widower, this motive, which is still present here, once again justifies the old man's modesty and his reticence. On the small staff that he has brought to the Temple like all the men of Judah who are "free of conjugal bonds," a dove alights, and at this sign of divine election everyone congratulates him. Here again, his entreaties do not dissuade the High Priest from placing the Virgin in his keeping until the day when he is to marry her. The decisive change occurred in the abridgment of this legend, which, written in the ninth century and long attributed to Saint Jerome, appeared under the title *Book of the Birth of the Virgin*.[73] Here Joseph's staff, influenced by Aaron's rod, bursts into bloom at the same time that it receives a dove, thus becoming a double miraculous sign that obliges Joseph—an old man whose widowerhood and previous fatherhood are no longer mentioned[74]—to receive Mary after their *sponsalia* have been celebrated on the spot. In his reelaboration of the *Golden Legend* Jacobus de Voragine once again treats the theme of the *desponsatio*, which obliges Joseph to return to his house "to make preparations for the wedding."[75] At this point, then—when the evolution of the written legend was complete and when its iconographical development was just beginning— an aged Joseph was chosen among all the unmarried men of Judah[76] to become the husband of the Virgin, thanks to the miraculous signs visited upon the "little staff" he had brought into the Temple. Under pressure from the Church the apocryphal theme of his widowerhood, which the Western theologians deemed incompatible with their doctrine of the purity of Christ's parents, had disappeared, yet it still seems to loom behind the old age that the Western legend continued to attribute to the saint. The other characteristically Western trait is the disappearance of the "placing" of young Mary "in Joseph's keeping" and the appearance of the theme of her betrothal[77] and later that of her marriage. This transformation took place between the ninth century and the end of the thirteenth century, precisely when the *sponsalia* were split into two phases.[78] The *Golden Legend* does not describe the forms observed in this marriage of the holy couple. But in seizing upon this theme, art was soon to give a precise account of these forms on the walls of Italian churches.

The iconography of this pious legend between the eleventh century and 1300 is based on very ancient and varied traditions.[79] Both north and south of the Alps certain earlier representations were not yet aware, it would seem, of the apocrypha, for they show an ordinary marriage observing the forms inherited from antiquity, in which a central figure joins the hands of a young Joseph with that of the Virgin in the traditional *dextrarum junctio* of the Romans. In other sculptures, acquaintance with the Eastern account of Joseph's election as transmitted by the protoevangelium of James or by pseudo-Matthew, can be inferred from certain details that were subsequently eliminated by later Western versions, although they appeared again and again north of the Alps well into the thirteenth century. They are the small size of the Virgin as a still not fully grown girl and the gesture of the High Priest, which corresponds better to placing Mary in the old man's keeping than to their union. The representations of the Marriage of the Virgin which, by the twelfth and thirteenth centuries, became more and more numerous in the French and German cultural spheres, finally, include more clearcut references to the *Book of the Birth of the Virgin*. Here Joseph as an old man often carries a leafy or flowering staff, sometimes crowned by a dove; useless staffs, abandoned by the men of Judah, are scattered over the ground and the altar; and the High Priest joins Joseph's and Mary's hands together.

Around 1300, these representations of the Marriage of the Virgin were very numerous north of the Alps, but almost unknown in Italy. It is true that Byzantine models had inspired a mosaic at Saint Mark's Cathedral in Venice (early thirteenth century) and a fresco in the upper church at Assisi, but the decisive renewal of this outdated iconography would be brought about at the chapel of the Arena in Padua by Giotto.*

In the cycle he devoted to the life of the Virgin, Giotto elaborated a most original synthesis of the preexisting models of the election of Joseph and of the *Sposalizio* by adhering faithfully to the *Golden Legend*. First of all, consider the setting: the scene takes place at the door of the Temple; the Byzantine altar where the staffs had been deposited in the expectation of the miracle is visible inside the building at whose threshold Mary's and Joseph's conjugal fate is decided. Some critics have viewed this scene as an allusion to Jewish customs: since marriage was not a sacrament, the scene could not be enacted in a consecrated space and therefore necessarily had to be moved outdoors under the open sky, although it had to take place near the Temple where Mary had grown up.[80] But it seems unlikely that Giotto or the donors of his painting were interested in a correct representation of the Jewish customs.

*For an illustration of Giotto's *The Marriage of the Virgin*, see *Annales E.S.C.* 34 (November-December 1979): 1229.

Surely, this would be to attribute to them a concern for historical accuracy that was far removed from the intentions of medieval iconography. Giotto's choice of the square in front of the temple as the setting of the holy wedding may well have been justified by more immediate reasons than such antiquarian scruples.

Consider also the protagonists. To the left stands Joseph, with the gray beard of an old man. The flowering lily stalk he holds in his left hand is weighed down by the dove that is perched on it. Mary, with her flowing hair, wears a wreath of flowers. The ages and the attributes to these two figures are obviously borrowed from the *Golden Legend*. Their respective positions also deviate from the Byzantine models Giotto might have seen not far from there. Joseph to the left and Mary to the right stand next to the High Priest, who, facing the beholder, is about to join their right hands together. The frontal position of the priest harks back to the schema inherited from the Romans in which *Juno pronuba*, and later her successor, *Christus pronubus*, presided over the *dextrarum junctio*, the symbolic gesture that came to prevail north of the Alps both in the ritual and in the iconography.[81]

Yet Giotto deviated from this tradition by representing in this painting the giving of the ring as practiced among his compatriots. His real innovation was the inclusion of this ritual object, which he placed in the center of the composition. The Virgin seems to be holding out the fourth finger of her right hand, which is supported by Zacharias, while Joseph's right hand, guided by the priest, presents the ring to her. This gesture, this finger, and this object would henceforth always be featured in the great flowering of representations of marriages after 1300, ranging from the mystical marriage of Saint Francis with Poverty and the marriages of the two Catherines with Christ, to marriages between lay people depicted on chests (*cassoni*) or in Italian miniatures.[82]

As for the other participants in the miracle of the staffs, the *Golden Legend* suggested their presence and their endorsement of the *Sposalizio*. In Giotto's fresco, the crowd of men of Judah pressing in behind Joseph comments rather excitedly on the event. One of the men breaks his barren staff over his knee, and seven others still hold theirs in their hands. While a certain disappointed surprise marks the faces of the unsuccessful contenders, most of whom are much younger than Joseph, they do not show any real hostility. This absence of acrimony is faithful to the apocrypha. One young man, it is true, raises his hand behind Joseph's back, but there is nothing threatening in this gesture. Raffaello Corso has correctly identified it as the representation of a popular ritual that was still condemned by the Italian synods in the eighteenth century, namely, the more or less violent blow struck on the husband's back by his *compater anuli* at the moment when the consent was exchanged.[83]

The fact that the Tuscan painter included this gesture of the popular ritual in his illustration of the apocryphal account underscores the independence of his pictorial representation and brings to light the image evoked in his mind by a ceremony he had witnessed many times. In this manner the *Golden Legend* and its models, which tell us nothing about the rite followed in the marriage of the Virgin, are completed by the painter. By depicting this gesture of his contemporaries, Giotto accomplished a radical updating of the nordic interpretations of the ceremony, for he anchored it in the reality of Italian life. Under these circumstances, one wonders about the relationship between this type of imagery and the conceptions the Church sought to impose on the ritual order of the wedding ceremony. Should the *Sposalizio* be considered an instrument of propaganda with which the Church intended to undo the popular ritual? Conversely, one also wonders to what extent the Church accepted the symbolic gestures of the popular ritual. We do know, in any case, that the extension and the development of Giotto's *mise en scène* and of his various inventions led the Italian painters, especially those of Tuscany, far afield in their interpretation of the legendary miracle, an evolution that, in a kind of backlash, led to a sharpening of the edifying and militant function assigned to the *Sposalizio* by the Church.

The setting, the actors, and the objects depicted by Giotto were destined to become extraordinarily popular in Italy. At first only the Tuscan painters vied with each other in giving prominence to certain details of his fresco.[84] By the fourteenth and fifteenth centuries all of them, whether Florentine or Sienese, adopted Giotto's conception and situated the scene near the entrance of the Temple, under its portico or in its atrium, at the foot of the steps, in the garden, or in the street running through the middle of the painting. Their quasi-unanimity is all the more striking as painters belonging to other regional schools would often use a different setting, the entrance or the interior of the church, when they treated this theme in the fifteenth century. Only the Umbrian school[85] would remain firmly attached to the tradition begun by Giotto; Raphael, emulating Perugino, was to give a convincing twist to this conception: in his painting at Brera, the triumphant bulk of the Temple, an autonomous and central structure, looms over the marriage that is enacted at the edge of the vast paved square in front of it.

The Tuscan, Umbrian, and many of the Lombard painters thus located the "*Sposalizio in facie ecclesiae*" and, more literally, "*ante foras ecclesiae*." Were it not that the church is outlined in the background, many of the Tuscan paintings might evoke the loggias of the old Florentine houses that sheltered the festivities that the great lineages wanted to celebrate with all the publicity and splendor they could muster, such as *giure*, peacemakings, and weddings.[86] Yet there is no evidence that the actual exchange of consent on the "ring day" normally took place in these loggias. The porticos of the Tuscan paintings therefore do represent the atrium of the sanctuary. One might wonder why these painters did not choose to locate their *Sposalizio* in the very center of the consecrated space, before the altar or at the entrance of the nave, as the Venetian and many Roman, Neapolitan, and even Lombard painters were to do. Recall that the Church was intent upon establishing a closer connection between the sanctuary and ecclesiastical control over the licitness of the union and the voluntary nature of the consent, and that these procedures were indeed carried out at the entrance of the church in medieval France and in certain regions of Italy, probably under the influence of the Norman ritual.[87] The portico of the Tuscan paintings is thus indicative of a desire to shift the *juridical* control over marriage to a representative of the Church; it does not convey an insistence on the religious blessing. A study of the gestures attributed to Zacharias confirms this contention.

Giotto's *Sposalizio* invests the giving of the ring to Mary with an undeniable religious tonality, yet it very much respects the gestures of the ritual practices of the Tuscans and therefore merely shows an ecclesiastical actor in the place where a layman officiated in actual practice. In the paintings of Tuscany and Umbria the priest always occupies a central position, but he merely guides the future spouses' hands toward each other, or even only advances Mary's hand toward Joseph's.[88] Before the sixteenth century the painters of these two regions almost never show the priest blessing the spouses. In other words, the painters assigned to Zacharias the place occupied by the registrar, but also by the father or the guardian of the bride, the man who handed her over to the husband on the "ring day."[89] In keeping with the Church's ambition to gain control over the domestic rite, the roles played in the Tuscan ritual by the notary and the father were united in the person of Zacharias; yet, curiously, he was not shown as the priest sanctifying the marriage through his blessing! In the *Sposalizio* the Church asserted the need for its intervention *before* the transfer of the woman to the husband, *before* the consummation of the marriage, and *at the moment* when the ring most forcefully symbolized the consent and the sworn faith of the spouses; yet in Tuscany it did not avail itself of this iconographical theme to preach the need for a religious blessing of the marriage, which it considered necessary but not indispensable for the validity of the union.

In giving this new twist to the popular rituals, the painters of the *Sposalizio* went very far indeed. Giotto's followers thus added secondary figures and details that, although unknown in the legendary story, reminded the beholder of gestures he could observe all around himself. Musicians and trumpeters at the wedding festivities, a "May branch" carried by a young man, little boys clinging to a woman's neck in a propitiatory rite—all of these secondary motifs, which were indicative of an ongoing exchange between the popular and the ecclesiastical culture, would eventually be either eliminated in later interpretations of the scene or given a new allegorical interpretation (viz., the *putto*, the little dog as an emblem of conjugal fidelity, or the dove of the Holy Ghost hovering far above the staff carried by the saint). But it is the manner in which the ritual blow was treated by Giotto's successors that provides the most telling illustration of how the openness of the iconography to popular practices came to undermine the exaltation of the religious marriage ceremony conveyed by the *Sposalizio*.

In point of fact, the Tuscan painters of the fourteenth century altogether changed the nature of Giotto's invention when they turned it into the sign of a heated confrontation between age groups. It was a long time before the Church, which rejected as apocryphal the story of the staffs, was able to lay to rest the incongruity of this interpretation. Throughout the fourteenth and fifteenth centuries, Tuscan painters and sculptors charged the group of pretenders with increasingly hostile, even hate-filled sentiments toward the saint who turned his back to them in order to bestow the wedding ring.[90] Shortly after 1300, Tadeo Gaddi already introduced a certain contained violence into the attitudes of the losing contenders. The staffs, now shown in much greater number, are being broken with alacrity by those who carry them, and the blow is administered more rudely with a closed fist by a young man to old Joseph.[91] Around 1360 a fresco by Giovanni da Milano, a pupil of Gaddi, in another chapel (that of Santa Croce in Milan), further exacerbates the behavior of the pretenders: by now two of them manhandle the saint, raising a hand or a fist against him. Agnolo Gaddi in his turn seized upon the motifs of his predecessors in the cathedral of Prato, where he placed even greater emphasis on the hostility—indeed, the fury—of the men of Judah. Two Sienese painters, Bartolo di Fredi and Niccolò di Buonaccorso, also stressed the frankly hostile attitude and the agitation of the men crowding the background behind Joseph.[92]

In all of these Tuscan paintings, Joseph wears the gray beard and the white hair of an old man. All the artists stress the contrast between this elderly bridegroom with his humble and reserved demeanor and the group of young bachelors, most of whom are beardless, curly haired, and foppish, and whose spite becomes more and more pronounced as one moves away from Giotto. By the fifteenth century, the *Sposalizio* had become the image of a conflict of generations, described with an ever-increasing wealth of detail. Spite, resentment, and blind violence pit these "youths" against the victorious elder. Two[93] and sometimes three[94] of them raise their fists against him with a fury that, by 1480–1510, distorts their faces. Children, who also carry rods, add to the agitation.[95] Finally, Signorelli, who shows the feelings of the young men against the elderly man who takes a beautiful girl away from them at their highest pitch, does away altogether with any reference to the miracle of the staffs. Henceforth, the conflict between age groups is their only motivation and it is no longer necessary to invoke the legend to justify the violent feelings of the protagonists.[96]

In going beyond the features of the legend and in accentuating and justifying the supposed hostility of the pretenders, the new interpretation of the ritual gestures depicted by Giotto at Padua, the Tuscan painters[97] were led to portray this hostility as the sign of the conflict of generations and the disapproval expressed by the young bachelors who objected to old men contracting legitimate marriages—a feeling akin to the disapproval expressed in the charivari. A misunderstood gesture of the popular ritual had cleared the way for other symbolic gestures also connected with the marriage ritual. An entire doubly apocryphal set of behaviors attributed to the witnesses at the marriage of an old man to a young maiden, a classic motif of the charivari, was thus grafted onto the central theme of the *Sposalizio*.

It seems important to me that the predilection of the Tuscan painters for the theme of "Saint Joseph's charivari" was tolerated by the Church until around the beginning of the sixteenth century. The Church probably accepted this embroidered version of the miracle of the staffs because it felt that it could put up with its exaggerated aspects as long as the proclamation of the marriage *in facie ecclesiae*, the assigned mission of the *Sposalizio*, remained its central theme. Outside of Tuscany, moreover, the references to the charivari were muted.* In Umbria and in the Marches the many painters who illustrated the Marriage of the Virgin and the miracle of the staffs in the years around 1500 removed all rancor from the gestures of the pretenders.[98] The Lombard painters of the sixteenth century also softened the expressions of the youths, making them vaguely unhappy or worried, sometimes even edified. Blows or fisticuffs are no longer to be seen, and one of the figures points with his finger to the exemplary husband, Joseph.[99] Joseph becomes younger, or his competitors become older, but in any case the opposition between age groups is attenuated.[100] When the reference to the miracle of the staffs was finally abandoned, the painters of Venice, Lombardy, and Rome—unlike Signorelli—used the *Sposalizio* as the occasion for an earnest meditation on marriage.[101] In one-fourth of the roughly 100 paintings examined, staffs and pretenders have disappeared, and a calm and collected atmosphere surrounds the witnesses to the scene, many of whom are old. These compositions, in which allegorical personages or simple worshippers are seen more and more frequently, rarely originated in Tuscany.[102] Becoming more prevalent by the middle of the sixteenth century, these compositions would carry the day with the Counter Reformation.

Why is it that the other Italian schools of painting did not stress the conflict between age groups as explicitly as the Tuscans? The main reason is that in Tuscany the development of this theme came earlier than its success in the various other provinces, where, generally speaking, it came into its own only by the end of the fifteenth century. In that later period, however, a veritable pro-Josephist offensive attempted to promote a widespread veneration of this saint by exalting his virtues. In the early fifteenth century the best-known

---

*For the illustration, *The Marriage of the Virgin* (School of Gentile da Fabriano), see *Annales* E.S.C. 34 (November-December 1979): 1234.

spokesman for this rehabilitation was the French author Gerson, but his efforts were to bear fruit, almost everywhere in Europe, only toward the end of the century.[103] At that time the person of the saint was cleansed of its comic or ridiculous aspects.[104] The emphasis was placed on the merits of Christ's foster father and the chaste husband of the Virgin. Henceforth it would have been unseemly to represent on the walls of churches or in the mystery plays of northern Europe young men maligning so noble a figure. The violence of the pretenders therefore turned into sweetness, their grimaces into smiles, and those painters who were still bold enough to show the fury of the unsuccessful competitors did so in order to ridicule the outrageousness of their gestures against the saint, that is to say, against the sacrament of marriage.

Thus, Francabiago in the church of the Annunziata at Florence and the sculptor Tribolo at Loreto would show little children breaking their staffs, crying with rage! Here the derision of the saint becomes derision of his detractors. Even before the Council of Trent, which would attempt to root out the last vestiges of the apocrypha—the miracle of the staffs, the old age of Joseph—the rehabilitated saint became, somewhat tritely, the very type of the good husband who goes along with a marriage ceremony that the Church alone can inspire. The earnest partners, fully aware of the solemnity of the moment; the active priest without whom the ceremony cannot take place blessing the couple and guiding their hands; the allegorical mutations of the bystanders and the setting within the sanctuary—all of this comes together to put an end to the plots woven around the story by Giotto's successors.

The central propositions of the iconography inspired by Giotto thus eventually converged with the evolution and the extension of the liturgy of marriage, which they probably accelerated but which in any case made them unnecessary in the end. By the time the Roman ritual made the blessing of the rings before the altar and the "guidance of the Church" mandatory throughout Christendom, the *Sposalizio* had quite simply become obsolete. The apocryphal legend and the popular ritual that had been brought into it by the artists lost their reason for being once the Church's new apologetics and liturgy became firmly established. By the same token the ambiguous wedding of the thirteenth century, in which a child-Virgin was handed over to an old man, gave way to the Catholic marriage of a mature and harmonious couple, in which the *subarratio per anulum* is accepted as the central symbolic gesture. Like the Church, the ring had won the day.

Perspectives for Research

By its insistence on some of the places, gestures, and objects involved in the wedding ceremony, art depicting the Marriage of the Virgin shows the areas in which the Church sought to anchor its presence. Having achieved this goal in the seventeenth century, it retired its old iconographical tool, the *Sposalizio*, a theme that had by then become neutralized and deprived of its explosive charge. By absorbing or integrating those elements of the popular ritual that could be made to fit in with the Church doctrine, by casting in allegorical terms those that it did not condemn as pagan (without, however, being able to integrate them into the liturgy), and by rejecting as anecdotal or apocryphal certain rites denounced as unseemly or violent, the clergy had the better of the artist's sensitivity to the practices of his contemporaries.

The purging of the irreducible elements that would become part of folklore and the enrichment of the religious liturgy appear to be two complementary and opposing aspects of the same process. However, shedding light on this twofold process in the restricted area of iconographical propaganda by showing how the *Sposalizio* was represented does not exhaust the problem of how rituals come into being and how they survive. This is true, first and foremost, because of the impact of social variables about which the materials analyzed here have very little to say. Yet these variables starkly pose the problem of how the Church, or other powers, may have taken advantage of differences between the people's practices and those of the upper classes in order to tighten their control over the rituals of alliance.

The function sometimes given to the priest and the setting chosen for the giving of the ring, the shorter intervals between the various episodes of the nuptial scenario, the elimination of the *giure* and the central importance of the giving of the ring appear to indicate that marriage among the popular classes was somewhat more in keeping with the Church's wishes than it was among the great and the wealthy. But if this were true, one would still have to define the conduits and the stimuli that prompted humble people, at least in the towns, to conform somewhat better to the model held out by the Church and to eschew the attraction and the aping of patrician customs, turning instead to the image of good Christian marriage. In order to become better informed about them, we will have to study the apostolate of marriage, the sermons devoted to this topic, and—to return to the *Sposalizio*—the character of the monastic orders, religious confraternities, and private individuals who commissioned painters to treat this subject. This also means that one must study the artist's autonomy in relation to his patron, whether lay or ecclesiastic, and indeed the autonomy of a lay patron in relation to the church for which he donated the decoration of a chapel.[105]

As for evidence of a possible direct influence of the religious model of marriage on the practices of the Florentine bourgeoisie, we have very little to go on. It is clear that the Church had nothing to do with certain reorientations of the ritual that found expression after 1470 in the increasingly frequent omission of certain phases and in the more intimate character of the wedding festivities. For Florence, the *ricordanze* suggest that the problem of the dowry had detached the celebration of the wedding from the consummation of the marriage, which had become more closely tied to the "ring day." In this manner the creation of the marriage through the *verba de praesenti* and its completion through the consummation were gathered together into a much more tightly knit set of ceremonies, making the wedding itself superfluous. The fact that unions were celebrated more and more often *alla dimestica*, almost secretively, seems to have been a direct response not so much to the Church's teaching as to economic pressures and the marriage market. In the course of the fifteenth century the solution of the dowry problem through the institution of the *Monte delli Doti* did more to change the marriage ritual of the upper classes than the intervention of the Church. In the same manner it was the prince's action that, paradoxically, gave to the marriages of the urban aristocracy a simplicity similar to that of the popular unions, which also lacked the festivities connected with the *giure* and the wedding. These examples show that the incentives for simplifying and shortening the nuptial scenario of the great families did not, for the most part, originate with the Church.

These internal modifications tended to make marriage a more private matter and did not imply any true internalization of the consensual nature of marriage. Very well aware of this, the Church insisted less on the essence of marriage than on the need for ecclesiastical supervision, which, as the Tuscan *Sposalizio* has shown, was closer in form to the Norman model than to models of active mutual giving by the spouses. Indeed, the very legislation concerning marriage did not really favor practices involving the free expression of consent on the part of both spouses. According to the best theologians of the time, the willingness of the family's son or of the bride could be expressed by a mere sign, or even by the very fact of their presence and by their failure to make a formal statement of opposition.[106] Searching out "indications" of consent obviously gave wide scope to interpretations that best suited the purposes of family and friends. The practical limitations of the doctrine of consent are equally evident in the Florentine synodal statutes of 1517. At that time, the Florentine clergy decided to combat the popular practices of "ignorant people who do not understand the power of words spoken by them, often believing that they are becoming betrothed when they speak the words of marriage itself." As a corrective that would restore these popular "betrothals" to their proper importance, the synod proposed that the parties be made to summon the parish priest or a notary who would ask the future husband whether he was willing to marry the girl when she or her family would ask him to do so. No question here of *verba de futuro*, spoken by the future bride, taking the place of formulas or popular rituals by which she pledged her own person.[107] In combating the ambiguity of the popular ceremony of betrothal, the Florentine Church of 1517 condemned—perhaps not altogether innocently—its reciprocal character. And by dismissing the betrothal as a matter to be celebrated in a domestic setting under the supervision of the notary or

the parish priest, the Church endorsed and actually contributed to the trick-
ling down to the lower classes of the practices of the ruling classes, who were
not interested in submitting their marriage strategies to the opinion of a
young girl.

The case of Florence thus reveals the belated, incomplete, and socially as
well as psychologically limited character of certain mutations that were to become more distinctive and more generalized by the end of the sixteenth century. In calling these mutations belated, I mean in comparison with France
and perhaps certain other regions of Italy, such as Venice and Rome. There
the Church had gained control earlier, while in Florence the marriage customs assigned a truly special importance to the "ring day" only beginning in
the fifteenth century; even then, the priest was not given a place at the core of
the ceremony except, perhaps, in the formal imagery of the iconography.

If I said that these mutations were incomplete, it is because the disregard
for the religious blessing shared by most of the Florentines brought them
down to the level of those "brutes" who were condemned by the preachers
and by the most attentive of their flock; as a domestic ceremony, the handing
over of the wife to the husband following the giving of the ring continued to
be governed by very old formalities of the marriage contract. These formalities, to be sure, were guaranteed by a representative of the community, the
notary, who made sure that the consent of both parties was given in accor-
dance with the rules; nonetheless, these formalities perpetuated the gestures
and forms of conduct in which the woman fundamentally remained a pawn
to be placed as advantageously as possible on the social chessboard.

Finally, these mutations were limited since they did not, in general, correspond to a very profound feeling for the sacrament of marriage and since, as
far as the laity was concerned, they were a response to financial and political
considerations as much as to Church doctrine. Moreover, their social impact
was quite limited, since the popular classes were naturally more responsive to
change than the "old good families," for whom alliances and therefore the
rituals designed to bring two families together remained vitally important to
survival and advancement.

What, then, were the factors and the structures that, as late as 1500, placed
Florence and Tuscany into a somewhat exceptional position? It seems to me
that ever since the twelfth century the great emphasis on patrilinear descent
in urban lineages, together with a true decline in the juridical and social status
of women and the triumph of the dotal system had maintained and anchored
down certain contractual and juridical formalities in the rites of marriage,
thereby retarding the emergence of an image of the couple and of marriage
founded on reciprocal giving and on a freely consented community. In an
ambiguous and still quite timid manner, the *Sposalizio* prepared the terrain
for the Church's participation in these rituals. Yet all it could do to influence
people's ideas and attitudes was to show them a priestly figure whose gestures

and functions were very close to those of the traditional wife giver and guarantor of the contract.

NOTES

1. M. Meiss, *Painting in Florence and Siena after the Black Death: The Arts, Religion, and Society in the Mid-Fourteenth Century* (1951; reprint ed. New York, Harper Torchbook 1964), pp. 60-61, 109-17.

2. Ibid., p. 61.

3. Cf. the synthesis presented by André Burguière in "The Marriage Ritual in France: Ecclesiastical Practices and Popular Practices (Sixteenth to Eighteenth Century)," in the present volume. Cf. also J. Bossy, "The Counter-Reformation and the People of Catholic Europe," *Past and Present* 47 (1970): 51-70.

4. L. Beauchet, "Etude historique sur les formes de la célébration du mariage dans l'ancien droit français," *Nouvelle revue historique de droit français et étranger* 6 (1882): 351-93; J. Dauvillier, *Le Mariage dans le droit classique de l'Eglise depuis le décret de Gratien (1140) jusqu'à la mort de Clément V (1340)* (Paris, 1933); A. Esmein and R. Genestal, *Le Mariage en droit canonique* (Paris, 1929-35); G. Le Bras, "Mariage," in *Dictionnaire de théologie catholique* (Paris, 1927), 9, pl. 2, pp. 2,044-2,335; P. Vaccari, *Il Matrimonio canonico: corso di diritto ecclesiastico* (Milan, 1950), rototyped copy.

5. J. Dauvillier and C. De Clerq, *Le Mariage en droit canonique oriental* (Paris, 1936).

6. Esmein and Genestal, *Le Mariage*, 1: 68 ff.

7. K. Ritzer, *Le Mariage dans les eglises chrétiennes du I^{ier} au XIe siècle* (1962), French trans. (Paris, 1970); R. Metz, *La Consécration des vierges dans l'Eglise romaine* (Paris, 1954), pp. 363-410; J.-P. Molin and P. Mutembé, *Le Rituel du mariage en France du XIIe au XVIe siècle* (Paris, 1974).

8. G. Duby, *Medieval Marriage: Two Models from Twelfth-Century France*, trans. Elborg Forster (Baltimore, 1978); R. H. Helmholz, *Marriage Litigation in Medieval England* (Cambridge, 1974); P. Toubert, *Les Structures du Latium médiéval* (Rome, 1973), 1: 743-49.

9. E. Chénon, "Recherches historiques sur quelques rites nuptiaux," *Nouvelle Revue historique de droit français et étranger* 16 (1912): 573-660.

10. F. Brandileone, *Saggi sulla storia della celebratione del matrimonio in Italia* (Bologna, 1906).

11. M. A. Altieri, *Li Nuptiali*, ed. E. Narducci (Rome, 1873).

12. P. Toubert, "Les Statuts communaux et l'histoire des campagnes lombardes au XIVe siècle," *Mélanges d'archéologie et d'histoire* (1960): 468 ff. For Florence, see *Statuti della Repubblica fiorentina*, ed. R. Caggesse (Florence, 1910-21); *Statuta populi et communis Florentiae (1415)* (Freiburg, 1778-81).

13. P.-J. Jones, "Florentine Families and Florentine Diaries in the Fourteenth Century," *Papers of the British School at Rome* 24 (1956): 183-205; C. Bec, *Les Marchands-écrivains à Florence, 1375-1434* (Paris and The Hague, 1967).

14. A systematic reading of about 120 unpublished family records preserved at the State Archives of Florence and at the Italian National Library, together with some thirty published books (listed in D. Herlihy and C. Klapisch-Zuber, *Les Toscans et leurs familles: une étude du catasto florentin de 1427* [Paris, 1978], p. 190 n. 3), has given me a sample of about 140 marriages.

15. See the remarks of J. Le Goff in "Le Rituel symbolique de la vassalité," republished in *Pour un autre Moyen Age* (Paris, 1977), pp. 348-420, esp. p. 365.

16. Examples have been published by J. Del Badia, "Fidanzamento e matrimonio nel secolo XV," *Miscellanea fiorentina di erudizione* 1 (1886): 189-92; G. Biaggi, *Due corredi nuziali fiorentini, 1320 e 1493* (Florence, 1899). Descriptions of the phases of the wedding in Italy in N. Tamassia, *La Famiglia italiana nei secoli XV e XVI* (Florence, 1966), pp. 188-93; G. Palupatoni, "Le Nozze," in *Vita privata a Firenze nei secoli XIV e XV* (Florence, 1966), pp. 31-52, Herlihy and Klapisch, *Les Toscans*, pp. 588-94.

17. Altieri, *Li Nuptiali*, pp. 50-51.

18. Some of these *scritta* were carefully copied by Florentine writers in their *ricordanze* in the years around 1500; cf. the examples edited by D. Fachard, *Biaggi Buonaccorsi: sa vie, son temps, son oeuvre* (Bologna, 1976), appendix (for 1509).

19. Altieri, *Li Nuptiali*, p. 51.

20. E. Westermarck, *History of Human Marriage* (London, 1891), French translation by A. Van Gennep, 5 vols. (Paris, 1934–38) 4: 183–86; R. Corso, *Patti d'amore e pegni di promessa* (S. Maria Capua Vetere, 1924); idem, "Gli sponsali popolari," *Revue des études éthnographiques et sociologiques* 1 (1908): 487–99.

21. Altieri, *Li Nuptiali*, p. 51.

22. This is the term used by the Tuscan notaries for the notarized contract drawn up at the *giure*. Cf. note 28.

23. Cf. the controversy over the place of this commitment in medieval law in E. Friedberg, *Ehe und Eheschliessung im deutschen Mittelalter* (Berlin, 1864); idem, *Das Recht der Eheschliessung in seiner geschichtlichen Entwicklung* (Leipzig, 1865); R. Sohm, *Das Recht der Eheschliessung aus dem deutschen und kanonischen Recht geschichtlich entwickelt* (Weimar, 1875); idem, *Trauung und Verlobung, eine Entgegnung auf Friedbergs Verlobung und Trauung* (Weimar, 1876).

24. Burguière, "The Marriage Ritual"; Ritzer, *Le Mariage*, pp. 373–402. See the ritual of betrothal of the second half of the thirteenth century published by Molin and Mutembé, *Le Rituel du mariage*, p. 299, "Ordo XI."

25. Even Antonino, repeating the position of Hostiensis, approves of this procedure for the *sponsalia*. It means that the choice is made by the father, who must subsequently propose one of his daughters, although he is not held to his promise if she is refused (*Summa*, bk. 3, title 1, cap. 18 [Venice, 1582], fol. 18).

26. Ibid., bk. 3, title 1, cap. 16, fol. 16 v° and 17 r°: waiving the banns is common "cum magnatibus quia eorum matrimonia cum magna deliberatione solent tractari per amicos." The oldest synodal constitutions of Fiesole (1306) or Florence (1310 and 1327) make it an obligation for the priests to announce the future marriage only once, so that possible objections can be brought forward; cf. R. Trexler, *Synodal Law in Florence and Fiesole, 1306–1518* (Vatican City, 1971), pp. 68–69. By contrast, the synodal statutes of 1517 firmly proclaimed the necessity of having the banns published by the parish priest, failing which no notary would be able to celebrate the *sponsali de praesenti* (Mansi), vol. 35, col. 248.

27. One example for the dissociation between the *giure* and the *anello* "per legiptime et buoni chagione et chon bolla di Chorte di Roma" dating from 1449 is found in the *ricordanze* of Uguccione Capponi, Archivio di Stato, Florence, *Conv. sopp. S. Piero a Monticelli*, 153, fol. 12 v°.

28. These are very numerous in the notarial registers: cf. S. K. Cohn, *"Community and Conflict in the Renaissance: Florence, 1340–1530"* (Dissertation, Harvard University, 1978). The author has assembled two sets of samples, one for the fourteenth century, numbering 523 *acta matrimonii*, and the other for the period 1450–1530, numbering 2,244 such acts. F. Brandileone (*Saggi*, pp. 213–16) has published a form used by the Florentine notaries of the fifteenth century as well as (p. 476) Rainerius of Perugia's text on these procedures for marriage.

29. Altieri, *Li Nuptiali*, p. 51. Cf. also the regulations concerning festivities and gifts in Florence in the *Statuta* of 1415, 3: 366–69.

30. Antonino, *Summa*, bk. 3, title 1, cap. 18, *De sponsalibus*, still reserves this term for "promises of future marriage."

31. The Florentine statutes of 1415, a compilation of texts from various dates, give rise to a certain confusion about their use of the word *sponsalia*. A shift in meaning is manifest in the writing of a certain Lapo Niccolini, for example, who wrote in his *ricordanze* in 1402: "E del decto matrimonio e sponsalitio è charta fatta . . . etc." (to be found in *Il Libro degli affari proprii di casa di Lapo de Giovanni Niccolini de' Sirigatti*, ed. C. Bec [Paris, 1969], p. 94). Lapo reserves the word *giuramento* for the ceremony preceding the commitment. The French word *épousailles* underwent a parallel evolution.

32. Altieri, *Li Nuptiali*, p. 53.

33. F. Brandileone, "Die Subarratio cum anulo: Ein Beitrag zur Geschichte des mittelalterlichen Eheschliessungsrechtes," *Deutsche Zeitschrift für Kirchenrecht*, dritte Serie 3 (1901): 311–40; L. Zdekauer, "Usi popolani dell Valdelsa," *Miscellanea storica della Valdelsa* 4 (1896): 64–66, 205–12.

34. The Church considered marriage an indissoluble bond and Antonino demonstrated at length, in his *Summa*, bk. 4, title 15, cap. 7, *De desponsatione Mariae*, fols. 299–301, that Joseph and Mary were united by a "verum matrimonium," since the first completion of a marriage is to consent "in copulam conjugalem, non autem expresse in copulam carnalem," and since the second completion is the raising of a child.

35. A. Van Gennep, *Manuel de folklore français contemporain*, new ed. (Paris, 1976), vol. 1, pt. 2, chap. 4, *Le Mariage*, pp. 376–648; N. Belmont, "The Symbolic Function of the Wedding Procession in the Popular Rituals of Marriage" in the present volume.

36. Saint Bernardino da Siena, *Prediche volgari*, ed. L. Banchi (Siena, 1880–88), 2: 359. Cf. the advice to the bride concerning her conduct at her wedding by Francesco da Barberino, *Del Reggimento e costume di donne*, ed. G. E. Sansoni (Turin, 1957), pp. 59–61.

37. Altieri, *Li Nuptiali*, pp. 66–67.

38. Ibid., pp. 51, 53, 55.

39. Ibid., pp. 73, 81.

40. G. Salvioli, "La Benedizione nuziale fino al Concilio di Trento," *Archivio giuridico* 53 (1894): 169–97.

41. I do not believe that the rise in the average age at marriage of women toward the end of the fifteenth century can account for the practice of advancing the consummation, which in the earlier period was put off until the bride had reached the canonical age. The canonical age of the spouse was in fact one of the conditions for pronouncing the *verba de praesenti*.

42. *Summa*, bk. 4, title 15, cap. 7, fol. 300.

43. Long before the Council of Trent, the synodal statutes of Florence of 1517 forbade the fiancé to visit his intended bride more than twice between the betrothal and the *verba de praesenti* (*Concilium florentinum*, Mansi, vol. 35, col. 248).

44. S. Bernardini, *Opera omnia*, ed. P. Collegii S. Bonaventurae (Florence, 1950–78), 4: 469–70.

45. Altieri, *Li Nuptiali*, p. 68. Here the author describes many rituals designed to overcome this threat (in particular, the eating of fish) or to ensure the couple's fertility (pp. 76, 79, 81, 83, 88). For these rites, see Westermarck, *History of Human Marriage*, French ed, 4: 203–36; also E. Le Roy Ladurie, "L'Aiguillette," *Europe* 52 (March 1974): 134–46.

46. Cf. Herlihy and Klapisch, *Les Toscans*, p. 592 n. 34.

47. J. Kirshner, "Pursuing Honor while Avoiding Sin: The Monte delle Doti of Florence," *Studi Senesi* 89 (1977): 177–258; J. Kirshner and A. Molho, "The Dowry Fund and the Marriage Market in Early Quattrocento Florence," *Journal of Modern History* 50 (1978): 403–38.

48. Over and over, one finds in the declarations of taxpayers in the *catasto* of 1427 complaints of parents who must keep their married daughter at their home since they cannot pay the dowry so that the husband will "take her away."

49. Archivio di Stato, Florence, *Conv. soppr.*, 95, no. 212, *Ricordanze di Bernardo di Stoldo Rinieri*, fol. 169 v⁰, as well as fol. 169 r⁰ (1483) and fol. 171 (1487). The simplicity of the wedding festivities was intended by Lorenzo de' Medici after 1472; cf. the *Ricordi storici di F. di C. Rinuccini dal 1282 al 1460 . . .*, ed. C. Aiazzi (Florence, 1840), p. cxlviii.

50. On this point, see F. Guicciardini, *Storie fiorentine*, chap. 9, ed. G. Canestrini (Florence, 1859), and idem, *Opere inedite*, 10 vols. (Florence, 1857–67), 3: 90–91. R. Fubini has found in the registers of the notary Michelozzi a very large number of these marriage contracts concluded under the aegis of Lorenzo. Cf. D. Kent, *The Rise of the Medici* (Oxford, 1978).

51. A few examples: G. Buongirolami, *Ricordanze* (Archivio di Stato, Florence, *Strozzi*, II, 23, fol. 129), the agreement concluded on 11 December 1499 and not followed by any *giure*; idem, for T. Guidetti, *Ricordanze* (Archivio di Stato, Florence, *Strozzi*, IV, 418, fol. 3 v⁰), 2 October 1481; Luigi Martelli (ibid., *Strozzi*, V, 1,463, fol. 119), 24 April 1487; Bart. Valori (Biblioteca Nazionale Centrale, *Panciat,* 134, fol. 7), 1 March 1474; fol. 8, 2 January 1476; fol. 9, 7 July 1476; fol. 10, 22 November 1481; Recco Capponi (Archivio di Stato, Florence, *Conv. soppr.* S. Piero a Monticelli, 153, fol. 24 v⁰), 20 February 1469.

52. Ritzer, *Le Mariage*, pp. 388–95; Molin and Mutembé, *Le Rituel du mariage*, pp. 283–300 (appendixes), have published about a dozen of these *ordines* of marriage.

53. *Statuti*, ed. R. Cagese, 1: 222. They were repeated in substance by the *Statuta* of 1415, 3: 366.

54. Archivio di Stato, Florence, *Strozzi*, V, fol. 105.

55. Cf. the synodal statutes of 1517: "Nessuno ardisca contrahere sponsalitii ne de futuro ne de presenti se prima non chiama al preto suo o vero un notaio, e qualé faccia le parole tra loro in questa forma" (Mansi, vol. 35, col. 247).

56. *Summa*, bk. 3, title 1, *De statu conjugatorum*, fol. 6 and 32 v°.

57. Edited by R. C. Trexler in *Quellen und Forschungen aus den italienischen Archiven und Bibliotheken* 59 (1979): 111–39. "Item perche abbiamo intesco in alchuno luogo in contado . . . da alchono ignoranti farsi le nozze prima senza la benedictione overo mess dil Congiunto secondo a ordinato la santa Chiesa."

58. Altieri (*Li Nuptiali*, p. 73) reports that in Rome couples often heard a nuptial mass celebrated *at the house of the bride* three days before the wedding, so that they would be able to consummate the marriage on the night of the wedding and also observe the three "nights of Tobias" as prescribed by the Church.

59. Macchiavelli, *Oeuvres*, Pléiade ed. (Paris, 1952), *Clizia*, act 3, scene 7, p. 265. For the religious celebration in Italy, cf. Brandileone, *Saggi*, pp. 88–96.

60. An example of a rural marriage of 1302 to be found in Pampaloni, "Le Nozze," pp. 35–36. Many unions among peasants had to do without formalities of any kind, like this marriage mentioned by a Florentine in 1409: "Ed è vero posto che la detta donna fosse stata con d. G. più anni, non era però fatto sponsalizio ne dato anello o confessato dota" (Biblioteca Nazionale Centrale, Manosc. 77, fol. 34).

61. Cohn, "Community and Conflict," pp. 15–19.

62. *Summa*, bk. 3, title 1, cap. 18, *De sponsalibus*.

63. Cohn, "Community and Conflict," pp. 15–19.

64. One example in the *ricordanze* of Piero Strozzi (Archivio di Stato, Florence, *Strozzi*, IV, 354, fol. 168 v°). On 31 January 1508 at the marriage of a poor girl dowered by charity, the husband "gave the ring . . . at Santa Trinità in the presence of the church's monks."

65. This we can see from *ricordanze* reporting on the marriages of servants, slaves, poor girls, and girls dowered by a charity.

66. Chénon, "Recherches historiques," pp. 23–31, 33–35; Brandileone, *Saggi*, pp. 318 ff; *Dictionnaire d'archéologie chrétienne et de liturgie*, article "Mariage," vol. 10 (1932), col. 1890–93.

67. Antonino clearly distinguishes the two occasions when the ring can be given: the *sponsalia* are concluded through the giving of the ring, "alicubi tamen datur anulus quando contrahitur per v. de pr. et tunc non sunt sponsalia sed perfectum matrimonium" (*Summa*, bk. 3, title 1, cap. 18, fol. 19).

68. Altieri, *Li Nuptiali*, p. 51.

69. *Dictionnaire d'archéologie chrétienne*, art. "Mariage," vol. 10 (1932), col. 1891–93 and 1931–42.

70. In the seventh century the bishops already wore a ring as a sign of their marriage to the Church (*Dictionnaire d'archéologie chrétienne*, article "Anneaux," vol. 1, col. 2, 181–86). For the ring worn by nuns, see Metz, *La Consécration des vierges*, (cf. n. 7 above), appendixes.

71. E. Hennecke and W. Schneemelcher, *Neutestamentarische Apokryphen*, 3rd ed. (Tübingen, 1959–64), pp. 277 ff.

72. J. Lafontaine-Dosogne, *Iconographie de l'enfance de la Vierge dans l'Empire byzantin et en Occident* (Brussels, 1964–65), 2: 135–53; L. Kretzenbacher, "Stabbrechen im Hochzeitsritus? Zur apokryphen Erzählungsgrundlage eines Bildmotivs im Sposalizio-Thema," *Fabula* 6 (1963): 195–212.

73. Lafontaine-Dosogne, *Iconographie*, pp. 135–36.

74. *Dictionnaire d'archéologie chrétienne*, article "Saint Joseph," vol. 5, col. 2,656–66.

75. *Legenda aurea*, ed. T. Graesse (Breslau, 1890), p. 589.

76. Ibid., "nuptiis habiles non conjugati."

77. This again is Antonino's interpretation in his *Summa*, bk. 4, title 15, cap. 7, referring to the Jewish customs.

78. Chénon, "Recherches historiques," p. 13.

79. Lafontaine-Dosogne, *Iconographie*; L. Réau, *Iconographie de l'art chrétien* (Paris, 1955–59), 2: 170–73, and 3: 752–60; E. Sépulchre, "Saint Joseph et l'intimité dans l'art médiéval: étude iconographique" (Dissertation, Brussels, 1952).

80. Réau, *Iconographie*, p. 171.

81. A. Rossbach, *Römische Hochzeits-und Ehedenkmäler* (Leipzig, 1871); S. Ringborn,

"Nuptial Symbolism in Some Fifteenth-Century Reflections of Roman Sepulchral Portraiture," *Temenos* 2 (1966); *Dictionnaire d'archéologie chrétienne*, vol. 10, col. 1,895 ff.

82. Meiss, *Painting in Florence*, pp. 108–13, reproductions no. 100–107; G. Kaftal, *Saints in Italian Art: Iconography of the Saints in Tuscan Painting* (Florence, 1952), pp. 235–47, reproductions 244, 247, 248. For the diffusion of the legend of Saint Catherine of Alexandria, see B. Beatie, "Saint Catherine of Alexandria: Traditional Themes and the Development of the Medieval German Hagiographic Narrative," *Speculum* 52 (1977): 785–800; for the *cassoni*, see P. Schubring, *Cassoni*, 2 vols. (Leipzig, 1915), analytical index; see also E. Callman, *Apollonio di Giovanni* (Oxford, 1974).

83. R. Corso, "Tre vecchie costumanze aretine: il baccio alla sposa, la rottura della scodella, il pugno allo sposo durante la celebrazione nuziale," *Reviviscenze* 1, ser. 6 (1927): 71–83; A. Basile, "Usi popolari nuziali nello Sposalizio della Vergine della grande pittura italiana: il pugno e la rottura della bacchetta," *Folklore* 10 (1956): 3–11. Synodal texts in C. Corrain and P. L. Zampini, *Documenti etnografici e folkloristici nei sinodi diocesani italiani* (Bologna, 1970), p. 49. Many communal statutes prohibit striking the bridegroom.

84. One hundred Italian paintings of the fourteenth to sixteenth centuries have been analyzed altogether. The following pages are in part taken from my article, "La *mattinata* médiévale d'Italie," published in its entirety and in an English version in *Journal of Family History* (1980). A shorter version appears in the collective volume *Le Charivari* (Paris, 1980).

85. The vogue of the *Sposalizio* in this region was based on the cult of the relic of Mary's wedding ring at Perugia, a cult that developed in the fifteenth century. Cf. A. Rossi, *L'Anello sposalizio di Maria Vergine che si venera nella cattedrale di Perugia: Leggenda* (Perugia, 1857).

86. F. W. Kent, "The Rucellai Family and Its Loggia," *Journal of the Warburg and Courtauld Institutes* 35 (1972): 379–401.

87. For these rites "at the church door" at Gaeta, cf. Brandileone, *Saggi*, pp. 77–79, 90–91.

88. Respectively, in one-half and one-third of the cases.

89. The representation of the marriage of a poor girl dowered by the charity of the *Buonomini de San Martino* is particularly interesting: the girl's father advances her right hand toward the husband while the "Bonhomme" places the dowry into the young man's left hand. The father and the giver of the dowry occupy the central place, the very spot in which other painters depicted Zacharias; to the left the seated notary draws up the *instrumentum matrimonii*. (Fresco by Francesco d'Antonio del Chierico, about 1478, in the Florentine church of S. Martino al vescovo.)

90. Cf. Klapisch-Zuber, "La *mattinata* médiévale."

91. Cf. also the medallion of Orcagna at Orsanmichele, ca. 1350.

92. Bartolo di Fredi worked before 1367; Niccolo di Buonaccorso died in 1388.

93. Cf. Andrea di Giusto (Prato, duomo, after 1450), Fra Angelico (S. Marco), Giovanni di Paolo (Rome, Galleria Doria), Benozzo Gozzoli (Vatican, predella).

94. Cf. Fra Angelico (Prado), Bartolomeo di Giovanni (Florence, Innocenti, predella).

95. For example, in the paintings of Ghirlandaio (Florence, Santa Maria Novella, 1488–90), Franciabigio (Florence, S. Annunziata, 1513), and Tribolo (Loreto, S. Casa).

96. This painting was probably part of a private collection. In that of the National Gallery at Washington, D.C., the agitation of the men who break their staffs causes a kind of free-for-all.

97. There are a few exceptions: Lorenzo Monaco (Florence, S. Trinità); D. Beccafumi, another Sienese painter of the early sixteenth century; and V. Tamagni of San Gimignano (1492–1530).

98. Antonio da Viterbo, surnamed Pastura (Tarquinia, ca. 1478), Marco Palmezzano (Milan, Museo Poldo Pezzoli), Pinturicchio (Spello, 1501; Rome, S. Maria del Popolo, 1490), Ragazzini (Macerata, ca. 1520–47), Andrea da Iesi il Giovane (Cingoli, S. Sperandio). On the other hand, Monaldo da Corneto (Detroit, Institute of Arts) and Lorenzo da Viterbo (Viterbo, S. Maria della Verità) do show the wrath of the young men. Perugino and Raphael are still the best examples of this school and its interpretation of the *Sposalizio* (their works can be found at respectively, Fano, S. Maria Nuova and Caen, Musée; and, at Milan, Brera).

99. B. Luini (Saronno and Milan, Brera) and the painters of the first sixty years of the sixteenth century: G. Marchesi, G. Romanino, O. Samacchini.

100. Masolino da Panicale (Castiglione d'Olona, 1435), Bartolomeo dei Rossi (Parma, Duomo), B. Loschi (Carpi).

101. The clearest example is no doubt the painting by Lorenzo Costa (Bologna, Pinacoteca),

which shows Joseph as a beardless youth. Cf. also, for the fourteenth century, P. Cavallini (Naples, Museo Civico); for the fifteenth century, B. Fungai (Florence, Berenson Collection; Gotha, Landesmuseum); for the sixteenth century, Rosso Fiorentino (Florence, S. Lorenzo, Sodoma, Subioco). This last painter, like Palmezzano (cf. n. 98), completely eliminates the priest: here the spouses truly administer the sacrament to themselves by their will alone.

102. This can be seen in the works of Rosso Fiorentino, Fr. Zaganelli, the Brescianino, G. Marchesi, V. Salimbeni, and E. Sameggia (although the last three painters still refer to the miracle of the staffs).

103. J. Seitz, *Das Josephfest in der lateinischen Kirche in seiner Entwicklung bis zum Konzil von Trient* (Freiburg, 1908); Sépulchre, "Saint Joseph," p. 20.

104. Sépulchre, "Saint Joseph," p. 51. The caricature of the saint was for the most part perpetrated by the artists and writers of Germany and Flanders. In Italy the mockery was rarely carried so far as to show him engaged in lowly woman's tasks; respect for the *paterfamilias* was too prevalent and too vigorous to permit this.

105. Cf. F. Haskell, *Patrons and Painters: A Study in the Relations between Italian Art and Society in the Age of the Baroque* (London, 1963); P. Burke, *Culture and Society in Renaissance Italy, 1420–1540* (London, 1972).

106. "In filiis familias sufficit tacitus cum expressione eorum in quorum sunt potestate." "Si . . . illa nihil respondeat, dico quod si mulier consentiat animo sed ex verecundia taceat, permittit tamen se subarrhari per anuli immissione voluntarie vel dotari ipsa taciturnitate et patientia consensus eius exprimitur etiam si lingua taceat . . . sufficit quod non contradiceat" (Antonino, *Summa*, bk. 3, title 1, cap. 19, fol. 20).

107. Trexler, *Synodal Law*, p. 125; cf. above, n. 55.

4
Baptismal Kinship at Minot (Côte d'Or)

Françoise Zonabend

Many anthropological studies have been devoted to baptismal sponsorship in the countries of Mediterranean or central Europe and in those of the New World. For western and northern Europe the scanty information that we have comes from the folklorists—who are primarily interested in the regional characteristics of the baptismal ceremony—or from the theologians, who are only concerned with interpreting the Church's doctrine in this matter. There are explanations for this lack of interest. Baptismal sponsorship, it is said, plays a secondary role in these areas, since the institution itself is in decline; although in other parts of the world it continues to exert a definite influence on the economic and social life of the group. Yet how can we account for our societies' attachment to this institution, an attachment so strong that when the French Revolution considered suppressing it, the institution was replaced by a republican version of sponsorship? Can we really relegate it to the rank of an archaic curiosity when we note, on the basis of a few published studies,[1] that it reveals significant differences from province to province and that it is marked by various evolutions and adaptations that keep it alive to this very day? All of these characteristics testify to its vitality and should convince us of the need to undertake for Western Europe ethnohistorical studies, not only of the forms of baptismal sponsorship but of all forms of ritual kinship.

In this article I hope to make a strictly local contribution to these studies. The data have been gathered at Minot, a village in northern Burgundy situated in an area of open fields and clustered dwellings. My approach has been both historical and ethnographical, so all the data of the past have been read in the light of the present and vice versa. Note that my analysis will be limited to the study of baptismal sponsorship, the only form of parallel kinship found

Annales, E.S.C. 33 (May-June 1978): 656–76. Translated by Elborg Forster.

in this village. I have found no trace, neither for the present nor for the past, in oral interviews or in the texts, of other forms of ritual kinship, such as adoption or voluntary brotherhood (*affrèrement*).

Baptism is characterized, as it is in all other parts of the world, by rituals, by the exchange of goods and services, and by normative models governing the choice of the godfather/godmother couple.

The high point of the rituals of baptism is the day of the ceremony; on that day the rituals assume their full symbolic weight. In reality, however, the ritual of that day is preceded by another—the occasion when the child's parents officially ask two persons to "baptize" the baby—and followed by other, more discreet rituals, which take place on specific dates throughout the religious calendar or throughout the life cycle. These rituals are thus made up of a sequence of more or less complex operations spread out over time. The ceremony of baptism is only the most spectacular and the best known among them.

The Asking

"The asking," a sober and quasi-domestic step, marks the beginning of every baptism. Formerly, the spiritual parents were not chosen before the birth of the baby; people would have feared to "upset" it. Today, the godfather and godmother are decided upon in the early months of the mother's pregnancy. Now, just as in the past, "the asking" still calls for a certain solemnity; the parents put on good clothes and jewelry before they set out on this errand. For it must be made clear that they have come to "ask you" to be godfather or godmother; this is something "one doesn't refuse," but "doesn't offer," either. Proper behavior dictates that the demand be explicitly stated in the course of the visit paid by the parents to the future godfather and godmother. Being asked implies the obligation to accept; to refuse would constitute a serious insult. However, one does not ask to become a godparent. In a conversation about this subject among a group of women who are neighbors in the village center and who have long met together, helped each other out, and exchanged services on a daily basis, one of the women, the mother of many children, expressed puzzlement and regret that she had never asked one of the others, who was childless, to be godmother to one of her children. The latter answered: "I thought about it, but I never dared to make the offer." In fact, the first woman had large numbers of relatives, so she was able to fulfill all of her ceremonial obligations.

Only outsiders to the family, often of higher social status than the biological parents, may offer themselves as godparents. Yet outsiders are not often chosen, and it is even rarer that the godparents are of much higher social status than the child's parents. In the last century, the notary of Minot and later his son, a great landowner, never served as godfathers to any of their tenants' children. People were surprised, therefore, when the owners of the farm belonging to the château became godparents to their tenant's fifth child. "They probably offered to do it," was the comment. The two sons of the drygoods dealer, who had come to the village from Savoy in the first decades of the century, were godchildren of the people who had welcomed their father when he first arrived: "The godfather had offered himself; he had said: 'I'll be the godfather,' because they [the parents] would never have dared to ask." There is no doubt that this connection facilitated the drygoods dealer's integration into the community: twenty-two years later, his son was to marry the granddaughter of his brother's godmother. Note this interrelation between marriage and baptismal sponsorship.

It should be added that outsiders will easily offer to become grandparents to the last children of a large group of siblings. When it comes to these children, the norms are no longer applied and the parents often have considerable trouble finding godparents for them,[2] so they will consider any and all offers, even those that are made in jest. Madame G. tells the following story: "I am godmother to one of Jean Chevalier's sons, and yet we're not related. But when he had his first baby, he came to the farm to tell us about it. I jokingly said to him: 'when you have your seventh, I'll be the godmother.' Well, when he did have the seventh, he came around to ask me!"

The Day of the Baptism

The ceremony of baptism consists of two parts. In both of these, the godparents, who complete certain symbolic itineraries and gestures and pronounce certain ritual words, essentially play the role of intercessors.

The main task of the godparents in the first part of the ceremony is to have the newborn received into the community of Christians and to have him cleansed of original sin: "One becomes a Christian through baptism, that second birth, the sacrament that effaces original sin and leads the creature out of the death of sin to the life of grace, snatching him from the fatal hold of Hell in order to place him among God's children and to give him his rightful place in His Paradise."[3]

The high perinatal mortality of past ages explains the haste with which the baptism was traditionally undertaken. A child was born; and if it lived, it was taken to the church on the same day, or the next, in order to be baptized. The certificates of baptism of the past still bear witness to this haste: "Etiennette . . ., born 28 May 1762, was baptized on the same day by me, the parish priest;" "Jeanne . . . born 24 September 1740, was baptized on the next day by me, the parish priest." If its life was in danger, the child was baptized on the spot by the midwife, by the "helping woman,"[4] or by the maternal grandmother, who was always present at her daughters' confinements. Marguerite, who, in the period between World War I and World War II helped all the women of the village in their deliveries, recalls: "I did it once, I baptized a baby that was going to die. I poured on a little holy water, saying: 'I baptize you in the name of the Father, the Son . . . ,' and then the child was buried at the church. I had heard that you can do this, and so I did it." If the child stayed alive, it was given a real baptism in church; but once it had been "emergency baptized" [ondoyé dans le danger][5] in this manner, it was not condemned to err in limbo for all eternity. Yet however strong the desire to baptize the child as soon as possible, every effort was made to avoid doing it on a Friday, the most unlucky day of all, on which nothing should be undertaken that had any bearing on the future.[6]

In the past, people believed that as long as the child was not baptized it remained vulnerable, exposed to all kinds of danger. Hence the discretion that surrounded the birth. Having emerged from the mother's body, the child was placed in a laundry basket rather than in its cradle;[7] those who were present avoided looking at it; no one visited it; and its first name was not pronounced. The procession that went to the church for the baptism was small, consisting of the godfather, the godmother, and the "carrying woman" (usually the woman who had helped the mother during the delivery).[8] As the documents show, the mother was never present, and the father too was often absent. This discreet character of the baptismal ceremony no doubt explains why one finds so few photographs taken at baptisms. In the lot of three hundred old photographs collected at Minot, only one records a baptism, and in this case the godparents were notables. Likewise, late-nineteenth- and early-twentieth-centuries engravings always depict groups "leaving the church," or the "return from the baptism." Only after the baptism had been performed did the neighbors come to visit the new mother and the baby, bringing a small bag of salt and an egg.[9]

Owing to the religious disaffection of the inhabitants and to the decline of popular beliefs one already finds increasingly longer delays between the birth and the baptism by the late nineteenth century. Today, three, four, six months or more may pass between the two dates. In the parish almanac of 1918, the parish priest already deplored this pattern of behavior: "Parents are waiting too long to have their children baptized. Christian parents, do not put off your children's baptism. Death may surprise them, and then, what a responsibility, what remorse for you. Your children must be baptized as soon as possible. Waiting longer than two weeks is a mortal sin." This last priest threatened not to have the bells rung for a belated baptism. This was a serious threat which, if executed, would cast doubt on the child's legitimacy. For it was only after the baptism that the bells were rung, their resounding voices announcing to the entire group the birth of a new member.

Since the bells themselves were solemnly baptized, anointed with holy oil and endowed with prestigious godparents,[10] they had a sacred and social character that conferred upon them a protective role for the community and the newborn child. Moreover, the language of the bells was enlisted to help with the learning of speech. While the bells were ringing their full peal, under the wave of their sound, the godfather and godmother were supposed to exchange a kiss under the entrance way to the church: "Godfather and godmother must kiss each other so that the baby will not be *niacou*, snot-nosed, drooling and stuttering." Thereupon the godparents would toss out to the assembled village children candied almonds, hazelnuts, and small coins. At Minot this manner of throwing fruits and sweets is called *tricöts*.[11] "When they came out the kids would be waiting and then the godfather and godmother they would toss out the goodies in all directions; they made them run for it and they would pick them up from the ground. In those days there were more hazelnuts than candied almonds and more small change than coins." A. Van Gennep sees this as a ritual of abundance:[12] by tossing out food that many children would scurry to pick up, one called down upon the village fertility and wealth. Van Gennep adds that this ritual can also be considered a "rite of passage of the category of the compensatory welcome."[13] With this sweet tribute, the godparents pay their dues to the group of the young to which they have just added a new member. Thus, as soon as the newborn leaves the church, the second act of the ceremony begins. It is essentially a matter between the local community and the godparents, who act as a mediators for the child.

The return from the church is followed by a meal at the child's parents' home. In the past it involved few participants: the child's parents and the spiritual parents, plus their spouses if they were married, and the woman who had carried the child to the church. The ample but simple meal—it included only one meat course—was prepared at home without the help of a cook from the outside.[14] After the meal, the godparents would walk through the village and stop at all the houses to distribute candied almonds. By way of thanks, the inhabitants would say: "If the baby falls into the mud, we will pick him up."[15] Today the grandparents only make the rounds of the neighbors. Many other changes in the baptismal ceremony can also be discerned.

The discretion that used to surround the birth, and the precautions that were taken to protect the vulnerable newborn, are no longer in style. The ceremony of the baptism, which takes place long after the child's birth, is attended by large numbers of relatives who all go to the church, as does the baby's mother. Grandparents, uncles, aunts, godparents, and cousins are invited to two meals (a luncheon and a dinner), prepared by a cook from outside and composed of many courses with fancy names.[16] Today there is little difference between the meal served at the first communion or the wedding and the meal of the baptism. These changes are recent; at Minot, they took place in the 1960s, and now one finds both the discreet ceremony followed by a meal with a few guests and the ostentatious ceremony followed by two meals attended by numerous guests.

In order to gain a better understanding of these modifications it will be helpful to consider all the rituals that punctuate the life of the individual, for together these rituals constitute an indivisible whole. The first communion, formerly a simple celebration attended only by the immediate family, has assumed a much wider scope and now brings together large numbers of relatives; weddings, formerly open to the community, are becoming restricted to the kin group and to one age group; and finally, a death now calls only for an assembly of the kin group at the church and no longer gives rise to a huge family repast. Thus the ceremonies connected with childhood, the beginning of life, have taken precedence over those connected with death, the end of life. Can we see this development as a consequence of the preponderant position acquired by children and adolescents in modern social life, or does it have to do with the more discreet place of death in our societies? This is not the place to answer this question; but in any case, we must realize that as the festive occasions that used to bring together the entire community or specific age groups throughout the calendar year are disappearing or becoming muted, the more specifically familial festivities take on a vastly inflated scope and assume such ostentatious forms that many older people are offended by them. Today's baptisms and first communions entail exorbitant expenses, borne by the more or less immediate family. People give presents and dinners among themselves, but in doing so they also show off to the community as a whole. This implies that each household within the local group lays claim to a place in the hierarchy among all the others; each one has a rank to maintain, and every familial ceremony reflects the place it holds or wants to hold. In the old days this kind of excessive rejoicing was reserved for the festivities of the patron saint's day, when every household, each according to its rank, consumed and made gifts to neighboring communities in the persons of the relatives it invited. Henceforth, the community is superseded by the family.

Obligatory Gifts

Between the godparents and the godchild, social relations, both formal and informal, will be established through a whole series of mutual gifts and services. The pseudoparents, always together, will be present and active at all moments of passage in their godchild's life cycle. At the baptism, the godfather and godmother share the buying of the candied almonds, which they subsequently toss out, together, to the children from the door of the church, and which they offer to the guests at the meal and then distribute to the neighbors. The meal itself is provided by the parents. The godfather gives the child a silver cup, fork, and spoon, and the godmother gives a chain and a religious medal. Should these presents be viewed as symbols of the godparents' respective roles? One of them acts in a materially nurturing capacity, whereas the other acts as a guide to the ways of piety. Only rarely does either godparent give a christening dress or bonnet. These items are considered "family heirlooms" and are passed from brother to sister, from cousin to nephew, until they wear out. At that point, the child's mother makes or buys a new dress, which again is passed down from child to child. "She has turned my dress! I lent it out many times in the family."

The godparents are, as a matter of course, the first ones to be invited to a child's first communion; at the meal they are seated on either side of their godchild. The godfather gives a watch, the godmother a missal and the rosary. The distribution of their roles is the same as at the baptism.

At the godchild's marriage, the godfather often acts as his or her witness. If the biological parents are no longer living, one or the other of the pseudoparents is called upon to lead the godchild to the altar. At the wedding banquet the spouses' godparents are seated between the young unmarried people (whether related to the spouses or not) and their parents, indicating that they are considered the first among the relatives. They always give a substantial present in keeping with the couple's taste.

Finally, if the godchild dies in infancy, the godparents carry the coffin: the godfather in the case of a boy, the godmother in case of a girl. If the godchild dies in childhood or adolescence, the pallbearers are members of his or her age group.

In these ways, the godparents are associated with all the important moments in their godchild's life, and they in turn associate their godchild with all the important moments in their lives. If one of the godparents marries, the godchild participates in the ceremony, occupying a place of honor, even if it is only symbolically: "When I was married my godchild was maid of honor; but as she was too young, her place was taken by a cousin." Later the silver or golden wedding anniversary of a godparent is celebrated in the company of the children and godchildren. If there are no direct descendants, the godchild will make the arrangements for the party: "Germaine and Maxime celebrated their fortieth wedding anniversary; they had a meal at a restaurant with us [first cousins] and Jocelyne [goddaughter] and her husband. Jocelyne made all the arrangements; she chose the restaurant and the menu. We will have our fiftieth anniversary this year, and we'll invite people in the same way, our cousins and my godson and his wife." The godchild substitutes for the absent child, just as the godfather or godmother is expected to substitute for the missing parent. When a godparent dies, the godson offers to be a pallbearer, unless he is too closely related, and he is always invited to the funeral meal attended by the immediate family.

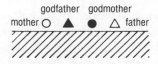

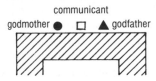

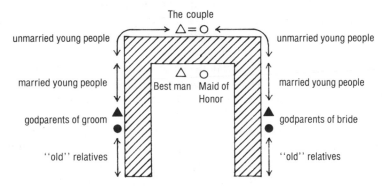

Figure 4.1. Seating of the godparents at the different ceremonial meals

Aside from these important occasions, when quasi-ritual gifts and services are exchanged, friendly and affectionate relations come into being between the spiritual parents and the godchild. For the godchild's birthday, for his name day, for New Year's or Christmas, the godparents give presents. In the old days, reports Van Gennep, "the godparents gave the *quignô*, or *quigneu*, (a piece of bread or cake) on Christmas eve; and on the first Christmas after the baptism the godparents would bring to the child a dress and a six-pound bread called an *époigne*; the following year the godchild would receive only a half-*époigne*."[17] At Minot people remember receiving only an orange and a few small coins. Today Christmas and birthday presents are more substantial.

It should be noted, incidentally, that these gifts are given only between spiritual parents and godchildren, to the exclusion of all other collaterals: "In our family we have decided not to give presents to the nephews and nieces, except for the godchildren." "The godchildren, well, we spoil them a little more than the others, we give them presents every year at New Year's and for their birthdays." Within the category of close relatives, there is thus a subcategory consisting of relatives bound together by spiritual kinship. Year after year, frequent exchanges of services, small presents, visits, or a regular correspondence contribute to the upkeep and the reinforcement of these relations. The high value placed on the social relations between spiritual relatives is confirmed by the terminology that sets these relations apart from the ordinary terms of kinship: "My father's brother is my uncle and my godfather, but I used to call him uncle." In the forms of address the spiritual kinship is effaced; the real kinship takes precedence over it.

One of the components of this special importance given to spiritual kinship and of this careful nurturing of social relations is of an economic nature. The villagers like to cite cases of godparents without direct descendants who left all or some of their property to a godchild: "Flavie had come to live with her aunt, who was her godmother, and later she inherited everything. Hélène Parent left more to Madeleine because she brought her up, and besides, she was her godchild, and she sure was given an advantage over the others. Godparents who don't have children always give an advantage to their godchildren and often leave them everything they've got." This rather important economic aspect no doubt explains why childless couples or unmarried older people are chosen as godparents more often than individuals who have children. Yet these choices are made only when the normal choices, which are mandatory for the two elder children, no longer apply. It should be emphasized, however, that these material considerations do not account for the pattern of behavior as a whole or for the choice of spiritual parents. Before pursuing this subject further, however, I should like to draw a few conclusions from my observation of these rituals.

At all the formal or informal occasions connected with these rituals, the godfather and the godmother are always present together and on an equal footing. This equality is established from the very beginning by the reciprocal exchange of gifts between them. The godfather gives to the godmother the "pretty box for the candied almonds" with which they will go from house to house; in middle-class families he will give her a "glove box." The godmother embroiders or buys for her *compère* [fellow godparent][18] a lace-trimmed handkerchief of fine batiste. Neither of them gives a present to the child's mother. In all the ceremonies that bring them together, one never has precedence over the other. In the past, both of them transmitted their Christian names to the child (see below); and to this day they share equally in the buying of the candied almonds for the baptism and in other expenses on behalf of the godchild. They are always invited together, and the godchild treats each of them in the same manner. To be sure, the relationship between spiritual parents and godchildren of the same sex will be freer and more affectionate; nonetheless, both godparents' importance to the godchild's parents and to the child itself remain of equal weight.

This equal sharing of honors and obligations is but the echo of another equality, namely, the systematic practice of choosing one spiritual parent from the paternal and the other from the maternal lineage (see below). This concern with equality is also evident in a number of manifestations of social life, such as the kinship system, which shows a general tendency to preserve a perfect symmetry in all family relationships, and the inheritance practices, which, until recently, mandated the equal division of the patrimony among all the children. Jean Yver,[19] in his *Géographie coutumière de la France*, stresses this egalitarian character of the Burgundian law, which went hand in hand with a very liberal attitude. In fact, one wonders whether a better understanding of this strict bilateralism might not be gained if one evoked—with all due caution, to be sure—the political configuration of Burgundy as a frontier area, located between the southern regions where Roman law obtained and the eastern regions ruled by Germanic law. This brings us back to history, which in turn leads us to an examination of the norms governing the choice of spiritual parents.

The Constellation of Pseudoparents

Baptismal sponsorship indivisibly associates five individuals: the godfather, the godmother, the father, the mother, and the child. It is in relation to the child that the parents chose the godparents. Hence the many strangely matched spiritual couples; for the choice is a matter not only of picking among the individuals designated by the norm those who will "best take care of the child," but above all of opting for those who are best suited to the exigencies of the family's long-range goals. Recent as well as old baptismal records furnish many examples of couples of spiritual parents belonging to two different generations. Thus we find as a child's godparents a grandfather and an aunt, a cousin and an uncle. It appears that whenever the relative required by the norm is dead or missing, his or her descendant or the closest collateral relative is chosen instead, regardless of age. This conformity to the norm is particularly compelling in the case of firstborn children. Take the baptism if Louis B. in 1910: the godfather should have been the father's brother and the godmother the mother's sister. The father had no brother, so his place was taken by one of his brother's grandsons, a "young cousin" of twenty-five. The mother's sister was deceased, but she had left a daughter, then five years old, who was chosen as the godmother to her first cousin. Since she was much too young actually to assume this charge, it was the woman who carried the child to the baptismal font who spoke for her at the church, although the name of the young godmother was duly recorded in the parish register.

There is no hesitation in bringing together a child and an adult, individuals of different generations, or a married and an unmarried sponsor. This is irrelevant, for in the formation of the pair of pseudoparents, marriage strategies are not involved. In this sense it appears that the godmother/godfather couple responds to an altogether different set of preoccupations than the best man/maid of honor couple, which is constituted for a marriage. On that occasion the choice explicitly testifies to a desire to strengthen the ties of alliance between two families and possibly to bring about a second marriage. The godfather/godmother couple, by contrast, is marked negatively as far as a marriage alliance is concerned. Although the Church has not prohibited marriage between the godfather and the godmother of the same child since the Council of Mainz (ninth century),[20] society rejects such alliances: "Godfathers and godmothers can't marry each other; this brings bad luck." This point is made forcefully in cases where a godfather/godmother couple is constituted by a boy and a girl who are "going together," although their not yet institutionalized relationship remains vulnerable. Their being bound together for a baptism compromises their future alliance; it "breaks up" their relationship. Such fragile pairings are unable to cope with the suspicion aroused by the forbidden. For all these reasons I do not feel that baptismal sponsorship can be associated with other forms of ritual relationships that have a bearing on the notion of the couple.

Choices and Norms

In the course of my research, which I have not been able to evaluate statistically, the kinship relations between the godparent and the child—paternal grandfather, maternal grandmother, paternal uncle, maternal aunt, child's brother, etc.—which are sometimes noted in the documents, as well as many reconstituted genealogies (see appendix, genealogies 1-3), permit me to assert that ever since 1642, the date of the first religious census of the village, the spiritual parents were essentially chosen from within the kin group, one from the paternal and one from the maternal line. This alternating choice from each lineage—and we shall see presently how it was organized—is, with very few exceptions, carried through systematically. If we fail to see it, we can assume that there is a conflict between the allied kin groups or, at least, a desire to sever the ties between the two lineages.[21] Let us take as an example the case of a certain farmer who was quarreling over an inheritance with his sisters, and to whom a son was born in 1968; this child was given as godparents a sister of the farmer's wife and her husband. Or take the couple in the early years of the century in which the man came from a family of woodcutters and

the woman from a family of farmers. This couple was in a peculiar geneologi-
cal position, belonging to each of the two social groups—woodspeople and
tillers of the fields—that constituted the village. They were constantly en-
deavoring to remain among the tillers of the fields, and one notices that the
children's spiritual parents all belonged to the mother's family. It is evident
that cutting all spiritual ties with a lineage will rapidly increase the distance
from that lineage—in terms of familial relations, that is. Today the eldest
daughter of this couple is not even aware that her first cousin on her father's
side lives in the neighboring village. These examples illustrate the political
role of baptismal sponsorship; and although this is only a matter of family
politics, to be sure, its consequences for a family's relative standing within
the village community can be considerable. They also underscore the role
played by spiritual kinship in bringing together and commemorating members of the kin group: to choose one relative is to threaten another with obli-
vion. Hence the equitable selection of godparents from among the two kin
groups; hence also the small number of choices with which it is possible to
gratify any given individual.

Who, then, are chosen as spiritual parents? Until World War II, the
model of baptismal sponsorship was the following: "For the first child one
took the paternal grandfather and the maternal grandmother; for the second
child the father's oldest brother and the mother's oldest sister, and then for
the others there was no pattern." In order to explain this model, one must
also consider the naming of the child or, rather, the giving of the first name.
Recall that at Minot, as everywhere in Europe, the spiritual parents gave a
name to the child and that until about 1860-70, the child received only one
Christian name. This single first name given to the child was that of the godfather for a boy, that of the godmother for a girl. The preference for the
paternal grandfather and the maternal grandmother and then for the paternal uncle and the maternal aunt, to the exclusion of the other pair of grandparents, seemed to correspond to an exigency connected with the transmission of the Christian name, for a man gave his name to the child of his son or
of his brother, but not to the child of his daughter or of his sister; whereas a
woman gave hers to her daughter's daughter or her sister's daughter and not
to her son's child. The Christian name was thus transmitted directly in the
paternal or maternal line, respectively, at least where the oldest children were
concerned. The rule for the transmission of Christian names thus resulted in
the sharing of the children by the uterine and the agnatic lineages (see
Figures 2 and 3). The boys were given the names of the men in the paternal
line and the girls those of the women in the maternal line. In this manner the
Christian name was marked by a double affiliation and the children were
equally distributed between the two lineages. Keeping in mind that the family name defines the individual as the heir of a single lineage, that of the
father, one realizes the importance of this double affiliation of the Christian

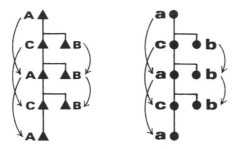

Figure 4.2. The old model: Baptismal ties and the transmission of the Christian name

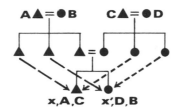

Figure 4.3. The new model: Baptismal ties and the transmission of Christian names x and x': freely chosen and usual Christian names; A, B, C, D: additional Christian names.

name, which, being transmitted from godparent to godchild, constitutes a veritable relational term[22] and results in a renewed affirmation of bilateral descent.

The mediating role of the godparent and the structural meaning of spiritual kinship thus used to be clearly expressed, especially in the transmission of Christian names. The rules for the giving of this Christian name have evolved, however, as has the selection of spiritual parents. Is there a relation of cause and effect between these two developments? This is probable, although these changes did not occur simultaneously. The rules for the transmission of Christian names were modified before certain categories of godparents were excluded, but there is no doubt that the first modification facilitated the second.

As for the naming of the child, a change has occurred from a single to multiple Christian names, the first of which is always chosen by the biological parents in agreement with the pseudoparents. However, the homonymy between godparent and godchild is disappearing. As for the second and third Christian names, the rule is shaping up as follows: the oldest of the boys receives his paternal grandfather's name as his second and his maternal grandfather's as his third name; while the oldest daughter is given her maternal grandmother's name as her second and her paternal grandmother's as her third name. The subsequent siblings are given as second and third names those of their godfather and godmother in feminine or masculine form, or that of a grand uncle or a great aunt from one or the other lineage (see appendix, genealogy 3).

As for the spiritual parents, a change is taking place in their actual selection, but the model remains unchanged. Even today the spiritual parents are taken from both lineages: "For the oldest one takes the father's brother and the mother's sister, for the second one takes the father's younger brother and the mother's younger sister, and then for the others there is no pattern."

The individuals who may replace these couples are, in order of preference, relatives by marriage—the wife of the father's brother, the husband of the mother's sister—who, in the day to day form of address, are in the category of consanguineous relatives for the godchild. Next are cousins of the father and the mother, and then come the child's first cousins and his or her older siblings. The selection is thus restricted to collaterals of the same or the next older generation. This choice of collaterals rather than ascendants constitutes a problem. At Minot, people have an explanation for this change: "We no longer take the grandparents because we noticed that they were elderly, that they were already old, and so one didn't have godparents for very long." It is difficult to accept this explanation, given the present life expectancy of the individuals in question. There is evidence that in the last decades the Church has insisted that children should have young godparents, but no one in the village has ever evoked this influence.

Let us return to the matter of the Christian name. Today the spiritual parents no longer automatically transmit their Christian name to their godchild, yet the ousted grandparents still see their Christian names perpetuated in the lineage. This change has led to several modifications in identification. The eldest children are doubly identified with the paternal and the maternal lineage, since the names of all four grandparents are now given to the grandchildren. Yet the old model is preserved through the second Christian name, which serves to mark the preeminence of the paternal line for the eldest boy and that of the maternal line for the eldest girl. The first of the Christian names, finally, which is left to the parents' free choice, becomes fortuitous. The important aspect of all this is the disjunction that has appeared between the institution of baptismal sponsorship, which is now assigned to the collaterals, and the function of transmitting Christian names. Henceforth, the circulation of Christian names in the genealogical chart is independent of the selection of godparents. This disjunction tends to prove that the transmission of the Christian name and the selection of the spiritual parents belong to two different areas of concern, which may have coincided for a time in the past. Today the transmission of the Christian name involves the identification of descent, whereas the choice of spiritual parents, as I shall show presently, is concerned with the area of marriage alliances.

How are these matters handled at the present time? The grandparents, although they have lost all spiritual responsibility, continue to play a preeminent role in the upbringing of their grandchildren: they teach the children how to perform many domestic chores, and part of the children's social standing continues to be transmitted through them. They have thus preserved a social role—indeed, a place of honor—within the kin group. They are always invited to the baptism, and today it is the maternal grandmother who carries the child to the church on the day of the baptism. Once the grandparents had thus been "taken care of," in every sense of that expression, baptismal sponsorship could evolve in a new direction; at the very least, one observes that tendencies which had existed all along were reinforced by this concentration on the collaterals.

What is the meaning of this modification in the norms governing the choice of godparents? It certainly involves a desire to break with tradition, with "the old days" and with the past—a time whose guardians are the grandparents. It also surely reflects a change in the temporal perception of the family, inasmuch as the genealogical distance between godparents and godchild has been shortened. In this manner, the collaterals are taking precedence over the ascendants. But what the family loses in depth it gains in collaterality. And, by eliminating the grandparents, a family renews its ties with *the cousins*, the descendants of the great-grandfather's brother. These cousins form the outermost circle of the consanguineous kin group. The awareness of kinship is expressed by referring to these individuals as cousins, but the origin of the relationship has become obscure. As I have shown elsewhere,[23] these cousins constitute a preferred category of potential marriage partners and, above all, a category of relatives who make it possible to reinforce existing marriage alliances, which are so highly valued by every family. It is through them that the consciousness and the memory of repeated alliances between lineages are kept alive. These cousins are the indispensable relays that will keep the system functioning, and hence it is important to stay in touch with them and to remember them. Using these relatives as godparents is the surest means of preventing them from disappearing or becoming estranged. In fact, it is often among these *cousins* that the godparents for the last-born of a group of siblings are chosen. It is precisely in these circumstances that spiritual kinship assumes its full meaning. These cousins are the only ones of the spiritual parents chosen from within the kin group to be referred to and addressed as "godfather/godmother." We have seen earlier that if a close family relationship exists between godparent and godchild, this relationship takes precedence over the spiritual kinship in the form of address: "My godfather was my father's brother—I called him uncle." If, by contrast, the terminology of the kinship relation is uncertain, if it does not clearly indicate the normal chronological distance between grandparent and godchild, then the terms "godfather" and "godmother" are used as forms of address. "My godmother was a [remote] cousin; I always called her godmother." Whenever the spiritual relationship unites nonrelatives, the terms godfather and godmother are used both as a form of address and as a reference.

Concerning these godparents who are remote cousins or not related at all, one notices, moreover, a possible extension of the terms of spiritual kinship, inasmuch as the godfather's wife becomes godmother to her husband's godchild, and vice versa. This extension also applies to the godchildren and their spouses, who call each other's godparents "godfather" and "godmother." In the same manner, this extension can involve siblings: "My brother's godmother is Madame B, she lives in the village; we're not related at all, but I call her 'godmother.' " In the form of reference each person returns to his or her place, but it seems to me that this liberty in the form of address gives spiritual kinship its full scope. For the spiritual ties between these domestic units of godparents and godchildren reinforce ties of kinship that were either about to disappear, since it was barely possible to put a name to them, or were altogether nonexistent. They create within these groups a fictitious kinship patterned after the model of real kinship: "They [her husband's godfather and his wife] addressed us as 'tu' and we always said 'vous' to them. To their daughter we say 'tu' and call her by her nickname. My husband and I have always called his godfather and his wife 'godfather' and 'godmother.' We often used to spend the evening at their house and they came to ours. Now that the family has left Minot, we are taking care of their graves."

Baptismal sponsorship thus calls for the same type of conduct and social relations as close ties of real kinship. Just as there is a way of dealing "as kin" with blood relatives and "as family" with in-laws, so there is a way of dealing "as spiritual kin" with certain individuals, whether they are related or not. Spiritual kinship constitutes a subsystem of the system of kinship, especially if one keeps in mind that baptismal sponsorship tends to become perpetuated either through reciprocation or through transmission within families (see figure 4). It is quite common, in fact, for the child of the godparent to become godparent to his or her godparent's child, or for the godparent's child to become godparent to the godchild's offspring. In that case people explain that they are "fishing for godparents where they have already caught some." Within the genealogical charts spiritual bonds thus become intertwined with bonds of alliance and consanguinity, forming loops and cycles, just as double marriages and repeated marriage alliances associate, unite, and reunite various lineages. It is perfectly obvious that there is a strategy of baptismal sponsorship, just as there is a matrimonial strategy. But while we can understand the reasons for the latter strategy, it is not easy to grasp the reasons for the former.

The effacement of the grandparents as godparents suggests that today families are perceived as consisting essentially of the collaterals, who must be con-

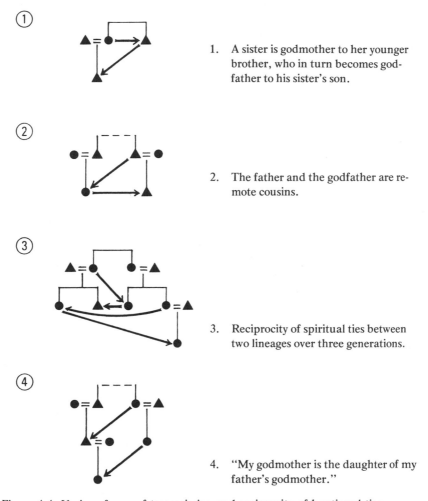

1. A sister is godmother to her younger brother, who in turn becomes god-father to his sister's son.

2. The father and the godfather are re-mote cousins.

3. Reciprocity of spiritual ties between two lineages over three generations.

4. "My godmother is the daughter of my father's godmother."

Figure 4.4. Various forms of transmission and reciprocity of baptismal ties

stantly kept together and reunited by means of the centripetal thrust provided by the ties of baptismal sponsorship. Therefore, it is the principal function of these ties to keep up the memory of lineages which would otherwise tend to become distant—in memory—from each other, owing to the increasing geographical dispersion of siblings. If families wish to keep up this memory, it is mainly because collateral lineages provide a favorable ground for renewed alliances. It therefore does not seem unreasonable to suppose that baptismal sponsorship is also considered as a means of finding a spouse for the godchild or his brothers and sisters. By bringing together distantly related lineages and by multiplying the occasions for encounters among distant relatives, baptismal sponsorship can play a role in the choice of spouses and in the marriage strategies of the various kin groups. This is not a new game, for a careful reading of the parish registers makes it clear enough that baptismal sponsorship and marriage have always been tightly interwoven, albeit indirectly. For example, a certain marriage, which in 1788 united the families of two tenants of outlying farms, had no doubt been prepared by spiritual ties established a few decades earlier between the two neighbors. Recall also the marriage of 1927 between the son of the drygoods dealer from Savoy and the granddaughter of his brother's godmother (see above). Three of the six children of Pierre Couturier, the surgeon at Minot in the late seventeenth century, found spouses among the relatives of their brothers' or their first cousins' godparents.

Although it is possible to reconstitute this intertwining of alliances and baptismal sponsorships from the parish registers, it is almost impossible to do this in oral interviews, for the memory of ritual ties does not last long. It covers no more than two, at most three, generations vertically (Ego, his children and grandchildren and, in the other direction, his parents) and one degree of collaterality (Ego's siblings). Ego never remembers his grandparents' godparents, and rarely those of his uncles and aunts. It is therefore quite difficult to reconstitute or to gather for a genealogy the complete information that would make it possible to establish the interrelation between baptismal sponsorship and the selection of marriage partners. For such a project, we would need to know the identity of all the godparents for a group of siblings, for the game involves not only the godparents and their godchild but all the godparents and all the siblings within a given kin group as well. The series of formal and informal obligations, the constant exchange of invitations and reciprocal visits that, as we have seen, regularly take place between the godparents and the godchildren, constitute so many additional occasions for meetings of kin groups. The plasticity of ritual kinship with respect to forms of address creates a kind of fictitious kinship and helps to keep up the contacts between domestic groups and age groups. And if today it has been found necessary to eliminate the grandparents, this was done in order to strengthen the ties with the collaterals and with remote cousins and in order to counterbalance, at least for a generation or two, the prevailing geographical dispersion of the kin group.

The change in the choice of godparents thus seems to be based on phenomena of a geographical and demographic order, and the reasons for it are, I believe, of a sociological order.

The traditional strategy that called for consanguineous marriages and repeated alliances within the village or the area of endogamy could be explained by the desire to add genealogical proximity to the proximity between properties, for it was essential to keep property circulating within the lineage.[24] Now that these alliances take place between geographically distant lineages, or even between genealogically unrelated kin groups, both of these exigencies have disappeared. At this point all that is left is the reference to a specific cultural identity, a shared social horizon, and "a certain similarity of two persons' cultures."[25]

The baptismal strategy that is practiced today between lineages dispersed far beyond the area of traditional endogamy and far beyond the limits of actual kinship is a means of arranging encounters between groups that share the same cultural origin and the same social milieu. The marriages that may ensue from such encounters make it possible to reproduce the existing cultural model. Through this spiritual kin group one meets "one's own people," people one knows, and persons with whom marriage is possible.

All of these observations lead me to conclude that spiritual kinship can be understood, in this region of France, only in relation to actual kinship. Its true meaning can be grasped only through reference to kinship ties, which are strengthened and continued by spiritual ties. The foreshortening of the vertical line that is taking place today, as well as the concomitant extension of the collateral ties, is essentially designed to foster a matrimonial strategy. The main function of baptismal sponsorship as it is practiced today in this village is to bring together groups of spouse-takers and groups of spouse-givers.

APPENDIX

Genealogy 1: Godparents of one of the village notaries

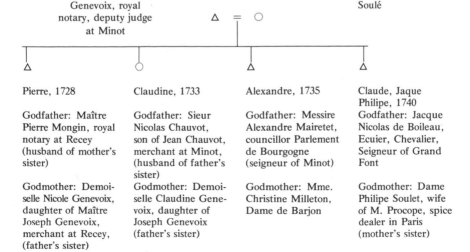

Pierre, 1728	Claudine, 1733	Alexandre, 1735	Claude, Jaque Philipe, 1740
Godfather: Maître Pierre Mongin, royal notary at Recey (husband of mother's sister)	Godfather: Sieur Nicolas Chauvot, son of Jean Chauvot, merchant at Minot, (husband of father's sister)	Godfather: Messire Alexandre Mairetet, councillor Parlement de Bourgogne (seigneur of Minot)	Godfather: Jacque Nicolas de Boileau, Ecuier, Chevalier, Seigneur of Grand Font
Godmother: Demoiselle Nicole Genevoix, daughter of Maître Joseph Genevoix, merchant at Recey, (father's sister)	Godmother: Demoiselle Claudine Genevoix, daughter of Joseph Genevoix (father's sister)	Godmother: Mme. Christine Milleton, Dame de Barjon	Godmother: Dame Philipe Soulet, wife of M. Procope, spice dealer in Paris (mother's sister)

This notary had established himself at Minot around 1720. Note the geographical dispersion (as far as Paris) of the relatives; nonetheless, all the godparents were chosen among relatives, except for the third child, whose godfather was the seigneur of Minot. At the time, this was the only child in the village to receive this honor.

Genealogy 2: Spiritual kinship between two groups of siblings issued from a double marriage: Two households of farmers, ca. 1740 (the Girardots in black, the Laillets in grey).

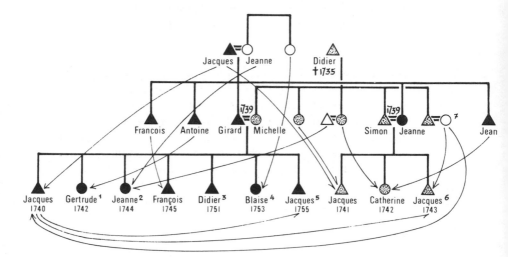

Note: Note that the selection of godparents extended over three generations (from grandfather to grandson); the double marriage that united these two kin groups had no influence on the choice of godparents; the couple godfather/godmother was often constituted by individuals belonging to different generations; the Christian name *Jacques* was transmitted to the male children of both groups of siblings; and all the spiritual parents lived at Minot, either in the village center or at an outlying farm close to that of the child's parents. The Girardot (black) line had been established in the village territory for two generations, and also had relatives in a neighboring village. The Laillet (grey) line had been present in Minot for a long time, but in every generation some of its members had gone to live in other villages. These relatives were not taken as godparents for the children; a godparent nearer home was chosen.

[1]Gertrude's godmother was Gertrude B, daughter of a farmer in the village center, no doubt a relative on her mother's side.

[2]Jeanne's godfather was Vincent V., a farmer at the same outlying farm as Jeanne's parents and her mother's brother-in-law.

[3]Didier's godfather was Didier M., farmer at a neighboring outlying farm, and his godmother was Françoise, daughter of a farmer at the same farm. The biological and the spiritual parents do not seem to have been related. But one often finds baptismal ties between outlying farms in the same vicinity or between farmers working at the same farm. They were the sign of the great value placed on mutual help within or among these outlying farms and served to weave among these families networks of spiritual solidarity that would eventually be consolidated by a network of alliances.

[4]Blaise's godfather was Toussaint L., farmer at a neighboring farm.

[5]Jacques's godfather was his fifteen-year-old brother. Older siblings often became godparents to younger ones, among farmers as well as among notables. Similarly, it was not unusual in the past for the children of a first marriage to serve as godparents to those of a second marriage. Was this a way of forestalling the scattering of families? Jacques's godmother was Magdeleine M., daughter of a farmer at the same farm. Ten years later, when a child was born to Magdeleine's father, Jacques's sister, Gertrude, would be the godmother.

[6]The godfather of Jacques, the second son of Simon, was Girard's first son, Jacques, who was three years old when his godson was born. The record indicates that he was represented by his father. Was this choice made necessary by the transmission of the Christian name?

[7]This couple had no children because the husband died young. His widow subsequently became godmother to at least four of her nephews and nieces.

Genealogy 3: The children of a farming family today

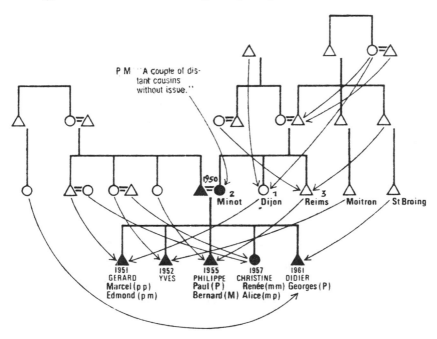

Note: In capital letters, the Christian name used by the child; (pm): mother/father; (pp): father/father; (P); godfather, (M): godmother. In the present generation, spiritual relations extend no further than to the immediately preceding generation and concentrate on wider collateral ties.

NOTES

1. There are few studies of this subject for northern France. The most recent are: M. Bouteiller, "Traditions folkloriques et parentés parallèles," in *Echanges et communications: Mélanges offertes á C. Lévi-Strauss* (Paris: Mouton, 1970), 1: 153–61; C. Karnoough, "La Parenté spirituelle, ses formes, ses rapports avec la terminologie de la parenté: un exemple français: La Lorraine,"

Actes du premier Congrès international d'ethnologie européenne, Paris, August 1971 (Paris: Institut d'ethnologie, 1972), microfiche 720048.

2. Popular fairytales offer many instances of parents who, unable to find godparents for the last-born of their numerous progeny, decide to take the first person they meet.

3. Lucien Febvre, *Problèmes de l'incroyance au XVIe siècle* (Paris: Albin Michel, 1968), p. 294.

4. A woman of the village who is present at all the moments of transition in peoples' lives: she helps with the confinement, gives the baby its first bath, cooks for the wedding feast, nurses dying patients, and washes the dead.

5. "On 7 February 1771, a female child, daughter of Claude——, a farmer, and Marie——, emergency-baptized at home by Anne——, her maternal grandmother, and deceased on the previous day, was buried in the cemetery of the said parish." "On 8 April 1789 a female child of Jean——, a gardener, deceased on the previous day after having been baptised in emergency by Hugues Rouhier, master of surgery at Minot, was buried in the cemetery." Extract of the parish register (Municipal archives).

6. "No one is baptized on Friday. One does not change shirts. One does not change the sheets on a Friday. There was a girl who had a doctor's appointment at Dijon, and she didn't change her shirt because it was a Friday." Friday is marked negatively.

7. Yet in the past the cradle was ready in advance.

8. By the end of the nineteenth century, it became customary to dress the child in a so-called christening dress, which was embroidered or lace-trimmed. Before that, the baby was simply swaddled and wrapped, I was told, in a "tulle veil." Was this a matter of recalling the mother's bridal veil and thereby signifying the child's legitimacy? No one remembers anything of the kind.

9. "When a child enters a house for the first time, one gives him one's house, that is, eggs and a bag of salt for good luck." A. Van Gennep, *Le Folklore de la Bourgogne* (Gap: Louis Blanc, 1934), p. 28. Eggs and salt do indeed signify good luck, but also fecundity and protection.

10. It is known that the great bell of Minot was recast on 17 May 1766, but its godparents are not known. It was taken down and recast once again in 1811, "but enough metal was added to obtain two new bells. The largest bell was given as godfather Pierre-Daniel-Cécile Massenot, son of the former royal notary, and as godmother Marie-Jeanne Joly [daughter of the former seigneur's steward, who had become a great landed proprietor]. The godfather of the smallest bell was the son of the deputy-mayor, Nicolas Nicolas. Its godmother was Claudine Ménétrier [daughter of a rich merchant of the village]." G. Potey, *L'Eglise Saint Pierre de Minot* (Dijon: Jobard, 1907), p. 35.

11. "*Tricöts*: candy and dried fruit tossed by the godparents to the children after a baptism." G. Potey, *Le Patois de Minot* (Paris, Droz, 1930), p. 52. A. Van Gennep, following F. Marion, reports that in the department of Côte-d'Or the *tricöt* is "the small christening meal attended by only four or five persons." Van Gennep, *Le Folklore de la Bourgogne*, p. 28.

12. A. Van Gennep, *Manuel de folklore français contemporain* (Paris: Picard, 1972), 1: 141.

13. Ibid., p. 142.

14. Here is a typical menu of the past: "*Pâté en croute*, fowl, vegetable, salad, sweet dessert."

15. It is difficult to find an explanation for this phrase. A Cévenol proverb says: "Those who have made you will pick you up," that is, those who have begotten you will bring you up (cf. J.-N. Pelen, "La Vallée longue en Cévennes," *Causses et Cévennes*, [special issue, n.d.], 184 pp). Does this mean that all the villagers will help bring up the child if he should be left alone?

16. Menus for christening meals:

For Olivier and Christophe, 30 March 1969

Luncheon	Dinner
Galantine truffée	Potage velouté
Cornet jambon Lucullus	Canapés maison
Poulet chasseur	Bouchées financière
Haricots panachés	Médaillons sauce Périgord
Filet de porc	Coeur de laitue
Salade de saison	Produits de nos tachetées
Délices de la ferme	Pithiviers
Pièces montées d'Olivier et Christophe	Fruits rafraichis

Marquise Lanvin   Brioche dijonnaise
Bons vins   Bons vins
Mousseux   Mousseux
Café-liqueurs   Café-liqueurs

For Xavier, 9 March 1969

Luncheon   Dinner

Galantine truffée   Crème Windsor
Jambon de Bourgogne   Friands maison
Suprême de colin sauce Nantua   Poularde sauce ivoire
Poulet chasseur   Rôtis sans plumes
Myrthos et flageolets   Ne fréquente que les huiles
Baron d'agneau Châtillonnais   Nos parfums de Provence
Coeur de laitue   Moka
Délices de nos tachetées   Ambassadeur au kirsch
Éclats de banquise et ses éventails Brioche mousseline
Pièce montée de Xavier   Corbeille de fruits
Millefeuilles
Bons vins
Champagne
Café-liqueurs

For Sylvie, 8 November 1964

Luncheon   Dinner

Hors-d'oeuvre choisis   Crème veloutée
Langouste á l'américaine   Poule sauce suprême
Friands truffés   Filet de Charolais sauce Madére
Dindonneaux rôtis   Salade de saison
Petits pois à la française   Plateau de fromages
Salade du jardin   Pièce montée
Plateau de fromages   Crème caprice
Moka   Brioche
Coupe Pompadour   Fruits de saison
Petits fours   Bons vins
Bons vins   Champagne
Champagne   Café-liqueurs
Café-liqueurs

17. Van Gennep, *Folklore de la Bourgogne*, p. 25.

18. The terms *Compère* and *Commère*, which today have a pejorative connotation, are used in jest between the godfather and the godmother.

19. Jean Yver, *Essai de géographie coutumière* (Paris: Sirey, 1966), p. 169.

20. Until recently and since the Council of Trent (1545–63), marriage was prohibited on the grounds of "spiritual kinship" only between godparents and godchildren, the person who administered and the person who received the baptism, and the spiritual and the biological parents.

21. In the case of illegitimate children, who do not have these two lineages—paternal and maternal—the mother does not dare ask her immediate family and so turns to her neighbor's children. "When Nanette's kid was born, the mother came to see my grandmother to ask us to be godparents, and my grandmother said: 'Don't worry, we'll let you have the children.' " Relatively unidentified with the social system, children (cf. note 22) are well suited to assume this role.

22. On the giving and the transmission of the Christian name, cf. F. Zonabend, "Pourquoi nommer?" in *L'Identité*. Papers from the seminar directed by Claude Lévi-Strauss (Paris: Grasset, 1977).

23. Cf. T. Jolas, Y. Verdier, and F. Zonabend, "Parler famille," *L'Homme* 10, no. 3 (1970).

24. Cf. T. Jolas and F. Zonabend, "Gens du finage, gens du bois," *Annales, E.S.C.* 28 (Janu-

ary-February 1973): 292. English translation in R. Forster and O. Ranum, eds., *Rural Society in France* (Baltimore, 1977), pp. 126–51.

25. "*Q.*: What are the conditions under which it [understanding between man and woman] will succeed?"

"*A.*: First of all, a certain similarity of culture. . . . I think that they must have the same cultural background, that both of them must be able to handle the same cultural materials. . . . I therefore think that the most important thing is a cultural equality and that both can express themselves, make themselves understood in their own cultural world, which is shared by both of them. They must see the world in the same way." "Entretien avec J.-P. Sartre," *Le Nouvel Observateur* 639 (1977): 65–66.

5

Christianization and Ritual Kinship in the Byzantine Area

Evelyne Patlagean

"Sai come si dice? Tre 'c' sono pericolose: cugini, cognati e compari. Le tresche più gravi si verificano quasi sempre nella parentela e nel comparatico."—L. Sascia, *A ciascuno il suo* (1967)

Kinship relations in Roman society and within the diverse ethnic groupings of the provinces of the Empire have usually been overshadowed in the eyes of historians by the highly visible civic relations. Nor have they attracted the attention of the anthropologists, who for a long time showed little interest in the self-contained field of classical antiquity. Yet here, too, kinship relations were an effective component of the social organization.[1] Kinship made for almost universal matrimonial exchange, showing, at least in the East, practical traces of preferential marriage between cousins; they were also characterized by the importance of relations between cousins and brothers-in-law.[2] This level of kinship was supplemented by voluntary kinship relations, adoption and fostering, a traditionally important ingredient of the Roman system,[3] and voluntary brotherhood (*affrairement*), documented as a provincial practice.[4] Christianization brought about a substantial elaboration of these ties. To begin with, there came into being, from the fourth century on, a whole set of marriage prohibitions on the grounds of kinship and alliance,[5] which was only the other side of the increased emphasis on the social functions of such relations. Behind the scriptural justifications one can discern the evolution of a society in which the time-honored network of civic relations tended to wear away. What is more, this ancient but fully elaborated, formalized, and newly revitalized system came to form the substructure of the system of voluntary bonds that were even more profoundly marked

Annales, E.S.C. 33 (May-June 1978): 625–36. Translated by Elborg Forster.

by the historical evolution. Spiritual descent through baptism and the development of spiritual brotherhood were added to adoption, which continued to be practiced.

Whether founded on the act of physical generation, on alliance, or on choice; whether going back to antiquity or newly created, all of these relationships exhibited the same characteristics by the time their historical elaboration had been completed: they were created by a decisive and compelling act of the Church and entailed civil consequences that might well be laid down in a contract; their creation in turn led to marriage prohibitions. However, they also gave rise to positive ties of solidarity, which played a considerable role in various areas of the social and political organization of Byzantium. Finally, the canonical definitions of these relations were upheld by the legislator and the publicly stated norms in these matters were recognized by Byzantines and outsiders alike as pertinent elements of the structure imposed on society by the powers of Church and State. Or, to put it more simply, the system of voluntary kinship, even more than that of kinship by blood and alliance, can teach us a great deal about the interchanges between the norms imposed by the legitimate powers of the Byzantine Empire and those that took shape in the actual practices of society, where they responded to a collective need that is thus revealed to the historian. I shall deal here only with lay people, who entered this system in one of three ways: through the continuation under Christianity of traditional adoption, through a new kind of filiation by baptism, and through voluntary brotherhood, which has become more clearly visible thanks to the written medieval documents of the Byzanto-Slavic area. For the sake of brevity, I shall leave aside, except for some necessary allusions, the father/son relationship between monks and laymen and the father/ children relationship between the superior of a monastery and his monks, but I do wish to draw attention to the importance and historical interest of such relations.

What I have just said points to the normative character of most of my sources. Yet one should not believe that all of these texts were equally official, for within this normative order different levels are perceptible. At the highest level one finds texts emanating from the core of political power: these are the canons of ecclesiastical councils; answers to canonical questions by the patriarchs of the capitals or by the bishops; regulations of the great monasteries; polemics against heretical fringe groups; and, also, the *corpus* of imperial laws. But more private and more obscure writings have also come down to us. The law of the State is reflected in practical reference works for the use of judges and legal practitioners. The law of the Church is presented in a whole range of forms: in numerous copies of ritual books, in accounts of the activities of preachers or missionaries, as well as in practical reference works, written in this case for the use of priests, although the elaboration of these writings still remains to be studied. Indeed, the two most important of these manuals are not yet available in critical editions that would show their successive accretions over time. These are the *Penitential*, ascribed to John the Faster (6th–10th centuries?)[6] and especially the canonical *Manual* of the *cod. Par. gr.* 2664, probably composed between the twelfth century and the fourteenth century, a work that seems closer to the ecclesiastical norms of the Slavs than to the major decrees of the official Byzantine Church.[7] Finally, the practices themselves and the use that society made of them are attested by the cases submitted to the canonical authorities, by the historiography of the time, by archival documents, and by the forms used by notaries and law courts. In this article, I have limited myself to setting up a few sign posts that will permit us to trace the historical evolution. I have looked for them not only in the Byzantine documentation but also in the Slavic margins of that society; for the elaboration of Byzantine forms of voluntary kinship proved to be a decisive criterion of cultural expansion and acculturation, if by culture one means, among other things, the system of powers and the relationships among them.

Although all the voluntary ties of kinship evolved in the same manner as to their form, their cultural and social significances turn out to be very diverse. I will quickly pass over adoption, noting only the recognizable impact of Christianization which, already marked by the time of Justinian (527–65), was spelled out by Pope Leo VI (886–912): adoption gave rise to certain marriage prohibitions, especially after it had become the object of a Church ritual (Leo VI, Novella 24),[8] which is attested in the law of Justinian, became mandatory in that of Leo VI, and can be found in many manuals of liturgy. Moreover, as in the case of marriage, the canonical criterion of voluntary commitment became completely binding with the same Leo VI, whereas in the classical Roman law, adoption was justified by the imitation of nature. In this manner Leo VI would extend the ability to adopt to eunuchs (Novella 26) and in the final analysis to "all those who have the misfortune to be without offspring" (Novella 27). Filiation by baptism, in contrast, was a new feature of the Christian societies, a logical extension of the definition of baptism as a new birth, which had existed from the very beginning.[9]

This is not the place to define the role of baptism as one of the rites of initiation of antiquity or to show in what ways it was different from the circumcision of the Jews, a masculine mark that was conferred upon the infant or the adult proselyte to signify his entry into the chosen group. I do wish to stress, however, that the definition of baptism could unfold all of its social consequences only when it was conferred upon infants shortly after birth. Except in the case of converted barbarians, to which I shall turn later, this was the form it took in the period under study here. The legislation of Justinian already instituted one marriage prohibition derived from baptism, the simplest and most evident among them, namely, the prohibition of marriage between godfather and goddaughter (*Codex Julianus* [hereafter cited as *CJ*] V, IV, 26, 2).[10] But a peculiarly Byzantine development was inaugurated by the

council held at Constantinople in 692,[11] the same council that brought significant advances in the matter of marriage prohibitions on the grounds of kinship by blood and alliance. It forbade (canon 53) marriage between godfathers and mothers of their godchildren, the penalty being the same as that
meted out for adultery, provided that the relationship was broken off immediately: "for kinship according to the spirit takes precedence over the union
of two bodies." This principle was of fundamental importance for the future,
and its meaning pointed in the same direction as the extension of adoption
beyond the imitation of carnal procreation. Proceeding from this starting
point, the extension of marriage prohibitions, a characteristic feature of Byzantine history, could logically assume an ever wider scope.

In the *Penitential* ascribed to John the Faster (Morin ed., p. 107), the prohibition is limited to the union between a godfather and his goddaughter or
her mother. But it applies to unions between the godfather's son and his goddaughter, defined as siblings by baptism, in the codifications of the Isaurian
emperors, the *Ecologè* of 726 (II, 2),[12] eventually encompassing unions between the godfather's brother and his goddaughter or her mother in Leo VI's
Novella 26. The twelfth-century canonist Theodore Balsamon, in his commentary to canon 53 of 692, noted a tendency to treat the impediments created
by spiritual kinship according to the pattern of kinship by blood, owing to
the superiority of the former.[13] In 1208, an opinion delivered by a patriarch
allowed a marriage in the direct line between the son of a godfather and the
daughter of his goddaughter; another opinion, written between 1261 and
1264, allowed a marriage between the son of a godfather and the sister of his
godson.[14] Finally, the *Manual* of Constantine Harmenopoulos, published at
Thessalonica in 1345[15] and considered to be the foundation of modern Greek
law, did limit the prohibition to the third or fourth degree, which included
the union between the godfather or his son and the mother or sister of his
godson (IV, VIII, 6). The collective pressure seemed to demand even stricter
regulations, however, as attested by the network elaborated in the Cotelier
Manual on the model of kinship by blood (1677 ed., ch. 182, ff.). Baptismal
kinship could be invoked after the fact as a reason for dissolving a marriage.
The historiographer John Skylitza[16] thus reports that, following a rumor spread
by the Palace, the patriarch Polyeuctes enjoined Nicephorus II Phocas (963–
69) to break the union he had just contracted with Empress Theophano, who
had become widowed. Incidentally, he was not obeyed (Thurn, ed., p. 261).
This possibility was also provided for the spouses in the collection of formulas
in use in thirteenth-century Cyprus under Frankish rule.[17] However, "those
who have fled the world and marriage" were forbidden to form ties of baptismal kinship by the monastic rules, as stipulated in the *Testament* of Theodorus Studita (9th century)[18] and the Regulations (*Typica*) of Athanasius and
Emperor John Zimiskes for Mount Athos (10th century).[19] For these men
there was another form of spiritual paternity, however, in which the monk

necessarily became the father of the layman, a relationship that had practical implications for the transmission of property, as several examples will show later.

In short, by the ninth and tenth centuries, filiation through baptism and the resulting marriage prohibitions appeared to be a long-standing and integral feature of the Byzantine cultural system. Also, this was precisely the era in which that system was exported as part of the great thrust of missionary diplomacy that gave rise throughout the area to the birth of young states for which Byzantium became the political as well as social model.[20] The pattern under discussion here was therefore integrated into the new structures in the Slavic area; its presence there must be considered all the more pertinent as it does not seem to have arisen naturally. The prohibition concerning a man's goddaughter and her mother, for example, was emphasized in a homily attributed to Methodius himself.[21] In this respect, public law acted as a means of propagation that connects the *Zakon Sudnyj Ljudem*, based on the Isaurian *Ecologe* cited earlier,[22] with the "statutes" of the Russian princes[23] that were subsequently incorporated into the Russian code of canon law *Kormčaja Kniga*.[24]

At first sight, voluntary brotherhood (*affrairement*) presents a number of similarities with the two relationships that have just been discussed: it too was instituted by a ritual and gave rise to marriage prohibitions. Yet it was different in one fundamental respect, and this difference is significant in a number of ways: voluntary brotherhood remained officially forbidden or, at least, unrecognized. In other words, it enables the historian to observe an instructive and, as we shall see, particularly powerful tension between the official norm in the matter of voluntary kinship and the actual practices that will be examined later. As early as 285 an imperial rescription (*CJ*, VI, XXIV, 7) declared that the adoption of a brother was inconceivable and that therefore its consequences for the transmission of property were nil. This position was confirmed in a manual of law that was widely used in the East, the *Book of Syro-Roman Law* (the title was given to it by its first editor), whose lost original version in Greek probably dated from the years 476–80 and which exists in a Syrian version, written in Mesopotamia around the eighth century, and in Arabic (Melkites of Egypt) and Armenian versions of the twelfth century.[25] The collection of tenth-century *Basilicae* expressed the same opinion (XXXV, 13, 17), although one scholium concedes that it is possible to adopt a kinsman as a brother; while another contrasts the categorical tradition of the rescription of 285 with a more ambiguous text from the *Digest*[26] (XXVIII, 5, 58, [56] 1),[27] which allows a man to institute as his heir, under the name of brother, one who inspires him with a "fraterna caritas." Yet, in the end, the widely documented practice of voluntary brotherhood was never recognized by the imperial law, because, unlike adoption and filiation through baptism, this relationship could not be considered an imitation of nature. The Church adopted the same position, which it asserted in a patriarchal opinion dating from the twelfth century at the latest,[28] or in the opinion delivered by the archbishop of Ohrida, Demetrios Chomatianos,[29] who in 1217 occupied this see near the frontier of the Empire. The patriarchal opinion underscores the strong suspicion of immorality attached to voluntary brotherhood, and one is tempted to make a connection between this judgment and the fraternal vocabulary which expresses a homosexual relationship in the *Satyricon*, where it seems to be used as a code. The author of the excellent study in which the pertinent passages of the *Satyricon* are cited probably should have attached an even more distinct meaning to this vocabulary.[30] However that may be, the collective demand seems to have been so strong at Byzantium that the dividing line between the norm and actual practices ran right through the normative texts themselves, since a number of them accorded a de facto recognition to voluntary brotherhood. This is the case in the collection of texts on jurisprudence by the judge Eustathius (mid-eleventh century),[31] which limits the incompatibility between voluntary brotherhood and marriage to the partners themselves (49, 11) in a practitioner's manual of southern Italy (*cod. par. gr.*, 1384, dated 1165/1166, fol. 171), which extends the marriage prohibition to the children of persons united in this relationship,[32] and the Cotelier *Manual*, which further elaborates the prohibition on the pattern of kinship by blood (ch. 187 f.). It is true, however, that here the use of the term "spiritual brothers" (παευωατικοί) is somewhat equivocal, and one sometimes wonders whether it does not mean the relationship between a godson and the son of his godfather. Finally, the monastic rules cited above forbade the monks to enter into voluntary brotherhood, just as they forbade them to act as godfathers.

The law codes of the Empire and the Church as well as the manuals of application thus substantiate the definition of the various kinds of voluntary kinship, the marriage prohibitions to which they gave rise, and the official incompatibility between baptismal sponsorship and the monastic state. Ritual books provide us with additional elements for the reconstruction of the system. In this area abundant material is available, thanks to Goar's old but fundamentally important collection, taken for the most part from the libraries of the West,[33] and to Dmitrijevskij's collection,[34] which, as a supplement to Goar's publication, is devoted to the libraries of the "Orthodox East." To be sure, a great deal still remains to be discovered in the light of recently published catalogs, especially those of the *Vaticani*,[35] which describe precious liturgical manuscripts from southern Italy; and it will certainly be necessary to multiply the descriptions of representative instances[36] before we can grasp the full range of gestures, words, and sequences and the personal or, on the contrary, formal structures of these rituals.

Yet a few unquestionable traits already emerge from the documentation available to us. The most important of these is the Church's claim, an intrinsic aspect of its function in society, that baptism cannot take place without a priest—who must not be the child's father, the Cotelier *Manual* (ch. 54) specifies—or outside of an ecclesiastical locale. These two criteria of orthodoxy became binding for baptism and for marriage,[37] a fact that is confirmed negatively by the successive denials of that claim on the part of the great current of heresy that had its source in Christian antiquity. We hear, for example, of a woman administering baptism in the age of Tertullian;[38] we hear of the refusal or deliberate downplaying of baptism imputed to the Bogumils by the priest Cosmas, who wrote against them in tenth-century Bulgaria (Vaillant ed., ch. 15, p. 81),[39] and by Euthymius Zigabenus, a monk in the Bulgarian capital under the reign of Alexius I Comnemus (1081–1118), who designated those who engaged in this practice by the antiquated name of "Messalians."[40] We are also told about secret derision by another Euthymius, a monk of the same monastery around 1050.[41] In addition, Euthymius Zigabenus described a counterritual in which the sacrament was administered to the new adept by the mixed conventicle and in which the water was replaced by the symbolic handling of the Book (Ficker ed., ch. 28, pp. 100–101).[42]

The manuals of liturgy show us a ritual for the adoption of a brother that conforms to the same criteria, even though the Church, as we have seen, disapproved of, or at least ignored, the practice itself. This ritual is found in texts ranging from the *Euchologe* (book of prayers) *Barberini* of the eighth century (see n. 33) to the *cod. Athon. Kutlum. 358* of the sixteenth century, including the *cod. Paris. gr. Coisl. 213*, which in 1027 laid down the usages of the Great Church of the capital.[43] The same ritual is also found in the oldest Slavonic liturgy, which was elaborated near the time of the Byzantine mission itself, as we can see from the Slavic *Euchologe* of Sinai, a copy of an older text executed in the tenth or eleventh century (Frček ed., fol. 9, r.-v., p. 658 f.).[44] The elaboration of this church ritual, founded on the joining of hands before the priest and the evocation of brotherly bonds among apostles and saints, may have been the Church's answer to the ancient practice of the mingling of two persons' blood, which is documented over and over, even after Christianization,[45] especially in Slavic countries, where voluntary brotherhood had always been of major importance.[46] In reality, as is so often the case, what happened was probably not so much that the old ritual disappeared as that a Christian ritual was superimposed upon it. This process in turn reflects the collective demand for ratification of existing practices by the Church; it also shows that the normative action of the Church consisted not only of elaborating directives at the center of political power but also of relating to all levels of the social spectrum and paying close attention to every local practice.

Finally, I believe that another Church ritual connected with adoption, according to the testimony of Leo VI, tended to establish a certain similarity between adoptive and baptismal filiation. The conditions imposed by the Church were thus the very ones that were considered necessary by the collec-

tive consciousness (excepting certain clusters of heretics) to ensure both the
validity of marriage and the validity of the mediating bonds of solidarity involved in voluntary kinship. In short, the Christian power structure and the
majority of its subjects came to share the same historical ground.

In view of this fact, one must turn to the basic aspect of the question at
hand, that is, to the role played by the system of voluntary kinship within the
social system of Byzantium, where it was a highly visible phenomenon. As we
have seen, its theoretical underpinnings were securely established only by the
end of the seventh century. It is not until the ninth century, however, that instances of concrete cases begin to appear with greater frequency in the historical writings, which mirror the aristocratic and imperial milieu of Byzantium.
In addition, that century also produced the oldest manuals of liturgy that
have been preserved, at least in the collections at our disposal. Was this con-
vergence historically significant or accidental? It is noteworthy in any case.

In looking for series of examples of the different kinds of voluntary kinship, one immediately notices a telling confusion in the vocabulary, suggesting that this set of practices had adopted a single repertory of terms based on
the notions of paternity, fraternity, and baptismal sponsorship. It appears
that the term υιοθεσιδ, which designated adoption, was extended to filiation
through baptism by the time of the Church Fathers. Conversely, fathers and
adoptive sons are called "spiritual" kin in the manuals of ritual: for example,
in a thirteenth-century collection of formulas from Cyprus (Sathas ed., formula 18, p. 629/2). The use of these terms in private documents, moreover,
reveals the existence of a kind of filiation that does not appear in the legislation at all, namely, the monk in the role of a father. Denied, at least officially,
the function of godfather, he could thus reclaim a position in the system that
would be commensurate with his cultural and social role; and, as we shall
see, this arrangement would have implications for the transmission of property as well. "Spiritual brotherhood," for its part, was produced not only by
voluntary brotherhood but also by membership in the same monastic community;[47] moreover, it also created a spiritual tie between a man's biological
son, his adoptive son, and his godson, as the marriage prohibitions indicate.
Only the relationship between a child's biological and his spiritual father
(compèrage) remained distinct in the vocabulary. Quite aside from the possible connections between these various forms of voluntary kinship and the
pursuit of marriage alliances, it is evident that baptism created the strongest
solidarity, considering that in addition to ties of filiation and brotherhood, it
produced a lateral solidarity that had no biological model, namely, relations
between biological and spiritual parents. Moreover, by way of a contradiction
that is only apparent, this society, which accepted the Church's marriage
prohibitions whenever they served to avoid unnecessary marriage alliances,
at the same time sought to reinforce its alliances by attempting to superimpose
the bonds of a marriage on those of a distant baptismal kinship. Here, how-

ever, the Church refused to go along. Canonical opinions, such as those delivered by Demetrios Chomatianos, testify both to the collective demand and to the refusal on the part of the Church (see, for example, response 13 to Constantine Cabasilas, Pitra ed., pp. 641–44).

The texts make us understand the concrete uses to which these ties of solidarity were put at all levels of Byzantine society. Their purpose depended on the partners. Ties of *compèrage* amounted to no more than a fellowship of pleasure seekers when Michael II (842–62) surrounded himself with an anonymous group of boon companions whose children he had held over the baptismal font and on whom he squandered public monies in the form of lavish gifts of gold specie (John Skylitza, Thurn ed., pp. 96–97). Generosity was also the basis of even more widespread ties created when Michael IV (1034–42) became godfather to many children whom he showered with lavish gifts, regardless, it seems, of their social standing; but his generosity was inspired by the vain hope that it would produce the cure of his epilepsy (ibid., p. 405). Moreover, the spiritual father seems to have occupied a position of eminence, not only in relation to his godson but in relation to his *compère* as well. This is evident in the moralistic tracts that enjoin the reader to honor him,[48] or in one of Agnellus of Ravenna's incomparable stories.[49] Two men, this story goes (Holder-Egger, ed., pp. 294/4-30), wished to conclude an alliance (*foedus*). One of them had a son, and the other offered to become his godfather; so they became "communiter patres, et dilectionem habuerunt in invicem in Spiritu sancto et obsculo pacis, quia et sic cundecet fieri qui inter se talia faciunt eo quod non homines sed Spiritum sanctum inter se mediatorem ponunt." The higher status of the spiritual father then made it possible for him to borrow 300 sols from the biological father without giving the usual security. The relationship between *compères* has the same implications in a story situated in Dalmatia, which is reported by Kekaumemos in the last quarter of the eleventh century.[50] A Byzantine strategus and a petty Slavic chief were trying to capture each other. The first showered the second with gifts, in exchange for which he received declarations of fidelity to the basileus [king]. Then he offered to become godfather to a son that had just been born to the Slavic chief; but he refused to come to the father's house for the purpose, and it was agreed that "the baptismal relation would be initiated" at the limit of the two territories. Despite this precaution, however, the strategus was carried off in the end.

At the center of imperial power and on its periphery, political calculation came into play. Leo VI, for example, was very careful in the choice of his son's godparents, one of whom was his own brother, the child's paternal uncle (Skylitza, Thurn ed., pp. 184–85); and as we have seen, Nicephorus II Phocas probably stood godfather to a child of Empress Theophano before he married her when she became widowed, disregarding the prohibition against such a marriage. Adoption for its part continued a long-standing political tradition. It was adoption that placed Alexius Comnemus, already a grown man, among the descendants of Empress Marie, to whom he was also related by marriage, while his brother Isaac received the hand of one of the Empress's nieces (Anna Comnema, *Alexiad*, II, I, 14).[51] Later Alexius received another offer of adoption from Nicephorus III Botaniatus, whom he actually succeeded (ibid., II, XII, 2). As for voluntary brotherhood, finally, which is so definitely dismissed by the official norms and so well attested in the rituals, I must admit that I have found only one instance of it in a historiographical text for the period of the ninth century to the eleventh century, but it is a major one, since it occurs in the *Vita* of the great Basilius I (867–86).[52] During his obscure youth, a rich widow in the Peleponnese—and this region may be of particular significance—miraculously informed of his future greatness, hastened to establish a bond of brotherhood between her own son and Basilius, upon whom she heaped her generosity. And indeed, when Basilius became emperor, he kept his spiritual brother near him and granted him his highest favor. Finally, the political use of spiritual kinship is most clearly apparent in the international constellation which in the ninth to the eleventh centuries attracted the young nations of eastern Europe to the orbit of Byzantium at a time when all of them were intent upon adopting the forms of a State governed by a sovereign and the formal structures of Christianity. At that time the emperor often became the godfather of a sovereign; it was a relationship, as we have seen, which implied a hierarchy: it was used in this manner by Michael III, who in 864 gave his own name to Boris of Bulgaria; the same meaning was attached to the baptism of Olga of Kiev at Constantinople in the middle of the ninth century. F. Dölger has presented this entire complex of facts in three studies, which can be criticized only to the extent that they tend to attribute metaphorical meaning to acts that in reality were fully efficacious symbols.[53]

Voluntary kinship also involved consequences for the transmission of property, as we can see most clearly in archival documents. Here is the last will and testament of a certain Genesios, preserved in the cartulary of the Italo-Greek monastery of Carbone.[54] In 1076 he bequeathed two pieces of vineyard to the priest Kalos, "my *compère*" (συγῖεαγος); no doubt the priest honored in this manner was the godfather of the legator's only, and illegitimate, daughter, whose existence is hinted at in the will. Ten years later, in 1086, Genesios made a new will: this time the daughter is acknowledged and provided for, and the will assigns only one piece of vineyard to "my *compère*" Ursus, probably the same priest Ursus who appears among the witnesses to the document. One wonders whether this is a second godfather to the same daughter, one of the cases of multiple godfathers that are attested later in Calabria by the *Liber Visitationis*[55] (Laurent ed., p. 50/2f.). As for adoption, its consequences for the transmission of property were differentiated in the thirteenth-century Cypriot collection of formulas depending on whether or not the adoptive parents had biological offspring or not (Sathas ed., pp. 628,

630). Particularly noteworthy is the role played by adoption in the history of the rural communities. One Novella that no doubt reflects practices of the tenth century attests that the *mighty* had themselves adopted by independent peasants and small landowners, a practice that enabled them to break into local communities for which they constituted a mortal danger.[56]

Acts establishing voluntary brotherhood, by contrast, are not to be found in any of the Greek source material that has been published so far, and this is not surprising. All we can find is a response by Demetrios Chomatianos at Ohrida (Pitra ed., p. 32) referring to a voluntary brotherhood between two military men (*stratiotes*) instituted by a will; but Demetrios reminds the survivor that such a disposition is null and void, a statement he repeats elsewhere as well (ibid., p. 713). Some of the documents of the Bessarabian princes,[57] on the other hand, do furnish—with the expected time-lag, to be sure—the examples for which we are looking. In Moldavia and Valachia, voluntary brotherhood was made to play the same role as adoption had played to the benefit of the great landowners of Byzantium.[58] Donations to a monk as "spiritual father," on the other hand, are well documented for Byzantium itself. In 1014 the Athnotite monastery of Lavra received the pledge of such a donation from a couple without offspring or heirs, to be paid after the death of the donors (*Actes de Lavra*, I, no. 18).[59] In 1016, one Glykeria addressed her donation to the monk Eustrathius, who by then had become the higoumen of Lavra, invoking his quality as her "spiritual father" (ibid., no. 20, cf. no. 16); however, the donation was shared among the "brotherhood" of the monks. Similar relationships are suggested by the fact that the function of witnesses to the wills of the grand princes of Moscow devolved on their "spiritual fathers."[60]

This, then, concludes my observations on the impact of Christianization upon voluntary kinship in the Byzantine Empire and its periphery at a time when such relationships became the basis of a particularly visible and effective network of social relations. This does not mean, however, that the question has been exhausted. At the very least, this history should be pursued to the point where it links up with still existing practices and sheds light on them. If this were done, one would become aware of the continued vigor of voluntary brotherhood in the Balkan and Slavic areas, and of *compèrage* in southern Italy. Might it not be possible, indeed, to discern regional tendencies? I can only raise the question.

NOTES

1. See the excellent illustration of these relations provided by R. Symes, *The Roman Revolution* (Oxford, 1939), at the highest levels of political competition at the end of the Republic.

2. Some indications in E. Patlagean, *Pauvreté économique et pauvreté sociale à Byzance, IV–VIIe siècle* (Paris and The Hague, 1977), pp. 118–28.

3. For the legal rules, cf. R. Monier, *Manuel de droit romain*, 6th ed. (Paris, 1947), 1: 263–70. The situation in a province is described in A. Cameron, "Θρεπτός and Related Terms in the Inscriptions of Asia Minor," in *Anatolian Studies*, ed. W. H. Buckler (Manchester, 1939), pp. 27–62.

4. Cf. N. Tamassia, *L'Affratellamento (αδελψοποιία): studio storico-giuridico* (Turin, 1886); C. A. Nallino, "Intorno al divieto romano imperiale dell'affratellamento e ad alcuni paralleli arabi," *Studi in onore S. Riccobono* (Palermo, 1936), 3: 321–57. Cf. also below, n. 30.

5. Cf. A. Esmein, *Le Mariage en droit canonique*, ed. R. Genestal, 2nd ed. (Paris, 1929), vol. 1; also J. Dauvillier and C. de Clerq, *Le Mariage en droit canonique oriental* (Paris, 1936), where the reader will find the legal rules whenever they are not expressly stated in the present article. See also K. E. Zacharia von Lingenthal, *Geschichte des griechisch-römischen Rechts*, 3rd ed. (Berlin, 1892).

6. J. Morin, ed., *Commentarius historicus de disciplina in administratione sacramenti poenitentiae*...(Paris, 1651), "*Antiqui Poenitentiales*", p. 84. For the manuscript tradition, cf. V. Grumel, *Régestes des actes du patriarchat de Constantinople*, vol. 1, *Les Actes des patriarches*, fasc. 1, *Les Régestes de 381 à 715* (Istanbul, 1932), no. 270. See also E. Herman, "Il piu antico penitentiale greco," *Orient. Christ. Per.* 19 (1953): 71–127.

7. J.-B. Cotelier, ed., *Ecclesiae Graeca Monumenta* (Paris, 1677), 1: 68–158 (hereafter cited as the Cotelier *Manual*). For the date, H. G. Beck, *Kirche und theologische Literatur im byzantinischen Reich* (Munich, 1959), p. 147.

8. P. Noailles and A. Dain, eds., *Les Novelles de Léon VI le Sage* (Paris, 1944).

9. For the beginnings of baptismal sponsorship, information can be found in M. Dujarier, *Le Parrainage des adultes aux trois premiers siècles de l'Eglise* (Paris, 1962).

10. P. Krueger, ed., *Codex Justinianus* (Berlin, 1877).

11. F. Lauchert, ed., *Die Kanones der wichtigsten altkirchlichen Concilien nebst den apostolischen Kanones* (Freiburg im Breisgau and Leipzig, 1896), pp. 97–139.

12. P. Zepos and I. Zepos, eds., *Jus graeco-romanum* (Athens, 1931), 2: 3–62.

13. Migne, *Patrologia graeca*, vol. 137, col. 700–704.

14. Grumel, ed., *Régestes*, vol. 1, fasc. 4, *Les Régestes de 1208 à 1309* (Paris, 1971), nos. 1208, 1373.

15. G. E. Heimbach, ed., *Constantini Harmenopuli Manuale legum sive Hexabiblios* . . . (Leipzig, 1851).

16. I. Thurn, ed., *Joannis Scylitzae Synopsis historiarum* (Berlin and New York, 1973).

17. K. Sathas, ed., *Μεσαιωνικη Βιβλιοθηκν* (Paris, 1877), 6: 557.

18. Theodorus Studita, *Testament*, 8 (Migne, *Patrologia graeca*, vol. 99, col. 1820).

19. These texts are conveniently arranged in the old edition by Ph. Meyer, *Die Haupturkunden für die Geschichte der Athosklöster* (Leipzig, 1894): *Typicon* by Anasthasius, p. 113/21–23; *Diatyposis* by the same author, p. 126/18; *Typicon* by Joannes Zimiskes, p. 146/23–27.

20. Very general indications of this are found in H. G. Beck, "Christliche Mission und politische Propaganda im byzantinischen Reich," in *La Conversione al cristianesimo nell'alto Medioevo*, Centro italiano di studi sull'alto Medioevo, Settimana . . . 14 (Spoleto, 1967), pp. 649–74. The best historical commentary on the conversion of the Slavs beyond the frontiers of Byzantium is that of A. Gieystor, "Paliers de la pénétration du christianisme en Pologne aux Xᵉ et XIᵉ siècles," *Studi . . . A. Fanfani* (Milan, 1962), 1: 329–67.

21. A. Vaillant, ed. and trans., "Une Homélie de Méthode," *Revue des Etudes Slaves* 23 (1947): 34–47; the author compares this homily to an episode of the Slavonic *Life* of Methodius (ch. 11), where such a union is punished by Heaven. The responses of Pope Nicholas I to the Bulgarians also attest to the importance of this criterion of Christianization (MGH, Epistle. VI [Berlin, 1925], p. 569): Nicolai papae Epistle. 99, 2, A 866 (Perels ed.). Cf. I. Dujčev, "I 'responsa' di papa Niccolo I ai Bulgari neoconvertiti," *Aevum* 42 (1968): 403–28.

22. For this text and the discussion concerning its Moravian or Bulgarian origin, cf. J. Vasica, "Origine cyrillo-méthodienne du plus ancien code slave, Zakon Sudnyj," *Byzantinoslavica* 12 (1951): 154–74; V. Prochazka, "Le Zakon Sudnyj Ljudem et la Grande Moravie," *Byzantinoslavica* 28 (1967): 359–75; ibid. 29 (1968): 112–50.

23. Fornication between godfather and mother of the godson is specifically forbidden by the *Statute of Jaroslav*, article 13 of the archetype reconstituted in the most recent history of these

texts, by J. N. Scapov, *Knjazeskie ustavy i cerkov v Drevnjeu Rusi, XI–XIV vv* [The statutes of the princes and the church in old Russia, XI to XIV century] (Moscow, 1972), p. 294.
    24. Cf. I. Žužek, S. J., "Kormcaja Kniga: Studies in the Chief Code of Russian Canon Law," *Orient. Christ. Anal.* (Rome, 1964), vol. 168.
    25. Chapter 86 of the Latin translation by Ferrini-Furlani, *Fontes iuri Romani anteiustiani*, new ed. (Florence, 1968), 2: 780. For this work see E. Sachau, ed., *Syrische Rechtsbücher*, 3 vols. (Berlin, 1907–14).
    26. H. J. Scheltema and N. van der Wal, eds., *Basilicorum Libri LX*, Series A (texts) (Groeningen, 1967), p. 1, 620. The scholium can be found in G. E. Heimbach, ed., *Basilicorum Libri LX* (Leipzig, 1843), 3: 606.
    27. Th. Mommsen, ed., *Digesta* (Berlin, 1877).
    28. Grumel, ed., *Régestes*, vol. 1, fasc. 3, n. *1034 (perhaps written by the patriarch Nicolas IV [1147–51]).
    29. J.-B. Pitra, ed., *Analecta Sacra*, (Paris, 1891), 6: 713.
    30. F. Dupont, *Le Plaisir et la loi* (Paris, 1977), pp. 164–69.
    31. P. Zepos and I. Zepos, eds., *Jus graeco-romanum*, 4: 7–260, Πεῖρα Εὐσταθίου τοῦ ῾Ρωμαίου.
    32. Cited by Tamassia, *Affratellamento*, p. 65, n. 5. On this manuscript, see L. R. Ménager, "Notes sur les compilations byzantines de l'Occident," *Varia* 3 (1958): 239–303.
    33. J. Goar, *Euchologion sive rituale Graecorum* (Venice, 1730), based on the Codex Barberini, III, 55, a patriarchal euchologe of the eighth century. Cf. A. Strittmatter, "The 'Barberinum S. Marci' of Jacques Goar," *Ephemerides Liturgicae* 47 (1933): 329–67.
    34. A. Dmitrijevskij, *Opisanie liturgičeskih rukopisej hranjaščihcja v bibliotekah pravosl. Vostoka* [Εὐχολόγια] (Kiev, 1901), vol. 2.
    35. Especially the *Codices Vaticani graeci, codices 1485–1683*, described by C. Giannelli (Vatican City, 1950), for example, ms. 1554 (twelfth century).
    36. For example, A. Jacob, "L'Euchologue de Porphyre Uspenski, Cod. Leningr. gr. 226 (Xe siècle)," *Le Muséon* 78 (1965): 173–214.
    37. Cf. for example, the decision under the date 1028, ch. 1 in Grumel. ed., *Régestes*, vol. 1, fasc. 2, no. 835.
    38. Tertullian, *Traité de baptême*, ed. Refoulé-Drouzy (Sources Chrétiennes 35, Paris, 1952), pp. 4–5, 17. See also the references assembled by H. C. Puech in his commentary to the *Traité* of Cosmas cited in n. 39, below, pp. 223–26.
    39. A. Vaillant and H. C. Puech, eds., *Le Traité contre les Bogumils de Cosmas le Prêtre* (Paris, 1945).
    40. Anathema 13 in Migne, *Patrologia graeca*, vol. 131, col. 45.
    41. Ἐπιστολή . . ., in G. Ficker, ed., *Die Phundagiagiten* (Leipzig, 1908), pp. 25ff.
    42. Euthymius Zigabenos, Ἔκθεσις περὶ τῆς αἱρέσεως τῶν Πογομήλων (sic) in Ficker, *Die Phundagiagiten*, pp. 89–111.
    43. For this manuscript, see J. Gouillard, "Le Synodicon de l'orthodoxie," Centre de recherche d'histoire et de civilisation Byzantines, *Travaux et mémoires* 2 (1967): 230–31.
    44. J. Frček, ed. and trans., *Patrologie orientale*, (1933), vol. 24 Cf. F. Dvornik, *Byzantine Missions among the Slavs: SS. Constantine-Cyril and Methodius* (New Brunswick, N. J., 1970), pp. 107–8, 363.
    45. Tamassia, *Affratellamento*, p. 68; Du Cange, "Les Adoptions d'honneur en frère et par occasion des frères d'armes," Dissertation 21a in Jean de Joinville, *Histoire de Saint Louis*, ed. Du Cange (Paris, 1668).
    46. Cf. J. Bardach, "L'Indivision familiale dans les pays du Centre-Est européen," in *Famille et parenté dans l'Occident mediéval* (Rome, 1977), pp. 335–53; H. H. Stahl, *Les anciennes communautés villageoises roumaines: Asservissement et pénétration capitaliste* (Paris and Bucharest, 1969).
    47. For example, in the donation to the monastery of Lavra by Glykeria, cited below in the text.
    48. For example, M. Bittner, *Der vom Himmel gefallene Brief Christi in seinen morgenländischen Versionen und Rezensionen* (Denkschriften der kaiserlichen Akademie der Wissenschaften, philosophisch-historische Klasse, 51/1, Vienna, 1906), pp. 18/13–14, 20, and passion.

49. Agnellus, *"Liber pontificalis ecclesiae Ravennatis,"* ed. Holder-Egger, *Mon. Germ. Hist. Scrit. rer. Langob. et Italic. saec. VI–IX* (Hanover, 1878), pp. 275–391.

50. *Cecaumeni Strategicon* . . ., ed. Wassiliewski-Jernstedt (Saint Petersburg, 1896), ch. 74, pp. 27–28.

51. Anna Comnema, *Alexiade*, ed. and trans. B. Leib (Paris, 1937–76).

52. *Vita Basilii*, in *Theophanes Continuatus*, ed. J. Bekker (Bonn, 1838), pp. 227–28.

53. F. Dölger, "Der Bulgarenherrscher als geistlicher Sohn des byzantinischen Kaisers" (1939); Dölger, "Die 'Familie der Könige' im Mittelalter" (1940); "Die mittelalterliche 'Familie der Fürsten und Völker' und der Bulgarenherrscher," (1942) in F. Dölger, *Byzanz und die europäische Staatenwelt* (Ettal, 1953), pp. 183–96, 34–69, 159–82. See also the recent publication by K. Hauck, "Formes de parenté artificielle dans le Haut Moyen Age," in *Famille et parenté dans l'Occident mediéval*, pp. 43–47.

54. G. Robinson, ed., "History and Cartulary of the Greek Monastery of St. Elias and St. Anastasius of Carbone" *Orient. Christ. Anal.*, fasc. 44, 53, 62 (Rome, 1928–30), docs. X–59 and XII–61.

55. M.-H. Laurant and A. Guillou, eds., *Le 'Liber Visitationis' d'Athanase Chalkéopoulos (1457–58)* (Vatican City, 1960).

56. P. Zepos and I. Zepos, eds., *Jus graeco-romanum*, 1: 203. For the problem of the date, see P. Lemerle, "Esquisse pour une histoire agraire de Byzance: les sources et les problèmes," *Revue Historique* 219 (1958): 266.

57. N. Iorga, *Anciens Documents de droit roumain* (with a preface containing the history of the Romanian customary law), vol. 1 [no further volumes were published] (Paris, 1930), document 32, dated 1516.

58. Cf. V. A. Georgescu, "La préemption et le retrait dans le droit féodal de Valachie et de Moldavie: Aspects de structure et de réception," *Nouvelles Etudes d'Histoire* 3 (1965): 181–203; H. H. Stahl, *Les anciennes communautés*, pp. 212 ff.

59. P. Lemerle et al., eds., *Actes de Lavra, I: Des origines à 1204* (Paris, 1970).

60. R. C. Howes, trans., *The Testaments of the Grand Princes of Moscow* (Ithaca, N. Y., 1967), doc. 1 (Ivan Kalita, ca. 1339, trans. p. 187); doc. 2 (Semjon Ivanovič, 1353, trans. p. 191).

6

From Sanctuary to Miracle-Worker: Healing in Fourth-Century Gaul

Aline Rousselle

When Adrien Blanchet used coin finds to date the Germanic invasions by relating the most recent dates of the coins found in treasures to the invasions known from written texts, he decided not to include the treasures and sacred hoards of the watering sanctuaries. These, he believed, had been destroyed by the Christians. A comprehensive study of the treasures and sacred hoards found in the sanctuaries of Gaul shows that their distribution and date of burial were related to the relinquishment of these religious centers and to the pauperization of the towns that had financed them, and thereby to the invasions. Yet, although most of these centers appear to be dead by the second half of the fourth century, some of them continued to attract the faithful well into the fifth century. As late as 585, the Council of Auxerre still prohibited votive offerings to springs, as well as the carving in wood of human feet or faces. After 511, Saint Gall saw a temple filled with statues, where patients were making wood carvings of the limbs that troubled them. When Gregory of Tours reports that the pagans would eat and drink to the point of vomiting, one wonders whether he refers to ritual drinking bouts or to classic medicinal practices. But we do know that many of the watering sanctuaries whose frequentation is attested by coin hoards were devoted to medical purposes.

This aspect of the faith of the Gauls can shed light on the circumstances that prompted their conversion to Christianity, for this conversion was in large part brought about by means of miraculous cures accomplished by miracle-working saints, the most effective and best known of whom was Saint Martin of Tours.

Annales, E.S.C. 31 November-December 1976): 1085–1107. Translated by Elborg Forster

Illness and Faith

Of the eighty-nine sanctuaries and baths that can be dated, twenty were sanctuaries for which the presence of sick patients is attested. Four of them were located in towns: Lutetia [Paris], Rennes, Lillebonne, and Bavai. Eight sanctuaries have left evidence of medical activity in the form of oculists' seals, although there is no evidence to prove that patients sought them out or that medical interventions were performed. Three of the sanctuaries have furnished only surgical instruments, and in seven cases only a number of thank-offerings have been found. The latter are indications of the presence of the sick, but not of the practice of medicine. The question is whether, in the absence of other proofs, it can simply be assumed that if the sick were there, physicians were there as well. Out of a total of twenty-four sanctuaries and baths for which the presence of either sick people or physicians has been established in this manner, only three were thermal springs. In all other cases, the curative properties of the water seem to have been strictly a matter of faith on the part of the patients, physicians, and priests assembled there. This is why one is tempted to see the illnesses that were cured there as psychosomatic illnesses. Moreover, it is difficult not to project onto these sanctuaries what we have learned about Asclepius.[1] His file consists essentially of inscriptions relating cases of cures. It thus speaks of conditions that could be cured. It also turns out that most of these cases are amenable to psychological explanations.[2]

In the case of the sanctuaries of Gaul, however, we are not dealing with cures. As we have seen, Gregory of Tours reports that the sick themselves made wood carvings of the limbs that troubled them. In most cases they had to buy these wooden, bronze, or stone objects in shops that manufactured and sold them at varying prices. The representation of the affected limb or organ was offered for sale as a token of hope for a cure. In short, the documentation that has come down to us concerns illness and faith, not treatment and cures. Yet the continued existence of these sanctuaries would seem to indicate that some of the sick went home cured.

It appears that the primary factor in a sick person's decision to go to a sanctuary was faith. The possibility of medical treatment in the cultic place of hope was secondary. This is why it seems useful to find out for which diseases the recourse to a sanctuary was considered indicated, and what their symptomatology was.

Unfortunately, the documentation for this investigation cannot be dated. It consists of thank-offerings that are often so crude that it is impossible to date them with any accuracy. I am basing my reasoning on the identification carried out by Drs. Bernard and Vassal of the diseases represented on the thank-offerings found at the sources of the Seine.[3] Foremost among them were eye diseases, known to us from bronze plaquettes with raised or recessed pictures. Also identifiable are diseases of the bones and joints, represented by deformed or ulcerated hands, arms, and legs. It is difficult to make a really accurate diagnosis of these conditions, for the sculptures are rudimentary, and in some cases the deformities may have resulted solely from the sculptor's handiwork. In other sanctuaries, however, a great many representations of fingers, hands, arms, legs, and feet have been found, so one can imagine gatherings of blind people, or at least of men and women unable to find their way without help, of the lame and the halt of all kinds, and of people afflicted with a goiter. Hernia trusses can be clearly seen on representations of torsos. Men and women sought help for diseases of their genital organs, and in one case a breast cancer is recognizable. Internal disorders are evoked by representations of certain organs in wood carvings whose identification may not always be certain; one sees lungs, as well as open or closed thoraxes showing the heart, the lungs, and the kidneys.[4]

This list does not by any means describe the entire morbidity of Gaul in the Roman era. It only presents those diseases for which people sought help in these religious centers between the first and the fifth centuries. To be eliminated from the outset are all acute diseases that rapidly ended in death, such as infections of all kinds, parasitosis, acute pulmonary tuberculosis, fatal tetanus, and snake bites (fatal in nine out of ten cases). The great epidemics, scourges that struck once in a generation or a century, swelled the ranks of those who came to the sanctuaries only to the extent that they caused serious aftereffects in some of the survivors. It must also be kept in mind that not all diseases were treated. Peasants became more bent over year by year. People were crippled by rheumatism, which periodically caused them pain. All of this was common, expected, and considered a normal part of life. People were patient. They had learned from childhood to put up with pain. They felt powerless to deal with a fever that might go away the next day. They also had recourse to remedies handed down through the generations: special diets, wine, herb teas, compresses. Only after all this had been tried, and only in cases of painful and protracted illness, did they seek out or summon the "specialist" of the village or neighborhood, a sorcerer, healer, or expert in plants or charms. In most cases, illness was dealt with only on these three levels. After all, one must try to imagine what was involved in making the journey to a sanctuary.[5]

In the eastern part of the Lyon region, where there was an abundance of sanctuaries, the distances were short: twenty to forty kilometers between two sanctuaries. Still, the patient might have to stay for some time. This raised the question of who would accompany the patient or the invalid, and what was to be done about the loss of work days if the patient and the person who accompanied him or her were still able to do some chores. Recall that this was a society where everyone was made to work and where the master or employer strictly controlled the comings and goings of the work force. A stay at a sanctuary was therefore possible only for those who practically could not work at all, owing to a motor handicap, weak vision, or chronic pain. The great quantity of poorly made wooden sculptures—along with a few good ones in stone—shows that by and large the patients were of lower class origin, most of them peasants or perhaps artisans.

In order to obtain the best picture possible of the morbidity of the lower classes in the era before Pasteur, I have used the lists of occupational diseases among present-day workers in agriculture[6] and the handicrafts. Within this category of diseases a distinction must then be made between the ordinary afflictions that were sometimes not even recognized as diseases and the severe but not acute disorders that justified a journey to and a stay at the sanctuary. Evelyn Patlagean has related some of the diseases mentioned in the hagiographical accounts of Byzantium to malnutrition in order to identify the poor among the clientele of the healing monks.[7]

The first example I shall treat is that of blindness. Generally speaking, one is surprised at the large number of cures among the blind and at the great number of blind people in the societies of antiquity and the Middle Ages[8] before the great advance of trachoma. To begin with, until 1846 there was a high incidence of blindness among children, due to neonatal gonococcus infection. Patlagean also mentions the effect of vitamin A deficiency on the eyes.[9] To these disorders one must certainly add the list of eye diseases specific to the rural environment. These are, on the one hand, lesions produced by heat and light and diseases caused by vegetal agents, and on the other, accidents due to blows or the piercing of the eye by vegetal or mineral matter. However, these causes were known to the peasant: he could feel himself being blinded, he could feel the impact of the foreign body on his cornea. A condition like harvester's keratitis,[10] however, which also threatens today's dockworkers and grain transporters, only produces its effects long after the harvest. In this condition, a minor and painless conjunctivitis is followed by a diminution of vision. The cause of the trouble remains a mystery, and although the symptoms may be more or less severe, they persist. These lesions of the eye, for which there was no known cause, must have been considered particularly amenable to a cure at the sanctuary, where the god was asked to give back what he had taken away, what had seemingly disappeared without an immediate and evident cause in the sense of an external pathogenic agent.

Aside from eye diseases, most of the thank-offerings suggest various kinds of paralysis, as does, incidentally, the hagiographical literature of the Christian era. All that was known about it at the time was the symptom. The only form of paralysis whose immediate cause was evident was hemiplegia following stroke. The fact is, of course, that paralysis has many causes. P. A. Sigal, who has studied the various forms of paralysis resulting from accidents of the nervous system, has called attention to Guillain-Barré syndrome, which may spontaneously regress after two to three years, and to multiple sclerosis, which may take the same turn even more rapidly.[11] Such improvements may account for at least some of the miracles. If one considers the etiology rather than the symptomatology of the diseases of agricultural laborers and artisans, one finds that many of them can cause paralysis, quite often of a localized form and sometimes susceptible to spontaneous healing.

Localized paralysis may be due to lead poisoning (Saturnism), arsenic poisoning, or mercury poisoning, the latter accompanied by tremors. Toxin-producing infections, such as diptheria, also give rise to local paralysis. Some diseases entail serious osteoarticular symptoms or aftereffects; among them are brucellosis, or Malta fever, which leaves the patient with severe pain in the spinal column, and chronic tetanus, which must be distinguished from acute and fatal tetanus. This chronic tetanus,[12] which was studied by Gui de Chauliac in 1963, is likely to heal itself. It takes the form of a localized contraction of the injured limb (monoplegic form) or extends to other limbs as well (paraplegic form). The incubation period may last several years. In this manner the immediate cause of the disorder may be hidden and forgotten. The continuing contraction eventually attenuates, and the lasting effects are more the result of the patient's immobility than of the tetanus itself. Another relevant form of deformity is caused by actinomycosis, which is contracted through marshes, rivers, and working with hemp and which can take various forms, among them an osteoarticular one. Finally, a kind of paralysis is produced by tuberculosis of the bones, which heals itself in three years but leaves subjects who have not been immobilized severely and incurably crippled. The localized paralysis of poliomyelitis with its attendant atrophy is also incurable.

It is clear, therefore, that paralysis has many causes and forms and that some varieties of it are amenable to cure or improvement. As in any therapy, the effectiveness of the treatment of paralysis is helped or hindered by the patient's psychic state. In terms of its symptomatology, paralysis is a spectacular phenomenon; the patient and his family know that it may be incurable, yet they also know that it can gradually or suddenly reverse itself. In the absence of a precise and in some cases reassuring etiology, it fully justifies the worst fears and the highest hopes of the patient and his family.

The agricultural milieu also produces the highest incidence of crippling and sometimes permanently disabling arthritis, as well as the highest incidence of chronic rheumatism in the joints. Deformations of the body were caused by the use of all the old farm implements, such as hoes, scythes, and mattocks, to the point that kyphosis is called "peasant's back."

The watering sanctuaries thus catered to invalids whose afflictions sometimes had unknown causes and an uncertain prognosis; the medications used to treat them had been developed over the centuries. Some of the physicians did not divulge the composition of their remedies, balms, and eyewashes, as we can see from the oculists' seals that have been found. The condition of the patients was desperate, though usually not fatal. Some of the diseases presented symptoms similar to those of known disorders and were treated accordingly. If the treatment produced different results, this was ascribed to the intervention of the divinity. The potential clientele of these religious centers was inexhaustible, for the inhabitants of rural Gaul brought to them not only their diseases but also their faith, which contributed to the therapy and the cures accomplished. The therapy itself was a combination of medication and prayer; but at this point we can only infer this from the presence in such cultic places of surgical instruments and the oculists' seals that testify to the practice of medicine.

Physicians and Medical Practices

The documentation concerning the medical practices and the physicians of Gaul falls into three categories: the names of physicians and medical schools, medical tools unearthed by archeology, and texts written by Gallic physicians or physcians who had spent time in Gaul. In all three categories the Greek element is paramount. Some forty Gallic physicians are known to us from inscriptions, and most of them have Greek names or surnames. Greek medicine was taught at the medical school of Rome, founded in 14 A.D. and in operation until the time of Theodoric. It was probably also taught at the schools of Marseilles, Bordeaux, and Saragossa, as well as at the school that must have existed at Metz. Whatever the origin of the physician, his medical language was Greek. One of them was Ausonius (d. 394)—the father of the poet—physician of the towns of Bazas and Bordeaux, and a Gaul who was more at ease in Greek than in Latin (*Epicedion in patrem*, 9-10). We know nothing of these physicians, except that they spoke Greek, had Greek names or surnames, and practiced in Gaul.

What kind of medicine did these physicians practice? In the case of the oculists, the documentation is somewhat more precise. The seals that served to mark the vials of their eyewashes bear the name of the oculist and the condition for which the eyewash was to be used, and properties of the collyrium were specified either by an advertising label such as "inimitable" or by mentioning the basic ingredient: "collyrium nardinum" or "collyrium diagessamias (of Samos earth)."[13] The indications furnished by the inscriptions of the oculists' seals, the finds of instruments used for eye surgery, and the formulas of eyewashes found in the textbooks thus add up to a fairly complete picture of the practice of medicine in the field of ophthalmology. It amounted to a rather simple type of surgery, which was capable of genuine accomplishments in removing the crystalline lens in cataract patients, supplemented by a wide variety of eyewashes, whose formulas were kept secret by each practitioner's dispensary.

As for the medical literature, it consists of no more than the works of two incompatible authors, Oribasius and Marcellus. Oribasius, a pagan, was born in Pergamum about 325. Julian [the Apostate] met him in 355 in Athens, attached him to his entourage, and brought him to Gaul. He was one of the few men who knew of Julian's seditious plans in 360. It was in Gaul that he wrote, upon Julian's request, his *Collectiones medicae* in seventy volumes, a compilation of other authors' and his own work. He wrote a short version of this work for his son (*Synopsis ad Eusthatium*) and a small guide to practical medicine dedicated to Eunapes. Written in Greek, these works could be read directly by the physicians of Gaul. They were so successful, and used for so long, that in the seventh century, when Greek was falling into disuse in Gaul, they were translated into Latin.

Oribasius's work was designed to facilitate the making of a sure diagnosis. In fact, this entire discipline must be qualified as diagnostic medicine. The essential operation is of an intellectual nature: it is a matter of understanding the disease. In order to practice it, the physician must be well versed in physiology and anatomy; he must be capable of observation and of asking the right questions of the patient and his family; and he must be able to account for the mechanism of the disease, partly by means of his knowledge of physiology and partly by means of a general concept of etiology that sees the human body in terms of the four elements. These skills are essential to the making of a physician. The actual treatment comes under three headings. The first, or mechanical part, deals with evacuations: bleeding and purging from the upper (emetics) or the lower part of the body (purgatives). The second deals with the prescription of pharmaceutical remedies, which are applied either externally or orally. The third is devoted to the design of dietary regimes and rules for leading a life that will prevent or cure disease. The same kind of medicine also appears in a letter by Vindicianus, physician to Valentinian I, which has come down to us in the guise of a foreword to Marcellus's book. Vindicianus also speaks about each case in terms of its diagnosis and treatment and relates both of these aspects of medicine to a general theory. Indeed, accounts of progress in medical science are always stated in terms of knowledge and diagnosis. The treatment as such is usually considered an accessory part of the art of medicine, which is why the pharmacopoeia of the different eras is of secondary interest in studies in the history of medicine.[14]

A very different kind of medicine emerges from the works of Marcellus. A Christian and a member of the senatorial class who became Chief Steward of Theodosius I in 395, Marcellus wrote for his sons a compendium of medical prescriptions, listing for each disease identified by its symptoms or by the affected part of the body, the formula of the appropriate remedy and the manner in which it should be prepared and administered. No anatomical descriptions or explanations for the pathology are given.

Marcellus intended to supply his sons with effective prescriptions, so that they would have no need to turn to charlatans.[15] He had contacts with a number of physicians, especially with the aforementioned Vindicianus. He freely ransacked the works of Scribonius Largus, a student of Celsus in the first century A. D. Celsus wrote the first treatise of pharmacopoeia that has come down to us. Scribonius Largus published the formulas of 271 remedies in a more general work called *Compositiones*. To the prescriptions taken from Scribonius Largus, Marcellus added certain remedies taken from the *Medicina Plinii*, which, compiled in the early fourth century, assembles the indications scattered throughout the *Historia naturalis* of Pliny the Elder. Marcellus's work, then, might be considered to be a textbook pharmacopoeia of the school medicine of the time, and as such part of the cultural community of the Empire, at least in the Latin tradition, just as Oribasius was the exemplary Greek physician trained in the classic medical tradition. In addition, however, Marcellus, a Gaul, wanted to give prescriptions that had proven effective in the countryside and for popular remedies.[16] But since he also says that he fears that his sons would turn to charlatans, he must have considered his book to be a medical compendium that would be both effective and learned.

Like Scribonius Largus, the official physician to Claudius and Messalina, Celsus was a scholar and not a charlatan. The *Medicina Plinii* describes the compounds of the remedies it mentions, but Marcellus, like Scribonius, indicates the weight of the different ingredients. Throughout most of his compendium, his pharmacy is of an experimental and quantitative nature.

A specifically Gallic flavor is imparted to Marcellus's book by the vocabulary of the flora and fauna used in his compounds and also by the use of Celtic words, written in Greek letters, in the magic formulas that enhance the effectiveness of the remedies. It is by no means certain that the formulas written in Greek were not also part of the Gallic tradition, and this is also true for the formulas written in Latin. Marcellus indicates in his preface that he owes a great deal to a physician by the name of Ausonius, who was closer to him in time than Celsus and Scribonius Largus. This physician may have been the father of the poet Ausonius.

In his chapter on sciatica and arthritis, Marcellus praises a treatment with which the same Ausonius had obtained good results. It is our only document concerning Ausonius's medical practices. This treatment enabled patients who had been prostrate and immobilized by pain to stand on their feet by the fifth day and to walk on the seventh. Here is the formula.

Gather a young he-goat's droppings on the seventeenth night of the waning moon, although dung gathered on another night of waning moonlight will be equally effective, provided the mixing is done on the seventeenth night. At that time, place into the mortar as many pellets as one hand will hold, provided it is an odd number. Add twenty-five well-crushed pepper corns, then one *hemine* of fine honey and one *setier* of very good aged wine. Mix all this with the handful of crushed droppings, then let the mixture rest in a glass container so that the remedy will be ready when needed. Keep in mind that its effectiveness will be greatest if all this is done on the seventeenth day of the waning moon and if its administration is begun on Thursday, Jupiter's day, and continued for seven consecutive days. The patient should be made to drink it standing on a footstool, his face turned toward the east. If this potion is administered as prescribed, and if these conditions are strictly observed, the patient, even if he is lying crippled and contracted in all his joints and in the hips, immobile and in despair, will surely walk by the seventh day (*De Medicamentis Liber*, XXV, 21).

This text must be cited *in extenso* if one is to understand the kind of medicine that was practiced by the physician Ausonius. The ingredients of the remedy, which strike us as rather surprising, were not so different from those known to us from other formulas; and in any case, they were of minor importance. But whatever the merits of this formula, with its precise quantities, it was composed and administered in a manner that betrays its magical power.

Physicians and Religion in Ausonius's Milieu

Ever since the third century, fiscal law had made a distinction between physicians and healers or exorcists. The *Digest* (I, 3) reproduces one of Ulpianus's texts concerning the fiscal situation of these practitioners. The first professionals to be exempted are the rhetors, grammarians, and geometers.

Physicians are in the same category as professors, and their cause is even better, since they watch over peoples' health, while the others watch over their studies. That is why their right to tax exemption must be acknowledged. A favorable hearing should also be given to midwives, who also appear to practice medicine. It is also possible, under certain conditions, to accept as physicians those who promise to cure some part of the body or a specific ailment, such as ear aches, fistulas, or tooth aches. Not to be included, by contrast, are those who work with incantations, imprecations and, to use the customary vocabulary of these impostors, those who perform exorcism. This has nothing to do with medicine, even if there are people who claim that it has helped them.

Ausonius's father claimed that he had a right to the title of physician, and his son echoed his conviction. The elder Ausonius was a member of the curia of Bazas, his native town (*Epicedion in patrem*, 4–5), since he owned property in the town's territory. He was also a member of the curia of the city of Bordeaux, where he must also have owned property. On what grounds did he enjoy tax-exempt status and honorary membership in these curiae? As a member of the senatorial class since his ennoblement, and especially his prefectship of Illyria in 375, he was an honorary member of the local senate even though he was no longer in office. His tax-exempt status therefore does not mean that Ausonius's father was considered a true physician under the definition of the tax law. Yet he must have been a physician. It is difficult to believe that at a time when magicians were ruthlessly hunted down even a very successful son could have obtained the ennoblement of a pagan exorcist and his elevation to a prefectship. It therefore seems likely that the medicine practiced by this physician Ausonius was a mixture of pharmaceutical remedies and magic. One must imagine that most of the treatments in which pharmaceutical and magical remedies were indissolubly blended together (by certain rites involved in the making of the remedy and by the ritual mode of administration) were prescribed by physicians qualified as such by the law. The only practitioners excluded from the medical definition were the exorcists, who did not dispense remedies along with their words.

The maternal grandfather of the poet and consul Ausonius, Emilius Magnus Arborius, is said to have been a druid or at least to have had ties to the druidic milieu.[17] This noble Aeduan, a learned astrologer, concealed his gifts and his knowledge (*Parentalia*, IV, 17–18), which were forbidden under the law. He knew how to draw up a proper horoscope, which was indeed a druidic specialty. Does this mean, however, that he was involved in any "Gallic religious resistance movement"?[18] This man, we are told by his grandson, was exiled because of his resistance to Victorianus during the revolt of Autun in 269 (*Parentalia*, IV, 9–12). In order to understand this, one must realize that Autun, the capital of the Aedui, had revolted against a usurper, even though the latter sought to gain control in order to shore up Rome's failing defense of the Rhine. Ausonius's grandfather had thus actively sided with Rome against Gaul, a fact of which his grandson was still proud long after Autun had been restored to the rule of Rome. Arborius, the noble druid and astrologer, was a fervent supporter of Rome, not a resistance fighter. During his exile he moved to Dax, a thermal station in the southern part of Gaul that had remained Roman,[19] where he married. One of his daughters was to marry Ausonius's father, the physician. The other daughter, Hilaria, never married and practiced medicine all her life (*Parentalia*, VI). Did her father teach her this science? The skills required in this profession were handed down from father to son. The exiled Aeduan worked hard for his livelihood (*Parentalia*, IV, 13–16), but Ausonius does not tell us what he did. He had his son Arborius trained as a rhetor (*Parentalia*, III).

Another member of Ausonius's circle who is known to us is a druid from northern Gaul who had moved to Bordeaux, a man belonging roughly to the same generation as the poet's Aeduan grandfather. This is Phoebicius (Comm. Prof. Burdach, X, 22–30), the head of the Belenos temple at Bayeux. His son Attius Patera (ibid., IV), professor of rhetoric at Bordeaux, obtained for him a position as grammarian in that city. It appears, then, that more or less brilliant families of the religious aristocracy of Gaul were particularly

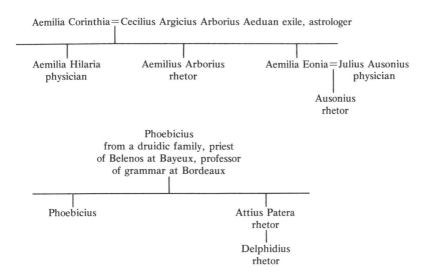

Figure 6.1. Two Gallo-Roman genealogies

loyal to the central Roman government,[20] and particularly well integrated into the Latin culture, inasmuch as they often became teachers of the Latin language and the art of Latin discourse. The members of Ausonius's family divided their occupational choices between a completely Latinized rhetoric and a medicine that preserved a markedly Gallic, ritualistic, and traditional character.

Baths and Therapy

I am inclined to believe that certain Greek elements were introduced into the practices of Gallic medicine because medical knowledge had been vested in the Gallic aristocracy and because that aristocracy was integrated into the Roman sociocultural establishment. The clearest example of this is the use of water in therapy.

Marcellus provides a few examples of the ritual and traditional uses of water in the prevention of disease and of the magic effects of plants growing in springs and rivers. "As soon as you see the first swallow, do not utter another word, run to the spring or well, bathe your eyes there and ask God to grant you that this year the swallows will not bring with them any tears and any pain for your eyes" (*De Medicamentis Liber*, VIII, 30). "Do not forget after each washing to throw water at your feet with both hands, and thereupon to lift your hands to your eyes, rubbing one corner of the eyes with each hand, and that three times" (ibid., VIII, 31). An inflammation of the eye must be attended to by "picking some peristereon, which grows by the spring; boil it until it is soft; you will be cured on the third day" (VIII, 29). Marcellus did not find these suggestions in Pliny or Scribonius Largus; it is very probable that they were traditional Gallic prescriptions.

The relationship between water and the sense of sight has been studied by E. Thévenot after the discovery of two oculist's seals at Les Bolards, where thank-offerings of eyes have also been unearthed. This was the first instance in which these two kinds of evidence were found together at the same site. Thévenot feels that it is Mithras, "a new interpretation of the indigenous Apollo-figures," who must be credited with curing disorders of the eyes in the watering sanctuaries.[21] Marcellus's suggestions show that in the cult of a sacred spring, hygienic measures and preventive magic were associated with curative magic, and that such cultic acts were part of a Gallic tradition untouched by any Roman interpretation.

If one brings this evidence to bear on the study of the watering sanctuaries, it becomes clear that in the fourth century the classic theory of medical science could only enhance the success of the Gallic therapeutic tradition and that it served to attract ever greater numbers of physicians and patients.

Amulets

Marcellus recommends for almost all of the diseases with which he deals in his book the wearing of amulets, that is, of an object or an animal, such as a lizard, or else formulas inscribed on a variety of materials, all of them to be worn around the patient's neck, waist, or finger. The physician himself will fashion the amulet; and he must be sure to be in a state of purity.[22]

Here is a list of the materials to be used for making amulets according to Marcellus. For eye infections, blood spitting, and sore throats, the material is not specified: "in charta virgine." It may be papyrus, but also another type of material. It is to be wrapped in a piece of linen cloth, which in some instances must be red (ibid., VIII, 56; X, 34; X, 71; XIV, 65–68; XV, 89). The heart and the liver call for a thin disk of lead (XXI, 2 and 8; XXII, 10); the kidneys, a virgin leaf enclosed in a gold or copper capsule (XXVI, 43–44), the eyes, the stone taken from a swallow's stomach and placed into a golden case, or the eyes of a male lizard in a golden locket (VIII, 45–50). The intestines call for a golden disk or ring (XXIX, 26). Intestinal troubles seemed to deserve a more costly cure than the others, but a cheap remedy was considered equally effective. The latter consisted of threading a string through a male lizard's eyes and knotting it around the patient's hips while reciting a formula (XXIX, 45). One of these formulas is preceded by a recipe for chrism [a mixture of oil and balsam] (VIII, 58).

The amulets found in the sites of sacred springs, like the eight disks of Amélie-les-Bains, are undoubtedly of this type.[23]

Marcellus's formulas that were to be inscribed on these disks or papers are usually written in Greek or Latin characters, but in the Celtic language.[24] The lead disks of Amélie-les-Bains were described in these terms by P.-M. Duval. In about 1847, when it was decided to increase the flow from the hottest spring of Amélie-les-Bains, part of the rock over which the water flowed out of a narrow crevice was blasted away. As a result, the spring ran more strongly and immediately flushed out a number of coins that were too corroded to be identified, as well as a few objects, among them a button and a round object. The latter is a capsule made of very thin lead to which an iron handle is attached. Also recovered were eight round and flat lead disks bearing inscriptions in Latin characters.[25] Duval has classified these inscriptions as texts in the Gallic language. It should be added that these were formulas designed to accompany, or indeed to take the place of, medical cures undertaken at the hot springs of Amélie, and that the patients, once they were cured, offered them to the water deity. This is all the more likely as a rite of departure was called for in all magical practices.[26] A lead disk of the same kind, inscribed with Latin minuscules, has been found on the chest of a body buried in a Gallo-Roman cemetery of the post-Constantinian period in Paris.[27] Moreover, Böhn, who edited the inscriptions on lead disks in the *Corpus Inscriptionum Latinarum*, refers the reader to Marcellus for a possible explanation of these formulas. Lead tablets were also found in second-century tombs at Chagnon in Saintonge.[28]

As we have seen, springs occupied a privileged position in the medicine of the later fourth century. If necessary, an amulet was sufficient, for the deity was all-powerful; and while the deity was officially Christian for Marcellus, a high official of Theodosius, it was nonetheless thoroughly pagan, given Marcellus's Gallic background. From one of his formulas an invocation of the Gallic *matrae* has come down to us: "The fool went to the mountain, the fool remained a fool. I beseech you, by the Mothers, not to respond with anger." (*De Medicamentis Liber*, X, 35)

I am also inclined to see an allusion to the medical watering places in the following epitaph of an eighteen-year-old woman of Lyon: "You who read [this epitaph], go and wash yourself at the baths of Apollo; this I did with my wife; would that I could do it again."[29]

It is clear, then, that the medicine practiced in the watering sanctuaries operating in fourth-century Gaul involved herbal potions, amulets, popular remedies prepared with crushed lizards' and doves' blood, and also ablutions. In short, the cures were based on remedies that we should seek to understand in an ethnographical perspective, rather than in terms of the history of medicine.

Faith and Healing: An
Attempt at Interpretation

The patients went to the sanctuary in order to cure a disease whose severe symptoms were considered to be somatic. Frenzy and melancholia were diagnosed by their physical symptoms and treated like all other diseases and with the same medications. In the medical textbooks, whether it be the *Medicina Plinii*, Marcellus's *De Medicamentis Liber*, or even Oribasius's *Collectiones medicae*, these conditions are never treated separately under the heading of mental illnesses or nervous disorders.[30] What these texts considered to be nervous disorders or illnesses caused by the nerves were the various forms of paralysis and the different forms of tremors. The nerve was considered a separate entity, a mechanical device that must be oiled and stimulated in order to be reactivated. In other words, only motor troubles were considered to be nervous disorders. In the part of Oribasius's work that has come down to us, mental illnesses are evoked only in the context of the classic treatments, bleeding and purges. "In the same manner I have arrested in several individuals epilepsy, apoplexy, melancholia and similar chronic ailments." "I know a man who will succumb to melancholia every year, unless he is purged, not only in the spring but also in the autumn." (*Collectiones medicae*, VII, 23) "The following signs indicate the need for a purge: vertigo, pressure and sudden pain in the head, continuous ringing in the ears, darkening of the vision, hardness of hearing, numbing of the other senses, sleepiness, lack of appetite, a bitter or otherwise disagreeable taste in the mouth after drinking a tasty beverage, anxiety without any special reason, weakening of a hitherto good memory, palpitation affecting various parts of the body, frequency of frightening and upsetting dreams, a quivering sensation of the skin, heaviness in the lumbar region."

We know that the most obviously psychosomatic illnesses, which manifest a neurosis or an illness involving a neurotic component, can present almost all the symptoms of other, so-called organic illnesses, including sensory, motor, dermatological, and internal disturbances (the latter most frequently involving the smooth muscles, the heart, stomach, intestines, and urinary tract).[31] But even the onset (theory of the favorable terrain) and the duration of any organic impairment are related, among other factors, to the patient's psychic state, so that there is no organic disorder whose eventual course is independent of both the organic and the psychic condition of the patient. The criteria I have cited as motivating the patient's recourse to a sanctuary—the unknown origin of the illness, prolonged stationary condition of the patient or recurrences, and intense pain—are also recognized as the syndromes present in psychosomatic illnesses. The religious aspect of the cure, which we will have to examine further, could have a much more powerful impact on the disease than any physician called to the patient's bedside. Under these conditions, the confusion of the symptoms could easily enhance the reputation of a sanctuary.

There was never any ambiguity as to whether a physician should be consulted, except possibly in cases of epilepsy. All ailments were brought before the physician, who dealt with all of them. Yet if one looks at the etiological theory of this medicine, one finds that he operated on two levels. The first was that of the mechanical functioning of the body, which was manipulated by the treatment (evacuations, diet, pharmaceuticals). This level was the only one considered in Oribasius's Greek medicine as expounded in his *Collectiones medicae*. The second level was that of the divine or demonic influence in triggering the disease and, hence, the course it would take. This level was dealt with in Marcellus's medicine, although he never referred to it in his book. We can deduce his etiology only from his therapeutics. The words of prayers and incantations indicated who it was that healed, prevented, or sent the illness. The evil that has befallen the body was willed by a power outside man; it can be made to depart by means of treatment, to be sure, but the effectiveness of that treatment is dependent on the divine will. Yet the divine or demonic power has not entirely taken over the patient; it acts upon him from the outside. He may therefore address himself to the deity and ask for deliverance through prayer and magic action.

Let us try to re-create the medical reality from the patient's point of view. He is suffering. He is given an explanation: in the wake of a certain illness, which is known to medical science, the evil has entered his body. The physician therefore makes him ingest certain remedies. At that point the patient is passive. Then the physician asks him to pray to the gods or to influence their decision. At that point the patient becomes active; the cure is placed into his own hands. He knows that the effectiveness of the formulas and amulets is related to the concentration of his own will. In practical terms, he thus undergoes a global therapy. He becomes a human being engaged, body and soul, in healing himself. He has also been given an explanation for his suffering: the evil is not within man, it is visited upon him by evil powers. This explanation is in keeping with the ambient cultural system as a whole and, as such, is perfectly rational. This is why patients suffering from the most serious illnesses betook themselves to a cultic place as a matter of course.

As far as the somatic illnesses—if indeed there is such a thing—are concerned, the fact that an explanation was added to the active aspect of the healing process enhanced the effectiveness of the treatment and could hasten the recovery. In terms of psychosomatic therapy, that is, in the most clearly psychically determined cases, this explanation acted as a kind of superimposed explanation, since it involved a power outside the patient. The acceptance of this explanation could contribute to the healing process, or at least to the suppression of the symptoms, if not their underlying cause.[32] This explanation does not hold the patient responsible. He has come under a spell, he is the plaything of unknown powers whose goodwill he can attempt to win. We know that superimposed explanations, as used in present-day psychoanalysis, are sometimes accepted by the patient with favorable results, although in other cases such an explanation itself becomes pathogenic because it forces the patient to face up to the causes inherent in his own life. The explanation of evil and disease in non-Judeo-Christian antiquity involved the patient's responsibility only to the extent that it suggested a failing in the performance of some ritual, but such a failing could be atoned for by other rituals.

The physician or priest intervened in this atonement procedure as an expert in formulas and remedies. He himself did not act as the medicine man. To some extent, the contact between the patient and the divine was established directly. It was inherent in the sacred place to which the human being had voluntarily betaken himself, and also in the sacred water flowing there, which was itself divine (the goddess *Sequana*), endowed with healing properties, and effective.

It is into this religious and medical context that one must place the success of the medical ministrations of Saint Martin of Tours, as well as the instrumental role of these cures in the conversion of the Gauls. In approaching this subject, one must be sensitive to the ambiguity of the word *conversion*, which designates both the will to convert people to a new religion and the act by which a person converts to a new faith. The same ambiguity spills over into the word *healing*, which in this instance is closely associated with the word *conversion*. The statement "Martin healed the Gaul who thereupon converted" is reversible into "Martin converted the Gaul who thereupon was healed."

Was Martin a Physician?

A well-known passage relating the healing of Paulinus of Nola's eyes by Saint Martin has long intrigued the interpreters of the *Vita Martini*: "Paulinus, the man who later was to set such a shining example, had begun to suffer severe pains in one eye, and already a thick veil had covered his pupil to the point that it was totally sealed up, when Martin touched his eye with a brush, thereby restoring him to his former health and eliminating all pain."[33] Regardless of whether or not Paulinus was suffering from a cataract, this text does seem to indicate, as J. Fontaine has pointed out,[34] that Martin treated Paulinus according to the rules of ancient medicine. But since Fontaine, like most other students of this text, was skeptical about the reality of Martin's qualifications in ophthalmology, he refused to credit him with a medical cure that appears credible when reported in terms of a miracle. Fontaine therefore proposed an allegorical interpretation, similar to those that have been advanced for the reliefs on the pillars of Les Nautes and Mavilly and for the Ra-

venna sarcophagus.[35] Indeed, there is a connection between the representation of a scene in which a patient's eyes are treated and the idea of a mystical
inner illumination, especially since the figures shown on these reliefs include
deities associated with sudden spiritual enlightenment. Fontaine's interpretation seems particularly plausible as Paulinus of Nola himself speaks of illumination in connection with his conversion to the ascetic life.[36]

Martin, we are told by Sulpicius Severus, did military service in the *Schol-
ares Alae*, first under Constantius and then under Julian (*Vita Martini*, II, 2).
No doubt he was part of the escort, or guard, assigned to Julian by Constantius when Julian left Milan for Gaul. Libanius tells us that the least valiant
members of this guard of 360 soldiers (Julian, 277 D) "spent their time mum-
bling prayers," as Julian is said to have put it (Zosimus, III, 3, 2). Sulpicius
tells us about Martin's qualities as a Christian soldier. His text is deeply inspired by the Gospel and deserves the literary study J. Fontaine has devoted
to it. Among other things, Sulpicius says that Martin "took care of the sick
and brought help to the wretched" (*Vita Martini*, II, 8). The literary character of this text does not prevent it from having a factual basis, for we know
that every soldier carried an emergency kit and that the soldiers dressed each
other's wounds. Medical officers were attached to each unit, and *capsaires*
guarded the medical supplies. In a sense, the army was thus the best training
ground for first aid volunteers. I do not mean to imply, however, that Martin
learned more than the technique of applying bandages and the formulas of a
few ointments.

Desiring to devote himself to the service of God, Martin obtained his discharge from Julian in 356. It should be noted that discharged soldiers, along
with the freedmen and the members of the senatorial class, were almost the
only individuals not locked into some occupation and therefore free to embrace an ecclesiastical career. Immediately after his discharge, Martin went to
Poitiers, where he joined Saint Hilary, who was at that time engaged in his
struggle against the Arian tendencies of the bishops of Gaul as well as against
the policies of Constantius II. In the framework of this article I cannot discuss the reasons why Martin became an exorcist rather than a deacon, a fact
that Sulpicius explains by Martin's modesty (*Vita Martini*, V, 2). I simply
want to point out that at the church of Poitiers Martin exercised an ecclesiastical function about which we still do not know very much, although we do
know that it did not exist at every church.[37] Jerome tells us (*De Vir. inl.*, c)
that Hilary composed an *Allegation to the prefect Sallustius against the physician Dioscurus*. This book has not come down to us, and neither its date
nor its content are known. But we do know the prefect Sallustius.[38] A Gaul,
he was appointed quaestor attached to Julian when the latter was sent to
Gaul in 356. A pagan rhetor, he gained the friendship and confidence of the
caesar,[39] who missed him when Constantius II recalled him in 359 (Julian,
Orat., VIII). In 361, when Julian seized power, and when the prefect of the

praetorium Nebridius, faithful to Constantinus II, refused to swear loyalty to the new regime, he entrusted the prefectship of the praetorium of all of Gaul to Sallustius.[40]

When and where could Hilary have written his *Allegation* to Sallustius? Hilary was exiled from Gaul in 356 or, assuming that it took some time for Constantius II's order to reach him, in early 357 at the latest. Hilary subsequently lived in Asia until 359, then stayed briefly in Constantinople, and returned to Gaul, with the consent of Constantius II, in 360. It is fairly certain that this was the time when Saint Martin joined him in Poitiers and moved to a hermitage at Ligugé (*Vita Martini*, VII, 1). Hence, it was during the few months of Sallustius's prefectship in Gaul that Hilary sent him his *Allegation* against the physician Dioscorus, a friend of Julian's. By that date, Julian had not yet declared himself a pagan, although he did protect the Nicean bishops against Constantius.[41] Since it is unlikely that Hilary would later have turned to a pagan prefect who shared Julian's view of Christianity, the *Allegation* must be dated 361. We also know that Martin, upon his release from Julian's army, had a first contact with Hilary in 356, when he was made an exorcist, and that he was again in Hilary's entourage between 360 and his election to the bishop's see of Tours in 370.[42] In about 365, Saint Hilary was to express his ideas about medicine in his commentary on Psalm 13. This text can be interpreted as an allegory, but the ideas may well have come from Martin and should probably be taken literally: *"In a lost world, one seeks out a physician*: We need a physician who can heal us by providing succor in one single and universal endeavor, who everywhere in the world can treat all ills, however varied they might be, and that not through science and techniques (for who has ever successfully turned to science and techniques?) but through the power of the Word. This is the physician for whom the spirit clamors and whose coming it awaits, for when he arrives, the fever abates, the blind see, paralysis ceases, and death withdraws" (*Tractatum in Psalmos*). Saint Hilary believed that Christian words had the power to drive out demons: "A word will stay, punish and drive out these invisible beings that we cannot understand" (*Tractatum in Psalmos*).

How can the presence of demons be detected? By definition, the unbaptized were considered to be the prey of demons and had to be exorcized. Yet Christianity continued to see all illness, madness, and all the tribulations that the pagans attributed to maleficent powers as signs that the demon had gained power over a creature, sometimes incited by evil spells cast by another person.

This was the official belief of the Church, personified by the meeting of its bishops in council. For instance, at the Council of Elvira, the Church refused to grant absolution, even in the hour of death, to those who had killed by means of evil spells. This belief was also held by literate Christians like Prudentius, who asserted that the pagans used magic to kill their grandmothers when they wanted her inheritance.[43] Theoretically, every Christian should have been able to perform exorcisms, but in the general context of the time the exorcist was at one and the same time the man who knew the formulas and the wielder of a charismatic power that healed the body and the spirit by means of religious and magic formulas referred to as incantations and imprecations.

When he was sent into exile, Martin settled at Milan, then retired to the island of Gallinara, where "he lived for a time on roots." One day he took some hellebore, "a poisonous plant, but when he felt that the violent poison had attacked him and that his death was near, he drove away the threat of this danger through prayer." In this passage Sulpicius Severus actually shows us Martin as a competent herbalist. Who, one might ask, would take hellebore if he knew what it was? To a large extent, the medical textbooks were devoted to the description of the plants used in the composition of remedies. Some of these plants were poisonous, at least in some cases. Celsus had taught that the poison of adders and hellebore is harmful when applied to wounds, but not when taken internally (*De Medicamentis*, V, 27, 3b). Oribasius's father and grandfather were of the opinion that hellebore is the best purgative, although they recommended that the patient make his will before he undertook the purge, since a number of those who had taken hellebore had suffocated and few had survived (*Collectiones medicae* VIII, 8). It was, in other words, a dangerous drug that had to be administered with due caution (ibid., VII, 26).

Restored to Hilary's entourage at Poitiers and settled at Ligugé, Martin resuscitated a catechumen by stretching out on the body that had lain lifeless for three days: "From that moment on, the renown of the blessed man began to assume great lustre. In this manner the world came to recognize him, who was already considered a saint by all those who knew him, as a powerful man, truly worthy of the apostles" (*Vita Martini*, VII).

Fontaine distinguishes four kinds of miracles performed by Saint Martin.[44] Briefly summarized, they are (1) objective miracles, which are most closely patterned on the Gospels—resurrections, healings, and exorcisms; (2) miracles ensuing from other actions; for example most of Martin's "thaumaturgical gestures" related to his assult on the paganism of the countryside; (3) folkloric miracles, issued from the stories handed down by the circles connected with Marmoutiers or from Sulpicius's literary reminiscences; and (4) purely literary miracles, "gratuitous and personal inventions on the part of Sulpicius." With some reservations, Fontaine places the restoring of Paulinus's sight into this last category.

Fontaine's schema concerns literary history and Sulpicius Severus as a writer. I should like to propose another, perhaps not quite so critical, classification of the miracles, one that attempts to grasp their reality before they became literature. In this manner I would distinguish between healings brought about by Martin's charismatic power and healings of a medical character.

Martin performed a second resurrection in the region of Ligugé. The slave of Lupicinus, a local notable, had hanged himself. Happening to pass by, the saint repeated the gesture that had restored the catechumen to life. He stretched out on the body and the miracle happened (*Vita Martini*, VIII), convincing the local population that he had special powers. Indeed, it was the people of Tours, having learned of this miracle-working power, who demanded that he be ordained as bishop, contrary to the wishes of the bishops convened to designate a new prelate. In order to make him leave his cell and to ordain him bishop, he was asked to visit a sick woman (*Vita Martini*, IX).

As bishop, Martin continued to perform healings: "But as for the healing grace, it was so powerful in him that almost none of the sick who approached him failed to recover their health" (*Vita Martini*, XVI, 1). Sulpicius reports six cases of healing that seem to bear some relation to the medical treatments of the time.

THE YOUNG GIRL OF TRIER (*Vita Martini*, XVI)

Martin is called to the bedside of a paralyzed girl by her desperate father. He begins by praying, "then, examining the patient, he calls for oil. After blessing it, he pours the virtue of this sacred brew into the girl's mouth, and she immediately recovers the power of speech. As the sacred oil comes into contact with her various limbs, life is gradually rekindled in them, until finally she stands firmly on her feet before the people." Oil was used as the vehicle of many medicinal substances. Oribasius used it to induce vomiting, precisely in cases of paralysis. As a preparation for this vomiting he advised the moistening of the body through abundant food and rest (*Collectiones medicae*, VII, 23). Then the patient must be asked to vomit, and if he is unable to do so, the physician must intervene: "Recognizing the imminence of danger, do not hesitate to rectify the situation by forcing aromatic oils into the mouth with the help of feathers" (ibid., VIII, 6).

THE COOK (*Vita Martini*, XVIII, 5)

As Martin was passing, also at Trier, by the courtyard of a house, a cook was seized by the demon. The unfortunate man was biting anyone who came near him. Martin ordered him to stop but "as the other growled with bared teeth and, with his mouth open, threatened to bite him, Martin thrust his fingers into his mouth saying: 'If you have any power, devour them.' Suddenly it seemed as if the possessed man's throat had been touched by a red-hot iron; he drew his teeth back from the fingers of the blessed saint, being very careful not to touch them. Forced by this punishment and these tortures to flee the body he possessed, but unable to leave through the mouth, he [the demon] was evacuated through a flux of the bowels, leaving behind repulsive traces." Here, by way of comparison, is Oribasius's procedure for purging in difficult cases: "In treating a patient who could not breathe and was about to die because he clenched his teeth and quivered like an animal that is being slaughtered, I have myself immobilized the teeth and kept the mouth open by means of wedges so that it would not close; then I inserted my hand and, finding the swallowing organs obstructed by a lump of mucus congealed in the form of a ball, I extracted it. This ball did not break when it was thrown upon the ground" (*Collectiones medicae*, VIII, 7). Martin used the same technique.

THE HEALING OF PAULINUS OF NOLA

Examined above.

THE SLAVE OF EVANTHIUS(?) (*Dialogues*, II, 2)

In the *Dialogues* of Sulpicius Severus, Gallus, a Gaul and retired military man (*Dialogues*, II, 1) who had served in the army with Martin, relates the miracles of the saint. A slave of Gallus's uncle Evanthius had been bitten by a snake. His master brought him to Saint Martin in an inanimate state, the poison having already spread throughout his body. Martin placed his finger on the wound and the poison came out with a spurt of blood. The slave got up, hale and hearty.

THE MUTE GIRL (*Dialogues*, III, 2)

This case probably took place in the region of Chartres or Rouen, for Martin was in the company of the bishops of these two towns, Valentinus and Victritius. A father brought to him his twelve-year-old child, mute from birth. In the presence of an excited crowd, Martin poured a little oil into the girl's mouth, holding her tongue with his fingers. The girl, of course, began to speak.

In the same category with these examples of medical treatment is the ointment prepared by an angel, which cured Martin's bruises after a fall (*Vita Martini*, XIX, 4). On the basis of these examples, I feel that Sulpicius's descriptions of cures must be taken seriously. It appears that Martin, an uneducated man, as his devoted biographer Sulpicius is the first to admit (*Vita Martini*, XXV, VIII), had some medical knowledge, which he had no doubt acquired in the army. He never denied his help to anyone. His achievements were attributed to the god who brought about the cure thanks to Martin's prayers, as he believed along with those around him. This belief gave rise to another type of cure, those that were due to the patient's faith and occurred without Martin's direct intervention.

The prefect Arborius placed a letter from Martin on his daughter's chest and her quartan fever ceased (*Vita Martini*, XIX, 1). A simple laying on of hands was sufficient to cure Tetradius's slave (*Vita Martini*, XVII). When Gallus's uncle was at death's door, he sent for Martin. As he went to meet him, he was suddenly cured (*Dialogues*, II, 2). Another notable, Lycontius, wrote to Martin that an epidemic had befallen his household. Even in his absence, Martin's prayers defeated the demon who had taken over the estate (*Dialogues*, III, 14).

The prettiest story is that of the nuns cloistered in the convent of Clion (Claudiomagus), a parish founded by Saint Martin. On the occasion of a visitation of the parish, the saint slept in the sacristy. After his departure the nuns came to touch everything that had touched him and divided among themselves the straw of his mattress. One of them was able to cure a possessed man by hanging one of these straws from his neck (*Dialogues*, II, 8). In short, as Sulpicius said in order to summarize Martin's activities, "he treated the sick and took care of people in danger" (*Epithet*, II, 12).

A pharmaceutical vase has been unearthed in the Vendée, at Saint-Martin-de-Fraigneau. Engraved on it with a stylus are the words "+Divi Martini Antistitis balsamum oleum pro benedictione." The paleography, we are told by H. Leclercq, is that of the fifth century.[45] If the reading is correct, two interpretations are possible. Either the vase contained oil whose recipe was given by or attributed to Saint Martin, or the inscription refers, as Leclercq supposes, to a custom reported by Gregory of Tours and Paulinus of Périgeux, in which vases filled with oil were deposited near the body of a saint, so that the divine grace would permeate it. Since the inscription is engraved with a stylus rather than molded into the vase, the possibility that it was a mass-produced article for the dispensary of a certain Martin must be ruled out. As we have seen, oil was used in the practice of medicine. We have also seen how Martin used it. Literary testimony indicates that Martin frequently blessed oil when he treated a patient, as in the case of the wife of the prefect Avitianus,[46] and also on the occasion when one of these vases filled with blessed oil fell to the ground without breaking (*Dialogues*, III, 3). It is thus possible that in his lifetime he used certain special formulas of his own.

The other interpretation can also be supported by literary texts, for Paulinus of Périgeux relates the healing of a paralyzed woman by means of an anointing with blessed oil placed near Saint Martin's tomb (*Vita Martini*, VI, 145-51).

What most impressed Martin's contemporaries were not his visions or his conversations with angels, but his healings. Paulinus of Périgeux shows that Martin's healing power survived him: "Large crowds often come to visit you, and in their presence your healing power is still alive" (866–67). There is little doubt, of course, that Julian's protegé Oribasius also engaged in divination and believed in the power of magic. But what about Martin? It was perfectly normal that as a Christian he should practice exorcism and lift spells, and indeed we are told that he insulted the demon when he cured the cook and that his healing involved the laying on of hands and prayer. Yet his technique, the use of oil, is too reminiscent of Oribasius's therapeutic procedures to be considered purely in terms of spiritual healing.

Martin's Faith and Faith in Martin

THE CROSS

Wherever his own or other peoples' salvation was concerned—material salvation from danger and spiritual salvation in the next world—Saint Martin believed in the total effectiveness of the sign of the cross and indeed of the word *crux*. When he asked for his discharge from Julian's army and refused to accept Julian's *donativum*, he was accused of cowardice, whereupon he proposed to go into battle protected only by the sign of the cross (*Vita Martini*, IV, 5). By making the sign of the cross he was able to stop a pagan funeral procession (ibid., XII), and it was the sign of the cross that deflected the fall of the sacred pine tree that was supposed to fall on Martin when it was felled (XIII, 8).

The most striking passage to this effect is Sulpicius Severus's dream (*Epithet*, II, 4) concerning Martin's impending death: "And I, having embraced his holy knees and asked for his blessing as was my wont, felt on my head the delicate caress of his hand and heard him uttering repeatedly amidst the solemn words of the blessing the name of the cross which was so familiar on his lips." Here we see that Martin believed in the value and the efficacy of the word *crux*, with which he no doubt interspersed the ritual phrases of the blessing. Martin also believed in certain gestures. Thus, he raised his hand to stop an angry cow that had strayed from the herd (*Dialogues*, II, 9) and breathed on the demon he saw behind the evil count Avitianus, who did not want to be exorcized (ibid., III, 8).

DREAMS AND VISIONS

Saint Martin, like all his contemporaries, believed in dreams, and modern psychoanalysis will not contradict him. He saw dreams as divine monitions. When he gave away half of his coat, a dream showed him Christ under the beggar's traits (*Vita Martini*, III, 1–5). A dream prompted him to return to Illyricum to visit his parents (ibid., V, 3). On the road he met with the devil, and I agree with J. Fontaine, who interprets this dream as a metaphor for an encounter with Constantius II's police surveillance.[47] Even though Martin often spoke with the angels, his dreams usually featured the devil in the form of Jupiter or, more frequently, in the form of Mercury and Venus and Minerva (*Vita Martini*, XXII; *Dialogues*, II, 13). Against this devil he used the sign of the cross. It is evident that Martin dreamed his desires and his fears. Jupiter, Mercury, and Venus, especially Venus as a mother figure, were the divinities most frequently found in the Celtic sanctuaries, together with the *Matres, Matrones*, and *Matrae* and with Apollo, although the latter is never evoked in the *Vita Martini*. It is also evident that Martin was greatly affected by his dreams and visions. In this connection it should be recalled that Oribasius recommended hellebore for persons subject to delirium and nightmares.

Martin thus emerges as a soldier, physically strong enough to subdue a possessed man, but also as a person with a compassionate heart and as excessively impressionable. Indeed, he was so impressionable that he devoted his life to the propagation of a religion about which he may have known very little, despite his personal contact with Saint Hilary.

FAITH IN MARTIN

Martin was perceived—against his will no doubt, although he himself came to share that view—as a man possessed by God, as *potens*, or powerful. This is the epithet used by all those who wrote about him.[48] The noun expressing his essential quality is *virtus*, which must be translated as "power."[49] This tradition was still alive in the days of Gregory of Tours, who wrote "About the powers of Saint Martin," that is, about the miraculous cures accomplished near his tomb.

Significantly, Sulpicius Severus never speaks about faith in God, only about faith in Martin. He cites Christ's word concerning the marvels that will be accomplished by those who have faith, and concludes from this passage that "those who have no faith in Martin's works have no faith in the words of Christ" (*Dialogues*, I, 26). Indeed, it is a sacrilege to say that Martin has lied (ibid., II, 13). Sulpicius Severus was to learn from Postuminanus, who visited him at Primuliacum on his return from the East, that his little book about the life of Saint Martin was known all over the world, but that some considered it to be a pack of lies (*Dialogues*, I, 26).

Faith in Christ thus passes through faith in Martin. Those who do not have faith in Martin are unbelievers (*Vita Martini*, XXV), infidels. The wife of Emperor Maximius, on the other hand, insisted on personally serving Martin when he visited Trier, cooked for him and mixed his wine before she presented the cup to him. After the saint had finished his meal, she faithfully (*satis fideliter*) gathered the crumbs he had left in order to serve them at the royal table. These crumbs are referred to as "illas reliquias" (*Dialogues*, II,

6). Should we understand this expression to mean "relics" or simply "left-overs"? Sulpicius Severus was probably inclined to use it in the first sense; after all, it was he who later initiated the cult of Saint Martin. He claims that those who will read his book without believing what it says (*infideliter*) will be sinners (*Vita Martini*, XXVII, 6; *Epithet*, 1, 5); and indeed, Sulpicius repeatedly shows us crowds that are only too happy to believe. There is the crowd from Tours and neighboring towns assembled to force the bishops' hands by demanding the election of Martin (ibid., IX, 1–3); the crowd at Trier gathered near the house where he will cure the paralyzed girl; the crowd that witnesses the resurrection of a dead man at Chartres; and the crowd present at his burial (*Epithet*, III, 17).

Martin's contemporaries believed in his power so fervently that some of them had visions themselves. The prefect Arborius, who had cured his daughter of quartan fever by placing a letter from Martin on her chest, one day saw Martin's hands becoming covered with jewels during Mass (*Dialogues*, III, 10). Also during Mass, a virgin, a priest, and three monks saw a globe of fire bursting forth from Martin's head, while the rest of the crowd did not see anything (*Dialogues*, II, 2). In this manner a dialectical relationship between faith and healing came into being. An unplanned event, the first resurrection, and Martin's successful medical treatments gave rise to further cures due to faith. Faith induced visions, and all of these factors converged to create Martin's success, to give him a notoriety that he himself attributed to God's power. Was it because he was sure of his power that he was able to impose his will on animals? When a group of tax collectors met him on the road, beat him and left him for dead, their horses ran away (*Dialogues*, III, 3). An angry cow stopped short before Martin (ibid., II, 9), and a water mocassin swam to the opposite shore (III, 9). People silenced dogs by crying out: "In the name of Martin" (III, 3). Also in an unplanned manner, he imposed his will on the elements; on the sea, on hail, and on fire (III, 14; III, 7; *Vita Martini*, XIV, 1). How, then, could he fail to perform miracles?

Healing and Conversion

This, then, is the psychological context in which we must see the conversions achieved by Martin. Convinced of the power of the Christian God, he wanted to convert the Gauls to this God; there is no doubt that his missionary zeal was greater than that of the other bishops of Gaul. Nor is there any doubt that his own accomplishments convinced him that God's power was within him; just as the crowds, in their desperate search for psychological security, were convinced that this man was a man of God.

Given these conditions, we will find two kinds of conversion: a few instances of conversion through preaching and, in most cases, conversion through miracles. Preaching convinced the brigand who had assaulted Martin in the Alps, but this was before his powers as a miracle worker were revealed (*Vita Martini*, V, 4). In the same manner he converted his mother and some inhabitants of Illiyricum (ibid., VI, 3). But as soon as he himself became aware of his vocation as a miracle worker, and as his accomplishments began to give him a reputation, the conversions he achieved were prompted by different criteria and brought about in one of two ways. An important person might call on Martin to cure a member of his family (*familia*), be it a slave or a child. This was the case with Tetradius. A pagan, he promised to convert if Martin would intervene (XVIII). The prefect Arborius, already a Christian, dedicated his daughter to God after he received an amulet from Martin (XIII).

Medical help was certainly one of the means by which entire households were converted, by contrast with the piecemeal conversion of Roman families. In another type of conversion an entire crowd of pagans might embrace the Christian faith. When Martin agreed to stand in the place where the sacred pine tree was supposed to fall, a whole crowd of pagans asked for the laying on of his hands after the tree had fallen to the other side (XIII). At Levroux, he demolished a pagan temple in the presence of a group of pagans who were unable to move (XIV); they recognized that they had been stayed by Martin's God and converted. In the Aeduan region, crowds of people became Christians (XV). In the town of Chartres, the name of Christ was unknown, but people had heard of Martin; so when his arrival was announced, a multitude gathered and Martin began to preach. This crowd watched as he resuscitated one man's only son and promptly kneeled down demanding to be made Christians. "Then and there he laid on his hands and they all became catechumens" (*Dialogues*, II, 4). No wonder that one of Martin's former comrades-in-arms living in Chartres invited him to his house, as Victritius of Rome had done (Paulinus of Nola, *Epithet*, XVIII, 7), no doubt in the hope of increasing his flock.

The source material concerning Martin, unlike the documentation for the watering sanctuaries, provides examples of cures rather than lists of diseases. These cures were therapeutic miracles, always occurring unexpectedly and suddenly.[50] The two cases of resurrection from the dead were due to Martin's initiative. On both occasions he asked everyone to leave the room, stretched out on the body, and prayed, having made no promises beforehand. On another occasion, Martin was already on his way to a certain notable's house. As he entered, he sensed a demonic presence. At this point a demon seized the household's cook, and Martin intervened spontaneously. In all other accounts of cures, however, his help was solicited; he was either asked to come or the patient was brought to him.

All his interventions, excepting the case of the mute girl who was presented to him as he was passing by, took place at the houses of notables and involved the notable himself, his daughter, or one of his servants. Let us look at the diseases for which these people had recourse to his power as a miracle worker. It was purely by chance that he came into the presence of a patient suffering an acute attack of gastrointestinal disease and that he arrived at Gallus's house shortly after a slave had been bitten by a snake. By contrast, his intervention was solicited in two cases of aphasia, one of them connected with paralysis, and in one case of incipient blindness. These are the very type of disorder for which treatment at a sanctuary would have been indicated.

In these well-defined cases of paralysis and blindness there was time to call a physician who would treat the patient at home. When he failed, the family cast about for alternate means. At that point, they appealed to Martin. Like the physician, he would come to the house and use comparable techniques. But his person was imbued with the power that paganism had attributed to the watering sanctuary. The oil he poured into the patient's mouth was a sacred liquid equivalent to the water of the sacred spring. It should be kept in mind that this was an aristocratic clientele accustomed to summoning a physician, and that these people called Martin on the strength of his reputation. However, the clientele that sought out Martin at Tours or in the other towns he visited was of an altogether different kind. With the exception of the mute girl who was presented to him in a town of western France, all other reported cases were cases of possession. An important point to be made in this connection is the failure on the part of Martin and his biographer to distinguish between the screams and the agitation of a person in the throes of an acute intestinal attack, as in the case of the cook, and the agitation of the possessed. We also hear of a group of energumens living in the church of Tours, waiting for Martin to pass by. Another energumen was cured by an amulet from Martin.

As far as his aristocratic clientele was concerned, then, Martin replaced the physician who could be summoned; whereas for the popular clientele, Martin himself became the focal point of the cure. During his lifetime, his power could be brought to the patient in the form of amulets and oils. After his death, a twofold movement became established: sanctified oil came to the patients and patients came to Martin's tomb, which had become the fixed locus of healing, comparable in every respect to the pagan sanctuary. The most interesting aspect of this development is Martin's lifetime, which marks a period of transition. Before we can proceed further, we must study the clinical signs distinguishing the energumens cured through Martin's intervention.

The cases of paralysis, blindness, and aphasia are described in terms of the individual, without any indications as to their etiology. Only once is the disease related to the demon, namely, in the account of an epidemic in the household of Lycontius. The other cases fall under two headings, which in themselves amount to a definition: demoniacs and energumens. Sulpicius relates only two cases in which Martin cured a demoniac. They were Tetronius's slave and the cook, in other words, two servants. Sulpicius describes the clinical signs: both are raving and furious, both lunge toward the by-standers and bite everyone who comes near. Both appear to be in the throes of cruel suffering. Pain, delirium, uncoordinated movements, panic—these symptoms could well be considered those of frenzy according to the classification of diseases found in Oribasius, Pliny, and Marcellus. In the case of Tetradius's slave, the crisis is identified as an attack of the demon by the pagan witnesses, who rush out to find Martin. In the other case Martin himself detects the demon, speaks to him, provokes him, and drives him out. A different category is that of the energumens. It is impossible to say whether they were epileptics only, or whether agitated patients of other kinds were designated by the same term. Its etymology points to possession. A god dwells within the epileptic. This is precisely the case of the group of energumens at Tours. When asked to give their names, they answer: "Jupiter, Mercury" (*Dialogues*, III, 5). In the case of the cook, Martin addresses the demon when he thrusts his fingers into the unfortunate man's mouth, saying: "If you have any power, devour them." It is well known that the pagan religions attributed epilepsy and delirium to the invasion of a patient by a divine power.[51] The Romans called these spirits lymphs and larvae and believed that they entered through the mouth or the nose. Magic practices were employed to dislodge them: a stake driven into the ground where the epileptic had fallen, ceremonies of purification for madness, sacrifices, and exorcisms. Other remedies included the recitation of special formulas, sometimes made up of Ephesian letters without apparent meaning, and of course the wearing of amulets to prevent a recurrence of the sickness or to bring down the vengeance of the god upon the enemy who had cast the spell.

The energumens of Tours did not call themselves lymphs and larvae. They acknowledged the names of the greatest gods of the Gallo-Roman pantheon, Jupiter and Mercury. These were the very gods who most often tormented Martin (*Vita Martini*, XXII). Mercury was one of the gods habitually worshiped in the watering sanctuaries[52] and mentioned on the tablets inscribed with imprecations.[53] The energumens, in other words, were possessed by the pagan gods whom Martin identified as demons. The sick people who had come to Tours were afflicted with what even paganism considered to be a demoniac illness, possession. Martin, like the Gallic gods before him, was asked to cure them. He had been asked for some time to deal with illnesses that called for treatment at a sanctuary, that is, paralysis and blindness; but the possessed who came or were brought to the church of Tours constituted a new category of patients, the possessed, although they were not defined as such. The saint used medical techniques to which sick patients were accustomed, administering oil as a technical means and using formulas, gestures, and prayers as they had been used in the magico-medical tradition of Gaul. What accounted for his therapeutic success?

Ever since the third century, the policies of the Empire had been shaped by the need for a strong defense. This policy demanded, of course, the recruiting of large numbers of soldiers and the payment of wages to unproductive men. Above all, these armies had to be fed. This situation induced a process of social degradation resulting from levies for the State that were farmed out to private individuals, the local notables. A major cause of insecurity for peasants living far from the front was their uncertainty concerning the amounts of agricultural products they would have to furnish each year in the form of dues or taxes. In other words, their own subsistence was never assured. By the end of the fourth century, this process had almost reached its limits. The peasants, especially in the western part of the Empire, relied on a patron to defend their harvests against the dues-collecting notables. They thus became more dependent on one man in order to become less dependent on an institution. But this dependence did not afford them security, neither with respect to taxes, which were henceforth collected in the form of dues, nor, above all, with respect to their military obligations.

If anxiety is indeed dealt with in one of two ways, by action or by security-giving dependence, one might see the Gallic peasant revolts [of that time] as examples of an active reaction. These revolts had always been pagan in character, and sometimes the attacks were directed against Christian buildings. On the other hand, the patterns of social dependence established in the fourth century failed to produce the hoped-for security. They were therefore bound to spawn ever greater anxiety, which was compounded by the military situation. The texts show that the manifestations of this anxiety, such as psychosomatic illnesses or phenomena related to possession, were becoming ever more prevalent. This social process took place over two centuries, two centuries filled with uncertainty and invasions occurring more than once in each generation, especially in northern Gaul.

These invasions did not demand an adaptation to a new social system, as would be the case after the barbarians had definitively settled on Roman soil. They were a matter of violent and episodic contacts, which were sure to happen again and again. To these troubles must be added the civil wars between emperors and usurpers, and the periodic revolts.

This situation was bound to produce anxiety. For all its scantiness, the documentary material at our disposal gives us two types of reactions of increased dependence due to illness, if indeed we agree that an unexpected and instantaneous cure reveals the psychosomatic aspect of a given illness. The first type, which is described for the notables, is psychosomatic illness assuming an organic character, that is, paralysis and aphasia. The second type expresses itself in symptoms of anxiety: fixed, and in many cases almost Parkinsonian, postures of the body, uncontrolled movements, panic due to precordial pain, or peculiar facial expressions, especially in the eyes.[54] These illnesses derive their historical interest only from their frequency and from their distribution throughout the social spectrum. Clearly, one cannot reduce Martin's activities to the curing of "illnesses" unless one attempts, as I have done here, to give a precise account of the illnesses that affected the different social groups.

Only in this manner is it possible to grasp the reasons for Martin's success and his advantages over the Gallic gods.

From the patient's point of view, Martin's therapy was cumulative. It made use of the most classic medical treatment, which was based on evacuation. But what was evacuated, through vomiting or defecation, was the demon. "Forced by these punishments and these tortures to flee the body he possessed, but unable to leave through the mouth, he was evacuated through a flux of the bowels, leaving behind repulsive traces" (*Vita Martini*, XVII). The evil that had entered the body was made to leave it by means of a medical technique wielded by the priest. A second element of Martin's treatment was the wearing of amulets and the recitation of formulas. However, there was one major difference between the therapy carried out at the sanctuary and Martin's therapy, and that was the substitution of a man for a place. A therapeutical relationship could develop between the patient and Martin. Indeed, this bond of dependency was intended and indispensable. Power was exclusively in Martin's hands, and the power he wielded was God's power over evil. The patient was thus at one and the same time acted upon by the demon that had entered his body and by Martin's counterpower that inaugurated the healing process; all he had to do was to give himself over entirely to the power of the saint. In this manner he could satisfy his craving for dependence. As in the etiology propounded by Marcellus and the Gallic medicine, an explanation of the evil was provided. In the Tetradius episode, the raving, possessed slave refused to be taken to Martin. Martin for his part refused to enter a pagan house. Tetradius promised to convert with his entire household and Martin forthwith expelled the demon by the laying on of his hands. By acknowledging the names of Jupiter and Mercury, the energumens made it clear that their sickness was paganism. In this case their conversion amounted to a magic act, and their paganism, once it was recognized as a wrong, amounted to an explanation of their illness. In this manner, the cause had become lodged within the patient, and he must spend the rest of his life purging himself of it by means of increased dependence on new rites and new institutions, for this dependence would not cease with the disappearance of the symptoms. It was as encompassing as the wrong that had caused the illness.

Yet the relationship with the miracle worker and the aura imparted by a miraculous cure offered a wonderful compensation for a patient in this desperate, anxiety-producing situation, since it provided security in a dependent relationship with the father figure of the miracle worker and even gave him social prestige.

NOTES

1. Emma and Ludwig Edelstein, *Asclepius: A Collection and Interpretation of the Texts* (Baltimore, 1945).

2. R. Herzog, "Die Wunderheilungen von Epidauros," *Philologus*, (Supplement 20), 3 (Leipzig, 1931): 71–112. See also A. J. Festugière, in *Histoire générale des religions, Grèce-Rome* (Paris, 1948), pp. 132–36.

3. R. Bernard and P. Vassal, "Etude médicale des ex-voto de la Seine," *Revue archéologique de l'Est et du Centre-Est* 9 (1958): 328–37; P. Lebel, "Complément à l'étude médicale des sources de la Seine," with a complementary note by P. Vassal, ibid., 13 (1962): 220–22.

4. S. Deyts, "Nouvelles figurations anatomiques en bois des sources de la Seine," *Revue Archéologique de l'Est et du Centre-Est* 20 (1969): 235–45.

5. It is not possible to make a study that would parallel P. A. Sigal's, "Miracles et guérisons au XIIe siècle," *Annales, E.S.C.* 24 (November-December 1969): 1522–39. In particular, it is not possible to draw up a map showing the geographical origin of the patients.

6. J. Albisson, *Contribution à l'étude des maladies d'origine professionelle en agriculture* (thesis in medicine, University of Paris, 1956), no. 143. In addition to the diseases listed in the official statistics, Albisson studies those that affect rural workers more frequently than other socioeconomic groups, suggesting that they be included in these statistics. Doctors Louis Fabre and Henri Arles of the Mutualité Agricole of Montpellier kindly examined for me the lists of agriculture-related occupational diseases, primarily in order to eliminate the diseases caused by contemporary chemicals. Their description of the symptoms and their knowledge of the after-effects of these diseases have been a great help to me.

7. E. Patlagean, *Recherches sur les pauvres et la pauvreté dans l'Empire romain d'Orient* (thesis in letters, University of Paris 1973), published by Service de reproduction des thèses de l'Université de Lille-III (1974), 1: 234–61.

8. Cf. Festugière, *Histoire générale des religions*, p. 136, n. 64.

9. Patlagean, *Recherches sur les pauvres*, p. 251.

10. Albisson, *Contribution*, p. 35.

11. P. A. Sigal, "Comment on conçevait et on traitait la paralysie en Occident dans le Haut Moyen Age (Ve–XIIe siècle)," *Revue d'Histoire des Sciences* : 193–211.

12. P. Gerbaut et al., "Le tétanos," in *Synthèses cliniques*, supplement to *Monographies médicales et scientifiques* 108 (December 1963): 53–55 in particular.

13. See the *Index nominorum* by Espérandieu, *Corpus inscriptionum latinarum*, vol. 13, III and *Revue Archéologique de l'Est et du Centre-Est* 9. One seal of an oculist named Balbinus was found in the department of Puy-de-Dôme: *Corpus inscriptionum latinarum*, vol. 13, part 3, 10,061, number 181. A pharmaceutical vessel found near Lapalisse comes from the dispensary of a certain Q. Julius Balbinus, who may have been the same man (ibid., 10, 011, 208). See Héron de Villefosse and E. Thédenat, "Note sur quelques cachets d'oculistes romains, *Bulletin monumental* (1881): 75–90, 259–85, 563–611 (1882): 5–55, 105–53, 603–718; (1883): 153–85, 308–59, for an analysis of names, remedies, and diseases.

14. J. Beaujeu, "La Médecine," in R. Taton, ed., *Histoire générale des sciences*, 1: 404: "The collections of authentic remedies and fanciful prescription disseminated by Pliny the Elder's *Historia naturalis* or gathered in Scribonius Largus's *Compositiones* need not be considered in a work on the history of science."

15. Marcellus, *De Medicamentis Liber*, in M. Niedermann ed., *Corpus Medicorum Latinorum*, (Leipzig-Berlin, 1916) vol. 5; also, cf. P.-M. Duval in *Les Sources de l'Histoire de France* (Paris, 1971), vol. 1, pt. 2, p. 630, bibliography.

16. Marcellus, "De Medicamentis," p. 3: "ab agrestibus et plebeis fortuita ac simplicia."

17. J.-J. Hatt, *Celtes et Gallo-Romains*, Collection Archeologia Mundi (Geneva, 1970), p. 300.

18. Ibid.

19. Ausonius, *Praefatiunculae*, V, 6. He married a girl from Dax, *Aquae Tarbellicae* and *Parentalia*, V, 12.

20. For the integration of druidic families into the Roman leadership structures at the beginning of the Empire, see M. Clavel-Léveque, "Le Synchrétisme gallo-romain: structures et finalités, in *Praelectiones patavinae* (Rome, 1972), pp. 113–14.

21. E. Thévenot, "Médecine et religion aux temps gallo-romains: le traitement des affections de la vue," *Latomus* 9 (1950): 416–20.

22. For example, in XV, 89: *Memineris ut mundus haec faciat.*

23. *Corpus inscriptionum latinarum*, vol. 12, 5, 367. This is Hirschfeld's reading, which

agrees with Bonnefoy's. A. Lebégue, in agreement with Bonnefoy, amended this reading and renders the inscription on the most complete of these disks as "Kantas Niskas, rogam (u)s et deprecamus (?) vos, et sanate." "Etude sur quelques inscriptions latines trouvées dans la Narbonnaise," *Revue Archéologique* (1882): 137.

24. For these formulas, see G. Dottin, *La Langue gauloise* (Paris, 1920), p. 214. Cf. P.-M. Duval, "Les Inscriptions gallo-grecques trouvées en France," *Actes du colloque sur les influences helléniques en Gaule* (Paris, 1958), pp. 63-69. See also bibliography of Marcellus's Gallic language in P.-M. Duval, *Les Sources de l'Histoire de France*, 1: 630-31.

25. Henry, "Lettre à Monsieur Prisse d'Avennes sur les inscriptions receuillies aux sources minérales d'Amélie-les-Bains," *Revue Archéologique* (1847): 409-14, which includes a facsimile that is all the more precious as the objects no longer exist.

26. R. Cagnet, "La Sorcellerie et les sorciers chez les Romains," *Annales du Musée Guimet: bibliothèque de vulgarisation* 15 (1903-04): 134-75. Although this article does not provide the actual references, many allusions to Marcellus can be recognized.

27. *Corpus inscriptionum latinarum*, vol. 13, III, 10, 029, 328, 6th ser. (1898), pp. 39-62.

28. C. Jullian, "La Question des piles," *Mémoires de la Société des Antiquaires de France*, vol. 57.

29. *Corpus inscriptionum latinarum*, vol. 12, 1,983. Iro Kajanto feels that this is an erotic epitaph: "Tu qui legis, vade in Appolinis lavari, quod ego cum conjuge feci, vellem sic adhuc possem." "Balnea, vina, Venus," in *Mélanges Renard*, vol. II, collection Latomus (Brussels, 1969).

30. Marcellus, *De Medicamentis* XXV for paralysis; XVII, 6 and I, 25-26 for *frenetici* and *lethargici*; *Medicina Plinii*, III, 18 for *lethargici* and III, 19 for *frenetici*.

31. See for example, M. Charcot, *La Foi qui guérit*, for ulcers and hysterical tumors; or Alexander, *La Médicine psychosomatique* (Paris, 1952).

32. I can only cite a fraction of the readings that have suggested or answered the questions I have asked of these texts. More useful to me than any history of medicine was *La Science dans l'Antiquité* by B. Farrington, French ed. (Paris, 1967). Similarly, J.-P. Valabréga's presentation of his *Théories psychosomatiques* (Paris, 1954) has influenced my work more profoundly than either specialized works or studies of individual cases of hysteria.

Ivan Illich's *Némesis médicale* (Paris, 1975) [Limits to Medicine] (London, 1976) contains, aside from a bibliography that focuses on the problem of healing and on the sick person rather than on advances in the knowledge of the human body, a number of ideas that the reader will recognize in the present study.

Concerning the superimposed explanation and its beneficial or harmful effect, J.-P. Valabréga, in *Théories psychosomatiques* (p. 44 ff.), presupposes that the explanation given is correct, i.e., scientifically correct, whereas in the present study I am dealing with explanations that are recognized as correct by the patient, whatever our opinion of their validity.

33. J. Fontaine, ed., *Vita Martini*, 19, 3, 1: 294-95.

34. Ibid., 2: 883 ff.

35. M. Renard, *Asklepios et Hygie en Gaule*, bibliography.

36. Paulinus of Nola, *Epithet*, 18, 9, Hartel, ed., *Corpus scriptorum ecclesiasticorum Latinorum*, 1: 136. It was written three years after his conversion, in 398. Cf. P. Fabre, *Essai sur la chronologie de l'oeuvre de de saint Paulin de Nole* (Strasbourg, 1948), p. 138.

37. H. Leclercq, s.v. *Exorciste*, in *Dictionnaire d'archéologie chrétienne et de liturgie*, ed. Cabrol and Leclercq 15 vols. (Paris, 1907-53), vol. 5, cols. 964-78.

38. K. F. Stroheker, *Der senatorische Adel im spätantiken Gallien* (Tübingen, 1948), p. 213. Cf. R. Etienne, "Flavius Sallustius et Secundus Salutius," R.E.A. 65 (1963): 104-13.

39. J. Bidez, *La Vie de l'empereur Julien* (Paris, 1942), p. 140.

40. E. Stein, *Histoire du Bas-Empire*, ed. J. R. Palanque (Paris, 1959), 1: 156.

41. Ibid., p. 158. Cf. Sulpicius Severus, *Chronica*, ed. Halm (Vienna, 1866).

42. Fontaine, ed., *Vita Martini*, 22: 661.

43. Council of Elvira, canon VI, in *Concilios Visigoticos et Hispano-Romanos*, ed. J. Vives (Barcelona, 1963), p. 3. Prudentius, *Contra Symmachum*, ed. M. Lavarende, Collection des Universités de France (1948), 3: 165, v. 165.

44. Fontaine, ed., *Vita Martini*, 1: 303. Cf. also J. Fontaine, "Une Clé littéraire de la Vita

Martini de Sulpice Sévère: la typologie prophétique," in *Mélanges Christine Mohrmann* (1963), pp. 84–96.

45. H. Leclercq, *Tours*, s.v. in *Dictionnaire d'archéologie chrétienne et de liturgie*, vol. 15, col. 2, 663. This inscription is not found in the *Corpus inscriptionum latinarum*, vol. 13 or in Le Blant, *Inscriptions de la Gaule*.

46. *Dialogues*, III, 3 and Leclercq, s.v. *Ampoule*, in *Dictionnaire d'archéologie chrétienne*, vol. 1.

47. Fontaine, ed., *Vita Martini*, in the form of a hypothesis.

48. On the occasion of the first resurrection, when all who were present, and Martin himself, became aware of his power. See *Vita Martini*, VII, 7; *Epithet* I, 5; *Dialogues*, I, 24, p. 177: "No one in Egypt is more powerful than Martin."

49. *Vita Martini*, passim and *Dialogues*, I, 23 and 27, and passim. Cf. Sulpicius Severus, *Chronica*, ed. Halm, index.

50. For unexpected cures in the context of mental illness, see, for example, H. Baruk, *Psychiatrie médicale, physiologique et expérimentale* (Paris, 1938), p. 633, 656–57; Jeanne Aboudrar, "Contribution à l'étude des guérisons inattendues au cours des maladies mentales" (thesis in medicine, University of Paris, 1964), no. 48. The problem of psychosomatic illnesses is evoked in most of the works on this subject. Bibliography in Valabréga, *Théories psychosomatiques*.

51. See Jobbé, *Les Morts malfaisants, Larves, Lémures, d'après le droit et les croyances populaires des Romains* (Paris, 1924); E. Masseneau, *La Magie dans l'Antiquité romaine* (Paris, 1934), p. 77 ff.

52. Thévenot, "Médecine et religion," p. 421 ff. and "Le Dieu cavalier, Mithra et Apollon, leurs affinités dans les cultes gallo-romains," *La Nouvelle Clio* 1/2 (1949): 615.

53. Wuensch, *Defixionum tabellae* (1897); R. Heim, *Incantamenta magica graeca et latina* (Leipzig, 1902).

54. P. Guiraud, *Psychiatrie générale* (Paris, 1950), p. 532.

7

The Birth of a Parisian Legend: The Miracle of Le Lendit

Anne Lombard-Jourdain

The miracle of Le Lendit is essentially Parisian. A host, stolen from the church of Saint-Gervais in Paris along with a ciborium and hidden by the thief on the road to Saint-Denis, was miraculously recovered in the Plain of Le Lendit by the assembled clergy of the two towns. The event seems to have been recorded only by two early seventeenth-century historians of Paris, Du Breul and Doublet.[1] Both assigned to it the date 1274, which was given by an inscription in the lower part of a stained-glass window in the church of Saint-Gervais. Their accounts are commentaries on this window, which no longer exists today.

An oral or written tradition can be the source of a work of art. On the other hand, legends are often spawned by an iconographic theme, by more or less artful or cleverly interpreted pictorial representations. Many examples exist of the interaction between sources of a literary character and pictorial monuments, and it appears that if a story can give rise to a work of art, the latter can also be the source of a legend. Which was the case here? It is interesting to observe in some detail how, on the basis of a pictorial stained-glass window and the meanings that could be given to it, the account of an event was embellished and exploited for purposes of edification. Nor is it without interest to use the example at hand to compare the credulity and the taste for the marvelous in vogue in the early seventeenth century with the critical attitude of Félibien a century later. In this particular case, finally, it is possible to give a precise account of the actual event, thanks to the discovery of a perfectly authentic and trustworthy text.

The "great stained-glass window" in which the story of the miracle was de-

Annales, E.S.C. 28 (July-August 1973): 981–96. Translated by Elborg Forster

picted "naively" but "at great length" decorated Saint-Pierre's chapel in the church of Saint-Gervais of Paris for almost two centuries. This chapel opened onto the north collateral aisle between the chapel of Saint-Magdalen and the chapel of Saint-Geneviève.[2] Built as part of the enlargement of the church undertaken by the vestry board of the church, it was completed in 1510, the year when Marie Favart, widow of Nicolas Leclerc, donated for the chapel the window that represented the miracle of Le Lendit.[3]

The donor of the window had been buried in Saint-Pierre's chapel. One of her descendants, François de Belin, councillor of the king, wished to be buried beside her.[4] In order to be included in the prayers said for Marie Favart, and "in order to manifest, continue, and renew every year the marvel of the said miracle," he founded on 23 June 1624 a low mass and an evening or vesper service to be celebrated every other year on 1 September in honor of the Eucharist. These services would complement the high mass sung every year in the choir of the church. The act of foundation, which has come down to us,[5] describes in detail the different services, the gratifications for the numerous members of the clergy who were to officiate, and the hymns that were to be sung, among them an *Exaudiat* as a prayer for the King." But the most interesting proviso for our purposes is the following: the low mass in honor of the Eucharist to be said in Saint-Pierre's chapel will be celebrated "by a preacher to be chosen learned and capable, and who will at the end of the said mass preach a sermon on the subject of the procession, the office of the said day, or [propound] other teachings on the miracles and effects of the said Eucharist." Surely the sermon preached in Saint-Pierre's chapel in full view of the "great window" of 1510 must often have treated the theme of the miracle of Le Lendit, embroidered upon the event, and commented on the details of the colorful transparent picture that the audience had before its eyes.

Du Breul in 1608 and Doublet in 1625 still saw this window in the church. At the time when Félibien wrote, in 1706, it had been removed "a few years ago." In fact, it disappeared, along with the opening that held it, during the construction of a chapel referred to as M. de Harley's chapel in Willaume's floorplan of 1735.[6] Chancellor Louis Boucherat, N. A. Harley's father-in-law, had a large opening made in the back wall of Saint-Pierre's chapel, which held the stained-glass window, in order to give access to the new chapel, where he was also buried in 1699. The stained-glass panel depicting the miracle of Le Lendit thus decorated a window in the church of Saint-Gervais between 1510 and 1699. Doublet cites the eight verses included in the picture, which he was "hardly" able to read:

In one thousand two hundred and seventy-four
When Saint Louis the king had died,
And when his son Philip ruled without fail

The miracle shown here occurred:
See how the good bishop of Paris
To the Plain of Lendit led his flock
For the sake of the body of Jesus
Purloined at Saint-Gervais by a thief.[7]

As for the scene depicted, we can imagine it rather well, thanks to the details furnished by both Du Breul and Doublet. It showed the host suspended in the air "by its own power" and ready to descend "onto the book" of the priest of Saint-Gervais, "as the processions arrived one by one at the field of Le Lendit" (Du Breul) or "as the processions arrived, among them that of Saint-Gervais" (Doublet). The master window maker had depicted the clergy of Notre-Dame and of the Parisian parishes, as well as the monks of Saint-Denis, passing in solemn procession before the multitude lining the road that cut through the Plain of Le Lendit near the *Leaning Cross*.

Du Breul's and Doublet's narratives are explanatory commentaries on the stained-glass window of 1510. Neither of them mentions another source. The memory of the miracle was kept alive in the minds of the faithful by the clergy of Saint-Gervais. Every year on 1 September, the anniversary of the day when the host was recovered, the clergy carried the Eucharist in procession around the church and then celebrated a solemn mass in its honor in the choir of the church. Moreover, as we have seen, a low mass including a sermon and an evening service were added in 1624, thanks to F. de Belin's foundation.

Let us now follow the elaboration of the legend. Under the title "Consecrated host miraculously elevated into the air for a long time," J. Du Breul tells the following story.

In the year 1274 the church of Saint-Gervais and Saint-Prothais was robbed during the night and, among other things, the thief took the sacred vessel holding the holy host and fled toward Saint-Denis. When he came to the field of Le Lendit, he began to smash the sacred vessel and at once the host flew off, flitting through the air in pursuit of the thief. When this was noticed by some passersby, they judged that it must be an act of God and therefore apprehended the thief who had the vessel. Informed of these happenings, the Abbot of Saint-Denis arrived on the scene with some of his monks and saw the sacred host still hovering in the air over the spot where the thief had been arrested. He ordered the thief to be taken to prison and soon after had him hanged and strangled on the gibbet of Saint-Denis. Nor did he fail to inform the bishop of Paris. Deeply impressed by such a great marvel, the bishop led a procession of his clergy to that spot, where the said abbot with his monks was already present. And when a number of hymns and lauds had been sung in honor of the said Eucharist, as the processions arrived each in its turn at the field of Le Lendit, it came to pass that the said host, suspended in the air, miraculously descended into the hands of the priest of Saint-Gervais and Saint-Prothais, causing great wonder among an infinite multitude of people who were there. Now there was contention between the abbot and the bishop as to who should have the host; the abbot wanting it because it was recovered on his land the bishop claiming it because it had been stolen in his city. In the end, it was agreed between them that it should go to the priest of Saint-Gervais as being his, considering that he had consecrated it. This with the proviso that he would celebrate or cause to be celebrated on every Friday of the year a high mass in honor of the Eucharist and that every year on the first day of September (the day when the said host was recovered) there would be held in the choir of that church the solemn service of the Eucharist and a procession around the church in which the Eucharist would be carried with all honor and reverence. And this is observed to this day, for every Friday there is sung in this church the mass in honor of the Eucharist, while in other churches it is said on Thursdays. And every year on 1 September a service is held as it is said above.

The story of the said miracle is depicted naively in a stained-glass window of Saint-Pierre's chapel in that church, which also shows some French verses telling a part of that story.

Doublet for his part also tells the story of the miracle of Le Lendit in his *Histoire de l'abbaye royale de Saint-Denis*, published in 1625. His account is considerably longer and more elaborate than Du Breul's; he offers a different interpretation of the window, and his account has the ring of a sermon. Recall that François de Belin's foundation was made on 23 June 1624. One wonders whether Doublet simply recorded the disquisitions of the preacher who gave the sermon on 1 September 1624, whether he recorded his own sermon, or even whether he meant to compose a sermon for the use of future orators. It is difficult to decide this question, but in any case he endeavored to amplify the story for purposes of edification.

He describes how the thief "stole *from the altar* the sacred ciborium *of gilded silver* containing the sacro-sanct host, which he went off to bury" at Le Lendit at the foot of the cross known in the seventeenth century under the name of the "Boundary Cross" [*Croix aux Fins*] or "Leaning Cross" [*Croix Penchée*].[8] The clergies of Notre-Dame of Paris and Saint-Gervais, on the one hand, and the monks of Saint-Denis, on the other—and here Doublet adds "the Court of Parlement in its red robes"—assembled in the Plain of Le Lendit. At that point "a dispute arose between the reverend Bishop of Paris and the venerable Abbot of Saint-Denis as to which of the two was entitled to lift up that sacred host for the reasons each of them alleged":

Once the place was found, and as the processions filed in, among them that of Saint-Gervais, o great and admirable marvel of the all-powerful nature of the divine presence and infinite Deity contained within that sacred viaticum, which by its own power had risen out of the ground and remained suspended in the air, it descended upon the book held by the priest of the church of Saint-Gervais, who reverently carried it back to the said church.

Du Breul had taken it for granted that the host had flown away in order not to be touched by the hands of the thief and that it had hovered in the air until the arrival of the priest of Saint-Gervais who had consecrated it. Doublet supposes that it was buried at Le Lendit by the thief and that it was able "by its own power" to "rise out of the ground" and to alight by God's will on the book held by the priest. Doublet thus slightly modifies the manner in which the miracle has occurred, but he does so with the purpose of lending credence to a second miracle. For he also wants to explain the "leaning" of the "Boundary Cross", which stood by the Estrée [road] between Paris and Saint-Denis, halfway between the two towns.

This cross marked the line dividing the abbey's road system and its jurisdiction from those of the city of Paris and the king.[9] It is shown on the oldest maps of the Plain,[10] and is often mentioned in boundary cases. Whoever traveled to Saint-Denis from Paris passed it. It was near the Boundary Cross that the gatekeeper of Saint-Denis would greet the bishop of Paris when he came to give the benediction at the opening of the fair of Le Lendit.[11] It was here that the same bishop, coming from Paris, would deliver to the abbot of Saint-Denis the remains of the kings and queens of France before they were enterred in the basilica;[12] and it was also in the vicinity of this cross that all important visitors were customarily received. It was called *Croix aux Fins, aux Fiens, Aux Feins,* or *Crux ad Fines*, that is, cross at the boundaries, and later *Croix qui penche* [the cross that leans], *Croix penchante* [leaning Cross], or *Crois du Lendit*. No pictorial representation of it has come down to us; and the stained-glass window of Saint-Gervais may have been the only one that ever existed.

We do know, however, exactly where the cross stood on the Estrée to Saint-Denis, and we know its size. Located a little ways south of the present impasse Chevalier, it was originally on the right side of the old Estrée, and later, after the road had been straightened in the first half of the eighteenth century,[13] on the left side of the avenue. Made of stone, it was "about twelve feet," or four meters tall. It owed its name to its "considerable inclination toward the said place of La Chapelle."[14] Sauval specified that "there was perhaps nothing remarkable about it, except that in order to kiss it standing at its base with one's feet closed, one had to hold onto it with one's hands."[15] It disappeared at the time of the Revolution.[16]

In 1624, François de Belin simply said that the host had been hidden "in a certain place on the road to Saint-Denis in France, from whence it miraculously and by its own volition took to the air." When Doublet brought in the Leaning Cross he may have done no more than record one of the popular beliefs that somehow spring up and gain credence. It is quite possible that travelers and passersby who followed the Estrée from Paris to Saint-Denis had already come up with the idea that the stone cross was tenderly and respectfully bowing to the Redeemer's body. It is also possible that the Parisian artist who executed the "great stained-glass window" of Saint-Gervais, wishing to locate the miracle precisely in the Plain of Le Lendit, which he "describes and depicts at great length" in his work, pictured the Leaning Cross because it was known to every Parisian. Whether Doublet accepted an assumption set before the parishioners of Saint-Germain every day in the glass image, or whether he propounded an idea of his own, he gladly seized upon this topic because he saw it as an additional means of edifying the faithful. "At this moment (o what a great and admirable occurrence!) it [the cross] bowed in reverence for its creator, which should make men blush with shame, who are more ungrateful in truth, more hard-hearted and more unfeeling than that stone when they do not want to recognize and adore their Lord and Savior in this most divine viaticum. . . . " Here Doublet's account goes one step further than the stories of miracles involving animals, which show horses, asses, oxen, bees, or dogs kneeling down before the Eucharist.[17] He shows an inanimate object manifesting its respect and adoration.

To the first miracle, the autonomous movement of the host, Doublet thus adds a second one, the respectful "leaning" of the cross. This is what Félibien understood in 1706 when he made use of Doublet's account.[18] "A year later [1274]," he writes, "we are told of a *two-fold* miracle which is said to have occurred on this occasion." Having told the story from Doublet's perspective, he gives free rein to his critical attitude:

Here we have a well-detailed story; yet it is to be wished that it were justified by *better proofs*. We hear *nothing about it in Guillaume de Nangis who lived at that time, nor in any of his continuators, even though they were very keen to record any unusual events*. Doublet does not adduce any other testimony aside from the stained-glass window of Saint-Gervais, where this story was depicted a few years earlier. These windows were *not old, as one can clearly see from the verses that appeared in them*. Moreover, everyone knows that *painters have always felt free to embellish the simplest stories with their own fictions*. All that we can conclude is that *the substance of the story seems to be true, but that the miracles look very much like a fable*. At the least, it cannot be denied that the proofs given are too slight to deserve any credence. Every year on 1 September a solemn service to commemorate the event is held in the church of Saint-Gervais; it seems to have been *instituted only with the aim of giving permanence to the act of atonement offered at the time to the desecrated host*.

This is a fine example of prudence and critical thinking on the part of Félibien. All the circumstances and possibilities are considered, all the so-called proofs are reduced to their true worth. Félibien calls attention to Guillaume de Nangis and his continuators and to the fact that the verses inscribed at the bottom of the stained-glass window and transcribed by Doublet are not "old," that is, written at the time of the event or shortly thereafter. As we have seen, they date from 1510. Nonetheless, Félibien concludes that if the details of the "miracle" seem fabulous, "the substance of the story seems to be true." We shall see that he was correct.

At the very time when the master glassmaker delivered his window to the church of Saint-Gervais, another artist also treated the theme of the miracle of Le Lendit. He was the designer of the cartoons for a series of tapestries woven for the choir of the church of Notre-Dame-du-Ronceray of Angers. Twenty-one scenes unfold on a tapestry 24.35 meters long and approximately 1.90 meters high. Unfortunately, this magnificent work, representing *La Figure et la Verité du Saint-Sacrement*,[19] was cut up and dispersed on the occasion of a sale on 2 October 1889.[20] The *Miracle du Lendit** was one of two panels bought by the Musée des Gobelins. It is preserved today in the Dépôt du mobilier national [National furniture collection].[21]

The first panel of the complete tapestry of Le Ronceray bore the coat of arms and the initials of Ysabelle de la Jaille, who was abbess of Le Ronceray from 1505 to 1518. We also know the donor, Louise Le Roux, from the abbey's obituary, which says: "decana et cameraria, quae donavit huic ecclesiae aulae sanctissimi Sacramenti figuris illustria." She died in 1523. Thus, the tapestry was executed between 1505 and 1523, and the cartoons were designed at the very time when the master glassmaker conceived the "great stained-glass window" of Saint-Pierre's chapel in the church of Saint-Gervais.[22]

The panel that concerns us here is occupied by a group of nine ecclesiastics forming a circle around the host, which is shown suspended in the air. One can recognize the bishop of Paris by his mitre and crozier and behind him the abbot of Saint-Denis. Some of the priests are shown with their hands folded, while others express their astonishment. To the right and in the foreground, the priest of Saint-Gervais, one knee touching the ground, prepares to receive the stolen host on his prayer book. Next to him a kneeling choirboy holds a candle. The sky, the trees, and the ground covered with grasses and flowers convey an outdoor atmosphere. In the upper corners of the tapestry two small scenes are designed to locate the miracle at Le Lendit and also to relate the earlier phases of the occurence. To the left one sees the thief, carrying the ciborium in his hands, climbing out of the window of the church of Saint-Gervais onto the roof of a neighboring house. In order to evoke the church of Saint-Gervais the artist has represented the chapel of Our Lady, which had just been built, as we know from the date, 1517, on the keystone of the arch. One recognizes one of its large windows, the shape of its broad roof, its heavy buttresses, and the houses nestled against its south-eastern side. "On this side the church was hemmed in by properties which had to be obtained through charitable donations."[23] The refurbishing and enlargement of the church had not progressed for more than a hundred years. In the right-hand corner of the tapestry the thief is depicted burying the stolen host along a road lead-

---

*For the actual illustration, see the original article in *Annales E.S.C.* 28 (July-August 1973): facing p. 982.

ing to Saint-Denis, which is seen far away in the blue distance. The route leads to a gate in the ramparts, of which one round tower is visible. In order to represent the abbey the artist has chosen to show "Suger's Gate," of which this is the oldest representation. It is clearly recognizable by the two large towers that jut out from it on either side, covered with watch turrets and separated by a high crenelated wall enclosing the gate. Behind it other identifiable buildings appear. The gate constructed by Suger to serve as the main entrance to the abbey was situated in its southwestern wing. It was destroyed in 1779. The first structure seen by those who arrived from Le Lendit, it appears in all the bird's-eye views drawn in the sixteenth, seventeenth, and eighteenth centuries, and some good pictures of it from the eighteenth century have come down to us.[24] The tapestry is framed on both sides by decorative columns, and a four line inscription below, executed in Gothic letters on red background, identifies the scene:

> From Saint-Germain a thief stole the host
> Which he hid at Le Lendit.
> The bishop of Paris went after it, and the abbot of Saint-Denis, too,
> But it was for the priest of the said place.

The miracle of Le Lendit would be known to us only from its pictorial representation in the tapestry of Le Ronceray, from the commentaries on a vanished stained-glass window by Du Breul and Doublet, and by the learned criticism of these texts by Félibien were it not for a manuscript of Rouen that has happily preserved an exact account of the facts. The author of the *Chronique parisienne anonyme de 1316 à 1339* was no doubt a member of the legal profession (barrister or attorney) and lived in the township of Saint-Denis.[25] An eyewitness to the event, he soberly and objectively recorded it as follows:

And in that very year, on Tuesday the feast-day of the Beheading of Saint John the Baptist [29 August 1329], a thief born in Auvergne, to his own misfortune, purloined in the church of Saint-Gervais of Paris, after high mass was sung there, a chalice containing twenty-four consecrated hosts, and proceeded to carry his booty to Saint-Denis; and as he was on his way, he took the chalice and broke it into several pieces. Arrived in that town, he took it to a goldsmith in order to sell it, and the goldsmith caught him right away. At Saint-Denis, where he was put into prison, he confessed to Robert Le Basnier, at the time bailiff of Saint-Denis, in the presence of several others, that he had purloined the said chalice and its contents in the church of Saint-Gervais in Paris, as well as several other thefts, such as of silver bowls and other items, together with twenty-four of his accomplices. When all of this had been found out and reported to the priest of Saint-Gervais, named Adam,[26] on Friday the first day of September, the said consecrated and blessed hosts were humbly returned to the said Monsieur Adam, priest of Saint-Gervais, by the abbot of Saint-Denis, Guy de Chaate-soubs-Mont-le-Hery,[27] and taken to Paris accompanied by a great crowd of people and many torches in a huge joyful procession which carried them to the said church of Saint-Gervais with full honors. And the above-said thief, on that Friday, at the hour of prime, in the presence of a great multitude from Paris and Saint-Denis, was hung for thievery from the highest gibbet of Saint-Denis.[28]

This unique and truthful account has until now gone unnoticed by the historians of Paris. In fact, even its editor fails to make any connection between the events it records and the miracle of Le Lendit.[29] Let us compare the objective account of the facts with the legend and try to discern how the legend came into being.

To begin with, the anonymous author provides us with an exact date: 29 August 1329. But the people of Paris and Saint-Denis remembered only that the sacrilege, the hanging of the thief, and the atonement procession took place "in the days of king Philip." This is why in 1510, when the master glassmaker was asked by Marie Favart to give form to the miracle of Le Lendit, inscribed it with the date 1274, substituting for Philip VI of Valois, Philip III (the Bold), son of Saint Louis. By contrast, the founding of an atonement ceremony to be celebrated every year in the church of Saint-Gervais correctly preserved the memory of the day and the month: 1 September.

The thief stole from the church of Saint-Gervais, "after high mass was sung there"—in other words, in broad daylight—a chalice containing twenty-four consecrated hosts. But people imagined that he *broke into the church at night*, stealing a ciborium *of gilded silver*, containing *one* host.

The contemporary chronicler of the fact simply stated that the thief, anxious to negotiate the chalice, made a clumsy effort to break it up into pieces as soon as he left Paris behind, although he did not succeed in making it unrecognizable to the expert eye of the goldsmith of Saint-Denis, to whom he offered it for sale and who had him arrested. In prison, he eventually made a full confession. None of this is in any way improbable. "And as he was on his way to Saint-Denis, he took the chalice and broke it into several pieces." Not a word is said about the precise spot where the thief broke the ciborium. Nor is anything said about the twenty-four consecrated hosts it contained. We are only told that they were returned three days later, on Friday, 1 September, by the abbot of Saint-Denis to the priest of Saint-Gervais, and that they were conveyed to Paris in a solemn procession followed by a multitude of people. No mention is made of the presence of the bishop of Paris on this occasion. But we do learn that the thief was hanged from the highest gibbet of Saint-Denis, which stood at Le Lendit, on that same Friday at about six o'clock in the morning, in the presence of the crowd that had flocked there from Paris and Saint-Denis. The author is so scrupulous about his facts that he even tells us that the criminal was from Auvergne and mentions the names of important officials of the time: Gui de la Chaate sous Montlhéry, the abbot of Saint-Denis, Adam, the priest of Saint-Gervais, and Robert Le Basanier, the bailiff of Saint-Denis.

Succeeding generations were more interested in the fate of the stolen host than in the thief. The precise details recorded by the author of the *Chronique anonyme*, such as the thief's place of origin, the exact time of the theft, the intervention of the goldsmith, and even the execution of the criminal, were forgotten when, at the end of the fifteenth century and the beginning of the sixteenth, the efforts at enlarging and beautifying the building undertaken by the vestry board of the church of Saint-Gervais focused attention on every aspect of the parish's history. To the popular imagination there was something miraculous about the recovery of the host that was still preserved at Saint-Gervais[30] and honored every year on "Restitution Day," celebrated on 1 September.[31]

In 1510 a female parishioner of Saint-Gervais wished to donate a stained-glass window to illuminate the recently completed chapel of Saint-Pierre. Advised no doubt by the clergy of the parish, she chose the subject matter for it: the miracle of Le Lendit. At that very time the author of the cartoons for the tapestries commissioned by the abbey of Le Ronceray of Angers also depicted this miracle in the series of miracles attributed to the Eucharist. It does not seem possible to me that one of these two craftsmen could have taken his inspiration from the other or that both of them could have used the same pre-existing model. Each of them has his own way of imagining and representing the mystery, and the resulting scenes are quite different in character.

In order to suggest that Le Lendit is located "halfway," the tapestry maker places the chapel of Our Lady that was recently built onto the apsis of the church of Saint-Gervais to the left, and to the right "Suger's Gate" at Saint-Denis. The glassmaker, for his part, sets the "Leaning Cross" into the center of the composition, since it was well known to all Parisians.

In order to tell the story of the miracle, the tapestry maker shows a group of important personages, ecclesiastics in their vestments, standing in a circle ready to receive the host suspended in the air and about to descend onto the book held by the priest of Saint-Gervais. The glassmaker, on the other hand, depicts the processions of the clergies of Paris and Saint-Denis as they arrive at Le Lendit. They reminded the viewers, to be sure, of the processions that set out to recover the miraculous host, but also of those that accompanied and greeted the bishop of Paris when he came to the Plain of Le Lendit each year in June to give the benediction at the opening of the fair.

G. de Tervarent was able to find the sources that inspired each of the panels of the Le Ronceray tapestry except in one case: that of the miracle of Le Lendit. It is not found in any of the collections of *exempla* that circulated at the time, recording proofs of the truth of the Eucharist taken from "the most obscure nooks and crannies of the Christian literature."[32] Moreover, in the original complete tapestry, the miracle of Le Lendit came immediately after another Parisian miracle, which is also attested by historical texts and represented on stained-glass windows.[33] This is the story of the sacrilege committed by the Jew Jean, or Jonathas, who in 1290 made a poor woman bring him a consecrated host which he stabbed and boiled; the host bled but emerged unharmed from these trials. This miracle was widely known in the Middle Ages and exists in a number of variants. *Le Jeu et Mystère de la Sainte Hostie*[34] had an enormous influence on the pictorial representations and the written versions of the story of the sacrilegious Jew. A version of it in French verse, printed in Paris between 1547 and 1568,[35] was certainly known to Gilles Corozet. Without pretending to trace the historical evolution of this other miracle,[36] I simply wish to point out here that it exerted considerable influence on the themes of the miracle of Le Lendit that was elaborated slightly later. This case is an interesting illustration of the phenomenon of contamination.

Gilles Corrozet was the first of the "historians" of Paris to mention the Jew's crime in the 1550 edition of his *Antiquités, histoires et singularités de Paris*.[37] The miracle of Le Lendit appeared only sixty years later, in the additions to the 1608 edition of Pierre Bonfons's *Antiquitez et choses plus remarquable de Paris*,[38] written by an octogenarian monk of Saint-Germain-des-Prés, Jacques Du Breul. It appears that many of the details of Du Breul's story are visibly inspired by Corrozet. The host, tossed into the fire by the Jew, "jumped out and flitted through the house"; when plunged into the kettle of boiling water, "through the power of the divine majesty it made itself visible in the chimney in the form of Our Lord Jesus crucified." In Du Breul's account of the miracle of Le Lendit the host flies about in the same manner, far from any contact. Doublet would make it come out of the ground unaided.

In the *Miracle of the Billettes*, a woman goes to the Jew's house to ask for fire in order to find out what is happening there and "having entered the said place, the host alighted in her little vessel," that is, a receptacle in which to carry embers.[39] At Le Lendit the host would descend unaided onto the book carried by the priest of Saint-Gervais.

The host that had been profaned by the Jew was promptly carried to the church of Saint-Jean-en-Grève, "where this host is still preserved, as one can see it depicted on the outside of the apsis of the said church."[40] A sculptural representation on the outside of the choir of Saint-Jean thus indicates the presence of the miraculous host within. This sculpture plays a role analogous to Marie Favart's stained-glass window at Saint-Gervais.

A court of law "found the host sound and whole" after its profanation by the Jew. Doublet was to add "the court of Parlement in red robes" to the processions that converged at Le Lendit.

Every year in June the miraculous host of Saint-Jean-en-Grève was carried through Paris in solemn procession, and on the first Sunday after Easter the chapel of Our Lady "of the Billettes," which had replaced the chapel of atonement, exhibited the "penknife" with which the Jew had "stabbed" the host.[41]

As we have seen, a procession of the Eucharist around the church of Saint-Gervais took place every year on 1 September.

Marie Favart's donation in 1510 and Sieur de Belin's foundation in 1624 testify to the fervor of the parishioners of Saint-Gervais and to the vitality of the miracle of Le Lendit. Yet it is certain that its reputation did not spread beyond Paris. Its memory was strictly localized. The stained-glass window of Saint-Gervais and the tapestry of Le Ronceray are its only known pictorial representations.[42] It is not mentioned anywhere but at Saint-Gervais or by anyone but the historians of Paris. If it was normal that it should be represented in the church from which the host was stolen and where a "Festival of Restitution" was celebrated every year, its appearance among the miracles of the Eucharist in the tapestry executed for the abbey of Le Ronceray is more surprising.

The scholars who studied this tapestry had varying views about its origin. L. de Farcy in 1889 thought that it was executed in Arras or Paris; H. C. Marillier in 1931 considered it a work from Touraine; G. de Tervarent in 1933 felt that he was dealing with Flemish workmanship.[43] To me, it seems more likely that it came from a Parisian workshop. A number of powerful arguments support my contention: (1) the miracle takes place in the plain north of Paris; (2) it was totally unknown outside the city proper and is not included in any of the collections of *exempla* that were usually consulted by the artists of the time; (3) in the series of tapestries of Le Ronceray it is shown next to another Parisian miracle, that of the "Billettes"; and (4) in order to situate the miracle between Paris and Saint-Denis, the author of the cartoons pictured in a very recognizable form two monuments that were well known to all Parisians, the Lady chapel at Saint-Gervais and "Suger's Gate."

The eyewitness account of the *Chronique parisienne anonyme* was not well known and the tapestry had been taken to Angers when Du Breul and Doublet produced their versions of the miracle of Le Lendit based on the stained-glass window of Saint-Pierre's chapel and the traditions extant among the people and the clergy of the parish of Saint-Gervais. Du Breul said that the host, refusing to be touched, fluttered in the air, thereby attracting the attention of the passersby and accusing the guilty party. Doublet imagined that the thief hid the host in the ground at the foot of the stone cross at Le Lendit, causing the cross to lean over piously, as could still be observed by everyone. Moreover, both of them invented out of the blue, each adding his own details, the ensuing dispute over the ownership of the miraculous host between the bishop of Paris and the abbot of Saint-Denis, which was a simple transposition of the many conflicts between them that had sprung up over the ages, precisely at Le Lendit.

In this manner we have been able to follow the transformation of a minor crime into a miracle, from the straightforward journal entry of an *honnête*

homme in the early sixteenth century to the literary developments added by
the seventeenth-century historians of Paris, by way of the pictorial representations of sixteenth-century artists and the indications furnished by a notarized document.

In explaining this transformation, one must first of all see the efforts to
validate the legend in the context of the needs faced by the clergy of the time.
The *Jeu et Mystère de la saincte hostie* was written and performed in order to
obtain contributions from the spectators as much as to explain the deposition
of the relic at Saint-Jean-en-Grève and to authenticate the "penknife" exhibited at Notre-Dame-des-Billettes. At the end of the performance one of the
actors addressed the spectators, to remind them that certain indulgences had
been accorded:

> . . . one hundred days will go to those
> Who willingly will give
> To have this holy jewel encased;
> God will reward them fair and square.
> And also now, good people here
> Be sure you don't forget
> That you have seen before your eyes
> A miracle great, not play:
> Do not forget it, if you please,
> And serve it with all your heart,
> By keeping up its brotherhood,
> Which surely is in proper place
> Where all this came to pass.

Collections were also taken at Saint-Gervais to complete the building of the
church, which had long been under way. Sermons exposing the history and
the virtues of the miraculous host inspired the faithful to give generously.

Oral traditions travel in all directions, become deformed, and can easily
die. But it so happened that various preachers, a playwright, and finally two
chroniclers gave to this tradition the pleasing form, complete with pictur-
esque and easily retained details, that made its fortune. Nonetheless, the
themes used by all of them were essentially the same. They were copied from
one work to the next, as if their familiar character made them true and as if
the authors were careful, from semiconscious deference rather than from
lack of imagination, not to improvise too freely in treating these edifying subjects.[44] The existing legends were collected, altered, and contaminated at the
time when the first "historians" of Paris were hard at work gathering, recording, and shaping them for their contemporaries and for posterity. The
Parisians' avid curiosity about their past, attested by the many guides to and
histories of their city dating from the sixteenth and early seventeenth centuries,
kindled the authors' zeal.

This was the time when all the *Antiquités, Choses remarquables,* or *Singu-*

larités of Paris assumed a form that would subsequently remain essentially unchanged. The *"verités"* established once and for all by Gilles Corrozet, Nicolas or Pierre Bonfons, and Jacques Du Breul would henceforth be repeated over and over again or endlessly paraphrased even until our own time, although in the eighteenth century some learned theologians, such as Dom Félibien and abbé Lebeuf, showed considerable reluctance to accept them.[45] Surely it is an old truth that a good story will always have more success with the public and with the writers that cater to it than straightforward facts.

The preceding analysis should motivate the reader to use the prudence that Félibien had already advocated in 1706. In the case of the miracle of Le Lendit, would we have been able to cut through the interpolations of Du Breul and Doublet without the unique text fortuitously preserved in the Rouen manuscript? Let us therefore be wary of proofs "too slight to deserve credence." But let us also be careful not to bring an excessively or totally negative attitude to apparently fabulous stories. Let us keep in mind, as Félibien recommends, that the "substance of the story" may be "true." A tradition, even one that has sprung up long after the fact and is suspect on this ground alone, may suddenly be confirmed by the discovery of archeological remains or a text. In this respect, the early Christian era is an inexhaustible reservoir of examples.[46] Certain legends are so far-fetched and their vicissitudes so fantastic that one is inclined to dismiss them out of hand; yet they are often imbedded in their place and time by a small element of truth: the name of a hero or the name of a place, the memory of a vanished building whose vestiges may come to light in an excavation,[47] a religious or legal tradition: all of these can bear witness to a people's roots in its soil and to the currents that have shaped its mentality.

APPENDIX

Foundation by François de Belin of several offices and ceremonies to be celebrated in Saint-Pierre's chapel of the church of Saint-Gervais in Paris.

Was present in person *noble homme* M[e]. François de Belin, councilor of the King and his attorney general, supervisor of the War-office in the governments of Paris and Ile-de-France, saying that it is well-known to all and sundry that by an old custom and a laudible tradition the reverend priests of the church of Saint-Gervais in Paris are under the obligation, which to this day they have always carried out, to have celebrated on every Friday of the year a high mass in honor of the Holy Eucharist and to hold every year on the first day of September a solemn procession, to carry the said Holy Eucharist in this procession, and to celebrate thereafter in the choir of the said church the mass of the Holy Eucharist in memory and thanksgiving of the miracle that occurred in Paris on the first day of September of the year M CC LXXIIII and of the recovery on the said day of the Holy Host which had been purloined in the said church and carried surrepticiously to a place on the road to Saint-Denis in France, whence it miraculously and by its own volition took to the air within sight of Messieurs the bishop of Paris, the abbot of the said Saint-Denis in France, the priest of the said church of Saint-Gervais, their clergies and an infi-

Source: Archives Nationales. Paris. Minutier Central, XXVI, no. 49, 23 June 1624.

nite number of people, as is depicted in the great stained-glass window of Saint-Pierre's chapel in the said church, which was given by the late dame Marie Favart, widow of Nicolas Leclerc, Bourgeois of Paris, as attested by the receipt of payment for the said window, produced by the said Sr. Belin, for the amount of one hundred and forty livres, dated 8 november one thousand five hundred and ten. Inspired by the zeal and charity of the said widow his predecessor, and wishing to be included in the prayers said for her, as well as in order to manifest more strongly, to continue and to renew each year the marvel of the said miracle by some acts of devotion, instruction, and public prayers beyond those that have already been instituted, the said Sr. Belin has by his right, pure, free and unrestrained will founded, and does herewith found, perpetually and for all times, in the said church of Saint-Gervais, and in every year on the first day of September, a low mass of the Holy Eucharist for or in memory of the said Sr. Belin in the said Saint-Pierre's chapel of the said church of Saint-Gervais, which mass shall be said and celebrated by a preacher who will be chosen learned and capable, and who will at the end of the said mass preach a sermon on the subject of the procession, the office of the said day or [propound] other teachings on the miracles and effects of the said holy Eucharist; and at the closing of this sermon the said preacher will recommend [to the audience] to pray God for the soul of the founder of the sermon, and the faithful will be called to the said sermon by the big bell; the preacher will be given six livres tournois and his assistant five sols tournois.

Item, [a foundation is made] for singing an evening or vesper service in honor of the said Holy Eucharist, to begin with the singing of the *Veni Creator* and to end, after a procession around the church in which the said Holy Eucharist is not carried, with the singing of the *Exaudiat* as a prayer for the King, the *Salve Regina* and the prayers to the Virgin and, lastly, a *Libera* and *De Profundis* as the customary prayers for the dead in Saint-Pierre's chapel over the tomb of Sr. de Belin or his predecessors. Present at this evening service or prayer for the dead will be the following gentlemen: the parish priest, his vicar, two deacons, four hooded monks and twelve other priests, each of whom will be given by the vestry board the following sum, to wit, . . . etc.

NOTES

1. Du Breul, in his additions to Pierre Bonfons, *Les Antiquités et choses plus remarquables de Paris* (Paris, 1608) p. 233. Bonfons told the same story in his *Théatre des Antiquitez de Paris* (1612 ed.), p. 807, and (1639 ed.), p. 601; Doublet, *Histoire de l'abbaye de S. Denys en France*. . . . (Paris, 1625), pp. 397–99.

2. Cf. the plan by Willaume (1735), reproduced in the appendix of L. Brochard, *Saint-Gervais, histoire du monument* . . . (Paris, 1938), p. 446. Today, Saint-Pierre's chapel opens onto the south aisle.

3. Receipt of 8 November 1510 for a sum of 140 livres, mentioned in an act of foundation to be found in Archives Nationales, Minutier Central, XXVI, no. 49 (Anciens notaires de la fabrique Saint-Gervais, J. de Monhenault) under the date 23 June 1624. See the text in the appendix to the present article.

4. Belin calls Marie Favart "his predecessor" and alludes to the burial plot of "his predecessors." He had in his possession and presented the receipt for the stained-glass window. Belin's desire to be buried next to Marie Favart is described in "an epitaph of marble stone or copper, which will be placed over the said sieur de Belin or placed against the wall above their enclosed pew which is in the said Saint-Pierre's chapel" (see n. 3 for the source).

5. See, in the appendix, the most important passage of this act of foundation. It is inspired by the devotion to the Eucharist that enjoyed such vogue in the seventeenth century and led to the foundation of the *Compagnie du Saint Sacrement* in 1627.

6. Brochard, *Saint-Gervais*, pp. 47–49 and floorplan.

7. Another set of stained-glass windows, attributed to Robert Pinaigrier (1490–1560), decorates the windows of the neighboring chapel, which is dedicated to the Virgin Mary and dated 1517. These windows depict scenes from the life of the Virgin and are also accompanied by verses in Gothic script. There are two verses under each of the four scenes represented in the two lancets of the windows, that is to say, eight verses altogether.

8. Since Doublet's account is much longer than Du Breul's, I can only reproduce its most important passages here.

9. This "little cross" marked one of the end points of the Paris Cross Roads (1400): Delamare, *Traité de la Police*, 4: 173. In the letters of King John (6 June 1354) one reads: "Ultra ad crucem Lenditi et quoddam quadrivium satis prope dictam crucem existens in itinere seu chemino Montis Martyrum" (Doublet, *Histoire de Saint-Denys*, p. 988). And elsewhere: "Two other marble boundary stones beyond the Cross of Le Lendit (called in the olden days the End Cross [Croix aux Fiens] and now the Leaning Cross [Croix qui panche]) on the highway by which one goes from Saint-Denys to Paris, and these stones are planted at the place of the Point Lisiart which marks the separation of the *banlieue* of Saint-Denys from the city of Paris and also the king's highway from that of Saint-Denys" (ibid., p. 418). Cf. also ibid., p. 398, and the report of the inspection of the pavement of Paris on 16 May 1636, cited in Félibien and Lobineau, *Histoire de la Ville de Paris* (Paris, 1725), *Preuves*, II, 2: 143[b].

10. See, among other documents, the *Plan du Terroir de Saint-Denis* by Inselin (1708), Bibliotèque Nationale, Cartes et Plans, Ge D 5492, and the *Plan de la Terre et Seigneurie de la Chapelle* (1704), by Jean Berthier, Archives de Saint-Denis, GG 144.

11. E. Roussell, "La Bénédiction du Lendit au XIVe siècle," *Bulletin de la Société de l'Histoire de Paris* 24 (1897): 68–79.

12. Doublet, *Histoire de Saint-Denys*, p. 398.

13. Archives Nationales, S 2245 B, nos. 3 and 10.

14. Report (procès-verbal) on the restoration of the *Leaning Cross* (4 March 1741). The cross had fallen into the road and it was decided that it should be restored because it marked the borderline to neighboring lands and because "it can be useful and even absolutely indispensable in various other circumstances" (Archives Nationales, L 865, dossier 6). See also Lambeau, *La Chapelle Saint-Denis, pièces justificatives*, no. 2, p. 578.

15. Sauval, *Histoire et recherches des Antiquités de la Ville de Paris* (1724), vol. 2, bk. 8, p. 350.

16. Following a deliberation of the commune of Saint-Denis on 21 September 1793, which decided to destroy all signs of feudalism and religion on the territory of Saint-Denis.

17. The tapestries of Le Ronceray of Angers represented several of these miracles. Cf. G. de Tervarent, "Les Tapisseries du Ronceray et leurs sources d'inspiration," *Gazette des Beaux-Arts* (6e période) 10 (1933): 79–99.

18. *Histoire de l'abbaye royale de Saint-Denis en France* (Paris, 1706), p. 251. Piganiol de la Force gives a résumé of Du Breul's account of the theft perpetrated at Saint-Gervais and no longer mentions the stained-glass window (*Description de Paris* . . . [Paris, 1742], 3: 510 [1765 ed.], 4: 128). In 1754, Lebeuf mentions together the profanation of the host by the thief of Saint-Gervais and by the Jews; he does not talk about the "miracles" and simply says: "These stories are very well known." (*Histoire de la ville et de tout le diocèse de Paris*, ed. Bournon [Paris, 1883–93], 1: 88). Sauval, who does not mention the miracle of Le Lendit, notes, in speaking of the miracle of Les Billettes, that he does not want to "furnish new laughing matter to the scholars and others who doubt the story of the Jew and the Host" (*Histoire et recherches*, 1: 117).

19. Another set of the same inspiration was created for Jacques Foure, bishop of Chalon from 1574 to 1578, for the choir of his cathedral. It is no longer extant. Cf. Pierre Saint-Julien, *Antiquités de Chalon*, p. 489.

20. The report of this sale by L. de Farcy has been published in the *Revue de l'Art chrétien* (1899): 143–46. For the history of this interesting tapestry, see also L. de Farcy in *Bulletin de la Société de l'Histoire de Paris* 24 (1897): 125–26; H. C. Mariller, "The Ronceray Tapestries of the Sacraments," *Burlington Magazine* 59 (1931): 232–39, and, above all, de Tervarent, "Les Tapisseries du Ronceray," cited in n. 17, above.

21. This panel measures 1.35 by 1.80m. It has been very well reproduced in color in *L'Illustration* of 3 December 1932, and very poorly in black and white in the article by G. de Tervarent.

22. As we have seen, Doublet expressly speaks of a "book." De Tervarent ("Les Tapisseries du Ronceray") thinks that this item was a corporale. Yet the use of a square corporale measuring 15 by 15 cm and covered with embroidered silk came into use in France only in the seventeenth century and was widely accepted only in the eighteenth. Cf. Corblet, *Histoire dogmatique, liturgique et archéologique du Sacrement de l'Eucharistie* (Paris, 1885–86), 2: 268–70.

23. Brochard, *Saint-Gervais*, p. 50.

24. *Pourtraict de la ville de Saint-Denys en France* by Belleforest (1575); map of the abbey of Saint-Denis in the *Monasticon Gallicanum* by Dom Germain (1690); map of the town drawn by Dumesnil, engraved by Inselin in 1704 and published by Félibien. Two sketches can be found in the Bibliothèque Nationale, Estampes, call number V^e 26 g fol. (Destailleur Collection). One of them is signed "Riquier"; the other is by F. N. Martinet and has been reproduced in a copper-plate engraving for E. Beguillet, *Description historique de Paris et de ses plus beaux monuments . . .* (Paris, 1779–81), 2: 122. It has been reproduced by J. Formigé, *L'Abbaye royale de Saint-Denis: Recherches nouvelles* (Paris, 1960), p. 34, figure 26.

25. Bibliothèque Municipale of Rouen, ms. 1146 (formerly Y.56), copy made by brother Jehan Raveneau at the request of the abbot of Saint-Wandrille in 1467. This copy was not made from the original, but from a copy that no doubt came from the abbey of Saint-Denis. Published by A. Hellot in *Mémoires de la Société de l'Histoire de Paris* 11 (1884): 126, para. 193; and pp. 6–10. The author who, in the first part, provides additions to the Chronicle of Guillaume de Nangis, does original work beginning with the year 1316. He writes in French.

26. He is mentioned on 29 March 1330 (new style) in an act of the *Cartulaire de Notre-Dame de Paris*, Guérard ed., 3: 257.

27. This was Guy, "called de Castres," or Guy I to distinguish him from Guy de Monceau (1363–98). He was elected [abbot] in March 1326 (new style), resigned his charge out of humility in 1343, and died in 1350. (Félibien, *Histoire de l'abbaye royale de Saint-Denis*, pp. 269, 274). The continuator of Guillaume de Nangis has this to say about him: "frater Guido de Castris, vir religionis honestate conspicuus, omnique morum honestate praeclarus" (Géraud, ed., appended to the *Chronique latine de Guillaume de Nangis* [Paris, 1843], p. 66).

The *Chronique parisienne anonyme* confirms what Lebeuf had advanced on other grounds: abbot Guy was from *Châtres sous Montlhery*, that is, from Arpajon, arrondissement of Corbeil. This town, originally called Châtres (*Castrae, Castris*), took the name of Arpajon, a community in the Cantal, only in 1720, upon the request of its new landlord, Louis, marquis de Severac. See Lebeuf, *Histoire de la ville et de tout le diocèse*, ed. Bournon, 4: 137.

28. The *Justice* [gibbet] of the abbey was located near the Estrée, at the level of Aubervilliers, and not far from the Leaning Cross. It can be seen on the maps by Inselin, abbé de la Grive, etc.

29. Hellot, in *Mémoires de la Société de l'Histoire de Paris* notes a number of "new facts" (p. 126, n. 1).

30. It remained there until the Revolution.

31. This celebration must have been instituted shortly after the event. It still takes place today.

32. The most important of these works was the *Promptuarium exemplorum* by Hérolt, of which forty-eight editions were printed between 1474 and 1500. When the panels of the tapestry were cut up, the letters *au* of the word *couteau*, which ended the third verse of the quatrain about the Jew's sacrilege, were left on the panel depicting the Miracle of Le Lendit. The document in which the official of Paris reported the event of 1290 was recorded in the *Chronique* of Jean de Thilrode, a monk of Saint Baovn of Ghent, written ca. 1294. It can be found in *Monumenta Germaniae Historica: Scriptores*, 15: 557. The text is cited by G. de Tervarent, who has brought together the documents concerning the Jew's sacrilege and a bibliography of the subject. In 1295, a chapel of atonement was erected on the site of the Jew's house. In 1299 Philippe Le Bel granted this chapel to the Frères de la Charité Notre-Dame, called the "Billettes." The eucharistic miracle was often called "the miracle of the Billettes." See Tervarent, "Les Tapisseries du Ronceray," and Corblet, *Histoire dogmatique*, 1: 477.

33. The miracle is shown on one of the twelve stained-glass windows, executed between 1612 and 1622 for the gallery of the old charnel house of the church of Saint-Etienne-du-Mont of Paris, as well as in the church of Saint-Alpin at Châlons-sur-Marne, and on a stained-glass fragment in the church of Saint-Eloi at Rouen, which is preserved in that city's museum. Cf. Corblet, *Histoire dogmatique*, 2: 542.

34. A version of it was performed at Laval in 1533. One version may have existed as early as 1444. See E. de Certain, "Chronique rimée de Guillaume Ledoyen, notaire à Laval au XVe siècle," *Bibliothèque de l'Ecole des Chartes* 13 (1852): 391 and n. 1.

35. "*Le Jeu et mystère de la saincte Hostie par personnages*, pièce en vers français imprimée à Paris pour Jean Bonfons, Rue Neufve Nostre Dame, à l'enseigne S. Nicolaś," n. d. in 8°, gothic characters, 36 fol. pp. Bibliothèque Nationale, call number Yf. Rés. 2915. Thanks to the indica-

tions noting the address, we can date this edition between 1547 and 1568. Cf. P. Renouard, *Répertoire des imprimeurs parisiens* (Paris, 1965), p. 42.

36. It is outlined by de Tervarent in "Les Tapisseries du Ronceray."

37. Pp. 94–95. Corrozet's account is repeated by Pierre Bonfons, in *Les Antiquités et choses plus remarquables de Paris* (1605) and in the augmented edition of the same work by du Breul (1608), chap. 29, p. 307, v°, with a few variants. The stained-glass window executed between 1612 and 1622 for Saint-Etienne-du-Mont is indisputably a precise and close illustration of the *Jeu et Mystère* published in verse by the Jean Bonfons publishing house.

38. It does not appear in the edition of the same work published in 1605.

39. "She makes the sign of the cross and takes fire, and the host jumps into her plate," stage direction for the *Mystère* published by Jean Bonfons.

40. Lebeuf, *Histoire de la ville et de tout le diocèse*, ed. Bournon, 1: 88, and Corrozet, *Antiquités et choses plus remarquables*, p. 95.

41. In the *Mystère* two bourgeois take with them the knife and the kettle, respectively, to be used as "relics, for here is a true miracle."

42. I should nonetheless mention a copperplate engraving (86 by 142 mm) signed: L. Fruitiers, sculp., which seems to date from the eighteenth century. To be found in the Musée Carnavalet, Estampes, Topogr. 62 E, P.C. It shows a person in rags inside a chapel. He holds in his hand a chalice and is about to flee through a window by means of a ladder.

43. L. de Farcy asserts that at the end of the fifteenth century the Parisian tapestry makers received other orders as well from the canons of the cathedral of Angers, and that Angers always commissioned its tapestries in Paris. G. de Tervarent, on the contrary, believes—and this opinion is held by most of the staff at the Dépôt du Mobilier national—that the tapestry was of Flemish origin. He notes that several of the miracles depicted in it are found in the *Fleur des histoires* by Jean Mansel, a work composed for a duke of Burgundy, probably Philippe le Bon (1396-1457), which was never printed.

44. This is, incidentally, so universally true that one could count them and establish a typology of miracles, as has been done for folkloric themes.

45. See n. 18.

46. Cf. H. Friedrich, "Die Anfänge des Christentums und die ersten Kirchengründungen in römischen Niederlassungen im Gebiet des Nieder- und Mittelrheins und der Mosel," *Bonner Jahrbuch* 131 (1926): 106-7. See also the examination of the legend of Saint Materna and the god Nam at Dinant by F. Rousseau, "Fausses étymologies créatrices de légendes," *Mélanges de linguistique romane offerts à Jean Haust* (Liège, 1939), pp. 355-73.

47. At Trier the discovery under the cathedral of the double basilica, erected ca. 326 on the site of a Constantinian palace, has lent weight to the tradition which claimed that Helen, Constantin's mother, ceded her palace to the bishop, who turned it into a church dedicated to Saint Peter.

8

The Iconography of the Sacred Universe in the Eighteenth Century: Chapels and Churches in the Dioceses of Vence and Grasse

M. H. Froeschlé-Chopard

Iconography, and especially the iconography of the retable that so often decorated the churches of the early eighteenth century, is an excellent tool for studying the religious sensibility of that period. A work on the baroque retables of Brittany has shown how one can make use of what appears to be a rich source for the historian who wants to find out which aspects of the doctrine were privileged and which particular devotions were most prevalent.[1] In the context of my work on the popular religion of eastern Provence, I have therefore examined the iconography of the local places of worship. I have used the records of the pastoral visitations by the bishops of the old dioceses of Vence and Grasse for the period 1680–1730, because these records are particularly detailed and mention the subjects and figures of every decorated panel.[2] I have also used the numerous altarpieces and retables that can still be found in this region.

I shall not deal with the problem of the schools and workshops that produced these works; nor shall I go into their morphology or their style. In short, this article does not pretend to approach the subject in terms of art history. Given the nature of my source material, I have dwelt only on what this art wanted to express, for the record of the episcopal visitation mentions no more than the "subject matter" of the altarpiece. I might well repeat what

Annales, E.S.C. 31 (May-June 1976): 489–519. Translated by Elborg Forster.

Emile Mâle said in his preface to *L'Art réligieux après le Concile de Trente*: "What I am studying in this book, as in earlier books, is the thought of the Church expressed in art,"[3] although in the case under study here the "thought" of the Church made many "concessions" to popular piety.

I should also like to point out that I do not dissociate the retable from its location in the church or chapel or from the place it occupies within each of these places of worship. This is why a detailed study of the structure of the sacred universe must be made before the iconographic themes are placed into their context.

Finally, I am treating the retable or the altarpiece as a whole, without separating its central and principal subject matter from its lateral and secondary subject matter, because I am attempting to grasp its global religious expression.

The Sacred Space

Forming the center of religious life and the center of the square around which the houses of these Mediterranean villages were clustered, the parish church contained within it a number of devotions, each of which had its own altar. In contrast to the church, the rural chapel constituted another, complementary and antagonistic pole of the sacred. Not only was it located in a remote place, in almost desert territory,[4] it was also a place of undivided sacredness, usually dedicated to one specific devotion. Yet this network of places of worship cannot be reduced to a simple duality. A more systematic study of the saints to whom these churches and chapels were dedicated reveals a structured space of the sacred.

CHURCHES AND CHAPELS

Occupying the center of this space, the church with its titular and its patron saint, each of whom had long been venerated by the community,[5] reveals the oldest stratum of devotion.

The outlying chapels, on the other hand, testify to more complex patterns of veneration. Some of them were similar to the church; for they too were dedicated to a saint of the Universal Church or to the Virgin. Whether old or new, their role was to manifest an unchanging devotion to the traditionally venerated saints. Such chapels were therefore more numerous in the foothills between the sea and the mountains, which was a more populous and expanding area, judging by the many petitions for chapels of ease [*succursales*]. The distribution of the thirty-six chapels dedicated to the Virgin is suggestive in this respect.[6]

Devotion to healing saints was also a widespread practice. The chapels devoted to Saint Anthony, Saint Roch, Saint Sebastian, and Saint Pons[7] form an impressively large group, larger than that of "Notre Dame" chapels. When charted on a map, these chapels are seen to be distributed throughout the territory. Much more uniform than that of the chapels dedicated to the Virgin, the distribution of these chapels is significant. Responding to an immediate and pressing need of the entire village community, the cult of these saints was found everywhere.[8]

A special case is that of the thirty-eight penitents' chapels, which were also evenly distributed throughout the area. Here the most prevalent devotion was to the Virgin as the Mater dolorosa (shading into the Descent from the Cross) or as Notre Dame of Mercy, on the one hand, and to Saint Bernardin, on the other.

The distribution of these three types of chapels was not a matter of chance. The penitents' chapels were located in the villages, near the church. The vigorous confraternities of penitents, which recruited 20 percent of the adult male population, and many woman as well,[9] made it a point to show a certain independence from the parish priest and constituted a rival group within the parish.[10] In terms of space this opposition was expressed in a meeting place that competed with the church, even though it was located very close to it on the same square. The chapels dedicated to traditional saints and to local patron saints, as well as the "Notre Dame" chapels formed a circle around the inhabited space, being located five hundred or one thousand paces from its boundaries. Along the path to the village, also within this protective perimeter, was the place of the healing saint. The special saint of each village was hidden at the outer limit of its territory or at the edge of the forest; it was this chapel that attracted processions and "pilgrimages."

Traditional saints, healing saints, and "pilgrimage" saints were thus located in space in a specific pattern along the lines of several concentric circles, whose center was the parish church. This pattern was the same in most of these villages (see figure 8.1).

THE INTERNAL STRUCTURE OF THE
PARISH CHURCH

Nor was the "central" church a homogeneous space; in fact, the distribution of the lateral altars in the parish church imposed a pattern on the multitude of sacred places within the village territory. It should be stressed from the outset that the parish church *always* made room for a variety of devotions.[11] The patron saint and the titular saint who gave the church its name had been associated with other cults, often in the very recent past. This process was so common that one can sometimes follow its development in the documents. In 1680, for example, a certain locality had only one chapel and one altar; in 1705 this chapel was elevated to a parish but still had only one

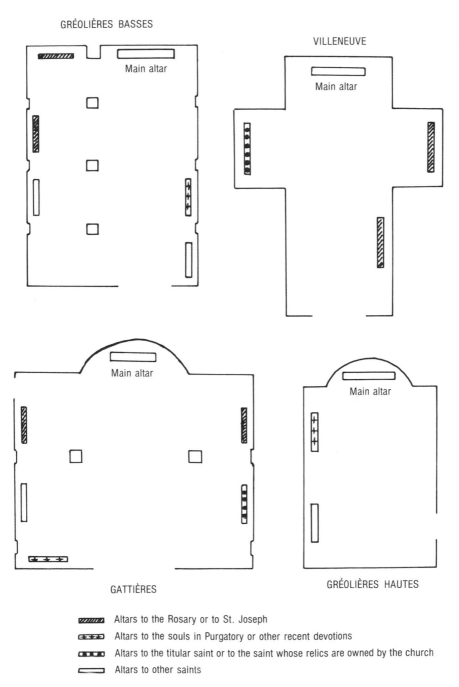

Figure 8.1. Examples of the disposition of the altars in churches

altar; in 1736 the bishop authorized the building of a third altar.[12] Thus, as soon as a church attained the rank of a parish church, it was considered important to multiply the shrines within the sanctuary. In such cases the additional altars were of two kinds: they either expressed the traditional devotions (cult of the patron saint, the titular saint, or the healing saint) or they introduced a new devotion (to the rosary, Saint Joseph, or the souls in purgatory). This opposition was expressed in space,[13] for the new devotions were placed in the front of the nave, whereas the healing saints were placed in the back. The latter were, as A. Dupront has called them, the "saints of the entrance."

This disposition, which can be observed everywhere, cannot have been fortuitous. The very terms used by the visiting bishops in the documents are revealing. Some of the altars are called "foremost," others are referred to as "in back" or "below." Moreover, the "foremost" altars were the most recent, for they were dedicated to devotions that came into their own after the Council of Trent. The spatial arrangements of a late seventeenth-century church was not a matter of juxtaposing various elements; nor were the new altars erected further and further away from the main altar. Quite to the contrary, this disposition was governed by precise rules grounded in a hierarchy of importance. The mind-set we encounter here is similar to that which informed the iconography of the great cathedrals, where the right side and the front of the nave were places of honor.[14] The clergy intentionally fostered this hierarchy, and one often sees the bishop giving orders for changing the location of a "badly placed" altar. As an expression of the intentions of the clergy, the disposition of the altars was bound to be marked by the Counter Reformation, and the new devotions spawned by that movement were bound to be placed at the top of the hierarchy.

In this hierarchy devotion to the rosary occupied the place of honor. Its altar was placed near or even adjacent to the main altar. A similar, though less rigid, place was assigned to Saint Joseph. These altars, as well as those dedicated to the guardian angel, the Holy Ghost, and to a lesser extent, the Child Jesus, were as important as the altars dedicated to the saints whose relics were owned by the church, often those of its titular or patron saint. Sometimes this rivalry was clearly marked in space, either through a contrasting addition, as at La Gaude, where the newly constructed altar to Saint Victoire was placed opposite the altar of the rosary, or through a substitution, as at Saint-Paul, where the sumptuous chapel of Saint Clement, whose altar was erected over the body of that saint, took the place of the altar to the rosary, which was moved "further back."[15] In the latter case, the ancient and tenacious devotion to relics resisted the advance of a new devotion.

Contrasting with this privileged group were the altars dedicated to the healing saints, located in the very back of the church. Midway between the two poles of the hierarchy I have outlined were the altars to the souls in purgatory, whose placement does not seem to have been entirely fixed. This trait is no doubt related to the very recent emergence of this devotion, for these altars were built only in the first years of the eighteenth century.[16] It also has to do with the fact that in certain parishes this newer devotion was substituted for another, earlier one, and therefore physically took its place as well.

The hierarchy of altars was a symbolic hierarchy, the fruit of clerical thinking. But it was reinforced and made visible to anyone who entered the church by the relative richness or modesty of the different altars. If one compares such extreme examples as the rosary, on the one hand, and Saint Anthony of Padua, on the other, striking differences are noticeable even in the framework surrounding the altarpiece. The altarpieces of the rosary are executed in the latest taste, decorated with columns of plaster or wood, and always sculpted and often gilded, whereas the altars to Saint Anthony show no decoration of this kind. Some of them, however, do have "retables" that might rival the retables or "wooden ornamentation" of certain altars to the rosary. But in these cases another difference appears, for the "retable" of Saint Anthony often turns out to be old, since it is painted on wood. When applied to an altar of the rosary, the term *retable* designates a very different thing, namely, a framework of plaster or wood surrounding a painting. Not quite as sumptuous as the retables decorated with columns, these frames, which in the great majority of cases surrounded a painting on canvas,[17] had one thing in common with the paintings: they were new. In short, the altars of the rosary were richly decorated, while those of Saint Anthony usually presented a simple, unornamented altarpiece. The altar dedicated to the rosary was thus elaborate and executed in the latest taste, whereas that of Saint Anthony was more modest and decorated in an old-fashioned style. Moreover, the richness of the altar of the rosary is uniformly observable in all the parishes under study here. In half the mountain villages and in half the coastal villages, the parishes were determined to have a beautiful altar dedicated to the rosary. Yet they did not feel this way about Saint Anthony, and in the poorer mountain villages these altars were neglected even more than elsewhere.

THE STRUCTURE OF THE SACRED
UNIVERSE AND HIERARCHY

The placement of the altars, their richness, and the age of their decor are so many material signs of a hierarchy. Within the sacred space of the church, concrete expression was given to a fixed order that every cleric, especially after the efforts of the Council of Trent, was expected to acknowledge. Nothing must equal the Eucharist placed upon the main altar, which was the starting point of every episcopal visitation. Then, in descending order of sacredness, came the rosary, Saint Joseph, and the souls in purgatory, the latter representing the only devotion that was for all practical purposes confined to the parish church. Also accepted, finally, were the local patron saints, whose placement in the church seems to have been a concession, and the healing saints.

This hierarchy was then carried over into the different sacred places of the village territory. The saint who in the spatial distribution was farthest removed from the Eucharist, whether in the church or in the countryside, could thus no longer be confused with God or given equal importance. The chapels that were located, sometimes for centuries, at the extreme limits of the village territory, where they protected cosmic and untoward places, were now seen as less sacred by the clergy; indeed, they became places where it was always tempting to look for suspect practices and "abuses." The internal arrangement of the parish church called upon the "people," that is, the laity, to make the same judgment. The iconography of the various places of worship only served to reinforce this hierarchy.

The Iconography of the Saints

All sacred places dedicated to saints, whether chapels or altars, presented the same characteristics: they were modest and plain.[18] Their altarpieces, which usually struck the visiting bishop as mediocre, all showed the same iconographic characteristics.

THE PREVALENCE OF THE TRADITIONAL ICONOGRAPHY

Tradition was most important in the allocation of space. Most of the altarpieces were divided into three compartments. This disposition can be inferred from the terms used to describe the altarpieces; in enumerating the saints pictured, the records of the visitations usually mention the most important saint first but suggest that other saints were included as well. In Saint Anthony's chapel in Cannes, a sculpted panel is presented as follows: "A very old retable depicting Saint Anthony, Saint Roch, and Saint Claude. Seeing that the image of Saint Anthony is held up by a small footstool, we have ordered that within a month a wooden pedestal is to be made to match those of the other saints."[19] This, then, was a group of statues standing side by side. The description is almost identical for an altarpiece painted on wood at Coursé-goules: "A fine old altarpiece, painted and gilded, showing Saint John the Baptist in the middle and Saint Petronilla and Saint Godard on either side."[20] Similarly, we hear of a painting on canvas "representing Saint Claude in the middle and Saint Sebastian and Saint Bernardin at his side."[21]

These descriptions, which show little variation, indicate that these altarpieces, whether old or new, were part of one and the same iconography. An inventory of the altarpieces still to be found today in places of worship in this area yields the following information.

The old altarpieces (sixteenth century), consisting of painted and gilded wooden panels, were sometimes the work of Bréa, and many seem to have been directly influenced by the Primitive School of Nice. All of them, whether it be the rich retable of the cathedral of Grasse, showing Saint Honorat in the middle with Saint Clement and Saint Lambert at his sides, both surrounded in turn by other saints,[22] or the one at Courségoules of which I have just spoken, present the same appearance. The panel is divided by arcades that surround each figure. Under these porticos the saints are shown either full face or in three-quarter profile; they are standing, and resemble the statues they may have replaced. Their posture is also hieratic. They all gaze toward an undefinable beyond. In the Courségoules altarpiece they are recognizable by a few attributes: Saint John the Baptist is carrying the divine lamb lying on a book, and his right hand, index finger extended, seems to point to the lamb. Saint Godard wears a bishop's garb, holds the crozier in one hand, and bestows the blessing with the other. Saint Petronilla does not have any particular attributes; she is absorbed in reading. Above these figures, placed into smaller compartments, we see a Christ of Mercy flanked by the Virgin and Saint John, while one of the lateral compartments depicts an Annunciation.

In the more recent altarpieces painted on canvas, the medieval porticos have disappeared. They are replaced by a uniform background, usually a sky with clouds that open to provide glimpses of celestial figures (angels, the divine lamb, the dove of the Holy Ghost). Yet the same figures, still appearing in threes, and with the same attributes, continue to occupy the space in the same standing position, the same rigid attitude, and with the same forlorn gaze (see figure 8.2).

These characteristics are also found in the much rarer altarpieces that depict only one subject. These show the saint alone, full face, standing, and in a fixed attitude. This is all the more striking when it involves a statue like the Saint Magdalen of Biot, the centerpiece of a decor that Bishop Mesgrigny called a retable with gilded framework. Yet this decor is baroque. The niche containing the statue is surmounted by a dais whose drapes open to show the saint. This decor in turn is framed by two pilasters supporting a rounded, very elaborate corniche, which holds up a sculpted dome. Two whorls at the foot of the pillars, corresponding in form to the cartouche at the summit, round out the composition of the ensemble. A contrast thus appears between the architectural decor of these retables, which is often baroque, and the more traditional central altarpiece. On the altars of Saint Lambert at Vence and Saint Claude at Cipières, the holy bishop bestowing the blessing is similar to the figures seen in earlier altarpieces, but the image is surrounded by a sump-

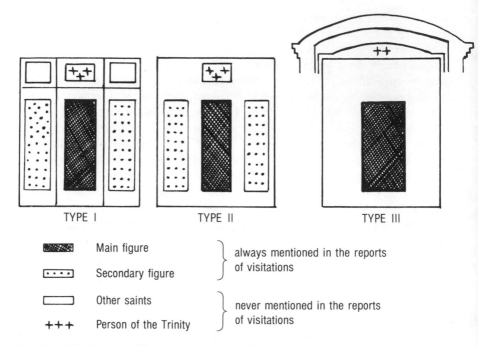

	Main figure	} always mentioned in the reports
	Secondary figure	} of visitations
	Other saints	} never mentioned in the reports
+++	Person of the Trinity	} of visitations

Type I: *Old altarpieces*: The saints are represented in distinctly separated compartments

Type II: *New altarpieces resembling the old ones*: The compartments disappear. The small scenes at the top often disappear

Type III: *New altarpieces showing only one figure or one subject*: The representation of the persons of the Trinity is shifted to the framework

Figure 8.2. Altarpieces of altars or in chapels dedicated to a saint

tuous decor and rich columns with composite shafts and telamon angels, respectively. These rich baroque decors, however, are rarely found in chapels or altars dedicated to saints, and most of the newer altarpieces reproduced the tripartite disposition of the old retables. It should be noted that one archaic feature fell into disuse: in the eighteenth century the central figure was of the same size as the lateral figures, while in the sixteenth century that figure's importance had been underscored by its taller stature.

INFREQUENCY OF NEWER REPRESENTATIONS

A newer iconography can sometimes be seen in altarpieces representing scenes. These subjects were treated infrequently, however, and there is no indi-

cation that such themes as the "Beheading of Saint John," the "Transfiguration," or the "Visitation" were treated in a modern manner. Two altarpieces
can be placed into this new current. The first is the "Death of Saint Claire"
at Saint-Paul. Here the figures are no longer uniformly distributed; appearing in greater number, they form two groups separated by an imaginary diag-
onal line; one side depicts the saint lying on a bed supported by her sisters,
the other shows the princes of the Church, among them the pope, who blesses
the saint. Even more characteristic is the alterpiece of Saint Véran in the
cathedral at Vence. It is a rather erudite canvas, in which the saint blesses a
crowd gathered about him in hierarchical order; the figure standing closest
to him and therefore the first to receive his blessing is a priest. This altarpiece
presents two new characteristics: the saint is depicted in a scene that he could
actually have experienced; and the episcopal function is magnified by means
of the anonymous throng of those who receive the blessing. Both of these features are clearly part of post-Tridentine art. Their appearance in the new
iconography is timid and belated, for they are only found in the cathedral,
and not before the eighteenth century.[23]

On the whole, then, these altarpieces were rarely designed to teach. The
art of "picturing" religious truths had not yet made any inroads. The art of
these altars and chapels dedicated to saints was one that "manifested" the
sacred.[24] It was to retain this character throughout the eighteenth century. In
1719, for example, an "almost new" altarpiece at Gréolières portrayed, en-
cased in a stucco framework of imitation marble that played upon contrasting
colors, Saint John the Baptist and Saint Eloi standing side by side in hieratic
attitudes. The same characteristics are found in an altarpiece at Courségoules
that cannot have been placed into the sanctuary before 1722, the date when
the chapel had to be enlarged.

THE ICONOGRAPHY OF THE SAINTS:
AN ART OF MANIFESTATION

"An art of manifestation." The altarpieces that feature several saints together permit us to take a closer look at this "manifestation" of the sacred.

The altarpiece over the altar dedicated to the titular or patron saint of the
parish usually featured all of the traditionally venerated saints. A good ex-
emplar of this type is the altar to Saint Véran in the cathedral of Vence described in 1716. It "represents Saint Véran in the middle, Saint John the
Baptist and Saint Magdalen on either side."[25] The latter two saints are frequently found throughout the region. Saint John the Baptist was the titular
saint of many rural chapels, and although there was only one rural chapel
dedicated to Saint Mary-Magdalen, she was the titular saint of a number of
parish churches. Many similar examples could be cited. The meaning of such

associations is evident: the altarpiece represented a group of protective saints and, behond these figures, a protective power that manifested itself. The altarpiece of the patron saint was the image of the protection that the patron saint *owed* the territory of the parish.

At the same time, however, one finds an even greater number of chapels and altars dedicated to healing saints. Here, too, different saints were associated in such a manner as to give presence to a power; not the power to protect the land but the power to ward off disease, above all the epidemics that decimated man and beast. The altarpieces in chapels dedicated to saints who gave protection against the plague were simply added to those of other saints who had an analogous function. For example, in a Saint Sebastian's chapel we find "Saint Sebastian, Saint Roch, Saint Anthony"; a Saint Roch's chapel features "the figure of the saint in the middle and at his sides Saint Sebastian and Saint Charles"; a Saint Anthony's chapel shows "Saint Anthony, Saint Roch, Saint Claude"; a Saint Pons's chapel shows "Saint Pons, Saint Claude, Saint Anthony."[26] Also present in these altarpieces are saints who protect against sudden death, such as Saint Christopher and even Saint Agatha, who gives protection against lightening.

Many altarpieces combined healing saints and local patron saints; in that case they became images of protection as such. A typical example of this is provided by Saint Margaret's chapel at Grasse, where this saint, who gives protection against sudden death in childbirth, is surrounded by Saints Mary-Magdalen, Catherine, Lazarus, Jacques, and Roch. In such associations of saints, certain more local saints assume the appearance of healers. Honoré or Honorat,[27] Aigous, and Saturin are examples of such saints.

The iconography of the saints, both in rural chapels and in the "entrance altars" in the church, has very specific characteristics. It was hardly touched by the Counter Reformation, for the altarpiece had no educational function. Never does one encounter any religious "propaganda." The saints are represented just as they were represented in the thirteenth century. Nor is this art baroque. That style is relegated to the surrounding framework. Never does one find a saint in ecstasy; on the contrary, the figures assume the hieratic attitudes of the old statues. This manner of representation, which runs counter to the aesthetic current of the time, cannot be explained solely by the remote location of the province. It was also related to the function of these altarpieces, which was to manifest the protective power of the saints. The altarpiece was assigned the function of giving presence and efficacy to a power. The immobility of the figures, their absent faces—everything manifested this power, which was the very meaning of the cult of the saints. Representations of the divinity were therefore not present or were relegated to a medallion at the very top of the altarpiece.[28] They were not needed, and the small space they occupy in the alterpiece as a whole is a telling sign of this assumption.

Iconography of the Virgin and the Crucifixion

Unless she was pictured as the Virgin of the Rosary, the Virgin, like the saints, was also confined to rural chapels, penitents' chapels, and the "entrance altars" of churches. There she assumed a number of different guises, being depicted as the Madonna, the Virgin of the Annunication, the Virgin of the Assumption, or the Mater dolorosa. In this last representation she was part of the Crucifixion, and the reports of the pastoral visitations often evoke her image in that context.

THE ICONOGRAPHY OF THE VIRGIN AND THE ICONOGRAPHY OF THE SAINTS

The chapels dedicated to the Virgin were often in better condition than those of the saints, but their decor was not appreciably different. Their altarpieces, which were not always beautiful or new, showed the same alignment of figures. Moreover, they depicted the Virgin surrounded by healing saints and local patron saints, the same ones we have studied earlier.[29] Placed in the center, her presence may have been intended to enhance the protective function of the altarpiece. One of these altarpieces, referred to in the records of pastoral visitations as "Notre Dame, Saint John, and Saint Anthony," is still to be found in the same chapel today, although "two folding doors painted on canvas and representing the mysteries of our redemption"[30] that covered this wooden panel have since disappeared. The existing panel shows a Virgin of Protection sheltering the Christian people under her cloak: to her right the world of the clerics, represented by its leaders (pope, cardinal); to her left the world of the laity, represented by the emperor in knightly garb and a king. In her right hand the Virgin holds a rosary and in her left, a rose. The chapel is called "Notre Dame del populo." This crowned Virgin of the people is a Virgin of Protection and a Virgin of the Rosary. In her central compartment she is taller than the two saints flanking her, who are recognizable by their attributes. Around these central figures small scenes of the life of the Virgin can be seen. In the gable the face of God the Father appears in a triangle. Although the Virgin is taller than the saints surrounding her, and therefore superior to them, she does not invalidate their intercession. She is the greatest protectress among other protectors. Altarpieces of this kind are not different from representations of other saints. They can also be found on the main altars of penitents' chapels, which often depict the Virgin together with other saints.

When she is represented alone, the Virgin appears as the mediatrix par excellence; her intercession and her protection are the most effective of all.[31]

Sometimes the visiting bishop refers to an altarpiece with the words "Notre Dame," or "the Holy Virgin"; but these expressions are too vague to let us imagine a specific iconography. Some of these "Notre Dames" are Virgins of Majesty, like the Virgin at Vence who, on an "antique wooden altarpiece" "holds in her arms a naked Infant Jesus."[32] This is certainly the same Virgin that was mentioned by J. Levrot in the early eighteenth century.[33] Once again, the grave and solemn bearing of the Virgin of Majesty indicates her similarity to the hieratic saints mentioned earlier. Other representations are the Virgin of Mercy; none of these altarpieces have been preserved, but they would no doubt resemble the "Virgin del populo" I have just evoked. This representation of the Virgin as a tutelary figure was more frequent than the records of the episcopal visitations would indicate. At Cagnes, for example, this figure appears in the frescoes of a chapel dedicated to Notre Dame de Protection. The very names of certain chapels recall this iconographical theme: Notre Dame de Consolation, Notre Dame de Grace, Notre Dame de Miséricorde, Notre Dame de Protection, Notre Dame del populo.[34] The Virgin as protectress is also one of the themes featured in the penitents' chapels, three of which are called Notre Dame de Miséricorde [of Mercy]. This devotion is sometimes depicted in altarpieces that happen to have survived. For example, one penitents' chapel, Saint Sebastian's, has as an altar frontal a naïve painting in which the Virgin shelters under her cloak two members of the brotherhood absorbed in prayer.[35] This medieval theme, which always shows the Virgin full face, immobile, and outsized in relation to the humanity she protects, indicates that even in the early eighteenth century the iconography of these chapels, along with that of the saints, was still overwhelmingly marked by the art that had flourished before the Counter Reformation and even before the Renaissance.

THE PREVALENCE OF SCENES FROM THE PASSION

The chapels dedicated to the Virgin frequently present the theme of the Mater dolorosa or the Descent from the Cross. These two titles cannot be disassociated; successive visiting bishops would apply these designations interchangeably to the same altarpiece or the same altar.[36] In doing so, they always highlighted the person of the Virgin, so the identification of altars and altarpieces becomes difficult. The "Descent from the Cross" mentioned in 1712 at Magagnosc may well be the altarpiece described in 1679 as "The Holy Virgin at the foot of the cross holding her son on her knees, Saint John, Saint Magdalen, and Saint John of Arimathea."[37] At Biot there still is an altarpiece that can be dated to the early eighteenth century on the basis of the records of visitations. It presents a Mater dolorosa similar to those that were current in the fourteenth century: the head of Christ falls backward, his right hand touches the ground, and his rigid body is supported on his mother's knees.

The existence of a large number of altars dedicated to the Mater dolorosa and their iconography reveals a world still marked by the late Middle Ages. In the same category are the altars of the Five Wounds of Christ, as well as the altarpieces representing the Crucifixion or what the visiting bishops call the "ecce homo"—although I was surprised to encounter this expression in connection with these altars. One of them, in fact, which can still be seen in the church of Châteauneuf, warrants the assertion that it is not an "ecce homo" but a Pietà. The figure of Christ does, to be sure, wear the crown of thorns, but his death is already accomplished, since his hands and feet are pierced. Moreover, the figure is surrounded by the emblems of the Passion.

The Mater dolorosa, the Crucifixion and the Descent from the Cross, and the Pietà all emphasize the Passion of the Son and the suffering of the Mother. They perpetuate the iconography of the late Middle Ages.[38]

THE ASSUMPTION OF THE VIRGIN
AND THE ANNUNCIATION:
THE EMERGENCE OF NEW REPRESENTATIONS

More modern representations only appear in scenes of the Assumption and the Annunciation. These themes, which are found quite frequently, no doubt replaced the old altarpieces that showed the Virgin surrounded by saints. The Assumption in particular often found its place on the main altar of Notre Dame chapels and penitents' chapels. In the latter the central subject is often accompanied by representations of protecting saints. Two examples of this are "Saint Martin, Saint Benedict, and the Annunciation" and "The Assumption and Saint Bernardin."[39] Two late altarpieces bring to light a curious mixture of new representations and survivals of the past. One of them, an Annunciation, places the figures into the atmosphere of soft, billowing clouds that is the hallmark of the new iconography.[40] Yet the Angel, while not "standing on the ground," does not float upon the clouds, nor is he accompanied by other celestial messengers. The intimate character of older Annunciations is still present in a few details, such as a chair or a sewing basket. The church of Grasse still has an Assumption dated 1787, which is marked by the new iconography. Here the Virgin rises to heaven unaided, her arms extended, seated upon a cloud. At this point, the Assumption begins to look like an Ascension. Yet the presence of two saints, shown larger in size than the Virgin in the lower part of the altarpiece, reduces the importance of the latter. This configuration harks back to the tripartite division of the old altarpieces, even though the holy personages are shown in the attitudes that were favored by the Counter Reformation, that is, with their eyes turned heavenward, in ecstasy.[41]

The iconography of the Virgin and of the Passion has many points in common with that of the saints. Whether depicted as the Virgin of Majesty, the Virgin surrounded by saints, the Virgin of Mercy, or the Virgin of the Assumption surrounded by saints, the Virgin always appears as the mediatrix par excellence, yet she is only the foremost of the mediating and protecting saints, one among the others. The suffering Christ also appears as a mediator who is asked to protect humanity from all evil, to protect it even beyond death. Here too the altarpiece is assigned the function of giving efficacy to a protection powerful enough to extend to the hereafter. Everywhere, the purpose of this art is to manifest the sacred.

The Iconography of the New Devotions

Unlike the "old" devotions we have studied so far, the "new" devotions were exclusively concentrated in the parish church. In this sacred precinct they had their shrines very close to the main altar and the Eucharist. Their pictorial representations indicate that they had a well-defined purpose and a specific role to play. I shall deal with the three principal and most widely practiced of these new devotions: to Saint Joseph, to the rosary, and to the souls in purgatory.

THE ICONOGRAPHY OF SAINT JOSEPH

Sometimes Saint Joseph is represented together with other saints in the characteristic alignment to which I have repeatedly called attention here. On a number of altars dedicated to Saint Anne he is included in an "extended Holy Family" showing, as at Grasse, "the Holy Virgin and the Infant Jesus, Saint Anne, Saint Joseph, Saint Joachim, and Saint John the Baptist."[42] The new devotion to Saint Joseph becomes more explicit in altarpieces depicting the Nativity or the Holy Family. The theme of the Holy family conceived on the model of the Trinity in heaven came into its own only after the Counter Reformation. It was Saint François de Sales who wrote in his *Entretiens spirituels*: "Mary, Jesus, and Joseph are a Trinity upon earth that in some manner represents the Holy Trinity." The altarpiece still to be seen at Saint-Paul is a perfect illustration of this statement. It represents in the center Jesus as a young boy, raising his right hand in a vague gesture of benediction. Standing to his right, the Virgin, looking at him, stretches her hand toward him; to his left Joseph, a man in the prime of life, holds his flowering rod. These three figures are depicted standing, full of majestic dignity. Above the child hovers a large dove of the Holy Ghost, the only luminous point of the altarpiece. At the very top appears God the Father surrounded by angels. Vertically, the altarpiece is thus occupied by the Holy Trinity; horizontally, it shows the terrestrial Trinity. The Child Jesus is the point where these two Trinities intersect. This alterpiece, which closely resembles a painting by Murillo, is dated 1679. This image, then, was quite new at the time of the pastoral visitations used as a source here.

Similarly, the men of that time, among them Saint-Cyran, saw an image of the Trinity in the stable of Bethlehem. This idea is also suggested by an altarpiece at Biot, depicting the Nativity where the Infant Jesus, in the center, is flanked in a strictly symmetrical fashion by the Virgin and Saint Joseph, who are bending over him. Together, the three figures form a triangle highlighted by a cluster of luminous little angels tumbling down. In both instances (Holy Trinity and Nativity) the focus of the heavenly Trinity is Jesus. But Jesus submits to the authority of Joseph and Mary. He is the model of every believer who submits to God, to the Spirit, and thereby to the Church as the incarnation of the divine. He is also the model of every child obedient to his parents and of every human being submissive to his superiors in the hierarchy.

The most frequently treated theme of the altars dedicated to Saint Joseph, however, is that of the Good Death, a theme that was popularized by Isolanus's book *La Somme des dons de Saint Joseph*[43] published in 1522. Many of the extant altarpieces illustrate this book. Saint Joseph is depicted lying down, sustained by the Virgin and Christ standing at the head of the bed. The Virgin is praying, while Christ supports the dying man with one hand and points to heaven with the other. Kneeling in prayer at the foot of the bed are the two archangels. In the sky appear the Holy Ghost and God the Father, who reaches down to receive the dying man. Saint Joseph is thus the saint of an exemplary death, lying in his bed surrounded by all those who are dear to him. A few details always locate this scene inside a dwelling: the bed and a window opening onto the next world. The importance of this devotion was such that the altarpiece allowed of little variation. It was therefore invariably evoked by the visiting bishop in the same manner: "The agony of Saint Joseph," "Saint Joseph on his deathbed," or "the mystery of Saint Joseph's agony." Yet these altarpieces are more than simple illustrations of the miraculous story of Joseph the carpenter conveyed by Isolanus's book. One important detail was added, namely, the presence of God the Father. The popularity of Saint Joseph was definitely related to the special power of intercession attributed to him since the sixteenth century, an intercession that could obtain the grace of a good death and thereby to avoid the suffering of purgatory. The popularity of Saint Joseph appeared late and was very intense, but it was similar to that of other intercessors.

The iconography of Saint Joseph, then, was quite different from that of the other saints (see figure 8.3). Saint Joseph is constantly placed in a special relationship with God the Father. He is God's image in the terrestrial Trinity and is received by him after his death. Having accepted the will of God, Saint Joseph dies well because he has known how to submit. His altarpiece represents

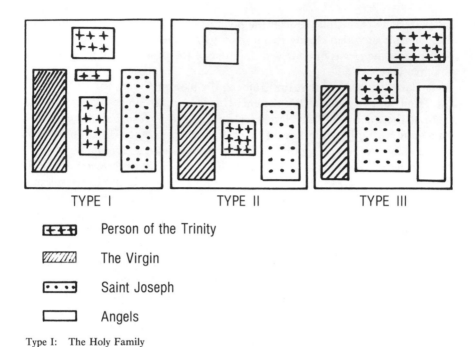

TYPE I   TYPE II   TYPE III

⊞⊞⊞   Person of the Trinity

▨▨▨   The Virgin

⌷•••⌷   Saint Joseph

▭▭▭   Angels

Type I: The Holy Family
Type II: Nativity
Type III: The Death of Saint Joseph

Figure 8.3. Altarpieces of the altars to Saint Joseph

a model, the model every believer must follow in order to obtain a "good death."

THE ICONOGRAPHY OF THE ROSARY

Like the new theme of the agony of Saint Joseph, the theme of the rosary is always labeled in the same manner in the records of pastoral visitations: "Notre Dame of the Rosary," "The mysteries of the Rosary," or "Notre Dame of the Rosary with the mysteries surrounding her." Almost all the extant altarpieces have striking common characteristics. They show the Virgin in the center, surrounded by the mysteries of the Rosary, which are shown on the periphery of the canvas. The latter are fifteen smaller paintings arranged in the following manner: starting at the upper center, the Joyful Mysteries are depicted at the right, the Sorrowful Mysteries below, and the Glorious Mysteries at the left. The central subject also shows very little variation. It is always a Virgin with the Child "distributing rosaries," as one vicar general put it, to Saint Dominic, in some cases, or to Saint Catherine of Siena in others, while the child also gives rosaries to one or the other of these saints.

This representation suggests the important role played by the Dominicans in the diffusion of this devotion. In this connection the texts establishing brotherhoods of the rosary are important. One of these texts, signed by the "Chief Bursar and Vicar General of the entire order of the Preaching Brothers,"[44] contains the following statement:

We moreover wish and order that the following provisos be strictly observed: to wit, that in the venerable retable or image of the said chapel shall be depicted the fifteen mysteries of our Redeemer and that in just and reasonable recognition of our concession shall also be painted on the same retable or altarpiece the venerable image of our Father Saint Dominic, the first teacher of the Holy Rosary, receiving upon his knees from the hand of the Holy Virgin the wreaths of prayer; all of the foregoing in such a manner that, should this not be done or neglected, our present letter shall be null and void for you and your successors.

The iconography of most of these altarpieces is in fact a homage to Saint Dominic, the saint who has given the world so useful a devotion,[45] as well as a résumé of the entire teaching of the Church in the representation of the mysteries of the Redemption. The adjunction of Saint Catherine of Siena only serves to enhance the Dominican influence. Yet on the canvas the Dominican saints are not represented alone; they are often shown as the principal figures of a throng in prayer. Sometimes that throng actually crowds in behind them, as at Tourettes; at other times it is simply evoked by its representatives, the pope to the right of the Virgin and the emperor to her left, as at Biot. The devotion to the rosary has been adopted by all Catholics, and the Dominican saints yield to the Virgin, who is placed high above them. As the Queen of Heaven who dominates the humanity that venerates her, the Virgin of the Rosary once again becomes similar to the Virgins of Mercy. Significant in this respect are the two altarpieces at Saint-Jeannet and Gattières, where the central theme is divided into two parts. The upper section treats the classic theme of the Virgin surrounded by Dominican saints, while the lower section shows the people in prayer in the same position as under the cloak of the Virgins of Protection. In the oldest altarpieces of the rosary, such as Louis Bréa's painting at Antibes, the Virgin standing in the center is a Virgin of Mercy with the Child in her arms, her cloak held up by angels. Dominican saints are not present (see figure 8.4).

The altarpieces of the rosary thus present a threefold aspect. The small scenes arranged like a halo of medallions around the Virgin amount to a teaching device. The doctrines depicted are sometimes evoked in the vocabulary of the visiting bishops.[46] Like an illustrated catechism, these scenes represent a whole series of mysteries taught by the Church. Yet the central and most important subject is still a more traditional theme, the Virgin and her

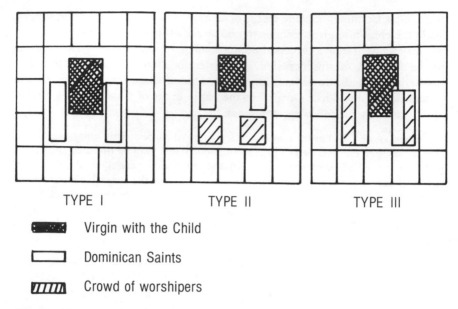

TYPE I   TYPE II   TYPE III

█▬▬█   Virgin with the Child

▭▭   Dominican Saints

▨▨▨   Crowd of worshipers

Type I: The crowd of worshipers is not shown
Type II: The altarpiece separates the Virgin and the saints from the crowd, which is shown at
          the bottom of the altarpiece
Type III: The most frequently found type. The crowd is placed behind the Dominican saints

Figure 8.4. Schemas of the altarpieces featuring the rosary

Child, the Queen of Heaven who assumes the characteristics of a Virgin of
Mercy even in the most recent altarpieces.[47] Although in this traditional subject the hieratic Virgin of the late Middle Ages has been superseded by the
figure of a friendly queen holding her child on her knees, the representation
of the people through its two medieval poles (pope and emperor) remains
prevalent. This hierarchical society, no doubt expressing on canvas the feelings and regrets of the seventeenth-century Church in the face of the demise
of the traditional hierarchy, had become the ideal image of society.

THE ICONOGRAPHY OF THE SOULS IN
PURGATORY

The very expressions used by the visiting bishops point to a rather wide variety in the altarpieces treating the theme of the souls in purgatory. One finds
the expression "Notre Dame interceding" [Notre Dame des Suffrages or
Notre Dame des Soufrages], and one of these altarpieces is described as
"Notre Dame and below the souls in purgatory." The altarpiece itself matches

this evocation. In the upper section it presents a compassionate Virgin with the Child standing on her knees, bending toward the souls. She no longer quenches the thrist of the parched souls with her milk, this subject having been judged indecent by the Counter Reformation,[48] but her right hand placed on her breast seems to recall that gesture. The purgatory presents the aspect of a quasi-hell it had assumed since the beginning of the seventeenth century,[49] for the souls are engulfed in flames. At the middle level, between the purgatory and the celestial world, at the center of the altarpiece, adult angels comfort the souls or deliver them. In one hand one of them brandishes a chalice showing a shining host, and with the other he pours refreshing water from a beaker.

This representation, in which the Virgin occupies the preeminent position, is also suggested by other expressions than "Notre Dame interceding." "The purgatory and the Holy Virgin in a glory" is one of these expressions. In the extant altarpieces corresponding to this description, the Virgin is always shown with the Child, her head haloed with light. This "glory" is delineated on the canvas by a wreath of small angels. The middle level is sometimes occupied by mediating saints, not, as G. and M. Vovelle have already pointed out, such official mediators as Saint Gregory, but traditional mediators or even the titular saint of the local church. This is the case at Gattières, where the kneeling bishop, who presents the poor, supplicating souls to the queen of the purgatory, seems to be Saint Blasius, the titular saint of the church.

The altarpiece at Saint-Vallier referred to as "The Mater dolorosa and the souls of purgatory" is more unusual (see figure 8.5). Three-fourths of its surface is occupied by a Pietà, a very close imitation of the Pietà by Annibale Carrachio. At the feet of Christ a tearful Saint Mary-Magdalen is holding his hand; behind him stand the Virgin and Saint John. In the background on a hill the three crosses of Golgotha are visible. This scene overlooks a pit holding the souls who are imploring the clemency of the Virgin, or perhaps that of her son. This altarpiece, which associates the Passion of Christ or of the Virgin with the salvation of the souls in purgatory,[50] leads into a second representation that is also frequently found in the area, emphasising not the Virgin but Christ and the Trinity.

With respect to these altarpieces the evocations of the visiting bishops are not always very clear. One of these altarpieces is described as "the deliverance of the souls in purgatory, Saint Prosper, and Saint Agatha." In this case the upper section of the canvas is occupied by a risen Christ showing his wounds. The two interceding saints are kneeling and Saint Agatha points to her breasts, which are shown on a platter, bathed in bright light. Here we see, once again, the importance of the protecting saints. Saint Agatha was venerated throughout the region, and Saint Prosper's relics were owned by the parish church. Other notations still emphasize the presence of the Virgin, even though she is only one among other mediators. Thus we hear of "the Holy Virgin praying

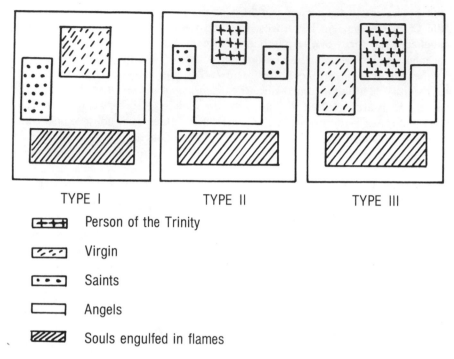

TYPE I   TYPE II   TYPE III

[+ + +]	Person of the Trinity
[/ / /]	Virgin
[• • •]	Saints
[ ]	Angels
[////]	Souls engulfed in flames

Type I: The Trinity is not shown, the Virgin is at the summit of the hierarchy
Type II: The Virgin is not shown
Type III: The Virgin is shown at the intermediate level of the intercessors

Figure 8.5. Altarpieces on altars to the souls in Purgatory

for the souls in purgatory." Here too, the figure of Christ probably occupied the center and the upper part of the canvas, as it does in the altarpiece of La Colle that can still be seen in the old penitents' chapel. The figure represents the same risen Christ I have cited above; his arms are stretched out and he is surrounded by the heavenly hosts. Kneeling to his right, the Virgin intercedes for the souls in purgatory, who are seen below and to the left. The souls present the tranquil appearance that has been shown by G. and M. Vovelle to be characteristic for the period 1730–90 in Provence as a whole. In the upper right corner of the altarpiece a monk is saying mass; he can be identified as Nicolas de Tolentino, the patron of the souls in purgatory. This is both an allusion to the history of that saint and an affirmation of the power of prayer and the power of masses for the dead ordered by the living. At times, the evocations of the visiting bishops are laconic, mentioning only "the souls of purgatory." One of the altarpieces "described" in this manner is that of Courségoules, which in the upper section shows God the Father, the dove of the Holy Ghost, and Jesus as a boy presented by the kneeling Virgin. Immediately below this Trinity there is also an abstract representation of Christ in the guise of a host floating above a chalice raised up toward the Father by a kneeling angel.

G. and M. Vovelle, who have cataloged the altars dedicated to the souls in purgatory for Provence as a whole, have outlined the following evolution: between 1670 and 1730, the Virgin as a mediatrix was replaced by the Virgin with the Child, and the intercessors tended to disappear; after 1730 the theme of the Madonna and Child receded, while images of Christ and the eternal Father became more prevalent. From my vantage point of the very early eighteenth century, I can confirm these changes.[51] However, G. and M. Vovelle cited as an exceptional case the altarpiece at Cagnes (1715), showing the Trinity and the symbolic image of a chalice surmounted by a host. As we have just seen, this representation existed in eastern Provence at the very beginning of the century. This remote area of Provence, where the new devotion took hold very late, appears to have experienced a more rapid evolution than the rest of the province.

Despite their diversity, the altarpieces treating the theme of the souls in purgatory present some striking analogies. The divinity usually occupies the place of honor, the center and the upper part of the altarpiece; whenever the Trinity is not depicted, this space is occupied by the Virgin. On the middle level are the mediating saints, and further down the angels who come to deliver the souls. Finally, at the very bottom of the altarpiece, the waiting people are depicted. This hierarchy is found everywhere, although one or the other elements may be missing. In this pictorial space the saint is no longer God's equal; he is represented, not for his own sake, but in relation to a divinity that is far above him. More than that, he is often replaced by the host or by a ciborium held by an angel. Here too the Church transmitted its message and glorified its power. The consecrated host has the power to efface sin, but only the priest, like Nicolas de Tolentino, raised up into the ranks of the mediators, has the power to transform the bread into the body of Christ.

In terms of their iconographical themes the new devotions are the complete opposite of the old ones. The Virgin and the saints refer to something that is beyond themselves: the Virgin of the Rosary refers to the mysteries of the Redemption, which are represented around her; Saint Joseph intercedes with God to obtain the grace of a good death for the faithful; the traditional saints pray for the deliverance of the souls in purgatory. A superior power, God or the Holy Ghost, is always pictured on the canvas. The saints no longer protect the faithful, they are reduced to the role of models. They no longer have a specific "virtue"; their effectiveness has become contingent on their relation with God. Underlying these pictorial representations is the desire to make all the faithful submissive to the Church—each individual to his superiors—for the essential value in every area of life has become obedience. In this didactic art—indeed, this propaganda—only the rosary, which attributes such great importance to the Virgin, retains some of the aspects of the old devotions. The devotions to Saint Joseph and to the souls in purgatory share one remarkable trait, namely, the representation of man's final destiny, or death, as the reward or sanction for his life in this world. Moral precepts thus became part of the iconography, just as they were emphasized in religion. They became the mainstay of the established society.

The Main Altar

After the Counter Reformation, then, a conflict arose between old and new practices, between *true* Christianity as defined by the Council of Trent and the pagan mentality, against which all missionaries and zealous prelates directed their concerted efforts.[52] The disposition of the altars that can be observed in the dioceses of Vence and Grasse and their iconography testify to this struggle, for it is clear that the new devotions were placed at the top of the hierarchy, while the others were relegated to locations further back in the church or to outlying areas of the village territory. In this context one wonders about the appearance of the main altar, the sacred focus of the church and the first altar to be inspected by the visiting bishop. Curiously enough, the iconography of the main altar appears to have been rather impervious to new influences.

Many of the main altars, 30 percent to be precise, were old. Half of these were in mountain villages, which thus appear to have been more conservative and poorer than the rest of the area. The themes of these altarpieces were similar to those of the altars dedicated to the saints. Here is how one of them is described:[53]

The retable consists of very old sculptures; the figures are gilded in most places and otherwise painted. The principal figure is that in the middle, representing Saint Mary-Magdalen, titular Saint of the said church. Below this figure is a sculpted chest serving as the tabernacle. On the Gospel side is the figure of Saint Peter the Apostle and on the Epistle side that of Saint Michael the Archangel.

All the descriptions of the main altars suggest that the saints were represented in the same alignment as in the rural chapels. Two altarpieces that are still in the same place confirm this assumption. They are wooden panels painted by Bréa or a member of his school, showing the different figures under arcades or in separate compartments and in the hieratic attitudes repeatedly evoked in the present study. One of these altarpieces unites three figures of equal importance: Saint Stephen in the middle, flanked by Saint John the Baptist and Saint Anthony. The other shows a number of saints grouped around Saint Jacques, and a Virgin and Child seated upon a throne, with the Virgin pictured above the apostle.[54]

Many of the canvases that can be identified by the vocabulary used to describe them as contemporaneous with these pastoral visitations, or at least as new at the time, show the same frontal and majestic disposition of the figures. Consider the description of the altarpiece at Gattières: "A painting on canvas representing the Holy Virgin carrying the Holy Child Jesus on her arm, with Saint Joseph and Saint Blasius to one side and Saint Anthony and Saint Nicolas to the other. This painting is embellished by a sculpted walnut ornament with two columns and a large cornice, and with other ornaments."[55] Today this altarpiece can be seen in the right-side aisle of the church; the canvas bears the date 1690. In the center it shows a Virgin similar to the Virgins of Majesty, seated on a throne with a Child Jesus carrying the globe in one hand and bestowing the blessing with the other. The surrounding saints form a circle around the Virgin and Child. The persons of the divinity appear only in the surrounding framework. The central medallion, for example, depicts God the Father holding the globe and bestowing the blessing. Below the capitals of the columns, Saint Blasius and Saint Nicolas are shown a second time. At Saint-Césaire an altarpiece of the same type is treated in a more "modern" manner: here the Virgin is less majestic, the Child plays with Saint John's rod, and the saints surrounding the Madonna are standing in less rigid attitudes. Although God the Father appears in the upper part of the painting rather than in the surrounding framework, the arrangement as a whole is the same.

Sixty percent of these altarpieces resemble those that are found in chapels dedicated to saints. The others, according to the records of pastoral visitations, depict various scenes; "The Assumption of Notre Dame," "The Nativity of Our Lord," "The Conversion of Saint Paul," "Jesus Christ Appears to Saint Mary-Magdalen," and so forth. Here again, the few altarpieces that are still extant show the persistence of the traditions. One example is the altarpiece at Caille, which represents the martyrdom of Saint Stephen. The saint is kneeling. He looks serene and is wearing the vestments of a deacon; he is surrounded by his torturers who are about to stone him. There is nothing terrifying about this scene. Its serenity is further enhanced by the presence of a small angel who presents the saint with his attributes, the palm frond and the crown.

Some of the altarpieces are more deeply marked by the Counter Reformation. They are those whose principal subject lends itself to a glorification of the papacy. According to the records of the visitations there were only two of these. One of them depicts "Saint Gregory the Great on Saint Peter's Chair," and the other is entitled, "Our Lord Giving the Keys to Saint Peter."[56] The latter, still to be seen at the church of Cagnes, is designed to emphasize the prime role of the pope. In the middle of the lower section, Christ hands the

keys to the kneeling Saint Peter; the two figures are surrounded by the other
apostles. In this canvas the keys are exactly in the center of the painting. Also
in the center, but in the background, one can distinguish Saint Peter's chair,
which is identical to the chair at Rome. Above that chair two little angels
hold aloft the tiara, and over the tiara hovers the luminous dove of the Holy
Ghost. Above this pyramid-shaped scene the sky is wide open, suffused in an
ochre-toned light, whereas the rest of the painting is rather dark. A powerful
figure of God the Father occupies most of this space, surrounded by the heavenly hosts. Clearly this figure was not added to the altarpiece as an after-
thought; on the contrary, it dominates its vertical axis (keys, chair, tiara,
dove) toward which everything converges.

THE ICONOGRAPHY OF THE MAIN ALTAR

The altarpieces of the main altars, seemingly so diverse in their subject
matter, if not in their iconography, nonetheless present a remarkable uniformity. They always feature the titular saint of the church. The latter is often
the center of the altarpiece if the panel features a number of saints, and he is
the principal figure when it depicts a scene. One even encounters altarpieces
that preserve the memory of a former titular saint. Sometimes the titular saint
is replaced by the Virgin who, as the universal protectress, has no doubt taken
over the specific protective function attributed to that saint. In such cases the
titular saint is represented at her side, as in the altarpiece at Gattières, where
Saint Blasius and Saint Nicolas, who flank the Virgin, were the titular and
the patron saint of the church, respectively.

Other saints appear, grouped around the titular and sometimes the patron
saint of the church. They are the special protectors of the community. Among
them are the saints who enjoyed particularly widespread veneration, such as
Saint John the Baptist, Saint John the Evangelist, Saint Peter, and Saint Anthony of Padua.

The function of the altarpiece on the main altar, then, appears to be similar to that of the altarpieces in chapels dedicated to saints, for it manifests
and calls upon all of the community's protective saints. Along with the titular
saints, healing saints are also featured. If the altarpiece sometimes makes
use of a more erudite iconography, as at Cagnes, where it is marked by the
ideology of the Counter Reformation, the fact nonetheless remains that even
there the altarpiece of the main altar is designed to give presence to the
church's titular saint, Saint Peter. The new art only made itself felt on the
main altar when it could treat a theme dear to the Counter Reformation by
means of the titular saint. This is what happened at Gréolières. In 1705 the
visiting bishop found there a "large and very old, painted and gilded retable
on which is represented Saint Peter with, at his right, the image of Saint Au-

gustin and Saint Catherine and, on his left, Saint John the Evangelist and Saint Sebastian."[57] Today, a canvas surrounded by a stucco ornament of imitation red and white marble shows only Saint Peter on his chair, borne by the four Doctors of the Church. This altarpiece was undoubtedly placed in the church in the course of the eighteenth century. The protective local saints and the healing saints have disappeared; only the titular saint is left, and he is used to glorify the Counter Reformation.

Like the altarpieces in rural chapels, the altarpieces of main altars are designed to manifest a power, the power of all the saints to whom the community has devoted itself. This attitude would seem to explain their resistence to new devotions, which could only be expressed on the lateral altars. It would also seem to explain the effacement of the persons of the divinity, who are often relegated to the surrounding framework, as at Gattières, and only rarely integrated into the composition of the altarpiece itself, as at Cagnes, where the subject matter happened to lend itself to such a treatment.

THE ROLE OF THE RELIQUARY BUSTS

Reliquary busts further accentuated the protective function of the main altar for the community. To begin with, their location is significant. Like the location of the different altars, that of the reliquary busts was strictly regulated. The niches and cabinets containing a relic were always very close to the main altar "on the Gospel side," or "next to the altar" [as the records put it]. When the parish owned two busts, they were placed at either side of the altar. Equally significant is the role of the reliquary busts. Placed close to the main altar, they reinforced its protective function. The records of pastoral visitations testify to the major importance of this protective function. They often mention, for instance, new relics placed into a bust representing the titular or patron saint of the parish. In this manner a new protection was added to the existing one. This alliance became so close that it did not take long for a new relic recently brought from Rome to be treated as the immemorial relic of the titular saint.[58] Conversely, newly acquired relics of a new saint soon caused that saint to become the patron of the parish.[59]

The most widespread form of the reliquary was the bust. Unlike the altarpiece of the main altar, the bust was a novelty whose progress can be observed through the records of episcopal visitations.[60] Busts seem to have become the most "decent" manner of housing relics. They were frequently arranged in pairs in the vicinity of the main altar: Saint Honoré and Saint Liberata, Saint Constant and Saint Felicisma, and so forth. If the church happened to have only two busts of male saints, a female bust might be added; otherwise the relics of a female saint were placed into one of the male busts. Here one senses a desire to create a balance between male and female protection. This phenomenon assumed an ever wider scope as the century progressed; today one frequently encounters heads placed at either side of the main altar, both of them without a name, but one of them male and the other female.

The saint represented in this manner had no recognizable attributes: the bust does not administer a lesson. One can barely recognize Saint Jacques by the scallop shells on his shoulders, or a holy bishop by the mitre he is wearing.

These busts were interchangeable objects. Visiting bishops implicitly acknowledged this when they demanded that the reliquaries be labeled or that each of them actually correspond to the relic contained within.[61] The bust was a presence. The attributes of the individual saint were of little importance; what counted was the existence of the relic.[62]

This is why the reliquary busts that can still be seen, whether they are old, like the bust of Saint Claude at Cipières (said to date from the fourteenth century and an exceptional case on other grounds as well) or new, like most of them, always show the same characteristics. The busts of saints were usually reduced to a head and a pair of shoulders, which made them less costly. Above a stand that contains the relic and above these armless shoulders appears a very stylized face supported by a heavy neck. The bust as a whole has the massive character of an object designed to be carried. Contrasting colors further accentuate the stylized shapes. The face is natural in color, whereas the eyebrows and the eyes are painted black, and clothing and tiaras are gilded. All the attention is focused on the very expressive eyes, which give the reliquary an almost threatening look. The saint it is purported to represent no longer has a human face; the bust is but a mask. It is the shrine that houses the protective relics of the parish, the means by which they can be touched and carried about.[63]

Present in almost every church, and destined to become ever more numerous in the course of the century, these busts, together with the main altar, perpetuated the traditional function of that altar, which was to manifest the protectors of the community. Here we seem to witness a kind of relay phenomenon, for at the very time when the altarpieces began to come under the influence of the Counter Reformation, the reliquary bust, though a novelty, became the vehicle of a tradition. It was often hidden in a niche closed with wooden doors or iron grillwork, but the decorations surrounding these niches reminded everyone that the protector was there, that he would be exhibited on solemn feast days, and that he would be carried in procession throughout the village territory on Rogation day.

* * *

At the beginning of the eighteenth century the iconography of the various sacred places within a village territory testified to an ongoing struggle. A "new religion," which stressed the persons of the Trinity and the authority of the Church and reduced the traditional saints to the role of intermediaries, endeavored to push aside an older one, in which the power of the saints was uncontested. A "new religion," which stressed personal morality and the role of the priest, endeavored to push aside an older one in which the "noncleric," whatever his merits, could reach God directly by appealing to the saints. This struggle was far from resolved at the beginning of the eighteenth century; it simply divided the church in half. On the one hand, we hear of rich altars, decorated with many candelabras, altarcloths, and altar frontals; on the other, of old altarpieces over altars supplied with the bare necessities, and at times not even that. This divergence resulted from a split that opposed the "true religion,"—the clerical religion that was adopted, as I have shown elsewhere,[64] by the village elite—to "superstition"—the religion of the "little people." This latter religion was relegated to the rural chapels, which were henceforth viewed with vague suspicion and distrust.

Yet the mirror held up by iconography shows that by the beginning of the eighteenth century this dichotomy was not yet complete. New devotions made use of the powerful appeal of the older ones to be better understood and more widely adopted. Some of the figures of this iconography assumed a dual role. Saint Joseph, though he had become the saint of the Good Death, was also a protector, the patron saint of a brotherhood like many another traditional patron saint. The Virgin of the Rosary was also the Virgin of Mercy, and although she was often depicted in the context of the new devotion, the Church's teaching became subsidiary to the old image of protection. The souls in purgatory were protected, as they had always been, by the saint whose relics were owned by the parish.

The real stake in this conflict between the traditional and the new current was the main altar. Its iconography usually did not focus on the Trinity or on the glorification of the Church but, rather, on a specific local devotion. The altarpieces of the main altar asserted the power of the titular saint, the foremost protector of the community, as well as that of the healing saints; in addition, reliquary busts presented the bodily remnants of new saints who promised new protection. But the main altar was also the place where the Eucharist was present, and if for some reason its decor had to be changed, the new altarpiece was made to glorify the tradition of the Church by means of the titular saint. Yet in the early eighteenth century, despite the clergy's well-devised efforts to establish a hierarchy in the spatial arrangement of the church, this dominant point of sacredness was still focused on all the existing devotions. In the unique and supremely sacred space of the main altar, the old devotions adjoined the Eucharist and thereby recovered a measure of equality.

APPENDIX A. Chapels in the dioceses of Vence and Grasse in the Eighteenth Century

Fig. A-1

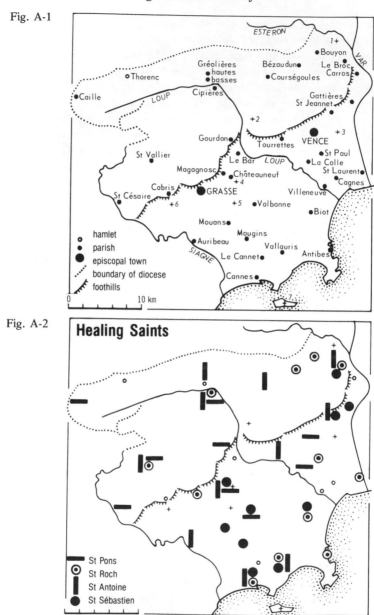

Fig. A-2

Note: Parishes of the eighteenth century that did not have a chapel listed in the documentation are indicated by a cross and a number. The latter refer to the following names: 1: Deux-frères; 2: Courmes; 3: La Gaude; 4: Opio; 5: Plascassier; 6: Peymenade; 7: Sainte-Marguerite.

Fig. A-3

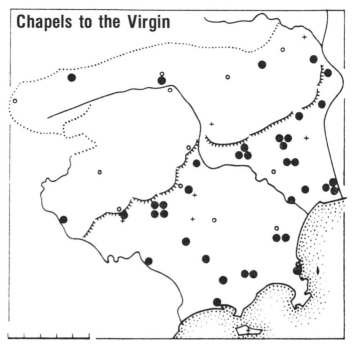

Chapels to the Virgin

Fig. A-4

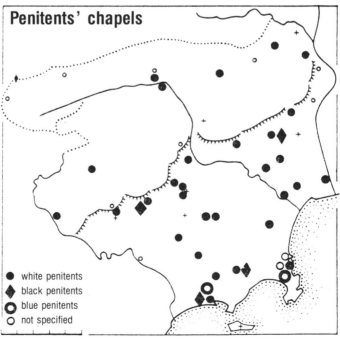

Penitents' chapels

● white penitents
◆ black penitents
◎ blue penitents
○ not specified

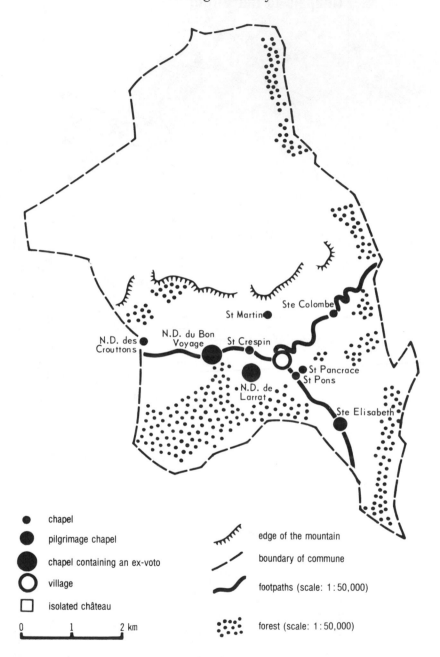

Fig. B-1 Vence

Fig. B-2 Tourrettes

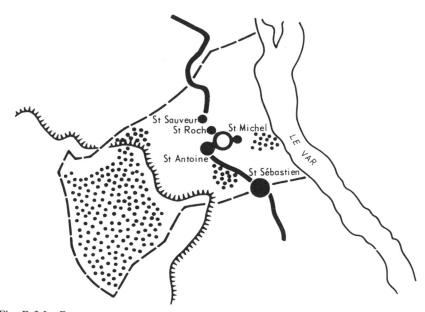

Fig. B-3 Le Broc

177

NOTES

1. V. L. Tapié, J. P. Le Flem, A. Pardailhé-Galabrun, *Retables baroques de Bretagne et spiritualité du XVIIe siècle* (Paris, 1972).

2. Pastoral visitations of the diocese of Vence: Théodore Allart (1682-85), Jean Balthazar de Cabanes de Viens (1686-97), François des Bertons de Crillon (1687-1714), Flodoart Moret de Bourchenu (1714-28); diocese of Grasse: Louis Aube de Roquemartine (1676-82), François Verjus (1684-1711), Joseph Ignace de Mesgrigny (1711-26), Charles Léonce d'Anthelmy (1726-52).

3. Emile Mâle, *L'Art religieux après le Concile de Trente* (Paris, 1931).

4. Maurice Agulhon, "La Notion de village en Basse Provence vers la fin de l'Ancien Régime," in *Actes du 90e congrès des Sociétés Savantes* (Nice, 1965).

5. List of titular saints: The Virgin (12), Magdalen (4), Peter (3), John the Baptist (2), Martin (2), Trophine (2), Stephen (2), Margaret (2); one each for Jacques, Catherine, Lawrence, Vincent, Mayol, Pandoise, Césaire, Andrew, Gregory, Blasius, Paul, and the Transfiguration.

List of patron saints: Magdalen (4), Stephen (2), Peter (2), the Virgin (2), Jacques (2), Lawrence (2), Trophine (2), Barnabas (2); one each for Anne, Catherine, Nicolas, Martin, Mayol, Vallier, Anthony, Veran and Lanbert, Blasius, John the Baptist George, and Marc.

6. See the distribution of these chapels in the appendixes.

7. Saint Pons protected the cattle. See visitation of Caille by Bourchenu, 30 August 1715. G 1257.

8. Contagious diseases and the plague were still raging during this period. The great plague of Marseilles, after all, took place in the years 1720-22. For the distribution of these chapels, see the appropriate map at the end of this article.

9. The records of the visitations often give the number of members in a brotherhood, but only for the men. In the two cases that do mention female membership, the number of women is higher than that of men.

10. I have dealt with this problem in an earlier article, "Les Dévotions populaires d'après les visites pastorales: Un example: le diocèse de Vence au début du XVIIIe siècle," *Revue de l'Histoire de l'Eglise de France* (June 1974).

11. A few exceptions to this rule can be found in parishes serving a small group of families living in "uninhabited" places.

12. Parish of Opio: visitation by Roquemartine of 20 February 1680 (G 24), visitations by Verjus of 28 April 1705 (G 25) and by Mesgrigny of 4 July 1712 (G 26), visitation by d'Anthelmy of 23 September 1736.

13. It is referred to in the record of the visitations by François des Bertons de Crillon and his vicar general Jean-Baptiste Olive (G 1250-53). The visitor speaks of the altars "on the Gospel side" and on "the Epistle side." Moreover, he ranks them for each side of the church in descending order, starting at the main altar, by using unequivocal terms such as "in the very front," "below that," and "in the very back." It is on the basis of that description that I have been able to reconstruct the interior of these churches. See the examples show in figure 1.

14. Emile Mâle, *L'Art religieux du XIIIe siècle en France*, 8th ed. (Paris, 1948).

15. G. Doublet, "Monographie de l'ancienne collégiale de Saint-Paul," *Annales Soc. A. M.*, vol. 18 (1901).

16. Neither for Vence in 1683 nor for Grasse in 1678-80, the dates of the earliest visitations under study here, can a trace of this devotion be found. It became widespread between 1687 and 1715. The establishment of new altars dedicated to it can be observed as late as the middle of the eighteenth century.

17. The visiting bishop often preferred the expression "sculpted ornament" to "retable." The expression "altarpiece on canvas" occurs very frequently. The newness of these decors is underscored by the approving remarks of the visiting bishops, such as "in good condition," "very handsome," "very neat," or "properly decorated."

18. Nonetheless, some rich chapels can be found in the two towns where the bishops resided and in the more prosperous of the small towns, such as Saint-Paul or Cannes.

19. Visitation of Cannes by Verjus, 6 July 1687 (G 25).

20. Visitation of Courségoules by J.-B. Olive, 19 August 1705 (G 1253).

21. Visitation of Saint-Jeannet by J.-B. Olive, 22 July 1705 (G 1253).

22. These other saints are smaller figures decorating the edges of the altarpiece. They are, on the right side, Saint Lawrence, Saint Agnes, and Saint Peter of Verona; and on the left side, Saint Sebastian, Saint Barbara, and Saint Bernard of Siena. All are shown with their attributes, which make them easily recognizable.

23. In 1716 this altarpiece had not yet replaced an old wooden one.

24. André Malraux, *Les Voix du silence* (Paris, 1951).

25. Visitation of Vence by Bourchenu, 30 June 1716 (G 1259).

26. Visitation of Mouans by Roquemartine, 21 October 1679 (G 24), of Saint-Paul by Crillon, 24 March 1699 (G 1251), of Cannes by Verjus, 6 July (G 25), of Saint-Césaire by Mesgrigny, 9 July 1712 (G 26).

27. There seems to be confusion between Saint Honoré and Saint Honorat. At Grasse, the altar ornamented by Bréa's altarpiece is called "Saint Honoré altar" in 1679 and "Saint Honorat and Saint Honoré" in 1712 and 1722, when it is "kept up by the brotherhood of the bakers." In the records concerning Saint Michael's chapel at Le Broc we hear in 1705 of an altarpiece representing "Saint Michael the Archangel, Saint Anthony of Padua, and Saint Honoré," whereas in 1715, the reference is to "Saint Michael, Saint Honnorat the Bishop, and Saint Anthony."

28. The altarpiece of Saint Claude at Cipières is a striking example. The same characteristics are found in old altarpieces such as that of Saint John the Baptist at Courségoules, and in the new ones such as Saint Anthony's at Châteauneuf.

29. Nine of the twenty-seven altarpieces whose subject matter is identified in the records of the visitations are of this type. Here are a few examples: "Notre Dame with the infant Jesus, Saint John the Baptist, Saint Pancratius, Saint Donatius, and Saint Blasius," "Notre Dame in the middle, with Saint Louis and Saint Claude," "Notre Dame, Saint Agatha and Saint Cler [Chaire?]."

30. Visitation of Bézudun by J.-B. Olive, 7 August 1705 (G 1253).

31. Eleven of twenty-seven altarpieces are of this kind.

32. Visitation of Vence by Crillon, 12 March 1699 (G 1253).

33. J. Levrot, *Catalogue de l'exposition rétrospective d'art régional* (Nice, Musée municipal des Beaux-Arts, 1913). Levrot attributes this altarpiece to Jacques de Carolis.

34. All these designations are used synonymously in P. Pedrizet, "La Vièrge de Miséricorde," except the last, which is a local expression. Perdrizet cites a Notre Dame of Mercy for a chapel called "Notre Dame du peuple" at Draguignan, and according to the records of the visitations two of the "Notre Dame del populo" chapels had retables representing Notre Dame of Mercy.

35. Saint Sebastian's chapel at Cabris.

36. Here are a few examples: The altarpiece in a chapel dedicated to Notre Dame of Mercy at Grasse is called "Descent from the Cross" in 1679 and *Mater dolorosa* (Notre Dame de Pitié] in 1712. The altarpiece does not seem to have been changed. This is also the case for two other chapels, as well as for the designation of the altars in a number of churches.

37. Visitation by Mesgrigny, 3 July 1712 (G 26), and by Roquemartine, 14 October 1679 (G 24).

38. Emile Mâle, *L'Art religieux à la fin du Moyen Age en France* (Paris, 1931).

39. Penitents' chapels at Grasse and at Cannes. Similar subjects are depicted at Châteauneuf and at Villeneuve.

40. Church at Gréolières, altarpiece dated 1730. A second altarpiece treats the subject in a similar manner; it can be seen at Gourdon.

41. This altarpiece originated in the old chapel of the black penitents of Grasse. The saints in question are certainly Saint Martin and Saint Benedict, who were mentioned in 1679. The church probably replaced the old altarpiece but stipulated that the same personages be represented. This was a fairly common practice.

42. Visitation of Grasse by Roquemartine, 9 April 1679 (G 24).

43. The author used a passage of the "Story of Joseph the Carpenter" in the Apocrypha, where Jesus says: "I sat down at his head and my mother at his feet. I held his hand in mine for more than an hour. The archangels Michael and Gabriel drew near to him and he joyfully rendered his last breath. I closed his eyes with my hands and the angels came to clothe him in a white robe." Quote taken from Mâle, *L'Art religieux après le Concile de Trente.*

44. This text, which establishes a brotherhood at Grasse and is dated 1 April 1588, is cited in Doublet, "Monographie de l'ancienne collégiale de Saint-Paul."

45. Presented as Saint Dominic's weapon against the Albigensians, this devotion became the weapon against all forms of heresy after the Council of Trent.

46. Visitation of Saint-Jeannet by Bourchenu, 12 September 1715 (G 1256): "Surrounding her in different separate and distinct squares are depicted the mysteries of the Incarnation and various acts of the Virgin that are mentioned in the Gospel."

47. The protective aspect of the Virgin that seems to be discernible in the altarpieces of the rosary is reinforced by the many statues decorating these altars. Twenty-seven of the thirty-one altars have at least one statue, but often there are more. In some cases as many as five statues decorate these altars. The "images" of Notre Dame of Protection are frequently decorated with presents. This popular homage to the protective and mediating Virgin shows that she was not eclipsed by the Virgin of the Rosary.

48. Cf. L. Réau, *Iconographie de l'art chrétien*, 2: 123.

49. Cf. G. Vovelle and M. Vovelle, "Vision de la mort et de l'au-delà en Provence d'après les autels des âmes du purgatoire," *Annales, E.S.C.* 24 (November-December 1969).

50. In the diocese of Grasse, altars dedicated to the souls in purgatory often replaced altars featuring the Five Wounds of Christ, the Crucifixion, and the Mater dolorosa. In 1715 the altarpiece at Tourettes represented "Jesus crucified and below the souls in purgatory." A *Mater dolorosa* [Notre Dame de Pitié] is also shown on the altar of the souls in purgatory at Antibes.

51. As we have seen, this devotion took hold in the region rather late. A few of these altarpieces can be dated as follows on the basis of the records of the visitations: The first reference, (Notre Dame interceding [Notre Dame des Suffrages]), is dated 1705; the altarpiece of Saint Vallier is mentioned in 1712; that of Châteauneuf, showing Saint Prosper and Saint Agatha, in 1712 (although the altar was new in 1700); the altar of the souls in purgatory at La Colle is mentioned in 1719; the altarpiece of Courségoules is mentioned in 1715 (although the brotherhood had been founded in 1705).

52. It is not too much to say that the entire Christian elite of the time felt that the people were not "Christianized." The bishops of the two dioceses studied here, some of whom sent out missionaries before they embarked on their rounds of visitations, would certainly have agreed with the judgment of Father Maunoir's biographer concerning Lower Brittany: "In a sense, teaching the Christian doctrine there amounted to implanting the [Christian] faith" (*Le parfait missionnaire*, 1697).

53. Visitation of Courségoules by J.-B. Olive, 17 August 1705 (G 1253).

54. Surrounding Saint Jacques in the lower part of the retable: Saint Benedict, Saint Jerome, Saint Mary-Magdalen, and Saint Peter of Verona. At the next level, at the feet of the Virgin: Saint Joseph as an old man, Saint Paul, Saint Peter, and Saint John the Baptist. Above: Saint Cosimus, Saint Anne, holding the Virgin as a child by the hand, Saint Francis, and Saint Damian. At the very top of the altarpiece: the Trinity (God the Father holding in his arms Christ on the Cross, overshadowed by the Holy Ghost), surrounded by the symbols of the four evangelists.

55. Visitation by J.-B. Olive, 25 July 1705 (G 1253).

56. Visitation of Tourettes by Crillon, 17 March 1699 (G 1251); visitation of Cagnes by the same bishop, 5 April 1699 (G 1250).

57. Visitation of Gréolières by J.-B. Olive, 21 August 1705 (G 1253).

58. At le Bar in 1687, two busts containing relics of "st Allexandre" and "ste Ephigénie" were mentioned. In 1693, one of these busts seemed to represent Saint Jacques. In 1705, the two busts were said to contain "the bones of Saint Jacques and Saint John with their authentic seals." Saint Jacques was the titular saint of the church and Saint John its patron saint.

59. According to the records of the visitations, the titular saint of the church of La Gaude was Saint Peter; but the parish also owned a bust and some relics of Saint Victoria. Today Saint Victoria is the titular saint (*Annuaire diocésain de Nice*, 1967).

60. A good example is Valbone. In 1678, the record mentions relics of Saint Blasius and of the "forty martyrs" in a shrine and relics of Saint Sebastian in an arm. In 1687 the parish owned two reliquary busts. Changes of this kind are recorded for many of these villages.

61. One often finds the visiting bishop leaving instructions similar to the following: "We have ordered a golden arm to be made for housing the relic of Saint Benedict the martyr, which must not remain in a bishop's bust, considering that the said Saint Benedict was only a martyr and not a bishop; or else that the mitre of the said bust should be removed and replaced with a martyr's crown." Visitation of Châteauneuf by Mesgrigny, 4 July 1712 (G 26).

62. Moreover, the new relics imported from Rome had no history. The saints were martyrs without specific individuality; but their relics nonetheless preserved all of their "virtue."

63. Although this was the general character of these busts, they are differentiated by their richness. The "poor" busts accentuate the compact character of the reliquary, while the richer ones are not quite so massive and show a certain concern for detail.

64. M. H. Froeschlé-Chopard, "Les Dévotions populaires d'après les visites pastorales," cited in n. 10 above.

9

Sociocultural Aspects of Religious Conflicts in Paris during the Second Half of the Sixteenth Century

Denis Richet

The dispassionate study of the religious clashes in sixteenth-century France is made difficult by our contemporary ideological blinders. Such a study is also burdened by the weight of historiographical traditions. Do the "ecumenical" trends that can be observed today in varying degrees within religious denominations—and especially within the Catholic Church after Vatican II—help us to understand the issues at stake in the past? This is probably the case, for the official ceremonies organized in Paris to commemorate the four-hundredth anniversary of Admiral Coligny's death reveal above everything else the cleavages that still persist. Nonetheless, benedictions took the place of musket shots. On the Protestant side, allegiance to the memory of the martyrs often goes hand in hand with an obstinate refusal to accept a history that tries to explain events. Witness the indignant reactions triggered by an article that a weekly publication asked me to write about the Saint Bartholomew's Day massacre.[1] Like the French Revolution, the long years of persecution experienced by the Protestants still disturb certain sensitive individuals to the point that they become locked into a purely commemorative frame of mind about the clashes that took place four hundred years ago.

Nor can historiographical pressures be neglected. Be they Catholic, Protestant, or agnostic, historians have long stressed three themes: the clashes between communities over dogma, the severity and absurdity of the persecutions, and the links between religious affiliations and social classes. Their re-

Annales, E.S.C. 32 (July-August 1977): 764–89. Translated by Patricia M. Ranum

search has often produced results that are remarkable,[2] although limited in scope and on occasion subject to revision. Indeed, certain simplistic sociologists, such as Hauser and Engels, once provoked a lively reaction from Lucien Febvre.[3] But the fact that a question is, as he called it, *mal posée*—wrongly stated—does not necessarily mean that it should be definitively buried. Still, if we read the works of some leading historians,[4] we might jump to the conclusion that there was no link at all between the Reformation and society.

Recent research[5] reveals a new orientation: integrate the fields in which historians have worked intensively (dogma, worship, and overt or latent antagonism) into a broader perspective which is partly inspired by such related social sciences as cultural anthropology, collective psychology, and even psychoanalysis. Studying a "culture" (in the praiseworthy or positive connotation of the word) as a civilization that only produced major texts is being replaced by studying conduct and value systems, or the relationships between the individual and the group or between individuals and groups.

I shall be more modest here. I plan to concentrate upon a few themes in the Paris of the "Wars of Religion" and to present a few hypotheses based upon a study of the Parisian *notables*, the city's leading citizens.[6] At that time Paris was experiencing the interpenetration of two conflicting situations, or a double cleavage. The more apparent of the two conflicts, and the least understood, pitted the *mal sentans* [those whose religious opinions were considered heretical] against the Parisian *notables* who remained attached to the Catholic Church. I am not going to discuss "novation" and "tradition," for this conflict was not couched in these terms and did not involve the same dynamics in 1594 as it did in 1559. Above all, this conflict cut across another cleavage that ran throughout the entire period. Although they expressed it at different times and in different ways, these divided *notables* shared a common desire to impose a more vital religion and a stricter moral code upon the lower classes and ensure a tighter control over their daily life. Could the common people's dissatisfaction with this elitist cultural aggression be expressed without clinging to the nostalgia and hopes of the social classes that separated them from the *notables*? These intermediate classes were close enough to the emotions of the common people to legitimate the meaning of those emotions and, as a result of their education and person-to-person contacts, were sufficiently linked to the world of the *notables* to gain a hearing.

* * *

I shall not go back to the beginning of the Reformation in Paris. Crespin's *Martyrologe*, Henri Hauser's research, and that of several generations of scholars have made it possible to reconstruct the general picture. In order to understand Catholic reactions, we must go back to the years between 1555 (the "implantation" of the Reformed Church of Paris) and March 1562 (the beginning of the first "War of Religion"), which have often been called a turning point. I believe that we must evaluate, if not measure, the nature and the results of the fundamental changes that took place during those years.

A brief recapitulation of the main events is essential. Most of them are discussed in the history of the Reformed Church of Paris that was written a decade after they occurred by Pastor Antoine de la Roche-Chandieu. After two years of silent Protestant infiltration (1555–57) came the "incident of the rue Saint-Jacques," in September 1557. Four hundred of the faithful assembled in the La Souche house, which belonged to Jacques Berthommier, a royal councillor.[7] Attacked by a mob, they were tried, and seven of them were burned at the stake.[8] The following year the shocking behavior of the Protestants spread to public sites: psalms were sung in the Pré-aux-Clercs [an uncultivated area adjoining the abbey of Saint-Germain-des-Prés]. King Henry II forbade these demonstrations, and the leaders of the Protestant church of Paris asked the faithful to refrain from singing psalms outside their homes. Shortly afterward (March 5) two people suspected of being Protestants were massacred in the cemetery of the Saints-Innocents, as a result of the Lenten sermons being preached in Catholic churches. In 1559 the effort to eliminate Protestants became overt and brutal.[9] Henry II intervened in the *mercuriale** of the Parlement of Paris and had Anne Du Bourg and four other councillors arrested. The edict of Ecouen intensified these harsh measures. Henry II's death in 1559 did not end the legalized violence. On 28 December 1559 Anne Du Bourg was executed. Not until Francis II's death in 1560 and the edict of Amboise did the monarchy openly acknowledge the increasing spread of the Protestant movement.

From that time on, Protestantism in Paris came out of hiding, triggering violence and incidents, the most notable of which occurred in the faubourg Saint-Marcel during the final days of 1561. The house called "The Patriarch," which belonged to Jean Canaye,[10] a wealthy merchant, was the scene of "conventicles"—secret or illicit meetings—and echoed with the sound of psalms, exasperating the priest and parishioners of the nearby church of Saint-Médard: "There was only a narrow street between the two localities." On 26 December the tocsin sounded, fighting broke out,[11] and one Gabaston, a captain of the city watch, led the Catholic "rioters" off to prison in the Petit-Châtelet. The following day, after protests by the royal attorneys before the Parlement, the prisoners were freed and it was decided instead that an expiatory procession would be held at Saint-Médard. The edict of 1562, which authorized Protestants to hold worship services in suburban homes, gave rise to numerous clashes.[12] After the massacre at Wassy (1 March) and the triumphant entry of the Duke of Guise into Paris (16 March), Catholic violence became quasi-official.

*The members of the various parlementary bodies would meet in plenary session each *mercredi*—Wednesday (hence the name, *mercuriale*)—to hear reports on the manner in which justice had been carried out.—Trans.

These events reveal a threefold change: a change in the social groups from which the members of the Huguenot (Protestant) community came, a change in the behavior of the faithful, and a change in the authorities' attitude toward them.

The fact that the Reformation had continued to recruit mainly craftsmen is proved by Crespin's membership lists and by the other lists that were preserved in documents of the period. But the important fact for the period 1557-62 is the overt shift of one segment of the elite to Protestantism and the hearing given the Protestants by the other *notables*. If we exclude the humanists of the 1520s, those burned at the stake had until then been chiefly craftsmen and small shopkeepers. After the execution in 1559 of Marguerite Le Riche, a bookseller's wife, members of the "establishment" were also burned at the stake.

That people of the time were aware of this phenomenon is extremely clear in the historical evidence supplied by both the Huguenots and their opponents. It is as if the definitive success or failure of the Reformation was going to depend upon one decisive issue: whether the *notables* would give Protestantism mass support. In a report sent to Geneva by the Reformed Church of Paris after the incident of the rue Saint-Jacques, we read: "The crowd that attended our assemblies included not only common people, with little education, but also a considerable number of the elite of France, as well as many nobles and magistrates. Honorable women and girls from the best families."[13] The list of the 159 individuals arrested at the time of this incident does not supply us with precise details, for occupations were rarely included; but it mentions 21 "damsels," several gentlemen, and royal officials.[14] Four years later, an uproar was created by the presence of one Desjardins, a *lieutenant de robe courte* and one of the chief magistrates in charge of the Paris police, at a conventicle held at "The Patriarch."[15] Among the evidence provided by Catholic sources I shall quote what I consider a very significant passage from the diary of Canon Bruslart:

Here I must omit nothing memorable that will show the deceitfulness of the new Evangelists and reveal their hypocrisy. On Friday the twentieth of the said month, they were given to understand that the Queen Mother [Catherine de Médicis] was going to watch them walk along the rue Saint-Antoine to their services. Notified of this, they summoned all manner of people to go to the services dressed in their finest garments and wearing *cornettes** in order to show the Queen that at their assemblies everyone was *respected and reputed folk* [Richet's italics]; and indeed most of them wore *cornettes*, even Du Moulin and Ruzé, attorneys at the [law] court, who had never previously worn such garb. And I must point out that the second-hand clothes sellers made a lot of money that day, because those who did not have fine clothes rented them in order to be considered of good repute.[16]

Cornette—a wide band of cloth that doctors of law wore about their necks and that hung down to the ground.—Trans.

What scandalized the canon was this claim to be *notables*. What worried him was the eventual impact that this spectacle would have upon the Queen Mother, and therefore upon those in power. Hence his desire to deny the changing social character of the Reformation.

These changes in Paris cannot be measured quantitatively.[17] Neither the lists of individuals arrested nor the lists of emigrants provide the required data. The *Livre des habitants de Genève*—the book of the inhabitants of Geneva—does not always give occupations, and the social sampling that it provides does not seem particularly representative of the Parisian community at that date. Those who remained in Paris did not necessarily belong to the same milieu as those who were forced to and were able to flee. Artisans and booksellers or goldsmiths seem overrepresented among the emigrants, as they later were in the lists of victims. Still, administrative and notarial sources do permit us to offer some answers based on qualitative information.

The milieu of the leading merchants, who were involved in international trade, was strongly affected. In a speech against the Cardinal of Lorraine that he attributed to a cloth merchant, Régnier de La Planche (who was very familiar with these merchant circles, to which his family belonged) gave both the names of certain merchants who had become Huguenots and a far longer list of people who were "sympathizers" or at least opposed to the policy of destroying the Protestants.[18] Among the former group were the Canayes, Nicolas Crocquet, and Jacquemin.[19] The second group, which totaled twenty-four names, were all *gens de bien* [people of probity and honor]. Robert Descimon and I found the same individuals in the ranks of the *échevins* [aldermen], the heads of one of the quarters of the city of Paris, and the leaders of the city militia. All of them belonged to what could be called the "two hundred families" of Parisian commerce.[20] This is not the place to go over these names one by one and attempt to evaluate their social "weight," although we could add many other names to those provided by Régnier de La Planche: for example, the great cloth merchants, Jacques Danès and Jean Rouillé, or the bookseller Oudin Petit.[21] I shall merely stress two points. First, during these years, when the Reformation in Paris was reaching its highwater mark, these families were only partly affected. Some members openly joined the Protestant cause, whereas others remained Catholics, leading to conflicts in the near future that would be both politico-religious and familial. Second, this involvement is revealed on the level of municipal institutions and, therefore, on the level of one of the groups entrusted with "policing" the city. By 1556 Sire Nicolas Perrot, the *prévôt des marchands* [provost or mayor of the city of Paris], and Guillaume de Courlay, one of the four *échevins* as well as notary and royal secretary, were acknowledged Huguenots. In 1558 and 1561, two Huguenots were elected as *échevins*.[22] Of the sixteen heads of quarters of the city, three were Protestants when the first civil war began. In July 1563 a riot broke out at the Saint-Antoine gate over *échevins* Ladvocat[23] and Le Prestre, who were accused of favoring the Huguenots. Both of these men were among the twenty-three sympathizers listed by Régnier de La Planche. Thus, the Protestant minority was a strong one and, moreover, had available a network of sympathizers or fencesitters, who were always suspect in the eyes of the Catholic throng.

We know that the high law courts did not escape "contagion," but to what degree were they affected? Here we can consult two lists with different origins. The first is an incomplete document (the beginning is missing) by an anonymous compiler.[24] On the basis of internal evidence, I have concluded that this document originated among the parish priests of Paris.[25] It is a list of officials who in 1562 were considered suspect for religious reasons. It includes thirty-nine councillors in the Parlement,[26] plus twenty-two *maîtres* or *présidents des comptes et généraux des aides*, which amounts to roughly one-fourth or one-third of the total membership of that court. This document is, of course, open to criticism. The list seems to have been padded, and the reasons for including an individual are rather vague: "Is rumored to be of the new religion"; "Is rumored to be, because he goes around with those of the new religion"; "Is rumored that he supports and favors them in everything"; "Very suspect because he goes about with Huguenots and is even related by marriage to other Huguenots"; "An upright man, but his wife used to go hear sermons regularly—it is very unfortunate that he took such a wife." Here we recognize the rumors that echoed through a quarter of the city, like tomtoms through the jungle. But this list also includes indications of a more serious nature: participating in worship services, refusing to celebrate Easter or recite the Creed,[27] eating meat during Lent, marrying in the Huguenot way, and so forth. I see this list as not so much reflecting that the Reformation had been implanted, in the strict sense of the word, into Parlementary circles, but that it had a broader audience prior to the time when a number of fencesitters, who initially were sympathizers, turned away.

We also possess an official document[28] containing the names of those members of the Parlement who were called upon to recite the Catholic creed on 8 June 1562. Thirty-four of them were absent "for religious reasons." These men were forced to go into exile. One hundred twenty made the required profession of faith. Yet among them were some indisputably Huguenot councillors, such as Roillard, Vaillant de Quélis, and Nicolas Perrot, and men such as Président de Harlay who appeared on the priests' list of suspects.

Beyond these statistics,[29] we must keep one observation in mind here, because it provides the key to the reactions of the monarchy and to those who triggered popular violence. These few years witnessed the maximum spread of the Gospel among the *notables* of Paris. All one's hopes or all one's fears seem likely to materialize: everything seemed about to topple.

The psychological changes that accompanied this social revolution were equally important for understanding the attitudes of the authorities. I see at least four attitudes that had important repercussions: a sort of "triumphalism," a point of view that took the offensive, overt scornfulness, and at the same time satisfaction over the consequences that the spread of the Gospel was having upon the behavior of the common people.

The triumphalism was linked to hopes for definitive and imminent success. Were not large numbers of distinguished individuals being won over to the Word of God? Was this not a proof—a supplementary but fundamental proof—that God was *with* true believers? This triumphalism can be observed everywhere, from Lyons to Rouen, from the region of Laon to Paris.[30] It can be seen in Huguenot hymns, in popular prints, and above all in deeds and in written words.[31] In addition to singing psalms in public, attending "Geneva-style" baptisms and marriages permitted this triumphalism to become visible, as did the wedding held in December 1561 that united the sister of Arnoul Boucher, seigneur of Orsay and first president in the Grand Conseil, and Jean Chandieu, registrar in the royal mint.[32] "It seemed that the cause of Our Lord Jesus, already so long condemned without a hearing, would this time obtain several decisions in its favor."[33]

Assuming the offensive arose from this vision of the future. After 1559 the martyrs who accepted punishment without defending themselves and who even experienced an intense joy in dying for God[34] were replaced by men who resisted. People took out their weapons, brandished their swords, and goaded their horses toward demonstrators on foot. Take, for example, the Huguenot account of the troubles at Saint-Médard:

At the first noises, a great troop armed with sticks appeared, coming from the direction of the fields; at whose head a troop of horsemen advanced; but as soon as they noticed them, all this riffraff withdrew in flight; and it is certain that such diligence shown by the gentlemen on horseback intimidated them with such fear that the people from the other quarters of the city, hearing the news, did not dare to get under way.

In April 1561 the municipal government became concerned about the disturbances being created by those attending the services held at the home of Sieur de Longuemeau in the Pré-aux-Clercs. When the authorities requested that the owner leave his house for a time in order to calm things down, the latter haughtily refused and surrounded himself with "more than three hundred men carrying pistols and weapons," among them Ruzé the lawyer, who, "clothed in a robe of purplish scarlet struck out at the poor *commune** with a very sharp sword."[35] I wish to point out that this move to the offensive had nothing in common with the "wild" aggressiveness of the Catholic mobs.

*In the sixteenth century *la commune* generally referred to what today we could call "the people." The word did, however, have a number of other meanings during the early-modern period. It could refer to bourgeois as contrasted with the nobility. It might refer to the militia established by the community. Or it might allude to the bourgeois of a city who had been granted a charter of self-government. Some, or all, of these meanings lie behind the use of this word in sixteenth-century texts. See also n. 37.—Trans.

Sure of themselves, the Protestant *notables* made certain that they stayed within legal limits and asserted that they were combating "rebellion" and "sedition." They in no way considered themselves conspirators.[36]

"Riffraff" and "rabble" on one side, *"commune"* on the other:[37] Protestant statements were in marked contrast with Catholic ones. This is another characteristic of the way the Huguenots thought on the eve of the civil wars. Their scorn for the crowd reveals their attachment to the old way of worshipping. Quotations revealing this scorn would fill a book. "These poor popular idiots," "the seditious populace," as the demonstrators at Saint-Médard called them. Under no illusions, La Roche-Chandieu added to our evidence: "The people of Paris, which is made up of ignorant rabble and given over to every evil." At the same time, however, Protestants exerted an acculturizing influence, which they took pleasure in stressing. The history written by the same La Roche-Chandieu reveals how these public demonstrations of the new piety had an exemplary function and a pedagogic force. "Some of the faithful being at the Pré-aux-Clercs, a public place, began to chant David's psalms in a small group, while others were frolicking. It so happened that all the games were immediately put aside and the majority of those who were in the Pré joined them in singing." The exaggeration matters little. What counts is the sought-after goal. In 1559 a schoolboy and two companions were denounced. Why? Because, "during religious festivities they were accustomed to meeting to rejoice in God and sing psalms and pray, while others were drinking and frolicking. Unhappy about this, the Devil raised up a traitor against them." These comments, which can be found in other sources as well,[38] seem to me important for two reasons. First, they show that attempts to modify traditional behavior were beginning in Paris. The Reformation achieved such modifications wherever it took root, especially south of the Loire River. They also help to explain the tacit cooperation given by many *notables* who had remained Catholic but who were concerned about ridding the city of its undesirable amusements.

We can, therefore, better understand why the authorities hesitated. As witnesses to the changes that had occurred in the sort of people joining the Protestant community, and partly won over to the cause and partly receptive to its moralizing effects, would the members of Parlement continue to punish blindly? Until 1559 the Grand' Chambre of the Parlement of Paris invariably sentenced unimportant people convicted of heresy to be burned at the stake. In that year Séguier and Harlay were appointed to preside over the Chambre de la Tournelle,* which tried four Huguenots, sentencing them to banishment and thus permitting them to escape execution. Milles Bourdin, the *procureur général* [attorney general], protested against the so-called Séguier

*The *Tournelle criminelle* was one of the chambers of the Parlement. It judged criminal cases that did not involve ecclesiastics, nobles, or royal officials—who were judged by the Grand' Chambre, the principal chamber of the Parlement.—Trans.

decree and criticized the two presidents for their lukewarm conduct, comparing the Tournelle—which had "merely banished two Lutherans who opposed the Roman Church"—with the Grand' Chambre, which "had no trouble burning Lutherans."[39] For this reason the chambers of the Parlement were called into plenary session for the famous *mercuriale*. Records of the lengthy debates that took place there have been lost, but, according to contemporary sources, for the first time there was talk in the Parlement of a council, of the Reformation, and of toleration. If we are to believe La Roche-Chandieu, "The majority either lightened the penalty or absolved them completely." The debate only ended when Henry II intervened personally. This was incontestably a crucial moment for the Reformation, a moment in which a certain vague sympathy for the movement was expressed in full Parlement and confirmed the attraction to the cause of the Gospel that Parisian *notables* had been experiencing for a number of years. It was also a factor in the bitterness of Catholics toward the members of the high courts, whose sincerity as Catholics and whose firmness in putting down the Protestants became suspect for several decades.

* * *

Violence on the part of the Catholics broke out in Paris prior to the first civil war and continued after the Saint Bartholomew's Day massacre. Between 1562 and 1572—the two years that represent the highwater marks—we can discern a typology of violence, determine its characteristics, evaluate its social aspects, and measure its consequences, both immediate and distant. Although in some cases this violence preceded the legal steps taken against the Protestants at the beginning of the first three wars (April 1562, September 1567, and August 1568), it generally followed such measures. Then, although it did not disappear, it lessened with each truce (March 1563, March 1568, and August 1570)—truces that were also edicts of "pacification." I should like to point out, however, that the edict of Saint-Germain did not end the ferment in Paris; the events that occurred there on Saint Bartholomew's Day did not come as a bolt of lightning from a clear blue sky.

We must draw a distinction between diffuse violence and massacres, butcherings, and drownings. Massacres followed a pattern that seems to break down into four stages. The first stage was the preparation of the faithful by preachers, above all preachers belonging to mendicant orders. Their role was to stir up public opinion by means of virulent sermons, especially during Advent and Lent, and thus to create such a climate of opinion that a move by the public authorities was enough to provoke mob violence. During periods of truce, when it was not disposed to give matters free rein, royal authority proved to be vigilant but often impotent in the face of such sermons. For example, on 10 December 1561 an incident occurred that is described in both Canon Bruslart's journal and the abstracts of the records of the Parlement.[40] "The Minim preacher for Advent at the Church of Saint-Bartélemy in Paris was taken this morning at ten o'clock by forty armed men to the king's court [of the Parlement], which excited the commune of the city of Paris, not knowing to what end the said Minim had been brought there; nonetheless, they have since had news that it was by the king's command." And indeed, Charles IX wrote the Parlement that the Minim should be replaced by a peaceable preacher, and the Prince of La Roche-sur-Yon came to declare to that court on 12 December "that this Minim had been rebuked the previous year for his brash remarks, and that there still are other preachers in Paris who speak with little discretion, among others a Carmelite preaching at Saint-Merry, the preacher at Saint-Eustache, and the one at Saint-Jacques-de-la-Boucherie. The latter had publicly complained that the town archers served as escorts for those going to hear [Protestant] services." But the Minim was released on 17 December and resumed preaching before a vast crowd. Once again, in March 1564, letters patent were issued in the Parlement against preachers: "We have learned that there are some preachers in this city of Paris who cannot control themselves and keep from mingling in their sermons many seditious and scandalous things that do nothing to edify the people but instead stir them up and excite them to sedition."[41] The king threatened to remove from the pulpit those who persisted after this warning, but it was a vain threat. These events repeated themselves after the peace of Saint-Germain [in August 1570] and, as we well know, during the years that preceded the second League.[42] Indeed, although preachers constituted a magnetic pole that focused public opinion, and although they were powerful enough to make royal authority bend when it attempted to restrain them, they were not powerful enough to provoke massacres when forbidden by royal authority.

The second stage was one in which the authorities seized the initiative. I wish to stress this point, which runs counter to any interpretation of the violence as "spontaneous." The initiative always came from above—from the king, from the princes, from the Parlement, or from the municipality. Sporadic bouts of agitation doubtlessly occurred during times of peace, but official acts made their spread "permissible." These official acts did not shed blood until the third war. The king exiled a certain number of Protestant *notables*; royal and municipal officials who were Huguenots were hounded out of office; the heads of the various quarters of the city and the captains of the city militia were ordered to draw up lists of suspects and to arrest them; and undesirable tenants were evicted from houses belonging to the city and replaced by good Catholics.[43] But until the executions in 1569 of Philippe de Gastines, his son, and his son-in-law, all respectable merchants of the rue Saint-Denis, the authorities did not directly shed any blood. They nonetheless unleashed the *grande levrière* [the great greyhound bitch, or the "dogs of war"]. Huguenots and Catholics opposed to violence naturally were aware of this—especially after the first war—and many of them did not wait for the anticipated events to transpire before fleeing. Once weapons were returned to the people, departures began. Thus, on 29 September 1567, after the ambush at Meaux [an unsuccessful attempt by the Huguenots to take the royal court into custody], Charles IX ordered the city government to distribute weapons.[44] Bouchefort wrote to the Duchess of Ferrera:

As for this city, I tell you that all those who belong to the [Protestant] Religion have left or are leaving today. The good people in Paris who are of the Roman religion are not rejoicing in this, and the bad ones see that they will not win them over by either treachery or blandishments. I see great and vast misery approaching, unless God intervenes. These poor people are asked, 'Why are you going away?' And they reply, 'Why did you give back weapons to all the people at the city hall? Was it in order to do good?'"[45]

Then the third stage, that of the "bad people," began, and it was a period of unbridled passions. It is clear that the crowd naturally interpreted the anti-Protestant measures as the lifting of an interdict. The short interval between dates is revealing. On 4 April 1562 Montmorency went off to Popincourt to destroy the pulpit in a house where Protestant services were being held. On 5 April, "An infinity of people went from Paris to Popincourt and razed the house by throwing stones at it; they tore out all the wood and beams and carried them to the front of the town hall, and there they burned them and cried out, 'God has not forgotten the people of Paris.' And if someone protested about it, he was fiercely beaten or else killed at once."[46] The decree issued in July provoked prolonged slaughtering. This did not yet constitute a seizure of sovereignty, but a seizure of justice [a development that troubled the judicial authorities]. "At six in the evening near Fort-l'Evesque the commune threw into the river two suspicious men whom they claimed they had been given and issued orders to dispose of since they were suspected of belonging to the new religion."[47] Given the choice between hunting people down and throwing them into the Seine, the people chose the more expeditious option. When a precise order was lacking, rumors spread by highly placed individuals were enough to legitimate the slaughter. When Guise and his friends went through Paris on 24 August 1572, Saint Bartholomew's Day, crying, "Kill them all, the King commands it," were they unaware how far their voices would carry?

During the fourth stage matters were again taken into hand. As soon as possible, the authorities regained control and raged against those who had committed the "excesses." Two acts were above all viewed as a danger signal: attacking persons of authority in the administration and the courts, and pillaging houses and possessions left behind by fugitives. Public order and property rights required respect. As early as 26 April 1652 Montmorency ordered the hanging of a thief who had pillaged a fugitive's house on the rue Saint-Denis,[48] and when a riot broke out in 1563 against two échevins accused of favoring the Huguenots, the city government ordered the newly organized municipal militia to intervene.[49] This militia actually served an ambiguous function. Created in 1562, at the height of the wave of repression, it was used both to discover and arrest people who were suspect for religious reasons and to maintain order in the face of the savage violence perpetrated by the Catholics.[50]

The events of Saint Bartholomew's Day followed the four stages in this pattern, but with even greater exasperation and conflict. First, public opinion became superheated as a result of sermons, the marriage of Henry of Navarre,[51] and the transfer to the cemetery of the Saints-Innocents of the cross that had been erected on the site of the Gastines's house.[52] Then, *in extremis*, Charles IX accepted the responsibility for the actions of Catherine de Médicis and the Duke of Anjou, which were limited to executing the leaders of the Protestant party. The massacre lasted for three days.[53] The monarchy attemped to justify events, vacillating between holding the house of Guise responsible, crediting the massacre to malice aforethought, and calling it a preventive measure. It finally attributed the events solely to the populace and reestablished order.[54]

Natalie Davis, Janine Estèbe, and Denis Crouzet have made the essential points about the forms that the violence took. I shall merely stress a few factors that highlight their cultural foundations.

First of all, we must draw a distinction between the violence itself (whether it is a question of a murder committed by an individual or of collective slaughter), and the multiple sorts of response to what the Catholic population perceived as aggression by the Huguenots, aggression against an inherited cultural equilibrium, against a way of behaving and a spontaneous way of worshiping.

The most striking thing about this period is that this response remained traditional and fit into a framework of institutions, methods, and ritual inherited from the past. (A decade later this was no longer true.) The great processions to expiate the crimes committed by the Huguenots remained official processions held in the presence of the public authorities. The role of church bells and of the tocsin remained fundamental, sometimes creating a veritable "war of sounds." To drown out the sound of psalms being chanted, the bells in Catholic churches would be rung a full peal. Let us turn to the anonymous narrator of the stabbing at Saint-Médard. "Those of Saint-Médard began with deliberate malice to ring all their church bells at once with such vigor that, since there was only a narrow street separating the two places, the sound reverberated so mightily in 'The Patriarch' that it was completely impossible to hear the exhortations."[55] "Genevan-style" baptisms were countered by rebaptisms. Although such second baptisms did not conform to the doctrine of the Catholic Church, they were occasions for great ceremonies. On 2 June 1562 a six-month-old girl who had been baptized by a Protestant minister was rebaptized at Saint-Germain-l'Auxerrois. "More than ten thousand people were present at this baptism. The bells were rung and the carillon was played as a sign of rejoicing. And several people who wanted to make the baptism more festive carried candles and tapers and cried out, 'God be praised for the recovery of this poor innocent little soul.' "[56]

To oppose the iconoclasts, as early as 1559 people held noisy worship services in the streets before the statues of the Virgin and the saints that adorned shop signs or stood at crossroads.[57] The scorn that the Catholic *notables* showed for these "superstitions" frequented by the "dregs of the people" clearly indicates that at this date there was still a great gulf between the way the populace worshiped and the demands for spiritual renewal being felt by the elite. Paris had not yet developed those strong Catholic organizations protected by certain factions of the elite that were already to be found in other cities.[58] Left to themselves or guided by their usual preachers, the people of Paris reacted according to time-tested patterns. After Saint Bartholomew's Day they began to seek miraculous cures when a hawthorn blossomed before the chapel dedicated to the Virgin in the cemetery of the Saints-Innocents. "Languishing" sick people came back "whole and cured of their illness." "It seemed," continued Claude Haton, "that by means of this miracle God was approving and accepting the sedition of the Catholics and the deaths of their great enemy, the Admiral [Coligny], and his family."[59]

It has been shown that the violence itself followed very old rituals and magical practices. Estèbe is correct in viewing Saint Bartholomew's Day as a ritual crime in which the accursed dead person had to undergo the purifying action of the four elements, water, earth, air, and fire. But we can see these purification rituals at work in the collective unconscious a decade earlier. The notion of "contamination" affected cemeteries, houses, and above all cadavers. When the house on the rue Saint-Denis where the Gastines family lived was torn down to raise on that spot a cross made from materials taken from the ruins,[60] was this not done in order to bring about the disappearance of a place that had been polluted by Protestant sermons and communion services? When cadavers of Huguenots were removed from their graves in cemeteries and dragged through the mud,[61] was this not in order to reestablish a sacrality that had been violated? The rituals involving the castration and disembowelment of cadavers was chiefly carried out by *young children*. Hanging was not enough to calm their emotions about the police archer called "Nez d'Argent" and his companions. On 2 May 1562 "small children threw an infinity of stones and mud at the said Nez d'Argent and, if he had had a hundred lives after his death, he would have lost them all."[62] A popular song gloried in this sacrificial violence.[63] Coligny's cadaver met an even more spectacular fate. "After it had had its head removed and its shameful parts cut off by little children, these same little children, some two or three hundred in number, dragged [the body] belly up through the gutters of Paris, as did the ancient Romans when they dragged tyrants *ad scalas gemorias unco*, which was the location of the sewers of Rome."[64] Why this special role for children?

Perhaps, as Crouzet suggests, because "children are bloodthirsty and enjoy cutting up bodies and disemboweling them, doubtlessly inspired by the scatalogical obsession that is part of child psychology." Instead, I see this as the reflection and symbol of an ideal purity held by society as a whole when confronted with some contamination, a purity that would soon become incarnate during the League in acts of quite a different sort.

A sociological study of the Huguenot victims of the repression is not easy to carry out. An inventory and evaluation of the sources must be made before any hypothesis can be advanced. Huguenots and people opposed to violence tended to refer chiefly to "people of reputation," whom they contrasted with the "dregs of the people." Preachers and Catholic "zealots" of the day were not very concerned about giving the social status of those rejected by the *commune*, a sort of urban entity. A certain number of incomplete and limited documentary fragments are extant. I chiefly used the following four sources:

1. A register of the minute books of the criminal registrar for the Parlement of Paris, edited and annotated by Paul Guerin.[65] It covers a mere two months (9 September to 9 November 1562) and contains only some twenty names of accused individuals. Fifteen of them were Parisian *notables*, including four lawyers and eleven important merchants, the latter sentenced in absentia and recipients of royal letters of surcease.[66] This register is invaluable for a study of Protestant *notables*, since we find in it the names of Nicolas Croquet and his wife, François Perrot, François Canaye, Jacques Gobelin, Jehan Petit,[67] and other merchants named by Régnier de La Planche. However, no statistical data can be compiled on the basis of this record book.

2. The jail books of the Conciergerie [prison] of the *Palais* [judicial Courts of Paris], now in the archives of the Prefecture of Police of Paris, part of which (September 1564 to June 1568, January 1569, and March 1569) were transcribed and published at the end of the nineteenth century by H. Bordier.[68] Although they supply us with information about more than two hundred heresy cases, including 138 involving residents of Paris, we must remember that the only people sent to the Conciergerie were those who were appealing a decision by a lower court such as the Châtelet or the courts of ecclesiastical seigneuries. These record books therefore contain only a part—undoubtedly a minority—of the decisions about religious cases made during the dates in question.

3. The extracts of the records of the Parlement of Paris listing the twenty-eight royal and municipal officials who were stripped of their offices in December 1568 and February 1569.[69] They are interesting for what they reveal about complicity within the world of officialdom, but they are restricted to those officials who had not yet fled Paris.

4. The list of the victims of the Saint Bartholomew's Day massacre. Although more complete than Crespin, Goulard's list[70] includes only 121 names,

a meager number compared with the lowest estimates of roughly two thousand made by contemporaries and compared with the number of victims in much smaller cities.[71] This is a select list of names drawn up on the basis of varied criteria such as reputation, age, sex, and family feuds.

The above information is clearly inadequate for showing a close correlation between any particular social category and the people selected as victims of the repression. We lack two sorts of information, without which we cannot measure the "isomorphy" of the violence. First, we do not know the overall socio-occupational distribution of the Parisian population; and second, we lack a complete list of everyone arrested or massacred. For example, it is clear that artisans (who accounted for one-third of the victims tallied after Saint Bartholomew's Day) were underrepresented on the various lists, while *notables* (noblemen, officials, and merchants known throughout the city) were given preference on the lists and were, therefore, overrepresented. Thus, it is difficult to agree with Estèbe that the chance to pillage the "rich" was a motivating force in the Saint Bartholomew's Day massacre. Although this motive undoubtedly played a role, as it does in every instance of a breakdown of urban order, it does not explain why some people were singled out to be massacred while others were spared. However, these sources do reveal that certain trades (shopkeepers, master artisans, and journeymen) were more affected, notably those who worked with precious metals, books, and leather. It is easy to see why the Catholic mobs focused their hatred upon the booksellers and printers of the Left Bank when we consider their role in the dissemination of works suspected of heresy. Was it owing to their wealth that many goldsmiths, gemcutters, gilders, or embroiderers in gold thread can be found on the lists of prisoners or among the victims of 24 August? This would not seem to be the case, for the majority of them do not appear upon the list of those paying the highest taxes in the capital.[72] We have reason to ask whether the very materials they transformed and sold did not, in the collective subconscious of the people, retain some essence of the accursed and did not mark them with the same infamous stain that had marked the Jews and the Lombards during the Middle Ages.

The judicial documents open another vista for us. We must look beyond the lists of those arrested or massacred and seek deviations from the norm revealed by certain incidents that seem anecdotal but that reveal traces of latent conflicts that would be expressed openly a few years later. The first conflict seems to me to be the one between the officials in the high courts who, if not suspected of heresy, were at least considered lukewarm Catholics, and the world of the *basoche* [law clerks] with its *procureurs*, beadles, notaries, minor lawyers, and sergeants at arms, who had sprung from shop- and stallkeeping families and felt frustrated in their ambitions to rise socially. The *basoche* jealously defended an orthodoxy that was consciously a leveling one. This was not a "class struggle" but a sharp conflict over social and cultural hegemony between two unequally matched segments of the Parisian bourgeoisie. In the struggle the "second bourgeoisie"[73] was clearly the underdog. It had neither honors nor positions, other than on the neighborhood level. But it benefited from its cultural links with the crowd and, in this position, was a good representative of the aspirations of the commune and of what it refused to accept. Better than any study of the dry lists, one specific case, the Fichard trial, sheds light on this social tension and the bitterness of the confrontations.[74]

In October 1562 President de Harlay presented his "complaint to the chamber of the Parlement" "because he had been notified that Fichard, *procureur* of the aforesaid [Parlement], was publicly insulting him when he saw him pass the *Palais* going to mass, saying words of this sort: 'Look at him now, going to mass. He's a big hypocrite, he's one of the biggest Huguenots. He doesn't budge from their services. I've seen him come out of Madame the Countess of Senthan's house.' And other scandalous words against the honor of the said president." Convoked, Fichard declared that he had obeyed the "admonition" of the vicar of his parish, Saint-Eustache, "and that in order to unburden his conscience he went to make declarations and revelations to the vicar of the said parish, in whose ear he whispered what he knew." At the vicar's request Fichard had put his denunciation in writing. When the court asked him to tell what it contained, "he replied that, if it please the court, he would not state it publicly and that he had put it in writing and abided by what it contained and would not change." He denied Harlay's statements, accusing him of trying to get his evidence withdrawn. "The said Fichard stated that these facts were false . . . and that two days earlier Monsieur the President [Harlay] had sent various people whom he would not name to him and that they had beset him and pressed him to take back his declaration from the said vicar, threatening, if he did not take it back, to cause him trouble and displeasure. Yet he did not want to take it back, fearing that he would offend his conscience." He added that Harlay's hostility had longstanding causes: "In addition he stated that for a long time the said Sieur President had wished him ill and that nine or ten years earlier he had slapped him and punched him in the hall of the *Palais*, when he was pleading a case before him."

At this point Fichard was locked up in the Conciergerie, and witnesses were summoned. His trial began on 9 November. The declarations of the accused and of certain witnesses provide a striking glimpse into the clime of 1562. First of all, let us listen to Fichard: "And when he was told that he should list the places and houses where he said he had seen the said Sieur President de Harlay, his son, and President de La Place[75] go to attend services, he replied that, if it pleased the court to order that he be questioned about his disclosures, he would name more than five hundred others who had attended them. He stated that all those who had made statements against him had been instructed beforehand and had 'pumped' him in order to get from him what he knew." Fichard named Maître Pasquier Noiret, Cardinal Lemoyne's priest, who was said to have laughed in the midst of other people upon seeing Harlay go to mass. Here is Noiret's reply to the judges: "Pasquier [Noiret] stated that one day, being at the *Palais* as the court was closing and Messieurs the presidents were going to mass, he saw that some people were laughing and stepping back to make room for them, saying that they had to make more room than usual and that they were accustomed to seeing only three presidents go by, and now there were four of them; and that Fichard had said, 'Here is President de Harlay, going to mass! Better late than never.' "

This episode enables us better to evaluate the effects of the terrorist pressures exerted by Catholic opinion, first upon those who wavered between Protestantism and Catholicism, and then upon those who were faithful to the Gospel. The network of sympathizers that we have seen take shape around the Huguenot community circa 1557 to 1559 progressively changed into a *peau de chagrin*.*

Related to royal intervention and molded by the priests and monks, this pressure not only dried up the supply of new adherents to the Protestant church in Paris but also provoked retractions or quiet returns to the old church. Councillors Du Four, Fumée, de Foix, and others arrested with Anne Du Bourg, recanted soon afterwards. We need only compare the names that appear on the black list of 1562 with a list of those present at the official Catholic ceremonies to see that many notables who had momentarily been attracted to Protestantism had returned to the fold by the beginning of the civil wars. Among them were such important figures as Marillac, a master of accounts, and Lamoignon, Lhuillier, Adrien de Thou, and Harlay himself, all councillors in the Parlement.[76] Starting in 1562 Protestant expansion was brought to a decisive halt.

Were declared Protestants better able to stand up against the persecution? We know examples of people who remained faithful despite severe trials.[77] However—and the lamentations of the authorities in Geneva confirm this— each persecution caused defections. Saint Bartholomew's Day triggered a massive number of conversions. If we are to believe Jean Rouillé,[78] who himself converted, more than five thousand conversions were recorded in Paris during one month. In Rouen, where Philip Benedict has observed that Protestant baptisms were reduced by five-sixths between 1565-66 and 1579-84,[79] the effects of the massacre were of a similar magnitude. Even though the figures are open to debate, it is difficult to contest the efficacy of the violence.[80] Prepared by ten years of latent persecution, the massacre of 24 August 1572, [Saint Bartholomew's Day] played a decisive historical role, although we may

---

Peau de chagrin—In Balzac's novel by that name, a magical piece of shagreen leather that had the power to make its owner's wishes come true. But with each wish, the owner's life span shortened.—Trans.

well question the sincerity of certain abjurations. A way to test this is provided by the list of those attending the Protestant church at Charenton after the Edict of Nantes [1598].[81] Although the Protestant community in Paris revived at that time, its numbers had been severely reduced. Families themselves were divided.[82]

Why these abjurations? The pastors and authorities in Geneva tended to stress fear of losing life and property. Indeed, this fear played a major role; but it must be viewed within the more complex psychological picture. We must not forget that for a decade these merchants or officials had been experiencing an almost permanent insecurity that made living a normal life almost impossible. Lack of security for office holders every time the war resumed forced departures from the family home, and threats of arrest followed by long imprisonment all contributed to making daily life difficult. The cumulative nature of the persecution has often been neglected by historians, but it is a major factor in the way consciences developed. Saint Bartholomew's Day provoked a profound reaction of despair. Protestants felt that henceforth God was no longer with them[83] and that all hope of success had evaporated. Society as a whole rejected an accursed minority: the *notables* who were being impelled in the opposite direction, the direction of integration, by their culture and their position in the economic, social, and administrative life. On 22 September 1572 Jean Rouillé, the Parisian cloth wholesaler, sent a letter to two merchants at Albi[84] that is very revealing of this unbearable fissure. I have selected a few of the most significant passages in this bill of exchange.

Honorable gentlemen, I received your [letter] through a merchant of your city who, according to your letter, had been instructed to supply me with 2,000 livres to be deducted from what you owe me. But he told me that he would not do so because you were of the new religion. . . . Meanwhile, gentlemen, I advise you that the King has given very ample testimony that he wishes and intends that in this realm there by only one faith, one law, one God, and one king, and to this end has exterminated and put to death all those who have prevented him from doing this. . . . It is no longer time to delay in a vain wait or hope of the contrary. . . . I beg you, as much as I can, if you wish to save your souls, assure your present life, save your possessions, and [keep] your family from poverty, take my advice, that is, as soon as you can do it, you and your entire family should make a personal profession of the Catholic religion . . . . Do not delay by waiting and hoping in vain for some sort of edict, for in truth you would be surprised. More than five thousand men in this city have done likewise. . . . If you do not take my advice, you are doomed, ruined, destroyed, you and your house, from attic to cellar, believe me.

If we put ourselves in Rouillé's place during the aftermath of Saint Bartholomew's Day, we can analyze the situation in terms of three essential considerations. The battle had been definitively lost for the majority of *notables* who had joined the Reformation or who had sympathized with it. The savage vigor of the Catholic reaction had borne fruit, but this violence stirred up by preachers and taken in hand by the *basoche* constituted a dangerous challenge. Until then those in power had made use of this violence, but they had not known how to channel it, control it, purify it. It was a great gamble. Since those in power had remained incapable of fulfilling this mission, they left to others the possibility of steering this violence toward terror and utopia.

* * *

I shall not trace here the events that rocked the Parisians' entire way of life between 1572 and 1592. Moreover, certain deep currents cannot be channeled into rigid chronological order. Until 1585 two important changes affected the *notables* in Paris, at a time when a veritable Huguenot state was being organized in southern and western France, and attempts at an armed reconquest by the champions of Catholicism were failing. The first change was the formation of the party of the *Politiques*, most of whose ideology has been presented to us by historians,[85] although their basic views may have been distorted. Far from having shown the least degree of religious skepticism, far from having been secretly sympathetic toward the Reformation, the majority of the *Politiques* hoped that the Counter Reformation would triumph. Being undoubtedly more lucid than the *Guisards* [those on the side of the Guise family], they considered the fight to be virtually won, but social order required that they close ranks behind a weakened monarchy whose future was threatened. A silent revolution occurred far below the surface during these decisive years. The steps taken by the Council of Trent were felt among the new generation of lawyers or merchants, owing notably to Jesuit secondary schools. The opening in Paris of the Collège de Clermont in 1564 permitted the sons of numerous officials in the high courts to prepare themselves to fit the mass into renovated forms of piety, devotion, and also culture.

After 1585 (and the formation of the second League) and especially after 1588 (which saw the Day of the Barricades and the execution of the Guises), political and social conflicts seem to have moved to the forefront: armed conflicts between Royalists and Leaguers, struggles between moderate and extremist Leaguers, and the formation of a party whose Catholic exclusiveness went hand in hand with specific political and social demands.[86] Less well known than these conflicts, but more important for the future, was the beginning of a veritable "Catholic action." It was during the time of the League that what was later to be called the *parti dévot* [party of the devout] took shape.

Abandoning a narration of events, I would like to evoke three problems briefly: the sociological aspects of League extremism, the shift from violence to terror, and the new forms of worship.

The sociology of League extremism has long been clouded by sources that were consulted to show one side to advantage. Not only were these sources almost exclusively literary, but this literature came above all from the circles opposed to the League (for example, Lestoile, Pasquier, Palma Cayet, J.-A. de Thou). Naturally, these writers tended to christen their enemies "vile populace," "rabble," "vile little shopkeepers,"[87] even when these enemies were members of social groups just beneath their own. Recent systematic studies of the *Registres des délibérations de l'Hôtel de Ville* [the records of the debates of the city government of Paris][88] have permitted Soviet and American historians to present a more accurate picture of the overall scene.[89] But even the most remarkable of these historians have encountered three difficulties. First of all, how can certain leaders be fitted into the various Parisian milieux if other sources, notably notarial and fiscal records, are not used?[90] Saying, for example, that Jean de La Bruyère, apothecary-grocer and supplier for the Hôtel de Ville, was a "rich" merchant means ignoring the fact that he was not among the leading families of Parisian commerce and that he represented a declining branch of a family whose other branches had already become solidly anchored in the high courts.[91] When La Bruyère's son, Mathias, replaced his Séguier cousin as *lieutenant civil* [royal judge of civil cases], it was, according to Lestoile, owing more to a "family quarrel" than to political motives. Not one of the five merchants "of wealth and status" that J. H. H. Salmon includes in his first table of "the Sixteen" belonged to the commercial aristocracy. *A fortiori* it is difficult to agree with A. A. Lozinsky when he excludes "civil servants" from the "bourgeoisie" or when he contrasts the "old style bourgeoisie" (*burgestvo*) with the "modern bourgeois class" (*bourgjoazia*). Someone's social status is not defined solely by his membership in a corporation or even by his wealth, but by a group of factors that together form the criteria for being a *notable*.

Moreover, all the members of the General Council of the League (1588), the Council of Forty (1589), or the Committees of Nine formed in each quarter after the murders of the Guises at Blois are not equally representative. The presence of Acarie, a *maître des comptes*, on the lists of 1589 and 1591 does not mean that the Chambre des Comptes [of the Parlement], which experienced a purge in 1591, supported the movement. We must also remember that the power of certain leaders declined. As was to be the case in 1789–93, those who founded the League in 1585 were rapidly surpassed by events, and many of them were considered traitors after 1591. Only after that year, when the entrance of a Spanish garrison into Paris strengthened them against the Duke of Mayenne [Guise's brother] can the Sixteen be studied as an autonomous movement. The individuals signing a collective letter to Philip II of Spain on 10 September 1591,[92] the ten members of the secret council that prepared President Brisson's execution in November, and the victims of Mayenne's repression in December represent the tough nucleus of those directing League radicalism.[93] Here we can be guided by Salmon's table, if we modify some of his data.[94] Of the forty-six individuals mentioned in sources, only one (Acarie) was a member of a high court; one (the goldsmith Turquet, colonel of his quarter's militia) was a merchant; and twenty-four belonged to the *basoche* or held minor offices. Lawyers, procureurs, commissioners, beadles, sergeants, and members of the regular religious orders or parish priests were the driving force behind the radicalism. Often linked to the world of shopkeepers, as the names of the witnesses on their marriage contracts prove, these minor officials were frustrated in their hopes for promotion. We know that the high courts tended to close their ranks to newcomers.[95] These minor officials were also aware that, in the eyes of the great robe or commercial families,[96] they embodied the *commune*.

As in any revolutionary period, we know only the leaders and the militant minority. To what degree did the common people, to whom constant reference was made, participate in the movement? I disagree with Lozinsky, for I do not think that the profound impetus came from the "lower levels of the people." Salmon is more prudent when he observes the almost total absence of artisans on the lists of the Sixteen, and thus leaves the question open. Here again chronology must be taken into account. In 1588 and 1589 the steps taken by the League found a large audience among the stable groups of the capital's population. As in the past, people working in the meat trade, and boatmen and "riverboys,"[97] supplied sizeable contingents. According to Nicolas Poulain, a "secret review of their strength" prior to the Barricades led the Leaguers to count on the support of thirty thousand men, which seems a high figure in a city with a quarter of a million inhabitants.[98] The conspirators did not, however, trust the lowest levels of the population, and it was to protect themselves from these people that the barricades were "invented."

It was pointed out that in the city there was a great quantity of thieves and people in the handicrafts, exceeding six or even seven thousand in number, who were not aware of the undertaking, whom it would be difficult to keep under control once they had begun to pillage; that their band would be a snowball that would continually grow and finally bring total ruin and confusion to the undertaking and to those who undertook it. On this advice, which seemed weighty and very pertinent, the invention of the barricades was proposed. That is, barrels full of earth would be placed near each chain [that was placed across streets at curfew to block traffic] to prevent passage and that, as soon as the word was given, no one could go through the streets other than those who knew the password and the sign. Only four thousand men would be able to cross the said barricades.[99]

In any event, as the author of the *Dialogue* acknowledged, support from the people lessened as the years passed. In October 1592 meetings of the various quarters of the city were held prior to the special citywide meeting. Thirteen of the sixteen quarters voted with the *Semmoneux* (those who wanted to *semondre*, that is, summon Henry IV to become a Catholic in order to negotiate with him).[100] Scarcity and the blockades of the capital were bearing fruit.

I shall not dwell here upon the program of the radical wing of the League as it is expressed in the *Dialogue* or in the works of Jean Boucher, a priest. Elsewhere I have stressed its three essential aspects: Catholic exclusivism, attachment to liberties and elections, and hostility to all forms of inherited notability. It is useless to stress the utopian and retrograde aspects of this vision of the world and of the city, a vision gleaned from scholasticism and running counter to the trend that had been growing stronger for centuries. However, I should like in passing to discuss the shift from episodic violence to organized terror that Crouzet has described so well.

The *basoche*'s old hatred for the officials in the high courts had several opportunities to be freely expressed. All but three of these officials had already been eliminated from the city militia and were to become victims of successive purges. On 16 January 1589 *Procureur* Bussy Le Clerc, who had been named governor of the Bastille after the Barricades, went to the Parlement at the head of an armed detachment and had some twenty magistrates arrested. Since other magistrates joined them in a gesture of solidarity, they formed an impressive parade through rows of jeering and satisfied spectators. Revenge, after so many humiliations! In 1590 and 1591, the arrests and, on occasion, executions of members of Parlement continued, although many of them had fled the capital and were hiding in their country homes.[101] Even more deserving of our attention than these violent acts is the terrorist climate that in many ways prefigured that of 1793. Informing became institutionalized, and the parish mass became the occasion for certain priests to denounce suspects and terrify their wives.[102] "Huguenots" were reinvented in order to legitimate the terror, a bit like the antisemitism without Jews that was recently observed in a certain country. As a result, not only the *Politiques* but even Leaguers became suspected of favoring heresy. The obsession with punishment and the fear of treachery became evident in the secret meetings that prepared Brisson's slaying in November 1591. A document of the time permits us to relive one of these after-dinner sessions held in Boucher's house on the rue de la Vieille-Monnaie.[103]

The priest of the church of Saint-Jacques, who was present, seeing that no one wanted to decide this issue,[104] spoke these words: "Gentlemen, it is well enough known. We must never hope for a favorable decision or justice from the court of the Parlement. We have endured it too long, we must put our knives into play." And then a bourgeois of the city called Gourlin rose from his seat and went to whisper in the ear of the said priest of Saint-Jacques, which some did not like. The said Gourlin returned to his place and then the said priest rose from his seat and said, "Gentlemen, I have been warned that there are traitors in this group. They must be expelled and thrown into the river."

Three days later, at another meeting, de Launay, canon at Soissons, denounced "the uncontrolled number of traitors who were in the city, whom so little effort is being made to prosecute." On 6 November Cromé, a councillor in the Grand Conseil and the possible author of the *Dialogue*, exclaimed, "No! No! Let us not fear, we have strong arms and hands to avenge manifest justice carried out before the eyes of each and every one."

A vigilant mistrust of the judicial system, a feeling of being submerged in a sea of traitors, and an appeal to direct action are the components of the terrorist psychosis that we can glimpse in this narrative.

If League extremism was limited to this sociopolitical program and to terrorist measures, none of it remained after the return of Henry IV. And almost all historians stress the failure of terrorism. Yet it seems to me that we ought not to neglect an essential aspect of League activities: the beginnings of a profound implantation of the institutions and methods introduced by the Council of Trent. If the phenomenon is less well known in Paris, and in the other cities of the North in general, than in the southern provinces of the kingdom, it is doubtlessly because the reaction against everything that evoked the League was more pronounced there. A certain loss of credit surrounded everything that seemed connected to theories of regicide and to social upheaval. In turn, this loss of credit contributed to the fondness for secrecy that many Catholic reformers showed during the seventeenth century.[105]

More than the Jesuits,[106] who were, however, the prime target of Gallican attacks, the mendicant orders played the decisive role during the years of the League. Although the Dominicans were the most involved in direct political activities, the branches of the Franciscan order had the greater influence.[107] Installed in the suburb of Picpus as early as 1575, the Capuchins had a monastery on the rue Saint-Honoré [in the center of the city, near the Louvre] by 1578 and promptly grouped confraternities or lay groups about them. During Lent of 1578 the Confraternity of the Holy Sacrament was founded for the purpose of "repairing the profanation" committed by the Huguenots. Henry III supported the creation of the Confraternity of the Disciples of Saint Francis in 1585. But the most lasting success, despite appearances, was the establishment of the confraternities of the *penitents*.[108] After the white penitents, who in 1583 were greeted by Henry III during a procession about which Lestoile has left us a sarcastic account, and after the blue penitents of Saint Jerome, the grey penitents established at the Capuchin monastery on the rue Saint-Honoré became the principal center of Catholic action.[109] During these same years Brétigny was making an attempt in Rouen to introduce the Carmelite order into France, a decade before the eventual success of Bérulle and Madame Acarie, the wife of the Leaguer *maître des comptes*.[110] Within these devout Parisian circles that coalesced around the Capuchins of the rue Saint-Honoré were members of the high nobility and from among the royal officials: Henri de Joyeuse, Benoît de Canfield, Bochart de Champigny, Michel de Marillac, and the young Pierre de Bérulle, all future leaders of the Counter

Reformation in Paris during the reigns of Henry IV and Louis XIII.[111] Indeed, it would be interesting to trace the sons or nephews of the Sixteen among those belonging to Bérulle and Condren's Oratory.[112] At the time of the League, social groups in these devout circles that had until then been separated, coalesced within the same confraternities and worked for the same ends. The channels of transmission that had long been lacking in Catholic reform were now in place.

Devotional forms also were renewed thanks to the League. Although it had begun two decades earlier, public and perpetual veneration of the Holy Sacrament, centered upon an oratory in which Christ's body was displayed and processions accompanying that body to the church, spread through Paris. Along with the official processions there appeared a new type of procession with hymn singing. Here we again find small children. During the first months of 1589, after the murders of the Guises, Paris witnessed extraordinary scenes that must have left a permanent mark upon the generation that was between ten and fifteen years old at the time. In every quarter of Paris crowds of children went barefoot to parish churches, where prayers were said for the "martyrs" [the Guises]. A general procession followed.

The next day, Tuesday, the tenth day of the said month and year [10 January 1589] for the weeklong festival of Madame Saint Geneviève, all the little children, both boys and girls, of the said city of Paris made a general procession; and they assembled in the cemetery of the Saints-Innocents, where prayers were said; and then, holding lighted candles in their hands, they were conducted by individuals appointed for this purpose from the said cemetery to the church and monastery of Madame Saint Geneviève on the Mount of Paris; at the entrance of which church the said little children, both boys and girls, who numbered about one hundred thousand, threw their candles to their feet and walked over them as a sign that this accursed tyrant [Henry III] had been excommunicated.[113]

Like the Huguenots of 1560, "zealous" Catholics benefited from the impact upon morals of these devotional practices. Although a *Politique* and very ironical about the League, Pierre de Lestoile noted in his journal for 14 February [1589], the day of the Mardi Gras.

Throughout the day there were in Paris fine and devout processions instead of the dissolution and trash of mascarades and Shrove Tuesday revelries with which people besotted themselves during previous years. Among others, one involved about six hundred schoolboys, from all the schools and divisions of the University, most of whom had not attained the age of ten or twelve at the most; who marched naked, wearing only a shift, and barefoot, carrying lighted candles of white wax in their hands and singing very devoutly and melodiously, and sometimes very much out of tune, through the streets and in the churches, which they entered to recite their prayers and the stations of the cross.[114]

A tract that appeared at the end of the month of January [1589] put into a *Politique*'s mouth the following admiring words about the League's measures against female luxury:

We see such a great reform in the reduction of luxury that those who do not witness it cannot believe it, and it seems rather that excess is now completely banished rather than chased out for a time, to the point that now a young lady is not only embarrassed to wear a ruff but even a simple linen band at the neck that is too long, or cuffs that have too much cutwork, or some other superfluous ornament, and the other young ladies throw themselves upon her and tear off her collar or rip her dress.[115]

The League in Paris undeniably expressed a desire to reform morals and behavior that would survive its political failure. The history of religious devotion during the "century of the saints" [the seventeenth century] must take into account this flamboyant period during which the Catholic Counter Reformation began to put down its true roots.

* * *

Despite the obvious discontinuities, beyond the social and political tensions, and in addition to the bouts of violence or institutionalized terror, we can thus see the profile of certain lines of action take shape in Paris during the Wars of Religion. Though divided on other issues, the *notables* of Paris demonstrated not only their anguished desire for a stronger faith and not only the desire to live better in that faith but also the awareness of an imperative mission to purify the city of its "trash" and its "mud" and to shape the earthly Jerusalem in the most faithful image possible of the heavenly Jerusalem.

NOTES

1. *Le Nouvel Observateur*, October 1972.

2. For example, Henri Hauser, *Etudes sur la Réforme française* (1909), and the fine series, *Bulletin de la Société de l'histoire du protestantisme français*.

3. We know that Hauser saw the Reformation as initially supported by the urban popular classes before it was taken over circa 1559 by a fraction of the nobility. Engels viewed it as the ideology of the "rising" bourgeoisie (see *The Peasant War in Germany*, 1850). See Lucien Febvre, "Une question mal posée: les origines de la Réforme française et le problème des causes de la Réforme," *Revue historique* (1929), later included in the anthology, *Au coeur religieux du XVIe siècle* (Paris, 1957).

4. Cf. Emile G. Léonard, *Le Protestant français* (1963); and Jean Delumeau, *Le Catholicisme entre Luther et Voltaire* (1971).

5. Some of this research remains unpublished. One outstanding example is the unpublished master's paper by Denis Crouzet, "La violence collective en France à l'époque des guerres de Religion" (University of Paris-Sorbonne, 1975), supervised by Pierre Chaunu. Another has recently been published: Philip Benedict, *Rouen during the Wars of Religion* (Cambridge: At the University Press, 1980).

Chief among other published works is the research of Natalie Zemon Davis, especially "The Rites of Violence: Religious Riots in Sixteenth-Century France," *Past and Present* 59 (1973). This and other articles by Davis are found in her anthology, *Society and Culture in Early Modern France* (Stanford, Calif., 1975). Another important work is Janine Estèbe, *Tocsin pour un massacre: la saison des Saint-Barthélemy* (1968).

6. This study, done as part of a seminar, owes a great deal to Robert Descimon's research.

7. The son of Pierre Berthommier, auditor in the Chambre des Comptes, brother of a canon at Chartres, uncle of François Petau, and councillor in the Parlement of Brittany.

8. La Roche-Chandieu, *Histoire de l'Eglise réformée de Paris*; and the article by Fernand Aubert in the *Bulletin de la société de l'histoire du protestantisme français* (1947), based upon research in the State Archives at Zurich, E II, 341.

9. This was also the year in which emigration from Paris to Geneva reached its peak. Of the 118 Parisians listed in the *Livre des habitants de Genève* between 1549 and 1560, 44 arrived in 1559. See vol. 1 of Geisendorf's edition (1957) of this document.

10. On the Canaye family, important dyers and drapers who were closely allied to the Gobelin family, see Charles Manneville, "Les Canaye," *Bulletin de la Montagne Saint-Geneviève*, vol. 5; and especially Robert Descimon, "Les Teinturiers de Saint-Marcel: Gobelin et Canaye," an unpublished master's paper done in 1969 under the supervision of Pierre Vilar. Note that Jean Canaye was in the southern province of Languedoc on business at the time of the incident. On 18 August 1562 he directed his brother Jacques, a lawyer in the Parlement, to protest his innocence. However, he had to abandon his house, "The Patriarch," in order that "it be given to the poor or used for other charitable works" (Félibien, *Preuves*, vol. 4). Jean Canaye settled in Geneva in 1572.

11. The Huguenot version of this battle is found in the anonymous "Histoire véritable de la mutinerie, tumulte ets édition faite par les prêtres de Saint-Médard," in Cimber and Danjou, *Archives curieuses de l'histoire de France*, vol. 4. The Catholic version appears in the "Journal de Pierre Bruslart, in *Mémoires de Condé*, vol. 1. The journal was actually written by Nicolas Bruslart.

12. Such clashes are discussed in P. de Pascal, *Journal de ce qui s'est passé en France durant l'année 1562 . . . Principalement à Paris et à la Cour*, ed. M. François (1950).

13. See Aubert's article, cited in n. 8.

14. In Lucien Romier, ed., *Origines politiques des guerres de Religion* (1913–14), 2: 254, from documents in the State Archives at Zurich.

15. Moreover, an arrest order was issued after Montmorency took this step (see the Registres du Conseil du Parlement).

16. Bruslart, "Journal," 20 January 1562.

17. Using chiefly parish registers, Benedict in *Rouen during the Wars of Religion*, has been able to show that the Protestants in Rouen made up 21 percent of the total population in 1565, and he has been able to sketch out the respective size of each group.

18. Louis Régnier de la Planche, "Le livre des marchands, ou du grand et loyal devoir, fidelité et obéissance de MM. de Paris, envers le Roy et Couronne de France" (1560), ed. Paulin Paris et Edouard Mennechet, *Histoire de France par les écrivains contemporains* (Paris, 1836).

19. The eighth of the nine children of Jehan I. Crocquet, Nicolas Crocquet was a merchant draper, a representative of his quarter and *échevin* of the city, husband of a Gobelin woman, and brother of two municipal councillors. He was sentenced to death twice in absentia during the first civil wars and was finally hanged on 30 June 1569 with Philippe and Richard de Gastines. Jacquemin was a merchant draper with ties to the leading commercial families of Paris.

20. Benedict, *Rouen during the Wars of Religion*, found a noticeably different situation in Rouen. There the middle-level shopkeepers were won over to the Reformation, while the top level remained faithful to the Catholic church.

21. In 1562, Jacques Danès was a member of the committee for the poor of the Reformed Church in Paris (*Bulletin de la société de l'histoire du protestantisme français* 1 [1852]: 225). He returned to the Catholic church and gave up business to become a royal secretary and acquired the seigneuries of Marly-la-Ville. On Jean Rouillé, Jacques Danès's brother-in-law, see Charles Pradel, "Un marchand de Paris au XVIᵉ siècle," *Mémoire de l'Académie des Sciences, Inscriptions et Belles Lettres de Toulouse*, 9th ser., no. 1 (1889) and no. 2 (1890); and Descimon, "Les Teinturiers de Saint-Marcel." Oudin Petit was a representative for the quarter of Saint-Séverin. He was assassinated on Saint Bartholomew's Day by his mother's second husband, Jacques Kerver, a representative of the quarter of Sainte-Geneviève, who also was a bookseller.

On the Petit family, see Philippe Renouard, *Documents sur les libraires parisiens*, which contains an inaccurate genealogy; and inventories made after death and documents providing for dividing up property, in the Archives Nationales, Paris [hereafter cited as A.N.], Minutier central, LXXIII, 78, and LXXIII, 42.

22. During the same period three of the six *councillor-échevins* at Rouen were Huguenots. See Benedict, *Rouen during the Wars of Religion*.

23. The estate of Henri Ladvocat, wholesale mercer on the rue Saint-Denis, and *juge-consul* in 1564, then colonel of the quarter of Le Sepulcre, reached the sizeable sum of 235,000 livres (1574-83). A.N., Minutier central, LXXXVI.

24. Bibliothèque Nationale, Paris [hereafter cited as B.N.], Ms. français 4047.

25. According to Canon Bruslart's "Journal," warnings *ad finem revelationis* about royal officials "who went to hear sermons and took communion or sacraments in a form other than that of the Catholic Church" went out in August 1562. During the trial of *Procureur* Fichard for libelous denunciation (see below), the accused replied that "a warning had been published and that to unburden his conscience he went to make declarations and revelations to the vicar of the said parish." See Guerin's article.

26. Another document, also in Cimber and Danjou, *Archives curieuses de l'histoire de France*, indicates that the parish priests objected to forty councillors [in the Parlement], "all of whom they claimed (untruthfully) were of the reformed religion."

27. This was the case for Adrien de Thou, councillor-ecclesiastic and canon of Notre Dame Cathedral and brother of Parlementary president Christofle de Thou, who refused to profess the Catholic faith on 15 June 1561.

28. Félibien, *Preuves*, 4: 803.

29. Benedict, *Rouen during the Wars of Religion*, points out that in Rouen the percentage of important Huguenot officials reached only one-tenth of the total membership in Huguenot groups.

30. Ibid. Benedict rightly points out the "exuberance and exaltation" of the Protestants who, during these years, thought that "the triumph of their cause was imminent." See also Antoine Richart, *Mémoires sur la Ligue dans le Laonnais* (Laon, 1869).

31. Jacques Pineaux, *La poésie des Protestants de langue française* (Paris, 1971). For popular prints, note, for example, the theme of the overturned pot, discussed in "Cinq siècles d'imagerie française," a catalog for the exhibit held in 1973 at the Musée des Arts et Traditions populaires.

32. Canon Bruslart, who recounts the incident in his "Journal," added: "Similar sacraments rather often were administered in this fashion before the eyes and in the knowledge of the Court of the Parlement, without, however, punishing them or bringing the matter before the courts."

33. La Roche-Chandieu, *Histoire de l'Eglise Réformée de Paris*.

34. There is a fine analysis of the "martyrological mimesis" in Crouzet, "La Violence collective." I do not share certain positions taken by Donald Kelley in "Martyrs, Myths, and the Massacre: The Background of Saint Bartholomew," *American Historical Review* (December 1972). The "martyrdom complex" can be observed before 1559 and again after 1572. The period between these dates is, on the other hand, one during which the "long suffering" Reformation became a "militant" one.

35. Bruslart, "Journal."

36. In his article in the *Bulletin de la société de l'histoire du protestantisme français* 119 (1973), Jacques Poujol shows that at the time of the Conjuration of Amboise, as in the majority of Protestant demonstrations of these years, it was a question of presenting the authorities with the articles of the Confession of the Faith of 1559. The truth was to be self-evident.

37. The word *commune*, which continually appears in Catholic accounts and in municipal records to designate the Catholic mob, has very important connotations. Founded upon the collective memory, during the League it became applied to a specific institutional project.

38. In volume 2 of his *Histoire ecclésiastique*, Théodore Beza told with satisfaction how in Rouen the Mardi Gras festivities disappeared when the Huguenots became masters of the city in 1562-63.

39. Bruslart, "Journal."

40. Félibien, *Preuves*, 4: 799.

41. Ibid., 4: 807.

42. Labitte, *De la démocratie chez les prédicateurs de la Ligue* (1966).

43. See *Registres des délibérations de l'Hôtel de Ville*, 8: 116, for a list of the officials stripped

of their charges in 1568 and early 1569, and ibid., 8: 16, for those renting houses on the Notre Dame bridge. For orders to draw lists of suspects, see Pascal, *Journal*, 2 June 1562.

44. Régnier de La Planche, "Le livre des marchands."

45. B.N., Ms. français 3347, fol. 24, which is quoted by La Ferrière, ed., *Lettres de Catherine de Médicis*, 3: 60.

46. Pascal, *Journal*.

47. *Registres des délibérations de l'Hôtel de Ville*, vol. 5, 21 October 1562.

48. Bruslart, "Journal."

49. *Registres des délibérations de l'Hôtel de Ville*, 5: 253, 9 July 1563.

50. It partly fulfilled this mission. The election of the officers of the militia produced very different results in the various quarters of the city. Certain captains were militant Catholics who made numerous arrests of suspected heretics. Thus, in the quarter of the rue de la Parcheminerie in 1562 such a man was Captain Tanchon, who later replaced the Huguenot Desjardins as *lieutenant criminel* [chief royal judge for criminal cases], then was arrested in 1564 for having pillaged the property of Protestants, and once again became *lieutenant criminel* in 1570–71. (See Guerin's article). The names of certain other officers in the militia who specialized in hunting down suspects frequently recur in the arrest records of the Conciergerie of the *Palais* (see n. 68).

51. *Journal d'un curé ligueur*, ed. Edouard de Barthélémy (Paris, 1865).

52. On the incident involving the Gastines cross, which led to riots, see *Registres des délibérations de l'Hôtel de Ville*, vol. 6; Cimber and Danjou, *Archives curieuses*, 1st ser., vol. 6; *Mémoires de l'Estat de France*, vol. 1; Crespin, *Le Martyrologue*; d'Aubigné, *Histoire universelle*, vol. 2, b. 1; and above all de Thou, *Histoire universelle*, vol. 6.

53. Concerning those responsible and the impact of the international situation, see Philippe Erlanger, *Le Massacre de la Saint-Barthélemy* (Paris, 1960), and Pierre Champion, *La France et le contrôle de l'Espagne* (1939). See also, Estèbe, *Tocsin pour un massacre*.

54. For the monarchy's attempts to distribute blame for the St. Bartholomew's Day Massacre, see the Royal declaration of 28 August 1572, and the letter from the Queen Mother [Catherine de Médicis] to the French ambassador in Madrid, 29 August 1572. Blaming the populace for the massacre, which was adopted as of September, aroused the indignation of the world.

55. "Histoire véritable."

56. Pascal, *Journal*.

57. De Thou, *Histoire universelle*, 2: 705–6.

58. Benedict, *Rouen during the Wars of Religion*, points out that this also occurred in Rouen, where a confraternity of the Holy Sacrament was founded in 1561 by twelve laymen, including five merchants and four members of the *basoche*.

59. Claude Haton, *Mémoires* (Paris, 1857).

60. Cf. de Thou, *Histoire universelle*, vol. 14. The Gastines's house was located on the rue Saint-Denis, in the quarter of Saint-Jacques-de-l'Hôpital. See B.N., Ms. français 11692.

61. On 20 March 1562, "a Huguenot was buried in the cemetery of the Saints-Innocents in the new fashion, but suddenly the papists came to disinter him and placed the dead body in the mud in the main street." Pascal, *Journal*. Other examples can be found in the *Journal d'un curé ligueur*.

62. Bruslart, "Journal."

63. "In the Halles of Paris/they rendered him justice;/then the little children/carried it out./ Soon he was taken down/after he had been hanged./When they had thrown him down/from the top of the scaffold/all the little children/came together again/and dragged him into the road./ Had he not deserved it?/They made their way/via the [rue de] la Feronnerie,/[with Nez d'Argent] tied and garroted,/leading a joyous life,/crying and singing happily:/'Nez d'Argent is coming.'/ When they had dragged him/into his cemetery/in the streamlet/that served as his bier,/they pulled out all his tripe/in order to burn it in a fire." The text of this song is given by N. Weiss, *Bulletin de la société du protestantisme français*, vol. 48.

64. *Journal d'un curé ligueur*.

65. See n. 50.

66. Among the four lawyers was Anne de Terières, sieur de Chappes, who appears on the list of suspects drawn up by the parish priests; and François de Marillac (see Guerin's article).

67. Nicolas Croquet's brother, Pierre, a municipal councillor, had been arrested by the offi-

cers of his quarter's militia, and was then authorized by the governor of Paris to withdraw to his home in order to "continue his business." The chamber ordered that first it should be determined "whether in the past he usually went to mass and to confession, celebrated Easter on the days specified by the Church, and did other Catholic acts and works" (see Guerin's article and also n. 19). François Perrot came from an old family of merchant drapers who became échevins by 1515. The son of a *prévôt des marchands*, François Perrot had spent a long time studying in Italian universities. See E. Picot, *Les Français italianisants au XVIᵉ siècle* (1906-7). Related to the Gobelins and the de Thous, he married Pierre Crocquet's daughter. He returned to Venice and then went to Geneva, where he appears in the *Livre des habitants* in 1573 (see Haag, *La France protestante*). François Canaye was a merchant dyer of the Saint-Marcel quarter, and second cousin of Jean Canaye (see n. 10). Jacques Gobelin was also a merchant dyer of Saint-Marcel. Jehan Petit was the son of Oudin Petit, the bookseller, and represented the quarter of Saint-Severin (see n. 21). He was connected with a bookseller in Geneva (A.N., Minutier central, XLII, 38, 13 December 1565).

68. Charles Read, *Bulletin de la société de l'histoire du protestantisme français* (1901); and Weiss, in the same publication, 1901 and 1923. Henri Bordier's transcriptions can be consulted at the library of the Société de l'histoire du protestantisme français in Paris.

69. Transcribed in the *Registres des délibérations de l'Hôtel de Ville*, 8: 117.

70. *Mémoires de Charles IX*, 1: 411.

71. Davis, "The Rites of Violence," gives a table with the figures available for several cities: Bourges, Meaux, Troyes, Orléans, Rouen, and Lyons.

72. I worked out a scale of contributions based on the forced loan of 1571, using B.N., Ms. français, 11692.

73. The words of H. Drout, *Mayenne et la Bourgogne* (Paris, 1937).

74. Guérin, in his article based on A.N., X^2 A924.

75. His son; Achille de Harlay, would later become first president of the Parlement. Pierre de La Place was first president of the Cour des Aides and a victim of Saint Bartholomew's Day. See the incomplete inventory of his personal property in A.N., Minutier central, *Thiruel*, 1572.

76. See his will in A.N., X114, fol. 252.

77. The same names are to be found in the prison records [of the Conciergerie] for 1564 and 1569, and on the list of the victims of Saint Bartholomew's Day.

78. See Pradel, "Un Marchand de Paris."

79. Philip Benedict, "Catholics and Huguenots in Sixteenth-Century Rouen: The Demographic Effects of the Religious Wars," *French Historical Studies* 9 (1975).

80. See Théodore Beza, "Deux lettres sur la Saint-Barthélemy," *Bulletin de la société de l'histoire du protestantisme français* 7 (1858).

81. J. Pannier, *L'Eglise réformée de Paris sous Louis XIII* (Paris, 1922).

82. Take the Arnauld family. Of the eight sons of Antoine I. Arnauld who were saved from the massacre by Catherine de Médicis, some returned to Protestantism (see the marriage contract of Isaac Arnauld, B.N., Pièces originals, 100, fol. 43). On the other hand, Antoine II, the famous lawyer, remained faithful to Catholicism. I plan to deal with this family in a projected study on Paris and the Estates General of 1614.

83. This was the justification for his apostasy made by Pastor Hugues Sureau, as quoted by Benedict in *Rouen during the Wars of Religion*. This feeling is revealed by the reappearance of the martyr's attitude; the victims of Saint Bartholomew's Day did not resist.

84. A document about Jean Rouillé, reproduced in Pradel, "Un Marchand de Paris." (See also n. 21.)

85. De Thou, *Histoire universelle*, to a large extent inspired by the political views of the Montmorency clan, exerted a great influence upon nineteenth- and twentieth-century historiography.

86. See Denis Richet, *La France moderne: l'esprit des institutions* (Paris, 1973).

87. In Estienne Pasquier's *Lettres*, written after the Barricades, we find the clearest example of this scorn. When the militia officers named by Henry II were replaced by new, elected ones, Pasquier was present and recalled: "They dismissed all the old captains and lieutenants, all honorable people, against whom those vermin, the common people, did not dare to stand up, and in their stead placed a certain Sire Guillaume, Sire Michel, Sire Bonadventure. Why am I saying sires? (for this word is applied only to leading merchants, but most of them are simple tavern-

keepers, cabaretkeepers, and other such breeds)." My analysis of the list of officers, by quarter, does not bear out Pasquier's assertion (see n. 20).

88. See A. A. Lozinsky, on the struggle for power in the Parisian municipality after the Barricades (1588–89), in Russian.

89. J.H.H. Salmon, "The Paris Sixteen, 1584–94: The Social Analysis of a Revolutionary Movement," *Journal of Modern History* (1973). Unfortunately, I have been unable to consult the doctoral dissertation by Peter Ascoli, "The Sixteen and the Paris League," University of California, Berkeley, 1971.

90. Descimon and I are preparing a study of *notables* based on all the lists of those "summoned" to the city meetings, complemented by the documents from the Châtelet and the A.N., Minutier central.

91. Salmon, "The Paris Sixteen." See also my unpublished dissertation on the Séguiers.

92. We know that there never was a council with sixteen members. It was given that name because there were sixteen quarters in Paris, which were unequally represented on the various councils. See also B.N., Ms. français 3960, for the letter to Philip II of 10 September 1591.

93. See Palma-Cayet, *Chronique Novenaire*, for Brisson's execution and Mayenne's repression.

94. I think that the category "minor functionary" should be incorporated into the one composed of lawyers and *procureurs*.

95. Or rather, to those newcomers who did not marry into established families. On the importance of women to social mobility, see Denis Richet, "La formation des grands serviteurs de l'Etat," *L'Arc* (May 1976).

96. *Le Dialogue du Malheustre et du Manant*. The author of this remarkable pamphlet, which is not well known because it is often confused with a royalist counterfeit, clearly expressed this three-part distribution of forces. On the one extreme there was the nobility, the upper clergy, and the leading families; and at the other, the "people," who did not remain faithful to the good cause. Between them were the Leaguers, who were faithful to God and heirs of the old freedoms. See Salmon, "The Paris Sixteen," for an excellent analysis of this source.

97. "Procès verbal de Nicolas Poulain," in Cimber and Danjou, *Archives curieuses*, vol. 11.

98. This is a very approximate estimate. Lestoile refers to a population of 200,000 inhabitants at the time of the siege of Paris, but he did so in order to make the League seem worse for having emptied the capital of *half* its population. The number 400,000, which he cites for an earlier period, is highly improbable.

99. "Procès verbal de Nicolas Poulain."

100. Lestoile, *Journal*; and *Journal historique sur les troubles de la Ligue*, ed. Fayet (1852).

101. See *Journal de François, bourgeois de Paris*, ed. Saulnier (1913), and Lestoile, *Journal*, passim. Only a minority of those who fled Paris joined the royalist Parlement that had withdrawn to Tours. Many continued to play a waiting game until late 1591. This was the case with President Séguier, who had difficulty gaining acceptance for the royalist nucleus at Tours. See Richet, unpublished dissertation.

102. Notably the priest of Saint-Séverin, a parish with many members of Parlement. Cf. Lestoile, *Journal*, passim.

103. B.N., Ms. français 3960.

104. I am referring to the Brigard incident. Named *procureur du roi et de la ville* after the Barricades, François Brigard became suspect. President Brisson merely banished him from the city, rather than having him executed as the Sixteen wished.

105. This loss of credit was felt until the late 1640s, during the days of the Fronde. Certain *mazarinades* [antiroyalist publications] reveal the Frondeurs' desire clearly to disassociate themselves from the Leaguers. On secrecy, see the article "Congrégations jésuites," *Dictionnaire de spiritualité*.

106. In reality the Jesuits were divided in their political choices. Although Father Commolet was among the great preachers of the League, others remained faithful to the end to Henry III. See H. Fouqueray, *Histoire de la Compagnie de Jésus en France* (1910), vol. 1.

107. After Henry III's assassination by the Dominican monk Jacques Clément, Father Bourgoing, prior of Saint-Jacques-de-Paris, was sentenced to death and drawn and quartered. Henry III's widow, Louise de Lorraine, asked Henry IV to forbid the Preachers order in France, and pressure had to be exerted to prevent this step. For the influence of the Franciscan order, see

Godefroy de Paris, *Les Frères Mineurs capucins en France: histoire de la province de Paris* (1937), vol. 1.

108. The defeat of the League brought about the official disappearance of the confraternities of the Holy Sacrament and of the Disciples of Saint Francis in the northern portion of the kingdom. On *pénitents*, see Marc Venard, *Les Confréries des pénitents au XVIe siècle dans la province ecclésiastique d'Avignon*, Mémoires de l'Académie de Vaucluse, 6th ser., I (1967).

109. Marguerite Pecquet, *Des Confréries des pénitents à la Compagnie du Saint-Sacrement, XVIIe siècle* (1965).

110. Benedict, *Rouen during the Wars of Religion*.

111. Identical measures were taken in other cities, especially in Rouen and Laon. See ibid.; and Richardt, *Mémoires sur la Ligue*.

112. See Charles Valois's introduction to the incomplete publication, *Histoire de la Ligue: oeuvre inédite d'un contemporain* (1914).

113. *Journal de François, bourgeois de Paris*, p. 40.

114. Lestoile, *Journal*.

115. Quoted by Saulnier in a note to his edition of the *Journal de François, bourgeois de Paris*.

10

Witchcraft, Popular Culture, and Christianity in the Sixteenth Century with Emphasis upon Flanders and Artois

Robert Muchembled

Witchcraft: Social Crime? Or Component of a Rejected Culture?

The chief difficulty in studying sixteenth- and seventeenth-century witchcraft in general terms is the inadequate sources dealing with the subject. Witches only left us accounts of what they did in the versions compiled by their judges, who took them over and broke them up according to the categories that had been carefully developed by their predecessors since the late Middle Ages.[1] We know most about the witchcraft that was punished and have no trouble viewing it as a "crime" against society.[2] Certain authors still follow Jules Michelet's lead, calling witchcraft the "child of poverty" and portraying it as social rebellion.[3] Others add nuances to this point of view and categorize witches as social outcasts.[4] I do not, however, view witchcraft prior to the final three decades of the sixteenth century as an outsider or an intruder. On the contrary, I see it as being deeply rooted in the way people thought and as revealing a cultural level, a sort of adjustment to the world that is closer to the "savage mind" of ethnography than to our own way of thinking. Also rooted in popular thought were recurrent paganism and what the elite or particularly the clergy called "superstitions." Therefore, in order to make the phenomenon once more to a certain degree autonomous, I have tried to analyze it before its prosecution in the courts and to study it during

Annales, E.S.C. 28 (January-February 1973): 264–84. Translated by Patricia M. Ranum

the first half of the sixteenth century by using information supplied both by modern specialists in folklore[5] and by two collections of northern French sermons of that century.[6]

Still, we must be distrustful, for these sources probably are not impartial. In order to avoid unconsciously adopting their viewpoint, I carried out my analysis in three stages. First of all, I copied from these texts whatever permitted me to describe the mental "climate" within which witchcraft developed, the climate that Jacques Toussaert called the "divine milieu" and that I would prefer to call the "magical milieu." I then tried to discern a double aspect of witchcraft and see it as both a phenomenon that involved deviating from the values being championed by the judges and inquisitors, and as an element that formed an integral part of another mental world, which we have since lost. Last, I analyzed a double role that I began to realize had been played by witchcraft, a role that served as a focus for the fears of a society in which the witch was the scapegoat and that also was an important element in the daily lives of the masses. This very ambiguity, which became increasingly clear during the course of the sixteenth century, makes the phenomenon valuable as an index of profound mental transformations.

The Magical Milieu

Today we are relatively well-informed about the religion of the Christian elites of Europe. And, since the first three decades of this century, historians of religion have been following the lead of Gabriel Le Bras and trying to reconstitute the exact picture of the religious lives of the masses.[7] This is a difficult task, for written evidence is scarce, especially for rural areas. In addition, many histories of the Catholic Church still give only limited coverage to demonstrations of popular piety.[8] It would, however, be unfair not to acknowledge the recent attempts, chiefly in France, to learn more about how the common people lived their Christianity.[9]

I will touch upon only those elements that will permit us to define the "magical milieu" that I believe gave birth to witchcraft.

THE IGNORANCE OF CHRISTIANS

First of all, the Christianity practiced by the common people was characterized by ignorance: ignorance of dogma and participation in the liturgy without always understanding the meaning of the sacraments or mass. Moreover, the majority of the clergy was also ignorant,[10] as an anonymous cleric who preached in the region of Béthune during the first half of the sixteenth century stated: "All the troubles of Christendom are occurring now because priests and confessors are ignorant of what they should know and neglect to learn it."[11] He added, in discussing prelates and parish priests, that "they must learn what they are supposed to teach others, for how is it possible to teach someone something that one does not know oneself?"[12] Jean Glapion expressed the same opinion in 1520 to the Duke of Lorraine at Nancy: "For the majority of us [priests] are ignorant of the articles of the faith."[13]

Many churchmen felt that this ignorance on the part of the clergy led to the people's ignorance of Christian belief and practices. Glapion proclaimed this.[14] "The preacher of Béthune referred to it in his discussion of the "Holy Sacrament of the altar," which, according to him, the Christians of the early Church received daily. Then people began to take communion only on Sundays, "and still later they became annoyed at going [to the communion service] so often, as a result either of the negligence of those who administer it, or the unworthiness or lack of devotion and laxity of those who receive it."[15] This indignation doubtlessly concealed a guilt feeling within the lower clergy. Discussing communion, which was held in such slight esteem that certain individuals "go ten or twelve years without receiving it," the preacher from Béthune strongly advised parish priests to require that people take communion at least once a year, "for priests are entrusted with souls. For they are held accountable for them."[16]

The people do not, therefore, seem to have been very religious. Toussaert asserts that this was true in coastal Flanders and in the Flemish-speaking "Westhoeck" until the early sixteenth century. According to him, the situation was no better in the cities. The parish of Saint-Jacques at Bruges included "ten percent of the population who were almost pagan, and forty percent who were Christian and worshipped at Easter with relative regularity."[17] Glapion said much the same thing in 1520: "In the Vosges mountains and in the mountains of Savoy there are so many simple folk who never hear their priest preach."[18]

The preacher of Béthune assumed an air of resignation, aware of the religious conventionalism of his listeners. "It is no longer a matter of listening to sermons. For after Easter no one pays any more attention to them than to overripe herrings."[19] Still, he commented, the crowd was large on Easter Sunday. Was this proof of the well-being of Christianity? Certainly not! "For where there is such a large crowd, it is very difficult to be reverent or devout."[20] Let us end with his conclusions about this sterile religious conventionalism: "They seem to think that it is enough when they have gone to church on Sunday and recited the Lord's Prayer and the hours, or when they have done some other pious act. I tell you that this is not sufficient."[21]

Le Brun doubtlessly is unduly pessimistic when he wonders "whether the French countryside was ever really Christian" prior to the seventeenth century.[22] Nonetheless, the principal characteristic of the religious life of the people at the beginning of the sixteenth century seems to have been its drabness.

FEAR

This rough sketch, which may be valid only for a small part of northwestern Europe, needs another dimension if it is to come to life. As far as Christianity is concerned, the world of religious ignorance was also the world of fear: fear of death[23] and fear of damnation and, by extension, of the devil and of hell.[24]

Priests and preachers identified fear of death with fear of the devil. At the end of the fifteenth century, Jean Tinctoris (Taincture) wrote a treatise entitled "Les Invectives contre la secte de Vauderie," invectives against the Waldensians. He forcefully denounced the devil's malevolence and exclaimed, "By the devil's wish death entered the world, and those who follow him experience it."[25] Churchmen or the masses of the Christian population at the end of the fifteenth century did not view death as a natural phenomenon. Calamities and catastrophes were credited to the action of evil, but also to God, who was in this way punishing sinners. For example, syphilis was considered a "chastisement sent from heaven to punish mankind, which had given itself over to excess sensuality."[26] Plague was considered the "divine punishment," the "ferocious and justiciary beast."[27] In discussing the plague at Tournai in 1400, an anonymous chronicler declared, "This thing having been done, it does not please God to withdraw His hand, but indeed [He] takes this pestilential rod and smites the people of the said city of Tournai harder than ever before, at random, because they have not turned to Him with their whole hearts."[28] Dancing was forbidden at Lille in 1489 in order to appease God.[29]

The priest of Cysoing also expressed these ideas clearly. "My friend, very often illnesses are sent to us by God for our sins. You must, therefore, cast them out of you through the confessional, in order to please Him and regain His love." Priests of this sort undoubtedly tried to frighten the crowds by referring to the "heat of the fires of Purgatory" and by requiring the sick who were near death's door to confess, "or otherwise I shall not bury you in holy ground any more than I would an animal."[30] Their sermons were permeated with references to the devil. This is confirmed by a sampling from the ten sermons written by the preacher of Béthune, for the word *devil* appears thirty-eight times and *devilry* appears four times.[31]

This theme was expanded upon chiefly in sermons dealing with the first two commandments: "Thou shalt have no other gods before me. Thou shalt not make unto thee any graven image" (Exodus 20: 3–4). Indeed, in this context the word *devil* or *devils* appears twenty-five times and *devilry* is used four times. At this point the connotations of the theme broaden. Until then, the word *devil* had only been linked with the idea of damnation. "The devil wages war against us"; "man is tempted by the devil"; "the thousand devils will carry him off." And the author stressed that baptism would free a person from "servitude to the devil." Then, preaching at length on the first commandment, he identified devilry with paganism ("to devils or idols"[32]) and with superstition.[33] The devil was shown to have enormous power. He understood perfectly "natural and outdoor things" and could therefore influence them—for example, "change the air and prevent it from blowing or raining."[34] Through the "devil's miracles"[35] he could also reveal what God has hidden from men.[36] It was easy for him to cure the illnesses that he himself had sent to mankind.[37] For Satan was "God's chief enemy."[38] He sought out "Waldensians, soothsayers, and witches and warlocks" as servants[39] and bound them to him by pacts and promises.[40] In order to avoid these traps, Christians were to refuse any pact or "trust in the devil or his followers."[41]

In this atmosphere dominated by a fear of omnipresent devilry, the uneducated lower clergy did not succeed in reassuring a populace that was even more uneducated. Perhaps the populace was looking for the consolation brought by magical practices? Perhaps it was trying to "tame" God by set forms and by words, to gain His good will.[42] Indeed, taking into account the fact that our documentation comes from a uniform source, it would seem that what witnesses called "superstitions" were a complex body of practices that were trying primarily to achieve concrete results, but that were not necessarily anti-Christian. Thus, the observer must attempt to study these "superstitions" and this "witchcraft," yet not get caught up in the thought processes of the witnesses without weighing the pros and cons. Ethnographers teach us to be prudent and advise that we adopt an outsider's viewpoint relative to both actors and witnesses.

The Content and Meaning of Witchcraft Prior to the Sixteenth Century

WITCHCRAFT AS VIEWED BY CLERICS AND JUDGES

At the end of the fifteenth century and during the first half of the sixteenth century, the two terms *witchcraft* and *superstitions* seem to have encompassed similar realities. They were not totally identical, for *witchcraft* clearly had a pejorative meaning,[43] whereas *superstitions* could be applied to deviance from Christian practice that clerics considered a venial, or pardonable sin.

The distinction seems to have developed slowly during the course of the Middle Ages. The first of the two terms to be used to any degree was *superstitions*. The Council of Leptines, in Hainaut, summarized circa 743–744 "pagan superstitions and customs," which included omens, sacrifices to saints, pagan festivals, fabric images, soothsayers, and spells.[44] At that time, *superstition* seems to have been synonymous with *paganism*. An eleventh-century penitential, "The Healer or Physician," written by Bishop Burchard I of Worms circa 1008–1012, included long lists of old and new superstitions and stressed witchcraft.[45] The penance for practices considered to be witchcraft does not seem to have been very onerous, in no way comparable to the burnings at the stake of the sixteenth century. During this period witchcraft doubtlessly was not seen as a counterreligion but as a combination of pagan survivals and new superstitions.[46]

The texts leveled at witchcraft became scarcer between the eleventh and the thirteenth centuries, then multiplied from the thirteenth to the fifteenth centuries.[47] At that point the Inquisition was unleashed, vigorously punishing heresy,[48] and the judicial mechanism that it had worked out was soon applied to witchcraft. In 1460 witches were tried and sentenced at Arras. They were labeled "Waldensians," although they no longer had any connection with the followers of Peter Waldo. This inaccurate terminology nonetheless reveals a new equation: heresy equaled witchcraft.[49] Treatises on demonology flourished during the second half of the fifteenth century. Jakob Sprenger and Heinrich Krämer's *Malleus maleficarum*, or *Hexenhammer*, of 1486 systematized beliefs on this subject.[50]

In the final analysis, the term *witchcraft* and the notion it embodied seem gradually to have shifted from paganism to heresy, that is, to a counterreligion. Are we not dealing here with merely an apparent transformation in witchcraft, a change that took place in the observer rather than in the subject being observed? There is no doubt that superstitions and witchcraft practices changed. But surely they did this slowly, whereas the discrepancy undeniably became more pronounced between the world that was the witches' cradle throughout the Middle Ages and the urban world where Christianity purified itself and became more demanding by the twelfth or thirteenth centuries.

The ignorance of the populace (which became increasingly evident to churchmen between the thirteenth and mid-sixteenth centuries), the increasing climate of fear in the West, and the proliferation of heresies were all interpreted by the inquisitors and the Christian elite as signs that God was sending to show His dissatisfaction.[51] Although I do not want to underemphasize the religious dimensions of the phenomenon, I can assert that the hunt for heretics—and then for witches after the mid-sixteenth century—was also a way of projecting religious anxiety and individual fear by focusing it upon something, by projecting it outside oneself.

A history of witchcraft along these lines is, however, incomplete. The time has come to question the witches themselves, to the degree that this is possible, or at least to study the tracks they have left behind them in their adversaries' words. We must try to excise and isolate these tracks, in order to put together the jigsaw puzzle of another lost discourse, similar to the one that Bakhtin pieced together for popular culture using the works of François Rabelais.[52]

WITCHCRAFT AMONG THE PEOPLE,
AND REAL LIFE

"Witchcraft" in the West of the fear-dominated fifteenth and sixteenth centuries seems at first to be a body of codes and beliefs permitting man an immediate grasp of the world. We seem, therefore, to be dealing with *magic* in the sense given the word by Marcel Mauss as: "any ritual that does not form part of an organized cult." According to Mauss, the notion of *mana*, which presents characteristics of secret power and mysterious strength, is an embodiment of the belief in "that state of anxiety and social sensitivity in which all the vague ideas, all the futile hopes and fears, float about."[53] In my opinion it is possible to study the countless folk codes described in books on folklore in the light of the "laws" of magic set forth by Mauss. A formula from fifteenth-century Picardy for increasing milk production by rubbing the vessel in which the milk would be collected with grasses growing in midsummer, at the feast of Saint John [June 24],[54] may be explained by the belief in the fundamental unity of the world: "Everything in it resembles everything else and everything in it is related." A contiguity exists between the grass collected under certain circumstances and the vessel that will be in contact with the milk. "Like produces like," and thoughts about magic thus shift directly from the grass, which the cow eats, to the milk produced by the cow. In like manner, the importance placed upon the saints who cure illnesses is also undoubtedly explained by this conception of a "sympathetic magic." Mauss sets forth the law of opposition: "Like makes like go away in order to give rise to the opposite."[55] As we know, in the early sixteenth century illness was generally considered a divine punishment. An appeal to the healing saints and to things sacred may have seemed the best way to get well. It tried to force God to alter the normal course of events. Such members of the clergy as the preacher of Béthune saw a danger involving the devil: "And so you who go to Saint Eloi's hammer, believing that it will cure you of some illness, you are idolaters, and if you should happen to be cured, it is not Saint Eloi's hammer that has cured you, it is the devil."[56]

He added that "superstitions about medicines" were increasing. "You must recite the Lord's Prayer, wear talismans, and stick your finger into a hole in a stone, and many other foolish things that are now being done in Christendom. It is all devilry."[57] Further on we read: "Idolatry reigns at present in so many people; some trust in wearing talismans, others in lighting candles, others in saying novenas in honor of Saint Chy or Saint La [nonsense names], and then they must eat two [of something], then one, and then put a bent coin into the water, which afterwards they must drink and then take it [the coin] to Saint I-don't-know-who; and all these things and others are nothing but superstitions of the devil. Such devilry comes from failing to hope and trust in God."[58]

I see this blend of superstition and Christianity as revealing an attempt to organize the world. We see this attempt as a nonrational classification, in which the supernatural and the real constantly collide and are indistinguishable. Yet such an attempt facilitated a transition to diabolical "witchcraft" in the pejorative sense that the word was given by those opposed to witchcraft.[59] The same is true for soothsayer-healers, village witches, and those who doubtlessly simply possessed magical aspects and formulas and who were the object of violent attacks by such men as Glapion[60] or the preacher from Béthune, who stated: "There are Waldensians, soothsayers, and warlocks and witches who want to become involved in knowing hidden things, such as who stole this or that or who did thus and so, or who want to know what will happen in the future; and for this they make pacts and promises with the devil, so that he will reveal to them whether or not I have stolen something; and make agreements and promises to do some service for the devil, and he will reveal to them the location of the lost objects."[61] These attacks shed light on a social function of the soothsayer within a rural community: he renders services and wards off "catastrophes" such as the one reflected in Glapion's reference to "those who make excuses about having beaten their wives and children by saying that it is because they married during a certain month."[62] I believe that in a rural society that was saturated with a fear of things holy, the soothsayer—who was in his own way holy—distinguished between the beneficial and the harmful, represented the cultural tradition, and passed on its codes of belief.

The priest saw the soothsayer as an obstacle, a competitor. In order to make the soothsayer detested, the cleric claimed that he belonged to the devil. "The devil can change and prevent natural things. Sometimes he makes the wind blow, at others he makes the earth quake, and many other happenings; the which he does to seize as much of God's customary power for himself as he can. For he wants to do things that exceed God's customary power, so that people will have recourse to him rather than to God, which is now being done by several people, which is a pity. And when they cannot know things through God, they want to know them through the devil, and they go off to a soothsayer or to a Waldensian."[63]

Thus, we may well ask whether witchcraft did not belong to a popular culture of which we have lost almost every trace, a culture that has left no written evidence and that was affected by the censure attached to witchcraft or to the sour aftertaste of paganism. In support of this hypothesis I see this culture as being receptive and open until the mid-sixteenth century. It evolved very slowly, at a pace that progressed in centuries-long stages, and it constituted a threat to a Christianity whose various elements it proved capable of assimilating and distorting, sometimes with the unwitting help of the clergy. When the priest of Cysoing said, "My friend, you must sprinkle holy water about frequently from devotion and from heartfelt need, and thus it will help you to *ward off enemies*,"[64] he did not realize that his parishoners might interpret the end of that sentence as involving magic. Is this so very far removed from the exorcisms of the seventeenth century? And from using such sacred things as holy water, the host, and relics to achieve healing or protection? And, by extension, for making up potions and ointments?

Witchcraft, Learned Culture, and Popular Culture

THE FEMALE WITCH: A SCAPEGOAT?

Between 1550 and 1570 the Church's attitude toward witchcraft changed abruptly. A veritable frenzy of persecution gripped the ecclesiastical and lay judges of Europe.[65] I see this as indicating a profound change in European civilization. It seems to reveal the accentuation of a growing divergency between a popular culture that was being suppressed and a "learned" Christian culture that, owing to the concurrent efforts of the Protestants and the reformers of the Counter Reformation, infiltrated the whole of the social body.

As I see it, this suppression of the common people's vision of the world, which was bathed in a "magical" climate, crystallized and became distorted during the course of the censure and annihilation of witchcraft. The female witch became the scapegoat who bore all the sins of a world turned upside down since the Reformation. Who could feel safe during the sixteenth century? The fear of death, which was already so evident during the fifteenth century, seems to have become exacerbated in the Europe of Luther and Calvin. Millenarist beliefs appeared, with their fear of the Antichrist's imminent arrival. Some people, like the Anabaptists of Münster in 1534, tried to gather together to await the end of the world. Others sought a victory over this obsession elsewhere, even if it was only a relative victory. Michel Foucault[66] has clearly elucidated a collective mechanism of compensation: "Madness is death already come. But it is also death's presence conquered."[67] Foucault specifies that madness is a ritual form of exclusion, which has replaced leprosy and which "indicates that the world is approaching its final catastrophe."[68] Were the witch hunters not thinking the same thing when they searched for the devil's mark on their own persons, not so much to keep the devil at bay as to persuade themselves of the impending victory of the Prince of Darkness? At the end of the sixteenth century, when Europeans began to place the insane in institutions,[69] did witchcraft take the place of madness, both as a ritual form of exclusion and as an awareness of the coming of the Apocalypse? There is nothing contradictory in this; the frenzy shown by those who persecuted witches permitted them to escape fear and prepare for the coming of the end of time under the eyes of an ever-frightening God.

Is it, therefore, surprising that they chiefly attacked women?[70] For woman embodied original sin, especially for the Christian elite, but also for the common people, who were told by the preacher of Béthune that woman was the personification of sensuality.[71] Glapion delivered an indictment against women in 1520 and referred to the "disesteem of women."[72] As early as the thirteenth century in Flanders, one Hadewijch, a woman who had been given a good education and who was influenced by the mystical movement of the *béguines* although she did not become a nun, implied in her "Chant XVI" that the only permissible love is love for God, since all other love leads to hell:

Hell: what torment I perceive,
It damns, it engulfs all.
None leaves it, no, none receives
The grace to see its end.[73]

Such a guilt complex, in such an intelligent woman. And, this guilt complex was still being encouraged by clergy and laymen alike during the sixteenth century, although a feminist trend was clearly beginning.[74] For example, in the "secret register of François de Boffle, lord of Souchez," we read that "nothing is more like death than a woman. All the more so since [like death] she flees her pursuers and pursues those who do not desire her."[75] In a similar vein, Mauss quotes the old Brahman saying, "Woman is death," in order to explain her fundamental role in all witchcraft.[76] Robert-Léon Wagner points out that in Europe the female witch was doomed to a "sort of degradation and scorn" that was not the lot of the warlock.[77]

Thus, witch hunting cannot be attributed solely to the clergy's discarded inhibitions and to a release of the repressed sexual impulses forced upon them by the Church's interdictions. Besides, prior to the enforcement of the decisions of the Council of Trent, clergymen often had concubines.[78]

To conclude on this point, it is possible to assert that every society that experiences fear finds its own scapegoats. In the twentieth century this aggressiveness is still focused upon people rejected by society, as shown in P. Fleischmann's film *A Bavarian Hunt Scene*, in which a homosexual is "rejected" by an entire village. According to the director of the film, this reveals a "profound disequilibrium" in the Germany of 1968. Analyzing leftism and French youth late in 1970, two journalists wondered whether our society is becoming "hostile to the young."[79]

As far as the second half of the sixteenth century and the seventeenth century are concerned, the historian's problem lies in tracing the sources of this fear, not merely in describing its effects. This search permits him to grasp, at least to some extent, the unconscious motivations of demonologists, but it sheds little light on the question of the relationship between the judges' discourse—in the linguistic sense of the word—*about* witchcraft and the original discourse *of* the witches themselves.

The latter is only available to us in the form of fragments congealed in the mold of someone else's mind, the mind of the man who accumulated the evidence. We must, therefore, collect these fragments and reassemble them, with the degree of subjectivity that this implies. In doing so we can discern the continuities in thought patterns or the slow changes in the way that an imperfectly Christianized rural society viewed the world. I believe that this will permit us to show that rural witchcraft developed within, and not on the fringes of rural society. It was one of the components of the "folklorized" popular Christianity that Jean Delumeau has been studying for so long.[80] This Christianity, which remained superficial and had not taken firm root in rural milieux, was competing with recurrent paganism and with non-Christian elements within the culture. This was the Christianity lived by the ignorant masses.[81] But when bishops, preachers, and the Christian elite saw this form of Christianity, they thought of it as witchcraft. Indeed, it was increasingly thought of as being witchcraft by Protestants and Catholics alike, who were fighting one another in the countrysides of Western Europe and who came into contact with this "magical milieu" that horrified Erasmus, Luther (despite his superstitious credulity), and the Jesuits.

COMPARISONS

I would like to point out that the reactions of the elite and of the masses can profitably be compared to the syncretic phenomena that took place between paganism and Christianity in Africa. Christianity had been introduced into the old kingdom of Kongo by the Portuguese by the end of the fifteenth century. In his study of this kingdom, Georges Balandier has shown that, by the reign of Alfonso I (1506–43), a "small minority" of the native population had been affected by Christianity, while the vast majority of the people viewed Christianity's "ceremonies, symbolism, church, and confraternities less as reasons for conversion than as opportunities for imitation. It only left a lasting imprint to the degree that it was able to *ally itself with traditional practices*." A syncretism took shape progressively, and although the people's daily life showed traces of Christianizing as early as the first years of the sixteenth century, this was only the case to the degree that "they assimilated it according to their needs and the rules of their logic." Crucifixes and holy statuettes were employed to assure fecundity or fertility; the cross was used for the magical protection of houses or individuals. "Alongside a *poorly rooted* and continually *threatened* Christianity, traditional religious pluralism and syncretic cults gave a direction to the religious life of the people of Kongo from the sixteenth century on." Popular knowledge preserved its aspect of being immediately efficacious. Balandier points out the importance of the *nganga*, the "priest, physician, surgeon, priestess," who possessed therapeutic secrets, knew natural remedies, and above all knew how to integrate them into a ritual that expelled the forces of darkness that were responsible for the trouble. "Fetiches" played an important role in everyday life. In one very small region they were used to treat "Haemoptysis, backache, convulsions, nervous ailments, and madness."[82] This is reminiscent of the vogue for village witches, relics, and healing saints encountered in Europe during this same period. This analogy may be merely superficial; only a comparative study of the mental images of sixteenth-century Europeans and of populations such as that of Kongo would permit an answer.[83] Such a study would clarify the reciprocal modifications experienced by an imported Christianity and a receptive "traditional" culture. It might permit us to analyze the physical and metaphysical conceptions that the mass of the European population had about the human being and his relationships with the world.

WITCHCRAFT AND POPULAR CULTURE

European witchcraft during the sixteenth century might be better understood as a part of the everyday life of these layers of the rural population. A first step was taken by Carlo Ginzburg, who has studied the *beneandanti* of Friuli between 1575 and 1650. As the basis for his study the author used trial records, but the region did not torture witches, even after 1620. It seems that the accused spontaneously narrated their activities. The witchcraft described by Ginzburg amounts to a pre-Christian fertility cult: a real or imaginary ritual battle would be held at night between a group of warlocks armed with sorgum stalks and the *beneandanti*, who carried branches of fennel.[84] The *beneandanti* were individuals who had been born with a caul* which they kept hanging at their necks as a talisman. The *beneandanti* came to be considered witches. [What happened to the *beneandanti* when the Counter Reformation reached these rural areas?] In 1634 one of them "confessed" to having attended a witches' sabbath.

Did the Inquisition succeed in gradually persuading these marginally Christianized peasants that they were witches? This seems to be a plausible hypothesis, but numerous studies still must be made to delineate the relationships among witchcraft, folklorized Christianity, and paganism.[85] Our current knowledge of rural witchcraft at the beginning of the sixteenth century can permit the historian merely to define a few essential characteristics of "popular culture," which was steeped in magic and superficial Christianity and which ran counter to a conquering Christian culture. Indeed, one might well ask whether there was only a single profile of values, a single ethos in

---

*A person "born with a caul," that is, with the amniotic sac still covering his head, was believed to possess special magical or extrasensory powers, such as the ability to predict the future.— Trans.

French society (or merely in the society in Flanders and Artois during the first half of the sixteenth century) or whether, on the contrary, two antithetical visions of the world were still dimly confronting each other.

It seems difficult to answer this question using the modes for analyzing a society's values that were worked out by Kluckhohn and Strodtbeck or by Talcott Parsons. These approaches are too theoretical and too general to permit us to grasp the subtle nuances existing between two groups within a single society.[86] Although I deplore the all-too-frequent lack of contact between historians and sociologists, I shall have to be satisfied with defining empirically a few characteristics that contrast the vision of the world held by the missionaries with that held by the poorly Christianized masses. In my opinion, this contrast can be deduced from the narratives written by churchmen who were denying, refuting, or condemning the practices and behavior of the common people.

In the eighth century Saint Bonifacius listed as the devil's works: "Magic potions, incantations and charms, believing in vampires and werewolves, carrying out abortions, disobeying one's lords, and wearing talismans."[87]

In a similar vein, the synodial statutes of Amiens, circa 1454, set forth the following proscriptions: "VII: Divinationes, sortilegia, fascinationes, per somnia, auguria, et alia quaecumque similia superstitiosa remedia, sive in precationibus et conjurationibus, siven in votis quos veneficia seu caracteres vocant, aut etiam in quibuscumque suspendendis vel ligandis consistant, tamquam damnata ab omnibus fidelibus nostrae civitatis et dioecesis observari aut fiere, eisque fidem adhiberi penitus prohibemus."[88]

These texts, and many others like them, express Christianity's values as far as the notion of evil was concerned. We can attempt to go beyond this concept of evil, which is itself Christian, and consider what the Church was rejecting as non-Christian values and as elements of a different vision of the world. In this way we can discern the rough shape of the original "popular culture," although by this time it had already been profoundly contaminated by the Christian vision of the world.

And so, when listing "what the devil can in truth really do and what he cannot do," in his treatise about invectives against the Waldensian sect, Tinctoris may have revealed some of the basic beliefs of the population of his day:[89]

What the devil can do	What the devil cannot do
—send serpents	—affect the "mutation of the heavens"
—send rain, wind, thunder, storms	—turn a man into an animal or an animal into another animal
—carry people in the air and "make them as if flying"	—cause a body to pass "through a closed lock"
—break locks, carry off the contents of chests	—"exercise the work of life in bodies"
—tempt people	

When contrasting beliefs that he considered pertinent with those that he held to be false, Tinctoris undoubtedly made his selection among the popular beliefs of the fifteenth century. It would seem safe to assume that what he rejected still formed part of a vision of the magical world, a world characterized by man's feeling of submission to nature, which was permeated with the divine. Nothing was abnormal in a nonrationalized world. Everything could be explained by the intervention of supernatural powers; God or the Devil. Tinctoris himself seems not to have totally shaken off these magical conceptions, which were partially integrated into a Christianity that cannot be compared conceptually with the Christianity of the twentieth century.

All in all, witchcraft can be viewed as a component in a vision of the world held by the common people. This vision is difficult to perceive and can only be glimpsed in a few broad characteristics: the continuity and influence of popular ways of thinking in the rural world, and the slowness with which they changed. At the beginning of the sixteenth century the majority of people in the West—including the country priests, who were scarcely more educated than their listeners and who were influenced by the same milieu—lived a Christianity that was different from that practiced by monks, theologians, or even city-dwellers. Parts of the Christian worship service were slowly sucked down into the troubled waters of this level of civilization, which shaped them after its own image. One fifteenth-century example is the veneration of Mary, which focused upon the protective aspect of the Virgin's voluminous mantle, which stopped the arrows of the plague. This theme even spread to the level of the elites, where it appears, for example, in paintings.

This world changed very slowly. Christianity, classical paganism, and witchcraft were fused in this melting pot. Around 1550–70, however, the discrepancy between this world and the world of the Christian elites began to appear more clearly than before. The missionary dynamism of the restructured, reorganized, and conquering Catholic and Protestant churches resulted in a brutal collision and a permanent contact between the two cultures. Popular culture could only meet the impact of this collision through the vast strength of passive resistance, further exasperating the Protestant and Catholic missionaries, who were aware of the importance of their task, since the Kingdom of God was at hand. The late sixteenth century and the entire seventeenth century provided proof of the great effort at restructuring attempted by the various churches, especially in France. They had to raise the cultural level of the masses and make their "crude" religious feelings coincide with those of the elites, which were continually being refined.

Their efforts were not, however, sufficient to erase every trace of witchcraft or popular culture. Survivals in folklore, severed from their early meanings, still exist, though their meanings have been forgotten by the common people. For example, in the department of Pas-de-Calais old ways are reflected in an interest in the supernatural and in soothsayers, and in the saying that "the devil is beating his wife" when it thunders. Of course, people today are far removed from this cultural level (this word is not restricted to civilizations with written cultures), from this original vision of the world that missionaries in the past and present have considered primitive but that was alive during the sixteenth century among the common people.

Witchhunts: An Index of Mental Changes?

We must, therefore, qualify our conclusions concerning witchcraft—or rather, witchcrafts. Ecclesiastics, judges—and perhaps simply city-dwellers in general—considered witches to be children of poverty and ignorance, that is, ignorance of the Bible. Witches frequented isolated places, mountains, remote spots, or hamlets that were far from churches.[90] But, to the degree that the twentieth-century historian can isolate witchcraft from the deprecating arguments made by sixteenth- and seventeenth-century witnesses, he can see witchcraft as existing on different levels. It was part of the "long-term practices that no one thought of overturning."[91] Indeed, the village witch, a "local notable," cured people in the community and protected them from what Mandrou calls "the practices of other, less well-intentioned henchmen of Satan,"[92] in other words, from the real or imaginary dangers that abound in this world. In this sense, everyone in rural areas—and sometimes even in towns—was a bit of a witch during the sixteenth century. All people were looking for an "escape," a "compensating activity," a waking dream that would reassure them and permit them to control the world. Thus, we could apply to witches and to their henchmen the admiring formula applied to the Rosicrucians during the seventeenth century by the *Mercure français*: "They are subject neither to famine, nor to thirst, nor to old age, nor to illness, nor to any other inconvenience." It seems to me that witchcraft did indeed represent an attempt to overcome the fears that were a part of daily life, and that the witches' sabbath (if it really existed in the sixteenth century) was a "magnificent hallucinatory contrivance."[93]

During such events people left behind them the *"solemnity of fear and suffering"*[94] and perhaps even challenged it and denied its existence, since, as Le Roy Ladurie has put it, a dream may be prolonged by the *schéma de l'inversion*—the pattern of inversion—exemplified by insurrection and witchcraft. This involved "turning the world upside down,"[95] which could lead to parodying the mass during the witches' sabbath. I wish to point out that during the Middle Ages popular folklore permitted this release of tensions through the dream world of festivals ruled by the insane, fools, or donkeys. Official interdicts and taboos disappeared during such festivities; laughter reigned and permitted the participants to overcome the mystical terror and, above all, the moral fear with which the Church had colored everyday life.[96]

All of this still does not help us to understand the abrupt change that occurred between 1550 and 1570, when the persecution of witches developed into a blind frenzy. Nourished by the "ideological sap that was authentically rural and that came from the depths of time and the depths of the soul,"[97] witchcraft does not, in my opinion, seem to have undergone much of an intrinsic change during the mid-sixteenth century. However, the way in which the judges and the Church viewed witches does seem to have changed at this point. The outburst of hatred toward witches may be explained on the individual level by the existence of latent aggressiveness among the judges. This anxiety was normal rather than pathological and is explained by some psychologists as man's constant oscillation between life- and death-instincts.[98] But the translation of this aggressiveness into social behavior, with its focus upon a specific scapegoat, permits us to presume that a change did take place in the way in which the population thought.

Can we establish a relationship between witch hunting and the increasing individualism of the sixteenth century? John Gilissen sees that century as bringing a shift in the balance between customary and written law in the old Belgian legal system.[99] He explains the decline of customary law and the growth of written law as resulting from the new need for security created by the emancipation of the individual during the sixteenth century. This meshes with Mandrou's observation that the many-sided and omnipresent fear affected hypersensitive temperaments and led to "ritual crime by entire communities."[100] All the more reason why "cultivated" individuals such as Jean Bodin or the inquisitors, who had lost contact with the majority of the basic solidarities of the rural milieu, should cast off inhibitions and eliminate fear through demonomania.

The rural world became a foreign world to the demonomaniacs who were trying to apply their own mental categories to it and who failed to take into account a popular culture they did not understand. Bakhtin has pointed out that in the age of the Pléiade [mid-sixteenth century] laughter in the popular sense disappeared and that Rabelais's jokes were no longer understood. The population no longer experienced that "universal and social sensation"[101] of having conquered fear and official seriousness. The decline of the popular humor and the mirth found during festivals[102] corresponded to the collapse of an old world and of a collective and popular mentality. Indeed, after the change during the mid-sixteenth century, this collapse has continued slowly until the present. The popular folklore that we see today certainly represents the incoherent traces of fossilized traditions, the debris of a "savage thought" that has disappeared. The new world that was born in the sixteenth century brought human progress in many areas: Christianization, capitalism, the state. But it no longer welcomed witchcraft, because the latter postulated a static, or almost static, world and a way of thinking that was based upon magical beliefs and that had roots in the world dominated by constant and multifaceted fear. Although the change cannot be reduced to this single dimension, it would seem that the persecution of witches and the effort to bring Christianity to the masses were ways of overcoming this fear.

A SCHEMATIC REPRESENTATION

A rough and incomplete interpretation is better able to portray my idea of sixteenth-century witchcraft than numerous pages. There was the witchcraft that the demonomaniacs thought and that they often clothed in grotesque disguises, and there was the witchcraft that the common people lived until the mid-sixteenth century; for they still partially lived it through their "incoherent" practices, which were alienated from the milieu where they had been raised and which they increasingly thought about with the guilt feelings inculcated by the demonomaniacs.

Prior to 1550-70, the Christianity of the masses and "popular" witchcraft were part of the same "magical milieu" and were only distinguishable from one another at the level of the Christian elites. The latter—who *thought* what was *actually being lived* by the masses and distorted it—could draw a distinction between popular Christianity (which was perfectible though imperfect) and witchcraft (which was to be condemned for the same reasons as superstitions and, above all, heresies).

After the mid-sixteenth and especially during the seventeenth century, the pictures of Christianity accepted by the elite and by the masses split into two different levels: the level of the saints and mystics and the level of the Christian masses of the population. These levels clearly were thought of as such. Superstitions, heresies, and Christianity's imperfections were crushed in the great attempt to win souls and their very essence was deprecated.

The Christian elites attracted large numbers of people from an increasingly Christianized population, causing these people to lose contact with the deep roots of their original popular culture and to censure and deny that culture. Witchcraft was lived to an increasingly smaller extent by these people and, thanks to the mental tools supplied by the demonomaniacs, was thought of in an increasingly deprecating manner and rejected as extraneous and pernicious. Only the "specialists"—the soothsayer-healers—who possessed secrets that were passed down from generation to generation, continued to practice and to live popular witchcraft for the peasant masses who no longer perceived its coherence. This created a tension for the majority of rural people, although they did not clearly perceive that this tension existed. A waning millennium-old popular culture influenced them to continue resorting to these dilapidated magical practices; yet at the same time, the demonomaniacs and priests were teaching them to view these remnants and these scraps of a culture that had become folklore as the greatest threat posed by the devil. Burning witches when war, famine, or the unusual death of an individual or an animal occurred was no longer a matter solely for judges; it could also unleash entire communities.

A Tentative Conclusion

Thus, as I see, it, the mid-sixteenth century saw the beginning of the continual but slow disappearance of an "incomplete world in the process of a transformation." This world was impervious to "completed, authoritarian, and dogmatic epochs."[103] This world was a popular western culture, perhaps simply a French one, or maybe even a culture restricted to Flanders and Artois.

I realize that studying witchcraft as a component of popular culture, as I have tried to do, necessitates many methodological precautions. Such precautions do not, however, eliminate the risk that the historian will make a subjective interpretation. And so, in lieu of a conclusion, I shall borrow a few words from the statement made in 1525 by rebellious Swabian peasants who were aware that they belonged to the incomplete, dynamic, receptive—in sum, not yet congealed—world that I have been trying to describe here: "We willingly agree to abandon those [of our twelve articles] that can be shown to disagee with this [holy] Word."[104]

In my attempt at a partial description of a world that has left us so few traces, I am aware that I may not have been impartial. Like the peasants, I agree to alter my vision of this world, for I do not consider it definitive.[105]

NOTES

I am greatly indebted to Bernard Delmaire, assistant in medieval history at the University of Lille III, and to Pierre Deyon, president of that university. Both agreed to read this manuscript and offered numerous criticisms and suggestions that led me to modify the text on many points. I thank them heartily for these stimulae.

I also wish to thank Jean-Pierre Chrétien, assistant in contemporary history at the University of Lille III, who shared with me his knowledge of African witchcraft. Lastly, I wish to thank Jean Delumeau, professor at the University of Paris I and director of studies at the Sixth Section of the Ecole Pratique des Hautes Etudes. My three years of study with him made me aware of the issues discussed in this article. The first part in particular is an application on a regional scale of a number of themes for study that he suggested.

It goes without saying, nonetheless, that I accept total responsibility for the opinions in this article.

1. *Le Nouveau Commerce* 17 (Fall 1970): 107–33, presents a "Manuel des Inquisiteurs," a translation into French, dated 1762, of the fourteenth-century handbook by Nicolas Eymeric.

2. The chief recent works on the subject are: Robert Mandrou, *Magistrats et sorciers en France au XVIIᵉ siècle: Une analyse de psychologie historique*, Collection "Civilisations et men-

talités" (Paris: Plon, 1968); Carlo Ginzburg, *I beneandanti, Ricerche sulla stregoneria e sui culti agrari tra Cinquecento et Seicento*, "Biblioteca di cultura storica" (Turin: Einaudi, 1966); Hugh Trevor-Roper, whose article—which first appeared in *Encounter* 28 (May-June 1967), was first reprinted in a collection of articles, *Religion, the Reformation, and Social Change* (London: Macmillan, 1967), pp. 90-192, and later published under the title *The European Witch-Craze of the Sixteenth and Seventeenth Centuries* (Harmondsworth: Penguin Books, 1969) (My references are to the Penguin edition); E. William Monter, *European Witchcraft* (New York: John Wiley and Sons, 1969), an anthology of selections from recent books on witchcraft with comments by Monter; Michel de Certeau, *La possession de Loudun*, Collection "Archives" (Paris: Julliard, 1970), an edition of the records of the case with bibliography, introduction, and notes; Maurice Caveing, "La fin des bûchers de sorcellerie: une révolution mentale," *Raison Présente* 10 (April-June 1969): 83-99, which is quite close to Mandrou's position and refers to a "change in the conception of the world" during the seventeenth century (p. 97) but is forced to admit that "these epidemics of witchcraft remain unexplained" (p. 98); Pierre Chaunu, "Sur la fin des sorciers au XVIIᵉ siècle," *Annales E.S.C.* 24 (July-August 1969): 895-911, who tries to blaze a trail for a study of rural witchcraft; E. William Monter, "Trois historiens actuels de la sorcellerie," *Bibliothèque d'Humanisme et Renaissance* 31 (1969): 205-13, who regrets that Mandrou's book dodges the issue of the reality of witchcraft (p. 211) and would like a study of the phenomenon "from the inside, from the peasants' point of view" (p. 207).

3. J. Palou, *La sorcellerie*, Collection "Que sais-je?" (Paris: Presses Universitaires Françaises, 1957), echoes Michelet's opinion as found in *La sorcière*, ed. Robert Mandrou (Paris: Julliard, 1964), the edition that I used for this article.

4. Chaunu, "Sur la fin des sorciers," p. 905.

5. Arnold Van Gennep, *Manuel de folklore français contemporain* (Paris: Picard, 1938), a monumental work, volume 4 of which is devoted to witchcraft and superstitions (see especially the bibliography at the beginning of that volume); and Paul Sébillot, *Le Folk-lore de France*, 4 vols. (Paris: Guilmoto, 1904-7). Works of this sort have assembled masses of precious—but rarely dated—citations that have as yet scarcely been used by early-modern historians. Delumeau can be credited with the idea of consulting these works.

6. Two manuscripts in the municipal library of Lille [hereafter cited as B. M., Lille] were used. The first is "Prones d'un curé de Cysoing" (department of Nord, arrondissement of Lille, canton of Cysoing), cataloged as Ms. 148 and listed as no. 105 in the *Catalogue général des bibliothèques publiques de France, Départements* (Paris, 1897), 26: 78-79 [hereafter cited as *Catalogue général*]. This quarto manuscript is paginated 215-414, with tables paginated B, C, E, F, and G. On folio B we find "Hunc librum scripsit Frater Matheus du Crocquet." The individual in question is listed in the obituary of Cysoing (Manuscript no. 70 in the *Catalogue général*, 26: 51-52): "Obiit frater Matheus du Crocquet, supprior, sacerdos et canonicus noster 1533."

The second manuscript is the anonymous "Sermons français," cataloged as Ms. 131 (and no. 106 in the *Catalogue général*, which states that the author undoubtedly resided in Béthune, the chief town in the arrondissement of that name, in the department of Pas-de-Calais). This in-4° manuscript is composed of 164 unnumbered folios written in a fine gothic hand dating from the first half of the sixteenth century. Various references (fols. 37vᵒ, 43, 61vᵒ, 121) indicate that the author was familiar with the region of Béthune and had preached there. Were these sermons intended for the inhabitants of that region? De la Fons-Mélicocq, "Les médecins et chirurgiens de la ville de Lille aux XVᵉ siècles," *Archives historiques et littéraires du Nord de la France et du Midi de la Belgique*, 3rd ser. (1867) 6: 197-221, believes the author to have been the Franciscan, Estienne d'Arras (pp. 211-14). He provides no reference, and I have been unable to verify this.

For practical purposes, I have added the punctuation and accent marks necessary to understand the excerpts from these manuscripts.

This type of source poses methodological problems. Although in this specific instance it is a question of sermons intended for the common people, we cannot assert that they accurately reflect the physical state of the body of Christian worshipers. Indeed, they seem to inform the historian about the "minimum" required of the faithful, and about their deviance and their superstitions. But, as Bernard Delmaire so pertinently pointed out to me, "there is a *rhetoric* for sermons that often stresses the least healthy aspects of the listeners' religious life in order to prompt them to repent." He added that collections of *exempla* existed during the Middle Ages and that preachers found themes and anecdotes in them. So, the sermons may involve the same shortcomings as the texts written by the judges about witchcraft: they may be harkening back to earlier models and may markedly diverge from the actual situation. Delmaire proposed that I read A. Lecoy de la Marche, *La chaire française au Moyen Age, spécialement au XIIIe siècle*, 2nd ed. (Paris: Renouard, 1886), and the excellent book by G. R. Owst, *Literature and Pulpit in Medieval England* (Oxford: Blackwell, 1966). To this I add J. Batany, "Paradigmes lexicaux et structures littéraires au Moyen Age," *Revue d'Histoire littéraire de la France* 5-6 (September-December 1970): 819-35, which states on p. 819 that "the sermon is almost the only literary work for which people were taught composition." The existence of a fourteenth-century collection of themes to be used in sermons, at B.M., Lille (no. 107 in the *Catalogue général*), tends to confirm this.

7. I am referring to various projects being carried out by the "school" of religious sociology, following Gabriel Le Bras's lead. See the work of Jean Delumeau, especially *Le catholicisme entre Luther et Voltaire*, Collection "Nouvelle Clio" (Paris: Presses Universitaires françaises, 1972), the key ideas of which were included over a period of several years in his seminar at the Sixth Section of the Ecole Pratique des Hautes Etudes; and Jacques Toussaert, *Le Sentiment religieux en Flandre à la fin du Moyen Age* (Paris: Plon, 1963).

8. One example: in "Réforme et Contre-Réforme," of *La Nouvelle Histoire de l'Eglise* (Paris: Seuil, 1968), vol. 3, 254 of the 624 pages are devoted to the sixteenth century. Aside from twenty-two very subtle and rich pages (pp. 232-54), and pages 41-42, in which H. Tüchle discusses the spirituality of laymen before the Reformation, the subject of popular religion is scarcely discussed. Thus, the five initial chapters by Tüchle seem to confirm the idea that we, above all, know about Christianity among the elite and seem to indicate that the Reformation rested almost exclusively upon this social level, which certainly is false.

9. E. Delaruelle, E. R. Labande, and Paul Ourliac, *L'Eglise au temps du Grand Schisme et de la crise conciliaire (1378-1449)* (Paris: Bloud et Gay, 1964), pp. 495-1231. Vol. 14 of the second part of Fliche and Martin's *Histoire de l'Eglise* has excellent chapters on religious life by Chanoine Delaruelle, which are more nuanced than Toussaert's. See also Jean Delumeau, *Naissance et affirmation de la Réforme*, 2nd ed., Collection "Nouvelle Clio" (Paris: Presses Universitaires Françaises, 1968).

10. See Jean Chelini, *Histoire religieuse de l'Occident médiéval*, Collection "U" (Paris: A. Colin, 1968). The author attempts to dig down to the level of the people and sketches out a "historical sociology for religious Europe during the Middle Ages," as Le Bras called it in his deservedly favorable review in *Archives de Sociologie des religions* 26 (July-December 1968): 151-56.

11. B.M., Lille, Ms. 131, fols. 40v° and 41. The theme of the clergy's ignorance is hardly original. Bernard Delmaire reminded me that it was a subject dear to the great reformers of the fifteenth century—for example, Gerson (1363-1469)—or to the numerous preachers such as Olivier Maillard (c. 1430-c. 1502), and Michel Menot (c. 1440-c. 1518). They worked chiefly in urban areas. Does this phenomenon reveal the beginning of a differentiation between religion in urban areas and religion in rural areas? Until the early sixteenth century the latter constituted a world of its own, while city-dwellers were becoming increasingly sensitive to Christian morality, the notion of sin, and even theology (although it is certain that this sensitivity was spread over a continuum). The synodical statutes, a source that has as yet been rarely consulted, might permit a partial answer to these questions. Cf. André Artonne et al., *Répertoire des statuts synodaux des diocèses de l'ancienne France du XIIIe à la fin du XVIIIe siècle* (Paris: Centre National des Etudes Scientifiques, 1963). I did not consult these statutes for this article.

12. Ibid., fol. 76v°.

13. André Godin, "La société au XVIe siècle, vue par J. Glapion (1460?-1522), frère mineur, confesseur de Charles Quint," *Revue du Nord* 47-182 (July-September 1964): 341-70. This remark by Glapion is quoted on p. 365.

14. Ibid., p. 365.

15. B.M., Lille, Ms. 131, fols. 58v° and 59.

16. Ibid., fol. 59.

17. Toussaert, *Le Sentiment religieux en Flandre*, p. 172. This generalization may be excessive. Nuances should be added for Flanders, and even more so for Europe in general.

18. Quoted in Godin, "La société vue par Glapion," p. 365.

19. B.M., Lille, Ms. 131, fol. 156.

20. Ibid., fol. 59v°.

21. Ibid., fol. 128.

22. *Nouvelle Histoire de l'Eglise*, 3: 246.

23. Cf. Léopold Genicot, *Le XIIIe siècle européen*, Collection "Nouvelle Clio" (Paris: Presses Universitaires Françaises, 1968), pp. 283–84. Page 284 refers to a religion "centered on Hell rather than on Heaven." See also E. Brouste, "La civilisation chrétienne du XVIe siècle devant le problème satanique," *Satan*, Etudes Carmélitaines, Desclée de Brouwer (1948), pp. 352–85; Delumeau, *Le catholicisme entre Luther et Voltaire*, and *Naissance et affirmation de la Réforme*; and Le Brun, in *Nouvelle Histoire de l'Eglise*, 3: 246.

24. A. Tenenti, "La vie et la mort à travers l'art du XVIe siècle," *Cahiers des Annales* (Paris: A. Colin, 1952); Jean Palou, *La peur dans l'histoire* (Paris: Editions ouvrières, 1958); and André Corvisier, "La représentation de la société dans les danses des morts du XVe au XVIIIe siècle," *Revue d'histoire moderne et contemporaine* 16 (October-December 1969): 489–539, which discusses the principal texts and engravings portraying the *danse macabre* from the fifteenth through the eighteenth century.

25. Quoted by Paul Fredericq, *Corpus documentorum Inquisitionis haereticae pravitatis Neerlandicae*, 3 vols. (Ghent and The Hague, 1896), 2: 271, document no. 165, dated 1477, with a reference to the Bibliothèque Nationale of Paris, Z 1365.

26. H. Brabant, "L'homme malade dans la société de la Renaissance," *Individu et société à la Renaissance* (Paris: Presses Universitaires Françaises, 1967), p. 260, a collection of articles from a conference on the subject held in 1965.

27. Ibid., p. 264.

28. The anonymous "Chroniques des Pays-Bas, de France, d'Angleterre, et de Tournai," in De Smet, *Corpus Chronicorum Flandriae* (Brussels: Hayez, 1856), pp. 115–569, and p. 333. See also L. Torfs, *Fastes des calamités publiques survenues dans les Pays-Bas et particulièrement en Belgique depuis les temps les plus reculés* (Tournai and Paris, Casterman, 1859).

29. E. Caplet, *La peste à Lille au XVIIe siècle* (Lille: Le Bigot Frères, 1898), p. 39. The *échevinage* [aldermanry] of Lille forbade dancing in order to "appease the ire of God, our blessed Creator."

30. B.M., Lille, Ms. 148, fols. 217v^o, 223v^o, and 217v^o respectively.

31. B.M., Lille, Ms. 131. My sampling is from the final ten sermons (fols. 87–162). Devil (*diable*): fols. 88, 92, 106v^o (twice), 107 (twice), 126 (twice), 129v^o, 131v^o, 132 (twice), 133, 137v^o (twice), 138 (five times), and 138v^o (five times); devils (*diables*): fols. 96, 97, 98v^o, 106v^o, 107, 117v^o, 118v^o, 131, 134; devilry (*diablerie*): fols. 123v^o, 132, 139, 140. First the author discussed ignorance of the divine law and of baptism (fols. 87–112v^o), then he preached about the first commandment (fols. 113–49v^o). The final two sermons (fols. 150–62v^o) deal with the second commandment. I am not satisfied with this brief study. It is nothing more than a simplistic approach to the subject. In order to avoid all subjectivity, one should *not* choose a theme but should first study the text without any preconceived ideas, making an exhaustive index with the help of a computer. The computer would then supply concordances, frequencies, and correlations based on an alphabetical index. Perhaps the theme of the devil would not prove to be a fundamental one. In this case, the researcher's presuppositions would become clear and would undoubtedly permit him to understand something about his own psychological makeup.

Semantic methodology applied to history has been the subject of numerous articles, including one by M. Tournier et al., "Le vocabulaire de la Révolution, pour un inventaire systématique des textes," *Annales historiques de la Révolution française* 195 (January-March 1969): 109–24. See also A. Dupront, *Langage et histoire*, Report to the Thirteenth International Congress of Historical Societies (Moscow: Naouka, 1970); and the special issue entitled "Méthodologies," of the *Revue d'Histoire littéraire de la France* 5-6 (October-December 1970), which contains articles by J. Proust on the use of computers (pp. 784–97), M. Duchet on computers as applied to texts (pp. 798–809), and C. Duchet and M. Launay on lexicology in the service of history and literary criticism (pp. 810–18).

32. B.M., Lille, Ms. 131, fols. 88; 92, 96; 106v^o and 107; and 117v^o respectively.

33. Ibid., fols. 123v^o, 132, 139, and 140.

34. Ibid., fol. 138v^o.

35. Ibid., fol. 138.

36. Ibid., fol. 132.

37. Ibid., fol. 126.

38. Ibid., fol. 131v^o.

39. Ibid., fol. 137v°.

40. Ibid., fols. 138, 139v°.

41. Ibid., fol. 139v°.

42. Cf. Raoul Allier, *Magie et religion* (Paris: Berger Levrault).

43. Robert-Léon Wagner, *"Sorcier" et "magicien": contribution à l'histoire du vocabulaire de la magie* (Paris: Droz, 1939), p. 146, links the word magic with "old age, maliciousness, and dirtiness," perhaps since the thirteenth century. Wagner tries to understand the notion of "magic," in reality a superior form of thinking centered upon alchemy, astrology, and so forth (According to him the word *magic* appeared at the end of the fifteenth century; see p. 26). His study of the vocabulary of witchcraft, however, which he sees as the ancestor of magic, is akin to my subject here. His book is a model of subtlety, culture, and intelligence and abounds in precious information about witchcraft and religion.

44. A Latin text, translated into French and included in Charles M. de La Roncière, Robert Delort, and Michel Rouche, *L'Europe au Moyen Age*, Collection "U" (Paris: A. Colin) 1: 110-11, document 49.

45. A text translated in Cyrille Vogel, *Le pécheur et la pénitence au Moyen Age* (Paris: Editions du Cerf, 1969), pp. 87-113.

46. See Wagner, *"Sorcier" et "magicien"*, p. 57, for a view of witchcraft as a counter religion. An example of a new superstition is impaling a newborn infant; see Vogel, *Le pécheur et la pénitence*, p. 110.

47. Wagner, *"Sorcier" et "magicien"*, p. 62.

48. See the three volumes of Fredericq, *Corpus documentorum Inquisitionis*.

49. Paul Beuzart, *Les hérésies pendant le Moyen Age et la Réforme, jusqu'à la mort de Philippe II (1598) dans la région de Douai, d'Arras, et au pays de l'Alleu* (Paris, 1912). Written from a Protestant viewpoint, this book includes numerous supporting documents, but the French have not yet written a careful history of these heresies, especially that of the Waldensians at Arras.

50. See H. C. Lea, *Histoire de l'Inquisition au Moyen Age* (Paris, 1901-2), especially 3: 589 ff.; and Trevor-Roper, *The European Witch-Craze*, pp. 24 ff.

51. The religious crisis, above all on the top level of society, has been described by Johan Huizinga, *The Waning of the Middle Ages*. See also Jean Delumeau, *La Civilisation de la Renaissance* (Paris: Arthaud, 1967), which studies the period 1320-1620 in an admirable synthesis, albeit focused upon the dynamism of the period and the level of the intellectual elites of the West.

52. Mikkaïl Bakhtin, *L'oeuvre de François Rabelais et la culture populaire au Moyen Age et sous la Renaissance* (Paris: Gallimard, 1970). I wish to point out that Rabelais was very receptive to demonstrations of popular culture, and that he did not judge that culture with the severity of a priest discussing witches.

53. Marcel Mauss, *Sociologie et anthropologie* (Paris: Presses Universitaires Françaises, 1950), p. 16. Author's italics. This book, with an introduction by Claude Lévi-Strauss (pp. vii-lii), is a collection of articles that first appeared between 1902 and 1934. My citations come chiefly from "L'esquisse d'une théorie générale de la magie" (pp. 1-141), which dates from 1902-3 and was written with the collaboration of H. Hubert.

For the concept of *mana*, see pp. vii-lii, lxv, and 131.

54. "The Distaff Evangile," cited by Van Gennep, *Manuel de folklore français contemporain*, 1-4: 1991.

55. Mauss, *Sociologie et anthropologie*, pp. 66, 64, and 63.

56. B.M. Lille, Ms. 131, fol. 126.

57. Ibid., fol. 123v°.

58. Ibid., fols. 131v° and 132. The meaning of the word *en*—"of it"—(must eat some *of it*) is not specified.

59. Roger Berger, *Le nécrologie de la confrérie des jongleurs d'Arras (1194-1361)* (Arras, 1970), "Introduction." This volume includes supporting documents, maps, graphs, and illustrations and was published as vol. 23 of the *Mémoires de la Commission départementale des Monuments historiques du Pas-de-Calais*. It describes the following custom at Arras. If put into water and drunk at Pentecost, the wax from the Holy Candle, or *Joyel*, would cure an epidemic of ergotism. This legend, which had traditionally been dated as originating in 1105, is undoubtedly much later—the late twelfth or early thirteenth century (pp. 39-41).

60. See a passage from "Contre les sorciers et les sorcières et ceux qui vont aux devins et devineresses," in Godin, "La société vue par Glapion," p. 353.

61. B.M., Lille, Ms. 131, fols. 137v° and 138.

62. Quoted by Godin, "La sociéte vue par Glapion," p. 354.

63. B.M., Lille, Ms. 131, fols. 138v° and 139.

64. B.M., Lille, Ms. 148, fol. 225v°. Author's italics.

65. For Flanders and Artois, see P. Vilette, *La sorcellerie dans le Nord de la France du milieu du XVIe siècle à la fin du XVIIIe siècle* (Lille: Faculté Catholique, 1956). See a review by Jacques Toussaert, *Revue du Nord* (1957): 87–88. See also Michelle Protin, "La sorcellerie en Flandre gallicane, 1581–1708," a typewritten paper done in 1963 under the supervision of L. Trénard at the University of Lille. The best synthesis on witchcraft in Europe during the sixteenth and seventeenth centuries is Trevor-Roper, *The European Witch-Craze*, although many points are open to dispute. See the review by Monter, "Trois historiens actuels," pp. 207–10.

66. Michel Foucault, *Histoire de la folie à l'âge classique*, abridged ed., Collection 10/18 (Paris; U.G.E., 1964), p. 28.

67. Ibid., p. 22.

68. Ibid., pp. 13 ff., and p. 29.

69. Ibid., p. 53.

70. Michelet, *La sorcière*, p. 21.

71. B.M., Lille, Ms. 131, fol. 102v°.

72. Quoted by Godin, "La société vue par Glapion," pp. 367 and 369.

73. Liliane Wouters, *Belles heures de Flandre: anthologie de la poésie flamande du XIIe siècle* (Paris: Seghers, 1961), p. 102. The word *Hell* is underlined in the text.

74. On the debate concerning women, on feminists, and on people inimical to women, see A. Cioranesco, *Bibliographie de la littérature française au XVIe siècle* (Paris, 1959), pp. 8 and 60–61.

75. Municipal library of Arras (department of Pas-de-Calais). Ms. 186, fol. 67v°. This manuscript dates from the second half of the sixteenth century. Souchez is a township in the arrondissement of Arras.

76. Mauss, *Sociologie et anthropologie*, p. 113.

77. Wagner, *"Sorcier" et "magicien"*, p. 145.

78. For example, in the departmental archives of Nord, at Lille, B[1741], fols. 196–97v° contain the revocation of a banishment in 1530 for murdering a priest of Lille called Sire Anthoine de Biach. The trouble began with a quarrel between the murderer and "Jehanne des Rosettes, called Moufflette, a loose woman and concubine of the said Sire Anthoine."

79. R. Badinter and J.-D. Bredin, "Un exorcisme collectif," *Le Monde*, 4 November 1970.

80. In his seminar at the Sixth Section of the Ecole Pratique des Hautes Etudes. See Delumeau's recent book on Catholicism from the sixteenth to the eighteenth centuries.

81. Bernard Delmaire advised me to qualify this assertion, in order to avoid being outrageously simplistic. He questions whether, despite the superstitions it incorporated, Christianity among the people was inferior to the more intellectual sort of Christianity that often had little affect upon the lives of a part of the elite (clergy, bourgeoisie, nobility, and so forth). The "Christian elite" of the early sixteenth century could accept an illiterate sheperdess but exclude the people. On the subject of defining the elite and the Christian population, see Francis Rapp, *L'Eglise et la vie religieuse à la fin du Moyen Age*, Collection "Nouvelle Clio" (Paris: Presses Universitaires Françaises, 1971), pp. 307–14; and for a discussion of the weakening and distortion of Christianity prior to the sixteenth century, pp. 315–31.

82. Georges Balandier, *La vie quotidienne au royaume de Kongo du XVIe au XVIIIe siècle*, Collection "Vie quotidienne" (Paris: Hachette, 1965), pp. 220–22, 258, 243, and 260 respectively. The italics are mine.

83. It must be pointed out, however, that the kingdom of Kongo was rather exceptional, concerning both the early date at which Christianity was introduced and the abundant written sources, especially those dealing with the sixteenth century; ibid., p. 283. Since documentation is often lacking, historians of Africa also rely upon oral traditions being recorded today. See J.-P. Chrétien, "Les tombeaux des 'bami' du Burundi: Un aspect de la monarchie sacrée en Afrique orientale," *Cahiers des Etudes africaines* 10, no. 1 (1970): 40–79.

84. Ginzburg, *I beneandanti*, and a review by Monter, "Trois historiens actuels," pp. 205–7.

85. Cf. Margaret Murray, *The Witch-Cult in Western Europe* (Oxford, 1921), reprinted in 1962 and cited by Monter, "Trois historiens actuels," p. 206.

86. See Guy Rocher, *Introduction à la sociologie générale*, Vol. *1*, *L'Action sociale* (Paris: Seuil, 1970), pp. 77 ff.

87. "Sancti Bonifacii sermones, "Sermo 15, *Patrologie latine*, ed. Migne, 89: col. 870 ff.

88. Monsignor Gousset, *Actes de la province ecclésiastique de Reims* (1842-44), 2: 700, col. 1.

89. Fredericq, *Corpus documentorum Inquisitionis*, 2: 271.

90. Emmanuel Le Roy Ladurie, *Paysans de Languedoc*, abridged ed. (Paris: Flammarion, 1969), pp. 242-43. He cites Thomas Platter's observations dated 1595, p. 243.

91. Robert Mandrou, *Introduction à la France moderne: essai de psychologie historique (1500-1640)*, Collection "L'Evolution de l'Humanité" (Paris: A. Michel, 1961), p. 325.

92. Ibid., p. 325.

93. Ibid., pp. 298, 34, and 323.

94. Bakhtin, *L'oeuvre de François Rabelais*, p. 102. Author's italics.

95. Le Roy Ladurie, *Paysans de Languedoc*, pp. 244 and 245.

96. See Bakhtin's thought-provoking observations, *L'oeuvre de François Rabelais*, pp. 96-98, 102, 103, and 108.

97. Le Roy Ladurie, *Paysans de Languedoc*, p. 244.

98. Juliette Boutonier, *Contribution à la psychologie et à la métaphysique de l'angoisse* (Paris: Presses Universitaires Françaises: 1945), p. 269.

99. John Gilissen, "Individualisme et sécurité juridique," *Individu et société à la Renaissance*, pp. 33-58.

100. Mandrou, *Introduction à la France moderne*, p. 338.

101. Bakhtin, *L'oeuvre de François Rabelais*, p. 99.

102. Ibid., p. 87, on the *risus paschalis* as a joyful resurrection of the common people after the fasting of Lent.

103. Ibid., p. 132.

104. Henri Peyre, *Les Douze Articles de la Guerre des Paysans* (Montauban: Granié, 1905), article 12, p. 34.

105. I wrote this article in February 1971.